LIST OF CONTRIBUTORS

Dr M Gurnell PhD FRCP
University Lecturer and Honorary Consultant Physician
University of Cambridge, Department of Medicine and
Addenbrooke's Hospital
Cambridge

Dr MZ Qureshi MRCP(UK)
Consultant Physician
Mid Cheshire Hospitals NHS Trust
Crewe
Cheshire

Dr RK Semple PhD MRCP(UK)
Wellcome Trust Clinician Scientist and Honorary Specialist Registrar in
Diabetes and Endocrinology
Institute of Metabolic Science
University of Cambridge
Cambridge

Dr JW Tomlinson PhD MRCP(UK)
Clinical Lecturer and Wellcome Clinician Scientist Fellow
Institute of Biomedical Research
University of Birmingham
Birmingham

Dr AM Wren PhD MRCP(UK)
Consultant Physician and Honorary Senior Lecturer
Chelsea and Westminster Hospital and Imperial College London
London

Royal College
of Physicians
Setting higher medical standards

Published by:
Royal College of Physicians of London
11 St. Andrews Place
Regent's Park
London NW1 4LE
United Kingdom

Set and printed by Graphicraft Limited, Hong Kong

First edition published 2001
Reprinted 2004
Second edition published 2008

ISBN: 978-1-86016-273-2 (this book)
ISBN: 978-1-86016-260-2 (set)

Distribution Information:
Jerwood Medical Education Resource Centre
Royal College of Physicians of London
11 St. Andrews Place
Regent's Park
London NW1 4LE
United Kingdom
Tel: +44 (0)207 935 1174 ext 422/490
Fax: +44 (0)207 486 6653
Email: merc@rcplondon.ac.uk
Web: http://www.rcplondon.ac.uk/

CONTENTS

List of contributors iii
Foreword vii
Preface viii
Acknowledgements x
Key features xi

ENDOCRINOLOGY

PACES Stations and Acute Scenarios 3

1.1 History-taking 3
  1.1.1 Hypercalcaemia 3
  1.1.2 Polyuria 5
  1.1.3 Faints, sweats and palpitations 8
  1.1.4 Gynaecomastia 12
  1.1.5 Hirsutism 14
  1.1.6 Post-pill amenorrhoea 16
  1.1.7 A short girl with no periods 17
  1.1.8 Young man who has 'not developed' 20
  1.1.9 Depression and diabetes 21
  1.1.10 Acromegaly 23
  1.1.11 Relentless weight gain 24
  1.1.12 Weight loss 26
  1.1.13 Tiredness and lethargy 29
  1.1.14 Flushing and diarrhoea 32
  1.1.15 Avoiding another coronary 34
  1.1.16 High blood pressure and low serum potassium 37
  1.1.17 Tiredness, weight loss and amenorrhoea 39
1.2 Clinical examination 42
  1.2.1 Amenorrhoea and low blood pressure 42
  1.2.2 Young man who has 'not developed' 43
  1.2.3 Depression and diabetes 45
  1.2.4 Acromegaly 45
  1.2.5 Weight loss and gritty eyes 47
  1.2.6 Tiredness and lethargy 48
  1.2.7 Hypertension and a lump in the neck 48
1.3 Communication skills and ethics 50
  1.3.1 Explaining an uncertain outcome 50
  1.3.2 The possibility of cancer 51
  1.3.3 No medical cause for hirsutism 52
  1.3.4 A short girl with no periods 53
  1.3.5 Simple obesity, not a problem with 'the glands' 54
  1.3.6 I don't want to take the tablets 55
1.4 Acute scenarios 56
  1.4.1 Coma with hyponatraemia 56
  1.4.2 Hypercalcaemic and confused 60
  1.4.3 Thyrotoxic crisis 61
  1.4.4 Addisonian crisis 63
  1.4.5 'Off legs' 65

Diseases and Treatments 68

2.1 Hypothalamic and pituitary diseases 68
  2.1.1 Cushing's syndrome 68
  2.1.2 Acromegaly 71
  2.1.3 Hyperprolactinaemia 73
  2.1.4 Non-functioning pituitary tumours 76
  2.1.5 Pituitary apoplexy 77
  2.1.6 Craniopharyngioma 78
  2.1.7 Diabetes insipidus 80
  2.1.8 Hypopituitarism and hormone replacement 83
2.2 Adrenal disease 85
  2.2.1 Cushing's syndrome 85
  2.2.2 Primary hyperaldosteronism 85
  2.2.3 Virilising tumours 87
  2.2.4 Phaeochromocytoma 89
  2.2.5 Congenital adrenal hyperplasia 92
  2.2.6 Primary adrenal insufficiency 94
2.3 Thyroid disease 97
  2.3.1 Hypothyroidism 97
  2.3.2 Thyrotoxicosis 100
  2.3.3 Thyroid nodules and goitre 105
  2.3.4 Thyroid malignancy 107
2.4 Reproductive disorders 107
  2.4.1 Delayed growth and puberty 107
  2.4.2 Male hypogonadism 111
  2.4.3 Oligomenorrhoea/amenorrhoea and premature menopause 113
  2.4.4 Turner's syndrome 115
  2.4.5 Polycystic ovarian syndrome 116
  2.4.6 Hirsutism 118
  2.4.7 Erectile dysfunction 120
  2.4.8 Infertility 123
2.5 Metabolic and bone diseases 125
  2.5.1 Hyperlipidaemia/dyslipidaemia 125
  2.5.2 Porphyria 128
  2.5.3 Haemochromatosis 130
  2.5.4 Osteoporosis 131
  2.5.5 Osteomalacia 134
  2.5.6 Paget's disease 136
  2.5.7 Hyperparathyroidism 137
  2.5.8 Hypercalcaemia 140
  2.5.9 Hypocalcaemia 141

CONTENTS

2.6 Diabetes mellitus 143
- **2.6.1** Management of hyperglycaemic emergencies 145
- **2.6.2** Management of hypoglycaemic emergencies 147
- **2.6.3** Short- and long-term management of diabetes 147
- **2.6.4** Complications 153
- **2.6.5** Important information for patients 160

2.7 Other endocrine disorders 162
- **2.7.1** Multiple endocrine neoplasia 162
- **2.7.2** Autoimmune polyglandular endocrinopathies 163
- **2.7.3** Ectopic hormone syndromes 164

Investigations and Practical Procedures 165

3.1 Stimulation tests 165
- **3.1.1** Short Synacthen test 165
- **3.1.2** Corticotrophin-releasing hormone test 166
- **3.1.3** Thyrotrophin-releasing hormone test 166
- **3.1.4** Gonadotrophin-releasing hormone test 167
- **3.1.5** Insulin tolerance test 167
- **3.1.6** Pentagastrin stimulation test 168
- **3.1.7** Oral glucose tolerance test 169

3.2 Suppression tests 169
- **3.2.1** Overnight dexamethasone suppression test 169
- **3.2.2** Low-dose dexamethasone suppression test 170
- **3.2.3** High-dose dexamethasone suppression test 170
- **3.2.4** Oral glucose tolerance test in acromegaly 171

3.3 Other investigations 171
- **3.3.1** Thyroid function tests 171
- **3.3.2** Water deprivation test 172

Self-assessment 174

4.1 Self-assessment questions 174

4.2 Self-assessment answers 180

The Medical Masterclass Series 185
Index 201

Since its initial publication in 2001, *Medical Masterclass* has been regarded as a key learning and teaching resource for physicians around the world. The resource was produced in part to meet the vision of the Royal College of Physicians: *'Doctors of the highest quality, serving patients well'*. This vision continues and, along with advances in clinical practice and changes in the format of the MRCP(UK) exam, has justified the publication of this second edition.

The MRCP(UK) is an international examination that seeks to advance the learning of and enhance the training process for physicians worldwide. On passing the exam physicians are recognised as having attained the required knowledge, skills and manner appropriate for training at a specialist level. However, passing the exam is a challenge. The pass rate at each sitting of the written papers is about 40%. Even the most prominent consultants have had to sit each part of the exam more than once in order to pass. With this challenge in mind, the College has produced *Medical Masterclass*, a comprehensive learning resource to help candidates with the preparation that is key to making the grade.

Medical Masterclass has been produced by the Education Department of the College. A work of this size represents a formidable amount of effort by the Editor-in-Chief – Dr John Firth – and his team of editors and authors. I would like to thank our colleagues for this wonderful educational product and wholeheartedly recommend it as an invaluable learning resource for all physicians preparing for their MRCP(UK) examination.

Professor Ian Gilmore MD PRCP
President of the Royal College of Physicians

PREFACE

The second edition of *Medical Masterclass* is produced and published by the Education Department of the Royal College of Physicians of London. It comprises 12 textbooks, a companion interactive website and two CD-ROMs. Its aim is to help doctors in their first few years of training to improve their medical knowledge and skills; and in particular to (a) learn how to deal with patients who are acutely ill, and (b) pass postgraduate examinations, such as the MRCP(UK) or European Diploma in Internal Medicine.

The 12 textbooks are divided as follows: two cover the scientific background to medicine, one is devoted to general clinical skills [including specific guidance on exam technique for PACES, the practical assessment of clinical examination skills that is the final part of the MRCP(UK) exam], one deals with acute medicine and the other eight cover the range of medical specialties.

The core material of each of the medical specialties is dealt with in seven sections:

- Case histories – you are presented with letters of referral commonly received in each specialty and led through the ways in which the patients' histories should be explored, and what should then follow in the way of investigation and/or treatment.

- Physical examination scenarios – these emphasise the logical analysis of physical signs and sensible clinical reasoning: 'having found this, what would you do?'

- Communication and ethical scenarios – what are the difficult issues that commonly arise in each specialty? What do you actually say to the 'frequently asked (but still very difficult) questions?'

- Acute presentations – what are the priorities if you are the doctor seeing the patient in the Emergency Department or the Medical Admissions Unit?

- Diseases and treatments – structured concise notes.

- Investigations and practical procedures – more short and to-the-point notes.

- Self assessment questions – in the form used in the MRCP(UK) Part 1 and Part 2 exams.

The companion website – which is continually updated – enables you to take mock MRCP(UK) Part 1 or Part 2 exams, or to be selective in the questions you tackle (if you want to do ten questions on cardiology, or any other specialty, you can do). For every question you complete you can see how your score compares with that of others who have logged onto the site and attempted it. The two CD-ROMs each contain 30 interactive cases requiring diagnosis and treatment.

I hope that you enjoy using *Medical Masterclass* to learn more about medicine, which – whatever is happening politically to primary care, hospitals and medical career structures – remains a wonderful occupation. It is sometimes intellectually and/or emotionally very challenging, and also sometimes extremely rewarding, particularly when reduced to the essential of a doctor trying to provide best care for a patient.

John Firth DM FRCP
Editor-in-Chief

ACKNOWLEDGEMENTS

Medical Masterclass has been produced by a team. The names of those who have written or edited material are clearly indicated elsewhere, but without the support of many other people it would not exist. Naming names is risky, but those worthy of particular note include: Sir Richard Thompson (College Treasurer) and Mrs Winnie Wade (Director of Education), who steered the project through committees that are traditionally described as labyrinthine, and which certainly seem so to me; and also Arthur Wadsworth (Project Co-ordinator) and Don Liu in the College Education Department office. Don is a veteran of the first edition of *Medical Masterclass*, and it would be fair to say that without his great efforts a second edition might not have seen the light of day.

John Firth DM FRCP
Editor-in-Chief

We have created a range of icon boxes that sit among the text of the various *Medical Masterclass* modules. They are there to help you identify key information and to make learning easier and more enjoyable. Here is a brief explanation:

> Iron-deficiency anaemia with a change in bowel habit in a middle-aged or older patient means colonic malignancy until proved otherwise.

This icon is used to highlight points of particular importance.

> Dietary deficiency is very rarely, if ever, the sole cause of iron-deficiency anaemia.

This icon is used to indicate common or important drug interactions, pitfalls of practical procedures, or when to take symptoms or signs particularly seriously.

ENDOCRINOLOGY

Authors:

M Gurnell, MZ Qureshi, RK Semple, JW Tomlinson and AM Wren

Editor:

M Gurnell

Editor-in-Chief:

JD Firth

PACES STATIONS AND ACUTE SCENARIOS

1.1 History-taking

1.1.1 Hypercalcaemia

> ### Letter of referral to endocrinology outpatient clinic
>
> Dear Doctor,
>
> **Re: Mrs Sally-Anne Cooke, aged 54 years**
>
> This 54-year-old teacher presented with loin pain to an acute urology take and was found on CT scanning to have several left-sided ureteric calculi. These have been managed conservatively, but initial investigation revealed a serum calcium of 2.8 mmol/L and an endocrinology opinion was suggested. I would be grateful for your advice regarding further investigation and management.
>
> Yours sincerely,

Introduction

Most urinary tract calculi contain calcium and most patients (~65%) have idiopathic hypercalciuria, but some 5% have underlying hypercalcaemia, as in this case, which ideally should be confirmed on an uncuffed venous sample. Although the differential diagnosis of hypercalcaemia is broad (Table 1), the presence of a renal stone usually implies that it is long-standing and therefore unlikely to be secondary to malignancy. The most likely diagnosis here is primary hyperparathyroidism.

History of the presenting problem

With increasingly frequent use of biochemical testing, hypercalcaemia is often found incidentally or as a result of directed screening, such as in this case. This means that frank symptomatology is uncommon, but symptoms of hypercalcaemia should be specifically sought. These usually occur when the serum calcium exceeds 3 mmol/L and comprise:

- thirst and polyuria;
- constipation;
- anorexia and general malaise;
- depression and anxiety.

More severe hypercalcaemia can lead to vomiting, severe dehydration, confusion and even coma (see Sections 1.4.2, 2.5.7 and 2.5.8).

Other relevant history

Careful enquiry should be directed towards possible causes and complications of hypercalcaemia. Bear in mind the conditions listed in Table 1 as you proceed.

Functional enquiry

A full systematic functional enquiry is needed. Respiratory symptoms might suggest sarcoidosis as the cause of hypercalcaemia. Gastrointestinal symptoms might be a consequence of hypercalcaemia, but could be causal if leading to

	TABLE 1 **CAUSES OF HYPERCALCAEMIA**[1]	
Frequency	**Type of disorder**	**Example**
Common	Primary hyperparathyroidism	–
	Malignancy	Carcinoma with skeletal metastases, eg breast, lung
		Carcinoma without skeletal metastases, ie humoral hypercalcaemia of malignancy
		Haematological disorders, eg myeloma
Less common	Vitamin D toxicity	Consumption of medicines/compounds containing vitamin D
	Vitamin D 'sensitivity'	Granulomatous disorders, eg sarcoidosis
	Excess calcium intake	Milk-alkali syndrome
	Reduced calcium excretion	Thiazide diuretics, lithium
		Familial hypocalciuric hypercalcaemia
	Endocrine/metabolic	Thyrotoxicosis
		Adrenal failure
		Phaeochromocytoma
	Other	Acute renal failure
		Long-term immobility
		Tertiary hyperparathyroidism

1. Note that artefactual hypercalcaemia is common and can be due to venous stasis at phlebotomy, hyperalbuminaemia or hypergammaglobulinaemia.

excessive consumption of milk or alkali. Any features suggesting malignancy should be explored, especially in patients presenting acutely.

Drug history

- Ask specifically about lithium: the mechanism of action remains unclear but may involve altered calcium sensing by the parathyroid glands and enhanced effects of parathyroid hormone (PTH).

- Thiazide diuretics: reduce urinary calcium excretion and potentiate the effects of PTH.

- Vitamin D intake (either oral or topical, for example for psoriasis).

- Milk, alkali, antacids.

> A detailed drug history, including use of over-the-counter treatments for indigestion ('white medicine') or of vitamin D-containing preparations, is essential in the patient with hypercalcaemia.

Family history

A family history of hypercalcaemia or a personal history of pituitary or pancreatic islet cell tumours may suggest the presence of multiple endocrine neoplasia (MEN) type 1 (see Sections 2.5.7 and 2.7.1). Familial hypocalciuric hypercalcaemia (FHH) should also be considered in familial cases of hypercalcaemia.

Complications of hypercalcaemia

These include peptic ulceration and acute pancreatitis. Is there a history of bone pain or pathological fracture? If not due to malignancy, these may be caused by long-standing hyperparathyroidism. Ask directly about urinary stones, which were the presenting feature of this case.

Plan for investigation and management

First explain to the patient that under normal circumstances you would perform a full physical examination looking for signs associated with the conditions described in Table 1.

Investigation

All patients presenting with hypercalcaemia should undergo the following investigations:

- routine haematological and biochemical tests, including FBC, inflammatory markers such as erythrocyte sedimentation rate (ESR) and C-reactive protein (CRP), electrolytes, and renal/liver/bone function tests;

- measurement of serum PTH;

- chest and abdominal radiographs.

Look for the following clues.

- Anaemia: may indicate malignancy, including myeloma.

- ESR, CRP: raised in malignancy, especially multiple myeloma.

- Impaired renal function: usually a consequence of hypercalcaemia, but remember that advanced long-standing chronic renal failure can cause tertiary hyperparathyroidism.

- Phosphate: low in hyperparathyroidism, raised in multiple myeloma (particularly when accompanied by renal failure).

- Alkaline phosphatase (bone isoenzyme): reflects osteoblast activation.

- Abnormal liver function tests: consider malignancy.

- PTH: suppressed in virtually all causes of hypercalcaemia except hyperparathyroidism, where a

detectable PTH level (normal or high) is inappropriate for the serum calcium level.

- CXR: look for primary or secondary malignancy, or hilar lymphadenopathy suggestive of sarcoidosis.

- Abdominal radiograph (kidneys/ureter/bladder): look for urinary tract calcification.

> A serum PTH within the 'normal' range is inappropriate in the context of hypercalcaemia and suggests that the patient has hyperparathyroidism.

Other tests will be driven by clinical suspicion and the results of these initial investigations.

- Serum electrophoresis, urinary testing for Bence Jones protein, and a skeletal survey: if multiple myeloma is suspected, hence a first-line test in any patient over the age of 50 years with hypercalcaemia.

- Isotope bone scan for bony metastases.

- Vitamin D levels: may be helpful if intoxication is suspected, but require careful interpretation given their wide seasonal variation.

- Urinary catecholamines, thyroid function tests and Synacthen test.

- 24-hour urinary calcium excretion: low in FHH (see Section 2.5.7).

In this case primary hyperparathyroidism is the most likely diagnosis, and after normal or high PTH is confirmed in the presence of hypercalcaemia, investigation should be directed towards assessing complications and, depending on local practice, identification of the overactive gland(s) (see Section 2.5.7).

Management

Hypercalcaemia associated with complications Specific treatment will depend on the underlying disorder. In this case, given the history of urolithiasis and assuming the diagnosis of primary hyperparathyroidism, definitive treatment should be offered. For a solitary parathyroid adenoma the preferred option is surgical excision. The only controversy is whether preoperative imaging should be performed, for example with ^{99m}Tc-sestamibi scanning and/or neck ultrasound; currently this depends on local practice/expertise (see Section 2.5.7). Postoperatively transient hypocalcaemia may occur, which can be treated with intravenous 10% calcium gluconate in the acute setting, or with a combination of oral vitamin D and calcium supplements in milder cases.

Asymptomatic hypercalcaemia With a diagnosis of primary hyperparathyroidism, a calcium level that is only mildly elevated (eg 2.8 mmol/L as in this case), in the absence of symptoms of polyuria and polydipsia or confusion, and with no evidence of urinary tract calcification, it is debatable whether any immediate specific treatment is required based on the biochemistry alone, other than ensuring adequate hydration. It would be appropriate to give the patient advice to drink around 3 L of fluid daily and monitor the serum calcium and PTH every 6–12 months (sooner if symptoms develop).

For details of the approach to the investigation and management of renal calculi, see *Nephrology*, Sections 1.1.8, 1.4.6 and 2.6.2.

Further discussion

Surgery for asymptomatic primary hyperparathyroidism

In recent years practice has changed, and it is now more common to offer early parathyroidectomy, especially as expertise in minimally invasive day-case surgery grows, rather than waiting for hypercalcaemia to become more marked or complications to develop. In the absence of symptoms or clinically overt complications, guidelines have been developed regarding which patients should be offered surgery based on evidence of hypercalciuria and bone mineral density loss (see Section 2.5.7).

Familial cases of hypercalcaemia/ hyperparathyroidism

If associated with suspected or confirmed MEN-1, then it is important to counsel the patient that hyperplasia of all four glands generally requires total parathyroidectomy (see Section 2.7.1). FHH is typically associated with a family history of mild hypercalcaemia: screening using the urine calcium/creatinine ratio is mandatory if inappropriate parathyroidectomy is to be avoided.

1.1.2 Polyuria

Letter of referral to endocrinology outpatient clinic

Dear Doctor,

Re: Mrs Jane Parry, aged 53 years

Thank you for seeing this hotel receptionist who has recently been troubled by passing excessive amounts of urine. She is very thirsty and drinking 'gallons of water' every day. Her migraine also seems to have returned of late, although she thinks that the headaches are somewhat different to previously.

Her past medical history includes a left mastectomy followed by radiotherapy 4 years ago for breast cancer. She is on tamoxifen and co-codamol. On examination she appeared somewhat anxious, but there was nothing else of note except for a slightly high BP of 148/93 mmHg. She has a normal fasting glucose level, and her electrolytes and creatinine are also normal. I am not sure as to the cause of her polyuria and would appreciate your advice regarding further investigations and management.

Yours sincerely,

Introduction

Polyuria is defined as the passage of an abnormally large volume of urine and must be distinguished from frequency of micturition. It is usually taken to indicate the passage of at least 3 L in 24 hours, a useful surrogate marker being nocturia on two or more occasions each night. If polyuria is confirmed, there are a large number of possible causes (Table 2), and the history, clinical examination and initial investigations should be used to direct more detailed study. In essence, diabetes mellitus (DM), chronic renal failure (CRF) and use of diuretics should be excluded before distinguishing between hypothalamic/pituitary (often referred to simply as hypothalamic) or nephrogenic diabetes insipidus (DI) and primary polydipsia

TABLE 2 CAUSES OF POLYURIA

Problem	Example
Osmotic diuresis	DM (glucose) Chronic renal failure (urea)[1] Intravenous infusions (saline, mannitol) Diuretics
Abnormal renal tubular water handling	Hypothalamic/pituitary (cranial) DI Nephrogenic DI
Excessive fluid intake	Primary polydipsia (dipsogenic DI) due to habitual excessive drinking or psychogenic polydipsia Iatrogenic

1. Polyuria is most likely in CRF associated with damage to the renal medulla, which prevents the elaboration of concentrated urine.
DM, diabetes mellitus; DI, diabetes insipidus.

(dipsogenic DI) with water intoxication.

History of the presenting problem

⚠️ The first requirement is to be sure that polyuria really is present: investigation for a problem that the patient does not have is futile. If there is any doubt, a 24-hour urine collection should be performed before embarking on other tests. The patient does not have polyuria if all the urine fits in one of the standard containers, although he or she may have the frequency associated with it.

Polyuria or frequency of micturition?

'Tell me about a typical day. For instance, how was it yesterday, starting with when you woke up in the morning?' Enquire about the frequency of visits to the toilet and roughly how much urine is passed on each occasion (small, medium or large amounts). How often does she wake up to pass urine during a typical night? If she can sleep undisturbed for 8 hours, then it is unlikely that she has primary polyuria. Does it hurt or burn when passing urine? Is there any accompanying discomfort in the

abdomen/loin/groin areas? All of these might point to a chronic urinary tract infection leading to urinary frequency.

Daily fluid intake

In all cases take a careful history of drinking behaviour. Exactly what did the patient have to drink yesterday, and why did she drink it? It is not at all uncommon for someone referred with polyuria to have drunk several cups of tea and/or coffee, one to two cans of fizzy drink and 0.5 L of water before lunch, the reason being recognised by them as 'habit' rather than thirst, but often also driven by a belief that it is good to 'keep the kidneys flushed'. However, even in cases where it seems immediately apparent that excessive fluid intake out of habit is the reason for polyuria, it is appropriate to look for evidence on history, examination and simple testing of the other conditions listed in Table 2, since it can be difficult to know which came first: the polydipsia or the polyuria; the chicken or the egg.

Thirst

Is the patient drinking because of a genuine thirst rather than because of a dry mouth such as that experienced with a head cold

and compensatory mouth-breathing? Patients with primary polyuria drink water/fluids to quench their thirst rather than as a matter of habit or routine. Does she have to get up and drink water (rather than just to pass urine) during the night? If so, this suggests that the problem is not psychogenic.

Common causes of polyuria

Ask directly about DM (already excluded in this case), CRF and use of diuretics.

Hypothalamic or nephrogenic DI

Table 21 lists many of the causes of DI. Questions should be directed at screening for these disorders, for example when considering pituitary dysfunction, a history of head injury, surgery or radiotherapy should be sought, together with evidence of anterior pituitary failure (lassitude, weight gain, cold intolerance, constipation, diminished libido).

Primary polydipsia (dipsogenic DI)

Compulsive water intoxication (rather than simple habitual non-psychiatric excessive drinking) is likely to be concealed and details may need to be sought from a relative, partner or carer (possible in routine practice, but not in PACES).

Other relevant history

Headaches

Although the patient has a history of migraine, the letter from the GP says that the current headaches are probably different from those that she experienced in the past, which may suggest alternative pathology. In which part of the head are the headaches localised? Are they constant or intermittent? Is there any visual disturbance? Are there any other features such as nausea, vomiting, aura or flashing lights? Patients with pituitary/peripituitary pathology may have frontal headaches ('behind the eyes'), bitemporal hemianopia and/or visual disturbance due to involvement of cranial nerves III, IV and VI.

Past history of breast cancer

Lung and breast cancers may metastasise to the pituitary and cause central DI. Are there any features that might suggest local or metastatic recurrence?

Psychiatric and drug history

> **When taking a history from patients with polyuria, ask directly if they have any psychiatric history or if they have taken lithium in the past. They may not volunteer this information unless asked directly.**

Primary polydipsia is most commonly seen in those with a history of psychiatric illness. Lithium, a cause of nephrogenic DI, is often used in the treatment of bipolar affective disorders and depression.

Plan for investigation and management

Explain to the patient that under normal circumstances you would examine her, and then proceed as follows.

> **Investigation of polyuria**
> - Confirm that polyuria is present before embarking on tests (if necessary with 24-hour urine collection).
> - Exclude osmotic diuresis (high glucose).
> - Exclude CRF (high creatinine and urea).
> - Consider hypothalamic or nephrogenic DI.
> - Consider primary polydipsia (dipsogenic DI).

Routine tests

- FBC (anaemia).

- Electrolytes and renal function (dehydration, hypokalaemia, CRF).

- Blood glucose (DM).

- Liver and bone biochemistry (specifically calcium, phosphate and alkaline phosphatase).

- Urinalysis for glycosuria (DM or renal disease), haematuria and proteinuria.

- CXR for evidence of granulomatous disease (eg sarcoidosis, tuberculosis) or possible metastases (particularly relevant in this case).

Further tests

These include plasma and urine osmolalities and the water deprivation test.

Having excluded an osmotic basis for polyuria, the diagnosis now rests between hypothalamic or nephrogenic DI and primary polydipsia. Begin with 'spot tests' of plasma and urine osmolality.

- Plasma osmolality: usually lower than 290 mosmol/kg in polydipsia, reflecting volume overload, and greater than normal in hypothalamic or nephrogenic DI, reflecting volume depletion.

- Urine osmolality: on the first voided sample of the day (especially if the patient has not drunk excessively overnight). May prevent the need for more detailed investigation. A value >750 mosmol/kg excludes significant DI.

However, often these initial 'spot results' are inconclusive, and it is necessary to proceed to either a water deprivation test or hypertonic saline infusion with measurement

of plasma antidiuretic hormone (vasopressin) (see Sections 2.1.7 and 3.3.2).

If hypothalamic/pituitary DI is confirmed, the pituitary and hypothalamus should be imaged by MRI and dynamic tests of pituitary function should be considered (see Sections 2.1.8 and 3.1). Patients with nephrogenic DI require more detailed tests of renal tubular function.

Management

Excessive drinking Patients who have simply got into the habit of drinking excessively should be reassured after simple screening that there is nothing seriously wrong and that their urinary volume, and any attendant embarrassment caused by the need for frequent micturition, will be eased if they can gradually decrease the amount of fluid they drink.

Hypothalamic/pituitary DI Symptomatic relief may be provided with the synthetic vasopressin analogue desmopressin. This can be administered orally, or more conveniently via a nasal spray (see Section 2.1.7). Any associated anterior pituitary failure should also be corrected with appropriate hormone replacement (see Section 2.1.8). If imaging reveals a structural abnormality, then specific treatment may be required, eg radiotherapy or chemotherapy for a patient with known metastatic breast carcinoma.

Nephrogenic DI Wherever possible, correct the underlying cause (eg electrolyte disturbances). In cases where a reversible cause cannot be identified, thiazide diuretics (eg hydrochlorothiazide) in combination with mild sodium restriction are often effective.

Amiloride may be of benefit, especially in lithium-induced DI.

Primary polydipsia (dipsogenic DI) in psychiatric disorders Polyuria can be controlled by limiting fluid intake, but this is easier said than done. Patients may have a known psychiatric disorder, and formal psychiatric input should be considered in those who do not. However, the reason for trying to restrain drinking and polyuria in this condition needs to be considered. Unless of massive degree, it is likely that the only complication of primary polydipsia is the inconvenience of urinary frequency, and reassurance to the patient, relatives and carers that there is no serious pathology may be the limit of useful medical contribution.

Further discussion

Pituitary metastases from lung, breast and other malignancies are well recognised, and occasionally DI may be the presenting manifestation. There may be accompanying symptoms and signs due to local mass effect, including optic chiasmal compression or cranial nerve palsies. MRI/CT does not always distinguish between metastases and other pituitary lesions (Fig. 1), but it is worth noting that pituitary adenoma itself rarely presents with DI. Accordingly, in a patient with hypothalamic DI and a pituitary fossa lesion it is important to consider other possible diagnoses, eg intrasellar craniopharyngioma, metastasis, infiltration. If there are no other obvious pointers to the diagnosis, then pituitary exploration and biopsy may be necessary.

1.1.3 Faints, sweats and palpitations

Letter of referral to endocrinology outpatient clinic

Dear Doctor,

Re: Miss Anne Davies, aged 46 years

Thank you for seeing this woman who has had recurrent episodes of light-headedness associated with sweating and palpitations. They are occurring with increasing frequency and are affecting her ability to perfom her job as a company director. She has a toddler at home and is finding the life–work balance a challenge. She has no significant past medical history and the only family history of note is that her mother suffers from type 2 diabetes mellitus. I am grateful for your assesment as to the likely cause of these episodes.

Yours sincerely,

Introduction

> ⚠ This presentation could be simply due to stress, but it would be most unwise not to explore the history carefully in routine clinical practice or in PACES.

A fundamental issue here is to determine whether there is a true organic basis for the presentation. In most cases such as this the diagnosis can be made after taking a thorough history, and clinical examination often adds little. Although the symptoms described may have no

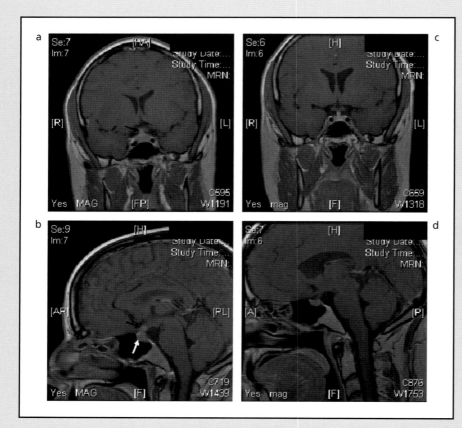

▲ **Fig. 1** Pituitary metastasis. Coronal (**a**) and sagittal (**b**) MRI scans demonstrating a pituitary mass (white arrow) with suprasellar extension (black arrow) in a 36-year-old woman with known metastatic breast carcinoma. Following radiotherapy (**c**, **d**) there has been a marked improvement in appearances.

TABLE 3 CONDITIONS PRESENTING WITH LIGHT-HEADEDNESS, SWEATING AND PALPITATIONS

Psychological/psychiatric 'Toxic'	Anxiety state Excess use of stimulants, eg caffeine Alcohol withdrawal Drug withdrawal
Cardiovascular	Primary arrhythmia Vasovagal Postural hypotension
Endocrine/metabolic	Menopausal vasomotor instability Hypoglycaemia Thyrotoxicosis Phaeochromocytoma

clear physical basis and simply represent a response to difficult social circumstances, a diagnosis of a non-organic disorder is a diagnosis of exclusion. In addition, 'light-headedness' means different things to different people: individuals with this symptom find their way into various clinics (neurology, cardiology, endocrinology, etc.) and a wide range of diagnoses need to be considered. The combination of light-headedness with sweating and palpitations is more specific in that it suggests enhanced autonomic sympathetic activity (Table 3).

History of the presenting problem

It is important to ask the woman to explain as precisely as possible the nature of the episodes of light-headedness, sweating and palpitations, and (in routine practice, but not possible in PACES) to obtain a report from a witness if available, since by the very nature of the problem the patient may not be able to give a lucid account. Ask both the patient and any witness about the following.

- When and how often do the episodes occur?

- What is she typically doing at the time?

- Are there any obvious precipitants?

- Are the onset and recovery sudden or gradual?

- What happens during an attack and how long does it last?

- Can she tap out how her heart beats at the time?

- Are some episodes worse than others?

Whilst answers to these questions may give a firm clue to one of the diagnoses listed in Table 3, it is also possible that the account given may broaden the differential diagnosis still further, and the full range of causes of presyncope, syncope or vertigo may need to be considered (see *Cardiology*, Sections 1.1.2 and 1.4.1; *Neurology*, Section 1.1.3).

Other relevant history

In addition to sweating and palpitations, enquire about the presence of any other autonomic symptoms, eg dry mouth, tremor, altered bowel habit. Consider the possibilities listed in Table 3 when talking with the patient.

Anxiety/depression

Does the patient experience pins and needles in the hands and feet, suggesting possible hyperventilation? Ask in detail about social circumstances, both at home and work, which seem likely to be relevant in this case from the information initially available. Does the woman have a long history of presenting with medically unexplained symptoms (see *Psychiatry*, Section 1.1.2)?

Alcohol/drugs

How much alcohol does the patient drink? Does she take any drugs, prescribed or non-prescribed? These questions must be approached with tact and care (see *Clinical Skills*, Clinical Skills for PACES). Is she 'addicted' to coffee?

Cardiac arrhythmias

Both tachyarrhythmias and bradyarrhythmias can be associated with light-headedness as a consequence of impaired cardiac output, and may be noted by the patient as 'palpitations'. Ask about shortness of breath, chest pain and any previous cardiac history (see *Cardiology*, Sections 1.1.2 and 1.1.3).

Endocrine/metabolic disorders

Autonomic symptoms can be the presenting feature of both common (eg thyrotoxicosis) and uncommon (eg phaeochromocytoma) endocrine and metabolic conditions. Ask carefully about symptoms that would suggest thyrotoxicosis, eg weight loss, tremor, dislike of hot weather. Neuroglycopenia is a possible cause of 'light-headedness' and hypoglycaemia must be considered in this woman (Table 4); if there is weight gain consider insulinoma.

Social circumstances

Whilst most of the history is directed at determining the accurate diagnosis, attention should also be paid to the impact that these symptoms are having on the patient's life, regardless of underlying aetiology, eg the ability to

TABLE 4 CAUSES OF HYPOGLYCAEMIA

Category	Examples
Diabetes treatment related	Inadequate carbohydrate intake, excessive exercise, pregnancy, inadvertent insulin/sulphonylurea overdose
Alcohol or drug induced	Salicylates, quinine, pentamidine
Tumour related	Insulinoma[1], non-islet cell tumour hypoglycaemia
Endocrine disorders	Hypopituitarism, Addison's disease, congenital adrenal hyperplasia
Hepatic dysfunction	Liver failure, inborn errors of metabolism, eg hereditary fructose intolerance
Reactive[2] (postprandial)	Idiopathic, post gastrectomy ('dumping syndrome')
Factitious	Sulphonylurea or insulin administration

1. A history of fasting or exertion-related hypoglycaemia in an otherwise healthy adult should prompt consideration of insulinoma.
2. Hypoglycaemia occurring within 5 hours of ingestion of food. In most cases the diagnosis is one of exclusion, with hypoglycaemia documented during the presence of symptoms.

perform her job and to look after her child.

Plan for investigation and management

In a case such as this your initial assessment is very important in gauging whether the symptoms have a psychological rather than physical origin, but beware of jumping to prejudiced conclusions. Always perform a full physical examination and relevant investigations unless the history is clear-cut.

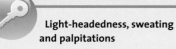

Light-headedness, sweating and palpitations

In anyone with episodic symptoms it is invaluable if the patient can be assessed during an attack. Priorities (after ensuring airway, breathing and circulation) are to observe the general appearance, check the pulse, measure BP, obtain an ECG rhythm strip, and test for hypoglycaemia with a fingerprick blood glucose monitor.

Carry out the following routine investigations:

- FBC (macrocytosis of chronic liver disease);

- electrolytes and renal function (low sodium and high potassium in Addison's disease);

- liver function (hepatic failure, metastases);

- fasting glucose;

- thyroid function tests;

- CXR (cardiac disease, metastases) and ECG (arrhythmia).

Further tests should be dictated by clinical suspicion.

- Cardiac disease: consider echocardiography and 24-hour tape (see *Cardiology*, Sections 3.3 and 3.10).

- Thyrotoxicosis (see Section 2.3.2).

- Phaeochromocytoma (see Section 2.2.4).

- Addison's disease (see Section 2.2.6).

- Hypoglycaemia (see below).

Hypoglycaemia

If hypoglycaemia is shown to be the cause of symptoms, then in most instances the aetiology (Table 4) can be readily identified without recourse to further studies (eg diabetes related, liver disease). Occasionally, however, additional investigations are indicated.

Insulinoma A supervised 72-hour fast with regular measurement of glucose and insulin profiles (every 6 hours, and at any time when the patient is symptomatic) will unmask hypoglycaemia in most cases. Biochemical confirmation of hypoglycaemia (laboratory blood glucose <2.2 mmol/L) should be accompanied by demonstration of inappropriate hyperinsulinaemia and elevated C-peptide levels.

If hypoglycaemia is found on a fingerprick blood glucose sample, immediately take a blood sample for laboratory estimation of glucose and a serum sample for storage for analysis of insulin, C-peptide and toxicological studies as appropriate.

The tumour may be visible on ultrasound (especially endoscopic ultrasound), CT (Fig. 2), MRI or angiography (Fig. 3), but up to one-third of tumours are sufficiently small to evade detection. Accordingly, some centres advocate localisation at surgery by palpation under direct vision. Intraoperative ultrasound aids detection of tumours that are too small to feel.

Factitious hypoglycaemia

Exogenous insulin administration causes hypoglycaemia with hyperinsulinaemia, but C-peptide levels are low because endogenous insulin secretion is suppressed. In contrast, the surreptitious use of sulphonylureas (which enhance endogenous insulin secretion) gives rise to a biochemical profile similar to that seen with insulinoma:

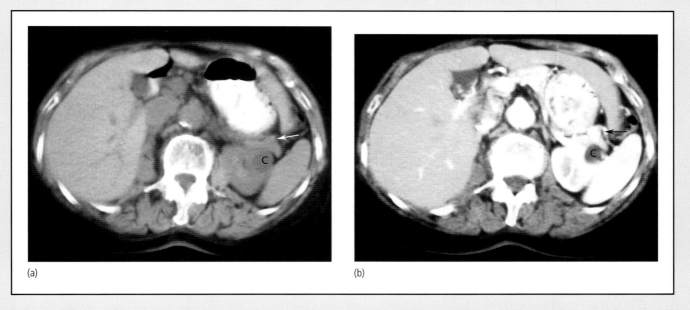

(a)   (b)

▲ **Fig. 2** Insulinoma. CT scans (**a**) before and (**b**) after contrast demonstrating an insulinoma (arrow) projecting anteriorly from the tail of the pancreas, in close proximity to an incidental left renal cyst (C).

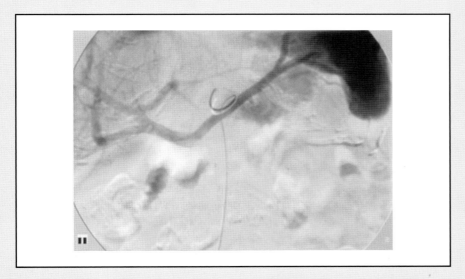

▲ **Fig. 3** Insulinoma tumour 'blush'. Digital subtraction angiogram of the splenic artery revealing the typical tumour 'blush' of an insulinoma within the tail of the pancreas.

diagnosis is made by assay of plasma or urinary sulphonylurea levels.

> ⚠ Factitious hypoglycaemia should be considered in those allied to the medical profession or, as perhaps in this case, where there is ease of access to insulin/oral hypoglycaemic agents (especially sulphonylureas).

Management

Insulinoma Surgical excision is the treatment of choice. Regular snacking will minimise the number of hypoglycaemic episodes prior to surgery. Diazoxide or somatostatin analogues, which inhibit insulin secretion, may be useful adjuncts in more refractory cases or in those considered unfit for operation.

Reactive hypoglycaemia Post-gastrectomy patients should be advised to eat little and often, avoiding rapidly absorbed carbohydrate. 'Idiopathic' (ie unexplained, but no sinister cause found) hypoglycaemia may respond to dietary manipulation with avoidance of refined carbohydrate and reassurance that there is no serious underlying disorder.

Factitious hypoglycaemia Treatment is difficult: confrontation often leads to denial despite convincing evidence. An underlying psychiatric condition is frequently present and appropriate referral is advisable, although often declined by the patient.

Further discussion

Multiple endocrine neoplasia type 1

Most cases of insulinoma are due to solitary benign tumours arising within the pancreas, but a small number have malignant potential and a few are seen in the context of the multiple endocrine neoplasia type 1 syndrome (see Section 2.7.1). The latter should always be borne in mind, and genetic counselling/ screening considered if there is a personal or close family history of hyperparathyroidism (ask about neck surgery, renal stones), pituitary adenomas or other neuroendocrine tumours (eg gastrinoma).

1.1.4 Gynaecomastia

Letter of referral to endocrinology outpatient clinic

Dear Doctor,

Re: Mr Lee Hopwood, aged 29 years

I would be grateful for your further assessment of this young teacher who complains of 18 months of progressive enlargement of both breasts, which are also intermittently uncomfortable. He is a keen sportsman who is increasingly embarrassed socially by his appearance. He is well in other respects, not having attended the practice for some 4 years. I would be most grateful for your advice on the cause and treatment of this problem.

Yours sincerely,

Introduction
Gynaecomastia is the presence of palpable breast tissue in a male. Clinically apparent gynaecomastia is found at about 1% of post-mortems, whilst corresponding histological changes have been reported in up to about 40%, suggesting that in many cases it may be a normal variant.

Gynaecomastia results from an increase in the net effective oestrogen/androgen ratio acting on the breast, either as a consequence

of a decrease in androgen production/action, or an increase in oestrogen formation (including conversion of circulating androgens to oestrogens by aromatisation). Physiological gynaecomastia may be seen in the newborn, at puberty and in the elderly. Other causes are listed in Table 5, but many cases are idiopathic.

The principal problems associated with gynaecomastia are cosmetic and psychological. In young men, gynaecomastia may lead to bullying and social isolation. In general, it is not associated with an excess risk of breast carcinoma, except in Klinefelter's syndrome.

TABLE 5 CAUSES OF GYNAECOMASTIA

Cause	Example/condition
Physiological	Neonatal Puberty Elderly
Idiopathic	–
Drugs that inhibit androgen synthesis or action[1]	Antiandrogens (eg cyproterone acetate, flutamide) or GnRH analogues (used in the treatment of prostate cancer) Digoxin Spironolactone Ketoconazole Metronidazole Cimetidine 'Recreational' use or abuse of anabolic steroids
Primary or secondary testosterone deficiency	Klinefelter's syndrome (XXY), Kallmann's syndrome Testicular failure secondary to mumps orchitis, trauma or orchidectomy Hyperprolactinaemia Renal failure
Increased oestrogen production (or increased aromatisation)	Testicular, adrenal or bronchogenic tumours producing hCG, oestrogens or androgens Chronic liver disease Starvation Obesity Thyrotoxicosis

1. Note that many other drugs have been implicated (some with no clear mechanism of action).
GnRH, gonadotrophin-releasing hormone; hCG, human chorionic gonadotrophin.

History of the presenting problem

When did the gynaecomastia start?
The age of the patient presenting with gynaecomastia is of great importance: this man is between puberty and old age, both times at which 'physiological' breast enlargement may be seen.
The duration and tempo of the enlargement should be noted, and the timing of pubertal milestones documented. Check whether the problem is unilateral or bilateral.

Has he noticed any other features?
Ask about tenderness, discharge and discrete lumps: lactation suggests hyperprolactinaemia.

What impact has this had psychologically?

It is very important to establish the reason for presentation and to document the degree of psychological distress caused by the problem.

Other relevant history

Has the patient gained a lot of weight over the course of the appearance of the breast enlargement? If so, this may be the reason.

Drug history

A careful drug history is essential, focusing on the drugs implicated in Table 5. In this case specific questioning about anabolic steroid use would be appropriate in view of the patient's involvement in sport: this is something that the patient might not volunteer in routine clinical practice, or in PACES, unless prompted to do so.

Testicular function

Evidence of testicular function should be garnered through questions about libido, shaving frequency, morning erections, and the onset of puberty. Whether the patient has been aware of any testicular lumps is also important.

Pituitary function

This presentation may be associated with invasive macroprolactinomas (and associated hypogonadism), hence ask about fertility: has he had any children? Does he have a partner and, if so, are they trying to have children? Also ask about any visual symptoms or headaches.

Other systemic diseases

Known liver disease, or risk factors for chronic liver disease should be sought, as should symptoms of thyroid disease.

Plan for investigation and management

Explain to the patient that you would normally conduct a full physical examination.

Investigation

Some experts argue that gynaecomastia is so common that it should only be investigated when breast enlargement is symptomatic, progressive, has no simple explanation or is accompanied by abnormal findings on examination. In these circumstances laboratory assessment should include:

- renal, liver and thyroid function tests;

- measurement of luteinising hormone, follicle-stimulating hormone and testosterone (with or without dehydroepiandrosterone sulphate as a marker of adrenal androgen production);

- oestradiol;

- hCG (± alpha-fetoprotein);

- prolactin (if other clinical features of hyperprolactinaemia);

- karyotype analysis, especially if gynaecomastia is accompanied by tall stature and small testes suggestive of Klinefelter's syndrome.

If oestradiol or hCG is elevated or testicular examination is abnormal, then testicular ultrasound is indicated.

Management

Where identified, the underlying cause should be treated, including withdrawal, where possible, of any drug that is implicated.

In idiopathic gynaecomastia, patients may simply need reassurance that there is no sinister underlying cause. Testosterone therapy is only effective in those cases associated with testicular failure. Tamoxifen may be of benefit in some patients, although this is an unlicensed use of the drug. For gynaecomastia associated with obesity there is a theoretical place for aromatase inhibitors such as letrozole, but again this is not a licenced indication. Cosmetic surgery (either liposuction or reduction mammoplasty) is the only effective definitive treatment.

> After taking a history, examining a patient and conducting appropriate investigations, do not underestimate the importance of reassuring a patient that nothing terrible has been found.

In practice it would be appropriate to arrange relevant blood tests and to review the patient again in clinic in 4–8 weeks to discuss any evidence for an underlying problem, and to explore his desire for therapy.

Further discussion

Most males with gynaecomastia find the condition distressing and a cause of social embarrassment, eg when taking part in sporting activities, as in this case. It can cause significant psychological morbidity, leading to teasing and social isolation in young men in particular. It is very important to address these concerns and to reassure the patient that you are arranging appropriate tests to exclude specific treatable conditions, although in many cases no underlying cause can be identified. Many men will appreciate reassurance that they are not becoming less masculine and more feminine, and it is also important to emphasise that even if no aetiological factor comes to light, then there are still a number of treatment options that can be considered.

1.1.5 Hirsutism

Letter of referral to endocrinology outpatient clinic

Dear Doctor,

Re: Miss Carly Denton, aged 33 years

Thank you for seeing this hairdresser with long-standing irregular menses who presents with gradually worsening hirsutism and weight gain. Interestingly, both the beautician doing her electrolysis and a fellow 'Weightwatcher' have suggested that 'there might be something wrong with [her] glands' and, accordingly, she is keen to seek 'expert' medical advice. I would be grateful for your views on diagnosis and treatment.

Yours sincerely,

Introduction

Knowledge of the normal biology of hair growth is central to the understanding of hirsutism, a common disorder in endocrine clinics. Although most cases represent predominantly a cosmetic problem, occasionally hirsutism is a sign of serious underlying pathology (see Table 40 in Section 2.4.6).

Hair

- Hair can be classified as either vellus (soft, non-pigmented) or terminal (coarse, pigmented). Before puberty most of the body is covered by vellus hair, notable exceptions being the scalp and eyebrows.
- At puberty, under the influence of androgens, vellus hairs are transformed into terminal hairs. In females this process is limited mainly to the pubic and axillary regions.
- The development in a female of terminal hairs in a male distribution (face, chest, back, lower abdomen and inner thighs) is referred to as hirsutism.
- Enhanced conversion of testosterone to dihydrotestosterone (active metabolite) through increased 5α-reductase activity in skin is believed to account for most cases of idiopathic hirsutism.
- Hirsutism should be distinguished from hypertrichosis, which is a generalised increase in vellus hair.

History of the presenting problem

Time course of hirsutism

How long have the symptoms been present? Polycystic ovarian syndrome (PCOS) typically presents with gradual onset of hirsutism and weight gain on a background of long-standing oligomenorrhoea, usually dating back to puberty.

Extent and previous treatment of hirsutism

Is the hirsutism restricted to certain body areas (eg chin, upper lip) or is it more extensive? Remember that the clinical picture may be modified by hair removal or make-up. Ask what measures the patient has used to control the hair growth (eg depilatory creams, waxing, plucking, shaving, electrolysis) and how frequently this is done. This will give an indication of the severity of the problem.

Other relevant history

Weight gain

A recent history of weight gain, as in this patient, is common and exacerbates the clinical features by promoting insulin resistance and suppressing sex-hormone binding globulin (SHBG) levels, thereby increasing circulating free androgens.

Virilisation

Increasing muscularity, deepening of the voice and/or clitoromegaly should prompt specific consideration of an androgen-secreting adrenal or ovarian tumour.

Disturbances of menstruation or concerns about fertility

A detailed menstrual history is critical, including current or previous hormonal contraceptive use. It is important to know whether the patient is currently concerned about fertility, as this may influence the course of treatment you recommend.

Oral contraceptive pill

Remember that many women on the combined oral contraceptive pill regard their withdrawal bleeds as 'normal periods' and will truthfully say that they are regular, but perhaps forget to mention that they are taking the pill.

Underlying disorders

Ask about symptoms of endocrine conditions, in particular Cushing's syndrome and hypothyroidism, and use of any prescribed or non-prescribed medications that may be associated with hirsutism (see Table 41).

Family history

Remember there are significant variations in the extent and distribution of body hair in normal women from different ethnic backgrounds. Ask about whether female relatives have had similar problems. PCOS is associated with insulin resistance, hence a family history of metabolic syndrome or type 2 diabetes should be sought.

Plan for investigation and management

Investigation

Opinions differ as to the extent to which women with hirsutism should be investigated. A suggested practical approach based on clinical findings is shown in Table 42. The features described in this case are suggestive of PCOS.

Investigation of hirsutism

- If suspected clinically, Cushing's syndrome and hypothyroidism require specific exclusion (see Sections 2.1.1 and 2.3.1).
- Dehydroepiandrosterone sulphate (DHEAS), a pure adrenal androgen, is useful in differentiating adrenal from ovarian sources of hyperandrogenism (see Section 2.2.3).
- If fertility is an issue, check mid-luteal (day 21 in a 28-day cycle) progesterone to determine whether cycles are ovulatory.

Management

Specific treatment will clearly depend on the underlying diagnosis:

- Cushing's syndrome (see Section 2.1.1);
- adrenal virilising tumour (see Section 2.2.3);
- ovarian virilising tumour (see Section 2.2.3);
- congenital adrenal hyperplasia (see Section 2.2.5);
- hypothyroidism (see Section 2.3.1).

Polycystic ovarian syndrome In the patient with PCOS, the following aspects are important.

- Communication: having excluded sinister underlying pathology, the patient should be reassured that although there is a slight imbalance between the male and female hormones in her body, all women have some circulating male sex hormones and she is not being 'masculinised' in any way. Patients with relationship problems or eating disorders may benefit from liaison counselling or psychotherapy.

- Weight loss: weight loss ameliorates all the symptoms of PCOS. Frequently, however, the patient has struggled to lose weight for many years, and may be unimpressed if, despite a hormonal imbalance being detected, there is nothing on offer other than a referral to the dietitian.

- Hirsutism: patients are usually experts on all forms of hair removal, having invested both time and money on a variety of cosmetic measures. Specific pharmacological options are discussed in Section 2.4.6.

⚠️ **Treatment of hirsutism**

Whatever treatment is given, patients are often disappointed that 6–12 months may pass before any benefit is seen. It is important to emphasise this before initiating therapy.

- Oligomenorrhoea/infertility: normalisation of the cycle can be achieved with a combined oral contraceptive pill, but ensure that you recommend a non-androgenic variety. Always enquire whether

fertility is currently an issue or likely to be so in the future: clomifene and/or metformin (see Sections 2.4.5 and 2.4.8) are likely to be more effective than the combined oral contraceptive pill in this setting!

- Other cardiovascular risk factors: patients with the metabolic form of PCOS may be obese and have impaired glucose tolerance. Other cardiovascular risk factors (eg hypertension, smoking, lipid profile) should be reviewed and treated as necessary (see Section 1.1.15).

- Review: the patient described has experienced a gradual onset of hirsutism with several features suggestive of PCOS and no worrying features to indicate malignancy. Having established that initial blood tests (luteinising hormone, follicle-stimulating hormone, testosterone, DHEAS, SHBG, 17α-hydroxyprogesterone) fit with the clinical diagnosis and agreed a management plan (in the first instance probably diet and exercise with or without co-cyprindiol; Dianette), it would be reasonable to arrange a follow-up appointment at 6 months. Significant effects are not seen before this time due to the long duration of the hair-growth cycle, with maximal effects not seen until 9–12 months.

Further discussion

Tailoring treatment for different needs

The patient has been referred with hirsutism, but she is 33 and her main concern may really be subfertility in view of her irregular periods. If this is the case she will need metformin or clomifene, with consideration of referral for specialist fertility treatment earlier rather than later as age restrictions apply for interventions such as *in vitro* fertilisation on the National Health Service. Patients' needs continually evolve and fertility should be discussed at each review.

Prognosis of PCOS

Whilst the patient's main concern may be cosmetic appearances, it should be borne in mind that this condition is associated with insulin resistance, type 2 diabetes and features of the metabolic syndrome. Cardiovascular risk factors should be sought and addressed, but this will require good communication with the patient as she may be unhappy coming away from clinic with several prescriptions, none of which helps her hirsutism!

1.1.6 Post-pill amenorrhoea

Letter of referral to endocrinology outpatient clinic

Dear Doctor,

Re: Mrs Tasmin Jayasena, aged 28 years

This woman presented after 2 years of failing to conceive. Her previous menstrual history is unremarkable, with menarche at 13 years of age and a regular cycle prior to going onto the oral contraceptive pill aged 18. However, she has had no menstrual bleeds since coming off the pill 24 months ago and she remains keen to start a family. I would be grateful for your opinion as to whether this is simple 'post-pill amenorrhoea', or whether further investigation is indicated at this stage.

Yours sincerely,

Introduction

The presentation is one of secondary amenorrhoea with infertility. 'Post-pill amenorrhoea' is not a diagnosis in itself: 6 months after stopping an oral contraceptive preparation, the risk of secondary amenorrhoea is no higher than in the general population, meaning that in amenorrhoea prolonged beyond this time some other pathology must be implicated. True secondary amenorrhoea may be related to failure at any level of the hypothalamic–pituitary–gonadal axis, whether functional (eg in the context of very low BMI) or due to direct neoplastic or inflammatory involvement of relevant organs, as detailed in Table 6.

History of the presenting problem

The history should begin by confirming that the patient had a normal menarche and regular menses prior to using the oral contraceptive pill (OCP) and establish whether there is any possibility of pregnancy (even allowing for the duration of amenorrhoea, pregnancy must be excluded in all cases).

Other relevant history

The rest of the history should be devoted to teasing out clues to the underlying problem, bearing in mind the conditions listed in Table 6.

Exercise/dieting/stress

Excessive exercise, weight loss or psychological stress can suppress the activity of the gonadotrophin-releasing hormone (GnRH) pulse generator. Patients may be evasive in their answers to questions concerning these issues. Similarly, severe illnesses with significant weight loss may also lead to hypothalamic amenorrhoea.

Pituitary disease

Secondary amenorrhoea can reflect direct damage to the gonadotrophs (eg pituitary adenoma, infarction) or hyperprolactinaemia (which disrupts GnRH neuronal activity). Enquire about galactorrhoea and other symptoms of pituitary disease, focusing on both symptoms of hormone hypersecretion and direct effects of a pituitary tumour, such as visual disturbance and new-onset migraine (see Section 2.1). If there is a history of previous pregnancy, then evidence of major haemorrhage or severe hypotension peripartum should be sought. Any general history of head trauma may also be relevant: the gonadal axis is particularly vulnerable to damage in both of these situations.

Premature ovarian failure

Most commonly autoimmune in origin and characterised by hypergonadotrophic hypogonadism.

TABLE 6 **CAUSES OF SECONDARY AMENORRHOEA**	
Cause	**Example/condition**
Physiological	Pregnancy Lactation Post-menopausal
Pathological	Polycystic ovarian syndrome (PCOS); (although more typically oligomenorrhoea) Hypothalamic–pituitary dysfunction (including excessive weight loss or exercise, stress, pituitary tumours/infiltration, hyperprolactinaemia) Premature ovarian failure Congenital adrenal hyperplasia Adrenal/ovarian neoplasms

Ask about menopausal symptoms (eg hot flushes, dyspareunia), check for a family history of early menopause, and also for any personal or family history of autoimmune disease.

Adrenal or ovarian tumours

Enquire about hirsutism and virilising features (see Sections 2.2.3 and 2.4.6). Given the regular menses prior to OCP use, both PCOS and congenital adrenal hyperplasia are less likely.

Exogenous sex steroids

It should be confirmed that the patient is not taking any exogenous preparations containing sex steroids.

Plan for investigation and management

In practice, it should be explained that the lack of periods is not due to an after-effect of the OCP alone, and that the problem may lie at one of various levels of the hormonal system controlling the ovaries.

Pregnancy test

> However unlikely it may seem, it is imperative to exclude pregnancy before embarking on further investigations for amenorrhoea. Explain this to the patient and obtain her consent to testing.

Routine blood tests

FBC, electrolytes, renal/liver/bone biochemistry and thyroid function will often have been checked before referral.

Specific endocrine assessment

- Luteinising hormone, follicle-stimulating hormone and oestradiol: to distinguish hypogonadotrophic and hypergonadotrophic hypogonadism.

- Prolactin: elevated in prolactinoma or with stalk disconnection.

- Testosterone and dehydroepiandrosterone sulphate: to exclude an androgen-secreting ovarian or adrenal tumour.

Further investigations will be guided by the clinical features and initial biochemical screen:

- hyperprolactinaemia and hypopituitarism (see Sections 2.1.3 and 2.1.8);

- PCOS (see Section 2.4.5);

- premature ovarian failure (see Section 2.4.3).

Management

Management will clearly depend on the diagnosis.

- Pregnancy: it is rare but not unheard of for pregnancy to present to an endocrine clinic. The chances are that you will not be the only surprised person in the room!

- Excessive exercise/weight loss/ stress: explain the physiological basis for the amenorrhoea and encourage moderation. Psychological/psychiatric input may be required.

For management of hyperprolactinaemia and hypopituitarism, PCOS and premature ovarian failure, see sections indicated above.

Further discussion

Advice for a patient with a pituitary tumour

> Patients with pituitary problems need to understand a little anatomy and physiology, otherwise their disease, its monitoring and treatment can seem very mysterious. They will often have their

own ideas about 'brain tumours': it is important to find out what these are and if necessary provide reassurance that their type of tumour will not spread elsewhere in the body and will not need treatment that results in baldness, etc. Patient information leaflets produced by the Pituitary Foundation (http://www.pituitary.org.uk/) are a useful aid.

Patients with microprolactinomas who are not trying to conceive need to be aware of the importance of complying with treatment to prevent osteoporosis: many women are quite happy not having periods when they know there is 'nothing to worry about'. If they find the side effects of bromocriptine upsetting, oestrogen replacement therapy is a good alternative.

1.1.7 A short girl with no periods

Letter of referral to endocrinology outpatient clinic

Dear Doctor,

Re: Miss Joanna Otai, aged 15 years

Thank you for seeing this young girl who has not started her menstrual periods yet. She is more concerned about her height and says that she is 'the shortest person' in her class. Her growth chart, maintained until the age of 9 years, shows that she has always been quite short. Her current height is 135 cm. She is otherwise healthy but it is quite obvious that she has not yet developed any secondary sexual characteristics. There is no family history of note and a recent set of blood tests, including FBC, electrolytes and renal function and blood glucose were all within normal limits.

I suspect that she has some hormonal cause for her delayed growth and puberty and would appreciate your evaluation and advice on further management.

Yours sincerely,

TABLE 7 CAUSES OF DELAYED GROWTH AND PUBERTY

Frequency	Condition
Common	'Constitutional delay'
	Chronic/severe illness
Rarer causes of short stature	Chromosomal abnormalities
	Single-gene defects
	Dysmorphic syndromes
	Endocrine disorders
Rarer causes of delayed puberty	Hypogonadotrophic hypogonadism
	Hypergonadotrophic hypogonadism
	Androgen excess

For further details see Table 37.

Introduction

'Delayed growth and puberty' are often linked presentations (see Sections 2.4.1, 2.4.3 and 2.4.4). In general, investigations should be initiated if there are no secondary sexual characteristics by 13.5 years in girls and 14.5 years in boys, and/or if the child's height falls below the third centile and is inappropriate for the height of the parents. There are many causes (Table 7), but remember that up to 3% of children exhibit constitutional pubertal delay.

History of the presenting problem

Birth and growth history

Enquire about birth weight and problems during pregnancy/at delivery: low birth weight is associated with short stature.

Are data showing the time course of growth failure available, eg child health records which include growth charts? In this case the GP's letter suggests that she has always been of short stature, but obtaining the actual charts allows you to determine whether there was a period of arrested growth from which she has never recovered the 'lost ground', or whether her growth velocity has been constant but low (Fig. 4). Has she experienced any dramatic changes in body weight?

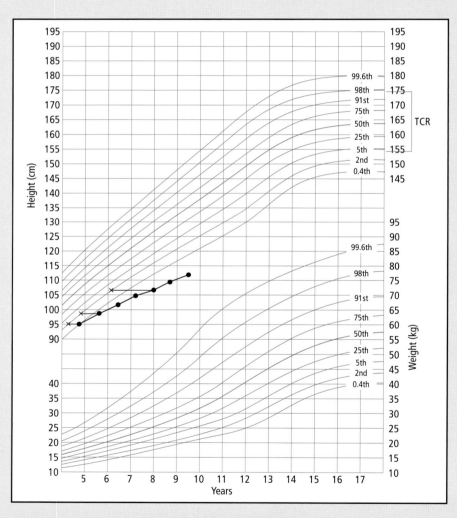

▲ **Fig. 4** Growth chart from a young girl with Turner's syndrome. The dots denote measurements plotted according to chronological age, whilst the crosses refer to bone age. TCR, target centile range.

Childhood/chronic illness

Does she have a history of other chronic illness, eg asthma, cystic fibrosis, Crohn's disease, chronic renal impairment, childhood cancer treated with chemotherapy and/or radiotherapy? Any of these can lead to short stature and/or delayed puberty.

Other relevant history

Past medical history

If Turner's syndrome is considered a possibility, ask about associated features: history of structural cardiac or renal disease; history of recurrent middle-ear infections or of hearing impairment; symptoms/signs to suggest hypothyroidism.

Family history

Enquire about a family history of short stature or delayed puberty. Ascertain the height of each of her parents.

Social history

Once you have gained the confidence/trust of the patient (and her parents) ask about eating habits: both nutritional deficiency and disorders such as anorexia nervosa may be associated with short stature and/or delayed puberty. Ask about her social circumstances: emotional stress can have adverse effects on growth.

Plan for investigation and management

Explain to the patient that under normal circumstances you would examine her fully. Recommended blood tests, imaging and further investigations are discussed in more detail in Sections 2.4.1, 2.4.3 and 2.4.4, but in brief may include the following.

Exclusion of chronic diseases

There are a number of chronic diseases that can be easily diagnosed and are worth screening for on a fairly universal basis:

- FBC (anaemia);
- electrolytes and renal function tests (chronic renal impairment);
- glucose (diabetes mellitus);
- C-reactive protein and/or erythrocyte sedimentation rate (systemic disorders);
- thyroid function tests (free thyroxine and thyroid-stimulating hormone);
- anti-tissue transglutaminase antibodies and IgA (coeliac disease);
- plasma bicarbonate and urinalysis (renal tubular acidosis).

Specific investigations

These will be determined by your clinical impression and initial screening tests, but may include the following.

- Bone age (typically plain radiograph of the wrist): can be compared with chronological age and may aid in the diagnosis of pubertal delay as well as in predicting future growth potential.
- Karyotype analysis: all girls with delayed puberty and growth should have a karyotype analysis as Turner's syndrome is not always clinically apparent.
- Paired luteinising hormone (LH), follicle-stimulating hormone (FSH) and oestrogen levels: will help to differentiate between hypergonadotrophic hypogonadism (primary gonadal failure as in Turner's syndrome) and hypogonadotrophic hypogonadism (secondary gonadal failure or constitutional delay).

Depending on the results of these investigations, more complex tests of pituitary function (eg gonadotrophin-releasing hormone test, see Section 3.1.4; assessment of growth hormone status, see Section 2.1.8) may be indicated, together with structural studies, eg MRI of the pituitary fossa, visual field assessment and pelvic ultrasound.

Management

Where identified, specific underlying disorders should be treated appropriately, eg juvenile hypothyroidism should be corrected with thyroxine replacement therapy. The management of Turner's syndrome is complex and requires a multidisciplinary approach as outlined in Section 2.4.4.

Further discussion

Children of parents with short stature

Children of parents with short stature and/or constitutional delayed puberty are at increased risk of being affected themselves. Determination of gonadotrophin (LH and FSH) and sex steroid (oestrogen or testosterone) levels together with assessment of bone age may help to establish the diagnosis. Low gonadotrophins and a relatively delayed bone age are more likely to be associated with normal (but delayed) pubertal development, whilst low gonadotrophins and a more advanced bone age are suggestive of underlying pathology, and require further investigation.

Turner's syndrome

Turner's syndrome occurs in 1 in 2,000 to 1 in 2,500 live-born females and is not always clinically apparent. All girls with delayed puberty and short stature, as a matter of rule, should have their karyotype checked. If the karyotype in peripheral blood-derived lymphocytes is normal but the clinical index of suspicion for Turner's syndrome remains high, then consider checking karyotype in a second tissue, eg skin fibroblasts, just in case the patient exhibits mosaicism.

1.1.8 Young man who has 'not developed'

Letter of referral to endocrinology outpatient clinic

Dear Doctor,

Re: Mr Gregory Clear, aged 18 years

Thank you for seeing this 18-year-old student who does not appear to have gone through puberty as yet. He originally presented to me with an upper respiratory tract infection, and at the time I noted a lack of facial and axillary hair. Subsequent examination revealed a general absence of secondary sexual characteristics, and his testosterone level has come back as very low.

Many thanks for your assessment.

Yours sincerely,

TABLE 8 CAUSES OF MALE HYPOGONADISM

Cause	Example/condition
Primary hypogonadism (ie testicular dysfunction)	Idiopathic Post chemotherapy, surgery, trauma or viral orchitis Klinefelter's syndrome (see Section 2.4.2) Systemic disorders, eg renal failure, haemochromatosis, myotonic dystrophy
Secondary hypogonadism (ie hypothalamic/pituitary in origin)	Constitutional delayed puberty Hyperprolactinaemia Hypothalamic/pituitary tumour/infiltration/surgery/radiotherapy Isolated hypogonadotrophic hypogonadism, including Kallmann's syndrome (see Section 2.4.2)

Introduction

The importance of the history in this case is firstly to confirm that the subject is indeed prepubertal, suggesting failure of onset of puberty rather than pubertal arrest (although there is overlap between these conditions, they should be considered as distinct clinical entities) and, secondly, to try to identify the underlying cause. Table 8 outlines the major groups of disorders associated with male hypogonadism, a term that denotes deficiency of both testosterone secretion (from Leydig cells) and sperm production (by the seminiferous tubules).

History of the presenting problem

Androgen status

Ask about frequency of shaving and beard growth, axillary and pubic hair development, deepening of the voice, and libido and erectile function (and where appropriate fertility).

Hypogonadotrophic hypogonadism

Enquire about problems with sense of smell (hyposmia or anosmia in Kallmann's syndrome), features suggesting other pituitary hormone deficiencies (Section 2.1.8), headaches/visual problems (hypothalamic/pituitary space-occupying lesion) and galactorrhoea (hyperprolactinaemia).

Hypergonadotrophic hypogonadism

Ask about testicular surgery/trauma or bouts of orchitis in the past, and gynaecomastia (Klinefelter's syndrome).

Other relevant history

Enquire about his previous medical history, in particular chronic illnesses during childhood and the teenage years. A family history of delayed puberty may be relevant in Kallmann's syndrome and in simple constitutional delayed puberty. Potential fertility may also need to be considered, although it would be appropriate to reserve this discussion for a later visit when the results of initial investigations are available.

Plan for investigation and management

Explain to the patient that under normal circumstances you would examine him to confirm his GP's findings. The objectives of investigation are firstly to confirm the presence of hypogonadism and then to determine the aetiology.

Routine blood tests

Unless the clinical features suggest a specific underlying disorder, some simple screening tests should be performed:

- FBC (anaemia);

- electrolytes and renal function tests (chronic renal impairment);

- fasting glucose;

- thyroid function;

- prolactin;

- liver biochemistry;

- serum transferrin saturation/iron studies (iron overload).

Gonadotrophins (luteinising hormone, follicle-stimulating hormone) and testosterone

The finding of a low testosterone level (ideally measured at 9 a.m.) on more than one occasion confirms hypogonadism. Measurement of luteinising hormone and follicle-stimulating hormone allows distinction between hypogonadotrophic (secondary) and hypergonadotrophic (primary) hypogonadism, although remember that the former may simply indicate constitutional delay.

Specific investigations

These will be guided by your clinical impression and preliminary screening tests, and are discussed in more detail in Section 2.4.2, but may include the following.

- Karyotype analysis: to exclude Klinefelter's syndrome.

- Assessment of pituitary function/ MRI pituitary fossa: in cases of secondary hypogonadism/ hyperprolactinaemia (see Sections 2.1.3 and 2.1.8).

- Genetic screening: if haemochromatosis is suspected (see Section 2.5.3), although this would be an unusual presentation for primary as opposed to secondary iron overload.

- Ultrasound of the testes: in cases of cryptorchidism.

- Semen analysis.

- Human chorionic gonadotrophin stimulation: to help differentiate primary and secondary gonadal failure.

- Bone densitometry (dual-energy X-ray absorptiometry): to help identify those at significant risk of fracture.

Management

The general principles governing management of the hypogonadal male are discussed in more detail in Sections 2.1.8, 2.4.2 and 2.4.8, but include patient and sympathetic explanation, treatment of any underlying disorder, correction/ replacement of hormone deficiency, and referral for specialist fertility advice if appropriate.

Further discussion

Testosterone replacement

Testosterone replacement can be efficiently delivered using patches (use may be limited by local skin reaction), gel (popular, although care needed to avoid transfer to partner or children), buccal tablet, intramuscular depot injection (3–4 weekly or 3-monthly depending on preparation) and implant. Oral preparations are not recommended as it is rarely possible to achieve therapeutic blood levels with this mode of delivery. Monitoring of testosterone replacement should include measurement of serum testosterone levels, liver chemistry and FBC (haemoglobin and haematocrit) and, where appropriate, prostate surveillance (digital rectal examination and prostate-specific antigen).

1.1.9 Depression and diabetes

Letter of referral to endocrinology outpatient clinic

Dear Doctor,

Re: Mrs Cynthia Scott, aged 72 years

This normally active widow was brought to our surgery by her daughters who are concerned about her mental state: they fear she is depressed. Her past medical history is unremarkable, although she is overweight and routine urinalysis has revealed glycosuria. Could she have an underlying endocrine cause for her problems?

Yours sincerely,

Introduction

Depression is very common. There may be several contributing factors, eg social isolation, neglect, bereavement, poverty and chronic health problems: all are major risk factors that should be sought in the history. Remember, however, that depression can be a manifestation of many physical illnesses, particularly in the elderly (Table 9).

History of the presenting problem

Is this depression?

What features have led the daughters to conclude that their mother is depressed? Has she directly complained of 'feeling down' or has she exhibited unusual thoughts/behaviour? Has she suffered any recent 'life events', eg bereavement, physical ill-health? How long have the symptoms been present for?

Primary depressive disorder

Enquire about physical and psychological features of depressive illness (see *Psychiatry*, Section 2.11). Also check if there is a personal or family history of psychiatric disease.

Depression secondary to underlying physical illness

Several physical disorders can present with or masquerade as depression, and accordingly a full medical history and systems enquiry is required to look for evidence of any of the conditions listed in Table 9. This will clearly involve

TABLE 9 PHYSICAL ILLNESSES WITH DEPRESSION AS A COMMON PRESENTING FEATURE

Type of problem	Example	
'Obvious'	Any condition causing severe physical debility	Malignancy 'Systemic illness', eg advanced cardiac/respiratory failure or chronic renal failure (dialysis) Parkinson's disease
	Any condition causing chronic pain	'Arthritis/rheumatism' Refractory headache Postherpetic neuralgia
'More subtle'	Endocrine	Hypothyroidism Hyperparathyroidism Cushing's syndrome Pseudo-Cushing's syndrome
	Neurological	Dementia

exploration of matters related to diabetes given that she has been found to have glycosuria. Has this been documented previously? Have there been symptoms of thirst and polyuria (see Section 2.6)? Has she recently gained or lost weight?

Also think about the following as you take the history.

- Cushing's syndrome/pseudo-Cushing's syndrome: type 2 diabetes is common in the elderly obese population, but when associated with mood change should prompt consideration of Cushing's syndrome. Enquire about symptoms of glucocorticoid excess, eg easy bruising, difficulty climbing stairs (see Section 2.1.1). Check for an obvious cause, eg exogenous steroid usage, and enquire about alcohol consumption. Remember that depression and excessive alcohol intake can result in pseudo-Cushing's syndrome (see Section 2.1.1). Care and tact will be required to elicit this history (see *Clinical Skills*, Clinical Skills for PACES).

- Hypothyroidism: mood change and weight gain are recognised

features of hypothyroidism (see Section 2.3.1).

- Hypercalcaemia: remember 'bones, stones, abdominal groans and psychic moans' (see Section 2.5.8).

- Dementia, eg Alzheimer's disease, multi-infarct dementia: may be mistaken for a depressive illness in the early stages (see *Medicine for the Elderly*, Section 2.7).

- Parkinson's disease: remember other physical features may go undiagnosed for some considerable period of time (see *Neurology*, Section 2.3.1).

Other relevant history

Enquire about home circumstances and social support.

Plan for investigation and management

Initial tests

- FBC and erythrocyte sedimentation rate (normochromic normocytic anaemia of systemic disease).

- Electrolytes and renal function: look for renal impairment; hypokalaemia (Cushing's syndrome).

- Liver chemistry and calcium (hypercalcaemia, metastases).

- Fasting glucose ± HbA$_{1c}$ (diabetes mellitus).

- Thyroid function tests (hypothyroidism).

- Consider performing a full dementia screen (see *Medicine for the Elderly*, Sections 1.1.2 and 2.7).

- CXR to look for evidence of bronchial neoplasia/lymphadenopathy.

- ECG.

Specific investigations and management

These will be directed by the suspicions raised on history, examination and initial testing:

- diabetes mellitus (see Section 2.6);

- Cushing's syndrome (see Section 2.1.1);

- hypothyroidism (see Section 2.3.1);

- hypercalcaemia (see Section 2.5.8);

- Parkinson's disease (see *Neurology*, Section 2.3.1);

- dementia (see *Medicine for the Elderly*, Section 2.7).

Further discussion

Coping with the diagnosis of diabetes

Many patients who are diagnosed with diabetes fear that this will inevitably mean insulin injections. Whilst this might ultimately be the case, it is important to emphasise that there are other ways to treat the condition, including diet, exercise and tablets, and that the diabetes may even regress with successful treatment of an underlying disorder such as Cushing's syndrome.

It is also important to consider whether the patient and/or her family would be capable of monitoring blood glucose levels and administering/supervising treatment, or whether a district nurse may need to visit each day.

1.1.10 Acromegaly

Introduction

Clearly a clinical suspicion of acromegaly in a patient awaiting carpal tunnel decompression must be taken seriously. However, the diagnosis has not been confirmed by finding a single 'high' growth hormone (GH) measurement. Normal GH secretion is highly pulsatile, with spikes of secretion every few minutes superimposed on a circadian rhythm, so random GH levels do not reliably discriminate between normal subjects and those with acromegaly unless markedly elevated.

History of the presenting problem

Symptoms of a GH-secreting pituitary adenoma are most usefully considered in terms of those attributable to direct local effects of tumour expansion, those that result from exposure to supraphysiological GH levels, and those due to associated hypopituitarism.

Symptoms due to local tumour expansion

Headaches, double vision and visual field loss.

Symptoms due to GH excess

- Changes in ring, shoe or hat size.

- Alteration/coarsening of features, or dental problems.

- Snoring, nocturnal apnoea, daytime somnolence: there is a high prevalence of obstructive sleep apnoea due to soft tissue overgrowth in the upper airway.

- Excessive sweating.

- Arthritis and arthralgia.

- Symptoms of cardiac failure.

- Symptoms of diabetes mellitus such as polyuria, polydipsia, tiredness and lethargy (GH antagonises the action of insulin). A rare difficulty in the clinical diagnosis of acromegaly is that patients with syndromes of severe insulin resistance may develop a strikingly acromegalic appearance (pseudo-acromegaly) without GH excess. This is believed to be due to cross-reaction of extremely high insulin levels with the insulin-like growth factor (IGF)-1 receptor, and perhaps also up-regulation of the receptor. A clinical clue to this condition is the presence of acanthosis nigricans, or diabetes requiring very large doses of insulin to control (>300 units/day).

- Hypertension: has his BP ever been measured? Hypertension is a major factor contributing to the excess morbidity and mortality seen in untreated acromegaly.

Symptoms due to associated hypopituitarism

Enquire about reduced libido and difficulties achieving/maintaining an erection (hypogonadism), tiredness and dizziness (adrenocorticotrophic hormone deficiency), weight gain and lethargy (hypothyroidism), and galactorrhoea (hyperprolactinaemia). Also see Section 2.1.8.

Other relevant history

Long-standing GH excess is associated with an increased risk of colonic polyps and carcinomas, so ask about alterations in bowel habit. Also remember that acromegaly can arise in the setting of multiple endocrine neoplasia type 1 (see Section 2.7.1). Check for a history of hypercalcaemia and ask about relatives with similar problems.

Plan for investigation and management

Covered in detail in Sections 2.1.2 and 3.2.4. In brief, after you have completed a thorough physical examination of the patient, consider the following.

⚠ Random GH levels do not reliably distinguish between normal subjects and those with acromegaly.

Growth hormone excess

- Oral glucose tolerance test: this remains the 'gold standard' investigation for confirming/excluding acromegaly, with the benefit also of establishing whether it has been complicated by the development of diabetes.

- IGF-1: levels are typically elevated above the age-related normal range and can be used to monitor the effectiveness of treatment.

Local tumour expansion

- MRI of the pituitary fossa: distinguishes macroadenomas from microadenomas and gives vital information about the proximity of the tumour to key anatomical structures such as the optic chiasm and cavernous sinuses. It is also important postoperatively to guide the choice of adjunctive treatment in cases where trans-sphenoidal surgery is not curative.

- Formal visual field testing: should establish the presence and extent of any temporal field defect.

Associated hypopituitarism

Luteinising hormone, follicle-stimulating hormone, testosterone, thyroid-stimulating hormone, free thyroxine, prolactin and an assessment of adrenal reserve, eg short Synacthen test or insulin tolerance test.

It is very unusual for diabetes insipidus to be a presenting feature of a pituitary adenoma, and polyuria in this case would be more likely to be due to previously undiagnosed diabetes mellitus. However, if there is any doubt, check electrolytes and paired serum/plasma and urine osmolalities and ask the patient to record fluid intake and output for a 24-hour period.

Complications of acromegaly

Further investigation will be determined by clinical findings and planned therapy, but formal polysomnography, or screening with overnight oximetry, will detect obstructive sleep apnoea in many patients with acromegaly and is of relevance to perioperative anaesthesia and airway management. Any clinical suspicion of colonic tumours should lead to formal examination of the large bowel endoscopically or radiologically. Do not forget to screen for other cardiovascular risk factors, eg dyslipidaemia.

Management

This is discussed in detail in Section 2.1.2. In brief, trans-sphenoidal surgery remains the mainstay of treatment for most patients with acromegaly, although there is increasing use of medical treatments: somatostatin analogues such as octreotide in sustained-release form (suppress GH secretion from the adenoma directly) and pegvisomant, a relatively recently developed GH receptor antagonist. In addition, radiotherapy remains an effective means of controlling tumour growth and lowering GH levels, although the latter may take several months/years to achieve.

Further discussion

Acromegaly

A picture is worth a thousand words (in routine clinical practice, but not available in PACES). Ask the patient to bring old photographs that may allow you to determine the approximate date of onset of the condition.

1.1.11 Relentless weight gain

Letter of referral to endocrinology outpatient clinic

Dear Doctor,

Re: Miss Kathy Macdonald, aged 24 years

Thank you for seeing this 24-year-old single mother who came to see me because she has gained 12 kg in weight over the last 7 or 8 months. Although she has always had a tendency to be slightly overweight, since the birth of her daughter her weight has increased at an alarming rate, despite the fact (she tells me) that she is hardly eating anything. Currently, she weighs 94 kg, which gives her a BMI of 35 kg/m². She has stretch marks over her lower abdomen. Her BP is 145/85 mmHg. I have checked her electrolytes, FBC and fasting glucose and they are all within normal limits.

I would be most grateful if you could see her to exclude an underlying cause for her weight gain.

Yours sincerely,

Introduction

Weight gain of such magnitude and velocity always warrants thorough assessment and evaluation to exclude possible secondary causes (Table 10).

History of the presenting problem

Time course of weight gain

Was there an event/trigger that started it off? She may have lost her

TABLE 10 CAUSES OF WEIGHT GAIN/OBESITY	
Cause	**Example/condition**
Lifestyle	Habitual/social overeating (quantity or quality, eg energy-dense foods) Excessive alcohol consumption Lack of exercise (voluntary or inability)
Psychological/psychiatric	Anxiety/depression Eating disorders, eg binge/comfort eating
Physiological	Pregnancy, post pregnancy Ageing
Genetic predisposition	Simple forms of obesity: likely to reflect interaction between the individual's genetic predisposition and his/her environment Severe monogenic obesity, eg congenital leptin deficiency Other syndromic disorders, eg Prader–Willi, Laurence–Moon–Biedl
Other	Endocrine disorders, eg hypothyroidism, polycystic ovarian syndrome (PCOS), Cushing's syndrome, insulinoma Hypothalamic dysfunction, eg tumour, infiltration, surgery Fluid retention, eg cardiac failure, nephrotic syndrome, cirrhosis Iatrogenic, eg glucocorticoids, lithium, antidepressants

job, contracted an illness, stopped smoking, suffered a personal/family stress or had a baby (as in this case). Was she overweight as a child or teenager? Has she been prone to fluctuations in weight?

Eating habits

Ask her to describe what she would eat during a typical day: both quantity and quality are important. Has there been any change in recent weeks/months? Ask (sensitively) about comfort/binge eating. Enquire about alcohol intake (current and past).

Exercise

Ask about formal exercise, eg gym, running, swimming, and also about exercise at home or at work. Does she have an active or sedentary job, or is she stuck indoors all the time with the baby?

Features suggesting an underlying psychological/psychiatric disorder

Check for clues to the presence of an underlying anxiety/depressive disorder, eg early-morning waking.

Underlying physical disorder

Consider asking about features of:

- hypothyroidism (see Section 2.3.1);
- PCOS (see Section 2.4.5);
- Cushing's syndrome (see Section 2.1.1);
- hypothalamic–pituitary dysfunction (see Section 2.1.8);
- insulinoma (see Section 1.1.3);
- cardiac impairment/nephrotic syndrome/cirrhosis.

Associated features

Ask about menstrual disturbance, eg oligomenorrhoea/amenorrhoea, and also features of androgen excess, eg hirsutism/androgenic alopecia, which are a consequence of associated insulin resistance.

Other relevant history

- Drug history: a full drug history should be taken (Table 10).

- Family history: ask about other family members who are overweight (especially if

childhood/early onset), thyroid disease, PCOS and type 2 diabetes.

- Social history: once you have gained the confidence/trust of the patient, enquire about social circumstances and employment/financial stresses.

Plan for investigation and management

Explain to the patient that under normal circumstances you would examine her and then proceed as follows.

Simple blood tests

- Electrolytes.

- Renal function tests (renal impairment).

- Liver function tests (hepatic steatosis, cirrhosis).

- Fasting glucose ± HbA_{1c} (diabetes mellitus).

- Fasting lipid profile (metabolic dyslipidaemia).

- Thyroid function (hypothyroidism).

Specific investigations

Depending on clinical suspicion and the results of preliminary investigations it may be appropriate to look for evidence of one or more of the following conditions:

- PCOS (see Section 2.4.5);
- Cushing's syndrome (see Section 2.1.1);
- hypopituitarism (see Section 2.1.8);
- insulinoma (see Section 1.1.3).

Management

Where identified, specific underlying disorders should be treated appropriately (see relevant subsections in Section 2).

Dietary assessment/advice Most patients who are overweight/obese will benefit from referrral for formal dietary assessment, especially those who claim that they are only eating lettuce and cucumber! Key issues to address include the following.

- Composition of current diet and total calorie intake: patients are often genuinely surprised at how many calories they are consuming each day (a food diary can be helpful).

- Food substitution, ie replacing current high-calorie energy-dense foodstuffs with healthier alternatives.

- Limitation of total calorie intake.

- Restriction of alcohol consumption.

Specific dietary advice will also be required if the patient is discovered to be diabetic or hypercholesterolaemic.

Exercise/lifestyle Encourage regular exercise, eg brisk walking, swimming or cycling for 30–40 minutes four to five times per week. Adjustments to work routines (eg taking the stairs rather than the lift) can also help.

> Most patients with simple dietary/lifestyle-related obesity require significant support in their quest to lose weight: encouragement and supervision can be provided through support groups (eg Weightwatchers), the GP practice or specialist hospital clinics.

Assessment of cardiovascular risk Other cardiovascular risk factors (eg hypertension, smoking, dyslipidaemia) should be reviewed and treated as necessary (see Section 1.1.15).

Medical therapy See further discussion below.

Surgery This is reserved for morbidly obese patients who are attending a specialist clinic and who have failed to lose weight or maintain weight loss despite intensive intervention and medical therapy. Two main types of surgery are available: 'restrictive', which limits the size of the stomach, and 'malabsorptive', which shortens the length of the gut by creating a bypass.

Further discussion

Drug treatments for obesity

Various agents are now licensed for use in subjects who are obese (BMI >30 kg/m^2) or overweight (BMI >27 kg/m^2 with a major obesity-related comorbidity, eg diabetes mellitus, hypertension) (Table 11).

1.1.12 Weight loss

Letter of referral to general medical outpatient clinic

Dear Doctor,

Re: Mrs Mandy Chang, aged 22 years

I would be grateful if you could see this healthcare assistant in your clinic. She has been previously fit and well and on no regular medications, but over the last 4 months she has lost more than 10 kg in weight and feels tired most of the time. There is not a lot to find on examination. I have arranged for her to have

TABLE 11 DRUGS USED TO TREAT OBESITY

Drug	Action	Comments
Orlistat	Gastric and pancreatic lipase inhibitor which reduces the absorption of dietary fat by ~30%	To prevent possible malabsorption of fat-soluble vitamins, co-prescription of a daily multivitamin is advised by some clinicians May potentiate the effect of warfarin Main adverse effect is faecal urgency/soiling, especially if non-compliant with dietary restriction of fat intake
Sibutramine	Centrally acting monoamine reuptake inhibitor that principally acts to increase satiety	Not recommended in patients with uncontrolled hypertension, pre-existing cardiovascular disease or tachycardia Concomitant treatment with monoamine oxidase inhibitors or serotoninergic drugs is not recommended because of the potential risk of serotonin syndrome
Rimonabant	Potent cannabinoid 1 (CB1) receptor blocker with both peripheral and central actions	In addition to promoting weight loss, rimonabant also ameliorates features of the metabolic syndrome, eg lowers HbA$_{1c}$, raises HDL-C and reduces triglycerides, effects which appear to be over-and-above those predicted on the basis of weight loss alone The most frequently observed adverse effects include nausea, dizziness, diarrhoea and insomnia An increased incidence of depressive illness was also reported in clinical trials, and the drug should be used with caution in those with a history of psychiatric illness, particularly depression or anxiety

HDL-C, high-denity lipoprotein cholesterol.

some blood tests, the results of which should be available for when you see her in clinic.

Thank you for advising on further investigation and management.

Yours sincerely,

Introduction

Weight loss is a non-specific symptom and may be the presenting manifestation of a large number of disorders (Table 12). However, the relatively short duration of symptoms in a previously fit young person makes some diagnoses, eg thyrotoxicosis, diabetes mellitus (DM), more likely than others.

History of the presenting problem

Allow the patient to explain what her major concerns are, then adopt a systematic approach with direct questions to screen for potential diagnoses for which relevant information has not been forthcoming.

General symptoms

Ask about other non-specific symptoms such as fever, night sweats and lymphadenopathy. Lymphoma is not uncommon in this age group and weight loss is one of the classical B symptoms.

Appetite and calorie intake

> Before embarking on a chase for causes of weight loss, it is always important to find out if the patient is trying to lose weight.

What is her attitude to eating and to her loss of weight? Appetite may be increased in hypermetabolic states, reduced in true anorexia of chronic disorders, and is usually normal in anorexia nervosa where the problem is food refusal. Has she ever made herself vomit?

Abdominal symptoms

Ask about dysphagia, vomiting/ regurgitation, abdominal pain or distension, and bowel habit (frequency, consistency, blood, mucus, difficulty flushing).

It may be that a clear lead will emerge to suggest malignancy, malabsorption or anorexia nervosa, in which case these possibilities should be pursued. Is it possible that other conditions listed in Table 12 are present? In this young woman consider the following.

Thyrotoxicosis

Ask specifically about the following.

- Heat intolerance: does the patient need fewer/thinner clothes/ bedclothes than those around her?

- Palpitations, breathlessness.

- Tiredness (mentioned by the patient), weakness, difficulty with sleeping.

- Mood: has she been irritable of late? Patients with thyrotoxicosis often report feeling unusually anxious/irritable/bad-tempered.

- Bowel habit: particularly increased frequency.

- Menses: especially oligomenorrhoea/amenorrhoea.

- Goitre: has there been any swelling or tenderness in the neck? Check for difficulty with swallowing/breathing.

- Eye symptoms, eg prominence, dryness/itching, double vision.

- Recent pregnancy: consider postpartum thyroiditis.

Diabetes mellitus

Elicit further symptoms, eg polyuria, polydipsia.

Other relevant history

- Past medical history: is there any history of previous surgery (especially abdominal) or chronic illness, or of any autoimmune disease.

TABLE 12 CAUSES OF WEIGHT LOSS

Type of disorder	Example
Hypermetabolic states	Thyrotoxicosis DM Acute sepsis/trauma
Anorexia of chronic disorders	Infections, eg gastrointestinal, HIV Systemic inflammatory disorders Malignancy, including lymphoma Addison's disease
Reduced calorie intake	Anorexia nervosa or other eating disorder Upper gastrointestinal tract pathology, eg oesophageal stricture Neurological disorders, eg motor neuron disease
Malabsorption	Coeliac disease
Increased physical activity	Female athletic triad

DM, diabetes mellitus.

- Drug history: check that she is not taking any non-prescription medications or herbal remedies that contain iodine or thyroid extract. Keep in mind the possibility of surreptitious use of thyroxine, laxatives, diuretics, etc.

- Family/social history: autoimmune thyroid disease may be associated with other organ-specific autoimmune conditions, so enquire about a personal or family history of thyroid disorders, DM, Addison's disease, pernicious anaemia, premature ovarian failure and vitiligo (see Section 2.7.2).

- Ask about recent travel abroad. If you suspect anorexia nervosa, concentrate on taking a careful social history. Ask about alcohol consumption and smoking; the latter can exacerbate dysthyroid eye disease.

Plan for investigation and management

Explain to the patient that under normal circumstances you would examine her, and then proceed as follows. Investigations should begin with 'screening tests', which are indicated in all cases of weight loss where the cause is not obvious.

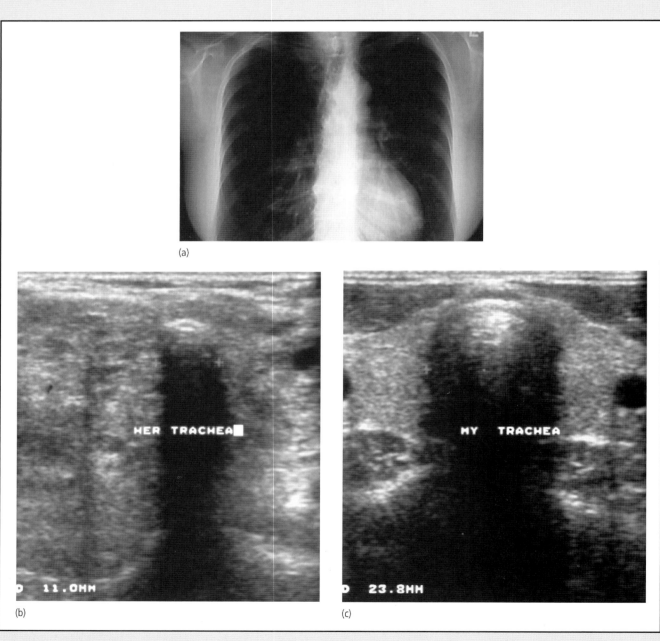

▲**Fig. 5** Retrosternal goitre with tracheal compression. (**a**) CXR and (**b**) thyroid ultrasound showing tracheal narrowing by a large retrosternal goitre. (**c**) Normal tracheal dimensions for comparison.

Routine tests

- FBC and C-reactive protein/ erythrocyte sedimentation rate (anaemia, infection, inflammation).

- Electrolytes and renal function (Addison's disease, anorexia nervosa, chronic renal impairment).

- Fasting glucose.

- Liver chemistry and calcium (intrinsic liver disease, malignancy).

- Haematinics (ferritin, folate, vitamin B_{12}).

- Thyroid-stimulating hormone (TSH).

- Anti-tissue transglutaminase antibodies and IgA (coeliac disease).

- CXR (lymphadenopathy, malignancy).

Further investigations should be directed by the findings on history, examination and screening tests.

Thyroid disease

If you suspect thyroid disease, check:

- free thyroxine (FT_4) ± free triiodothyronine (FT_3);

- TSH;

- thyroid autoantibody titres (see Section 2.3).

Radioisotope scans are not routinely performed in most centres but may help to differentiate between the various causes of hyperthyroidism when the clinical picture is not clear, eg in the absence of dysthyroid eye disease (see Section 2.3.2).

The presence of a retrosternal goitre and associated tracheal compression/deviation may be evident on plain radiography (Fig. 5a) and can be confirmed if necessary by ultrasound (Fig. 5b) and/or flow–volume loop analysis.

Other specific investigations

Consider Addison's disease (Section 2.2.6), lymphoma (*Haematology*, Section 2.2.5) and HIV; the latter diagnosis will need to be considered if no other explanation for weight loss emerges but needs to be approached carefully (see *Clinical Skills*, Clinical Skills for PACES).

Management

Thyrotoxicosis The various available treatment options are discussed in detail in Section 2.3.2. Reassure the patient that she has a treatable condition that is not malignant. However, it is important to point out that she might not feel completely back to normal for some time, whilst fine adjustments are made to the medication. It may be useful to explain the concept of an autoimmune disease. For a woman of childbearing age, as in this case, it is important to find out whether she could be pregnant or is planning a pregnancy in the near future, as this limits your treatment options (see Section 2.3.2).

Other specific disorders Where identified, other specific underlying disorders should be treated appropriately (see relevant subsections in Section 2).

Further discussion

Graves' disease

Features that would point to Graves' disease as the likely cause of this woman's thyrotoxicosis include the following.

- Age: toxic multinodular goitre is unusual in young females, although other causes of thyrotoxicosis (eg solitary adenoma, thyroiditis) must be considered.

- Family history of thyroid or other autoimmune disease.

- Dysthyroid eye signs: exophthalmos, ophthalmoplegia, periorbital oedema, chemosis.

- Pretibial myxoedema.

- Thyroid acropachy (looks like clubbing).

- Diffuse symmetrical goitre: clinically and on radioisotope scanning.

- Positive TSH receptor antibodies.

1.1.13 Tiredness and lethargy

Letter of referral to general medical outpatient clinic

Dear Doctor,

Re: Mr Charles George, aged 54 years

Thank you for seeing this 54-year-old businessman who is no longer able to meet the demands of his job. He has become excessively tired over the last 6 months and complains of extreme lethargy. The only past medical history of note is that of palpitations, which are now well controlled on amiodarone. It may be that he is simply trying to work too hard, but I would be grateful for your opinion as to whether there could be a medical explanation for his symptoms.

Yours sincerely,

Introduction

Tiredness and lethargy are non-specific symptoms, which most of us

TABLE 13 DISORDERS PRESENTING WITH TIREDNESS AND LETHARGY

Type of condition	Common or important example
'Normal variant'	Hard work Childcare
Psychological/psychiatric disorder	Anxiety Depression Alcohol dependence Chronic fatigue syndrome
Chronic/systemic illness, usually obvious in this context	Malignancy Heart failure Respiratory failure
Systemic illness, not always obvious	Anaemia Thyroid deficiency (or occasionally excess) Diabetes mellitus Primary hyperparathyroidism Addison's disease Hypopituitarism

experience from time to time – just think of the average junior doctor! A key part of the history is to try to determine whether tiredness and lethargy are features of an underlying medical disorder rather than everyday life. The differential diagnosis is broad, including those conditions listed in Table 13.

History of the presenting problem

Tiredness and lethargy
Exactly what does the patient mean by 'tiredness and lethargy'? When did the symptoms first appear? Have they been continuous or intermittent? Do they stop him doing anything that he would like to do? What activities has he had to cut out?

If the problem is that he falls asleep every night at 7 p.m., then this is certainly unusual; if he is unable to sustain working from 7 a.m. until midnight for five or six nights a week for very long, then few of us are able to do this and they (or their boss!) expect too much of themselves.

> **⚠** With any presentation that could have a 'physical' or a 'psychological/psychiatric' basis, always consider 'physical' conditions carefully before making a 'psychological/ psychiatric' diagnosis.

Specific diagnoses
Consider the diagnoses listed in Table 13 as you take the history.

- Anaemia: is there any history of indigestion or peptic ulcer disease? Carefully pursue any suggestion of altered bowel habit. Consider other causes of anaemia.

- Thyroid disease: both hypothyroidism and hyperthyroidism (see Sections 2.3.1 and 2.3.2) can present in this manner. This is likely to be of particular importance in this case since the patient is on amiodarone, which can be associated with both conditions (Fig. 6). Although unlikely, consider the possibility that his original palpitations

were a manifestation of thyroid hormone excess, now followed by thyroid hormone deficiency (a feature of thyroiditis; see Section 2.3.2).

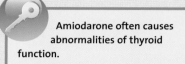

> **🔑** Amiodarone often causes abnormalities of thyroid function.

- Diabetes mellitus: excessive tiredness and lethargy are well-recognised presenting features of diabetes. Elicit further symptoms, including polyuria, polydipsia and weight loss (see Section 2.6).

- Adrenal insufficiency: tiredness and lethargy may be the only presenting symptoms of hypoadrenalism (see Section 2.2.6).

- Primary hyperparathyroidism: tiredness and constipation are common manifestations of chronic hypercalcaemia (see Section 2.5.7). Has the patient had urinary stones?

- Hypopituitarism: tiredness and lethargy are extremely common findings in subjects with hypopituitarism, frequently reflecting combined hormonal deficits (see Section 2.1.8).

- Anxiety and depression: ask about the physical manifestations of depressive illness such as early-morning wakening and poor appetite; also regarding the psychological/social factors that may be causative, eg stress at the office/home.

- Chronic fatigue syndrome: this is a difficult diagnosis that remains one of exclusion. Ask about poor concentration and memory, irritability, altered sleep and muscle aches.

The antiarrhythmic agent amiodarone has a high organic iodine content (approximately one-third by weight) and bears structural similarities to both T_4 and T_3:

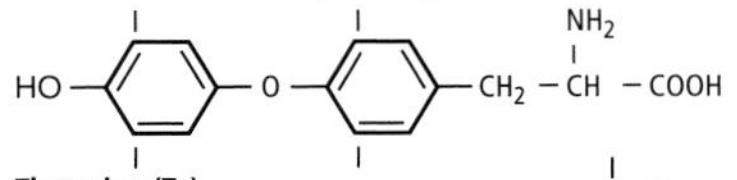

Thyroxine (T_4)

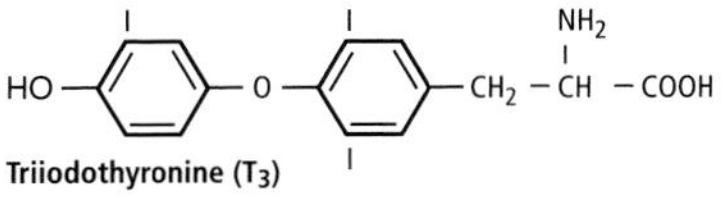

Triiodothyronine (T_3)

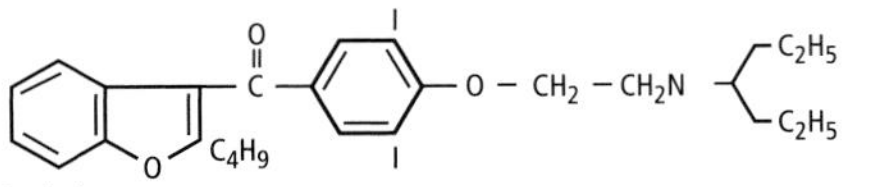

Amiodarone

Standard maintenance doses of amiodarone (100–200 mg/day) result in a massive expansion of the iodide pool and can influence thyroid physiology in various ways:

1 Abnormalities of thyroid function in clinically euthyroid individuals:
- ↑ T_4 and rT_3
- ↓ T_3 } through inhibition of the type 1 deiodinase
- ↑ TSH during early stages of treatment (? an effect on the pituitary type 2 deiodinase)

In the absence of overt symptoms of thyroid disease, specific treatment is usually not required, but thyroid function tests should be monitored periodically.

2 Amiodarone-induced thyrotoxicosis occurs in some patients and can arise through several mechanisms including:
- stimulation of excess hormone synthesis in response to an iodine load (more common in iodine deficient regions and may represent unmasking of occult thyroid disease, the so-called Jod–Basedow effect)
- destruction of thyroid follicles with subsequent release of thyroid hormones (essentially an inflammatory thyroiditis). Treatment can be difficult since it is often not possible to stop amiodarone. Medical therapy including antithyroid drugs and glucocorticoids may be necessary, with surgery reserved for difficult cases.

3 Amiodarone-induced hypothyroidism is more common in iodine-replete areas and in those with detectable thyroid autoantibodies. Again various mechanisms have been invoked, including the Wolff–Chaikoff effect in which high intrathyroidal iodide concentrations inhibit thyroid hormone biosynthesis. Treatment is generally easier than for thyrotoxicosis since amiodarone can be continued if necessary, and T_4 replacement therapy given.

Accordingly, it is wise to check thyroid function tests (FT_4, FT_3 and TSH) prior to commencing amiodarone and to periodically repeat them during treatment. Moreover, in light of its long half-life, abnormalities of thyroid function may persist for several months after discontinuation of therapy.

▲**Fig. 6** Amiodarone and thyroid function.

Other relevant history

This should include details of chronic/systemic illness, any autoimmune illnesses in the patient or his family, other medication (eg beta-blockers) and alcohol consumption.

Plan for investigation and management

First explain to the patient that normally you would perform a full physical examination looking for signs associated with the conditions listed in Table 13. The presenting symptoms here are vague, so initial investigations may need to cover a broad range of conditions.

Screening tests

- FBC (anaemia).

- Electrolytes and renal function (chronic renal impairment, Addison's disease).

- Liver chemistry and calcium (chronic liver disease, metastases, hypercalcaemia).

- Fasting glucose and thyroid function tests.

- CXR (malignancy).

- Inflammatory markers including erythrocyte sedimentation rate and C-reactive protein.

Specific investigations

Further investigations should be directed by the findings on history, examination and screening tests. In some cases, psychiatric assessment may be needed if depression or anxiety are felt to be key features.

Management

Where identified, specific underlying disorders should be treated appropriately (see relevant subsections in Section 2).

Further discussion

What if no cause for tiredness is found?

If all the initial investigations are negative and there are no other specific clinical pointers, then there is little to be gained by 'blind investigation', eg whole body imaging. In many cases an underlying medical cause for symptoms of tiredness and lethargy cannot be found, and lifestyle really is to blame. In these circumstances (which often form the basis of a communication skills scenario in Station 4 of PACES) it is important to explain the results of investigations that have been performed and to explain why you are not planning to arrange any further tests at this stage. Whilst some patients might be reassured that there is nothing physical amiss, others will be unhappy that no cause for their symptoms has been identified, especially if they sense that an underlying psychological cause is being inferred. Make sure that the patient knows that you have taken the symptoms seriously, but at the same time explain why continued 'blind investigation' is not justified nor in the patient's interest (inappropriate radiation exposure, the possibility of identifying an 'incidentaloma' that does not account for the presenting symptoms, etc.).

1.1.14 Flushing and diarrhoea

Letter of referral to endocrinology outpatient clinic

Dear Doctor,

Re: Mr James Hill-Wheatley, aged 50 years

This man has been unable to enjoy the recent festivities over Christmas because any over-indulgence with alcohol has resulted in severe facial flushing. He has also been troubled by rather watery diarrhoea. We would both be grateful for your advice on his further investigation and management.

Yours sincerely,

Introduction

Although it is important to bear in mind the possibility that the symptoms of flushing and diarrhoea are unrelated, taken together they suggest a number of specific diagnoses (Table 14).

History of the presenting problem

Flushing episodes

Can the patient describe a typical episode? How often do 'attacks'

happen, and how long do they last? Which areas of the body are affected, eg whole body, face, hands? Are there any precipitating factors, eg alcohol, tea/coffee, exercise, 'stressful' circumstances? Does he experience any other symptoms at the time of an 'attack', eg palpitations, sweating? What tablets/medications is he taking? For example, calcium channel antagonists and the sulphonylurea chlorpropamide are recognised causes of facial flushing.

Bowel symptoms

First find out what the patient considers to be his normal bowel habit, and then ask him to explain what he means by 'diarrhoea' (eg increased frequency of stool or loose motions). Has there been any blood or mucus with the stool? Are there any precipitating factors, eg specific foods, alcohol, 'stressful' circumstances? Has he travelled abroad recently?

Also check for other systemic symptoms, eg weight loss, malaise.

Other relevant history

Bearing in mind the possible diagnoses in Table 14, ask about the following if the information is not forthcoming spontaneously.

- Anxiety attacks: these would almost certainly be the commonest cause of this presentation. Are there other features to support this diagnosis? Has he had pins and needles affecting the hands and feet, 'atypical' chest pain or a history of medically unexplained symptoms?

- Thyrotoxicosis: enquire about weight loss, heat intolerance, tremor, proximal myopathy, etc. (see Section 2.3.2).

- Diabetes mellitus (DM): gustatory sweating and altered bowel habit are recognised features of diabetic autonomic neuropathy, but this is a feature of long-established diabetes and not a presentation of this condition (see Section 2.6).

- Carcinoid syndrome: most carcinoid tumours arise from enterochromaffin cells of the intestine. In general they are slow-growing and many are asymptomatic until metastases develop. Carcinoid syndrome only occurs when there are hepatic metastases or (rarely) a pulmonary primary releasing 5-hydroxytryptamine (5HT) directly into the systemic circulation (thereby circumventing first-pass metabolism in the liver).

TABLE 14 CONDITIONS ASSOCIATED WITH FLUSHING AND DIARRHOEA

Condition	Comment
Anxiety attacks Thyrotoxicosis Carcinoid syndrome	Common
Diabetic autonomic neuropathy Side effect of medication	Gustatory sweating and diarrhoea
Systemic mastocytosis	Very rare

Note that true 'flushing' episodes are not typical of phaeochromocytoma, although the pallor and profuse sweating that accompany catecholamine release may be perceived/interpreted as such by patients or their doctors.

It commonly leads to flushing (which may be spontaneous or precipitated by food, alcohol or stress) and recurrent watery diarrhoea. Other less common characteristics include abdominal pain, wheeze, right-sided heart disease and pellagra (dermatitis, diarrhoea and dementia due to niacin deficiency).

- Phaeochromocytoma: ask about related symptoms, eg anxiety, palpitations, hypertension (see Section 2.2.4).

Plan for investigation and management

Initial tests

- FBC.

- Electrolytes and renal function.

- Liver chemistry.

- Calcium.

- Fasting glucose ± HbA$_{1c}$.

- Thyroid function tests.

- Inflammatory markers (erythrocyte sedimentation rate and/or C-reactive protein).

Specific investigations

These should be guided by the patient's presentation: for thyrotoxicosis see Section 2.3.2; for DM see Section 2.6; for phaeochromocytoma see Section 2.2.4.

Carcinoid syndrome Look for biochemical and structural evidence using the following investigations.

- 24-hour urinary 5-hydroxyindoleacetic acid (5-HIAA) excretion: 5-HIAA is a metabolite of 5HT. A 24-hour collection is a sensitive (~75%) and specific (approaching 100%) test for carcinoid syndrome.

False-positive 24-hour 5-HIAA results

A variety of foods (avocados, bananas, plums, walnuts, pineapples, tomatoes, aubergines, cough medicine) can cause false positives in measurement of 24-hour urinary 5-HIAA and need to be avoided during the collection period.

- Fasting plasma gut hormones including chromogranins, a marker of neuroendocrine tumours.

- Ultrasound/CT: once the diagnosis has been confirmed biochemically, the liver should be imaged with ultrasound or CT. If the liver is clear, perform a chest CT to look for a pulmonary primary.

- Octreoscan: using radiolabelled octreotide about 85% of tumours can be visualised (Fig. 7). Uptake indicates that the tumour may respond to treatment with somatostatin analogues.

The carcinoid primary

Note that in a patient with hepatic metastases there is usually little to be gained in undertaking a protracted search for a primary carcinoid tumour unless it is causing symptoms in its own right, eg intestinal obstruction.

Management

This will clearly depend on the particular diagnosis. For anxiety/panic attacks the patient may respond to reassurance that there is no sinister diagnosis, but consider referral for specialist psychological/psychiatric input if symptoms are persistent and intrusive (see *Psychiatry*, Section 2.7). For thyrotoxicosis see Section 2.3.2; for DM see Section 2.6; for phaeochromocytoma see Section 2.2.4.

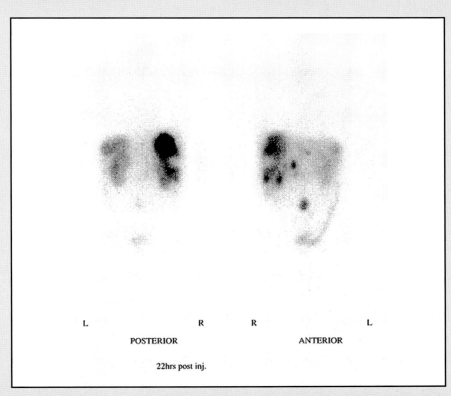

▲ **Fig. 7** Octreoscan. Radiolabelled octreotide scan demonstrating focal uptake centrally within the abdomen (primary tumour) and multiple areas of hepatic uptake (metastases) in a 67-year-old man with carcinoid syndrome.

Carcinoid syndrome The condition is rare, few doctors have much experience of it and it is best managed in a specialist centre. The patient's management will involve a multidisciplinary team that may comprise an endocrinologist, interventional radiologist, pathologist, oncologist, surgeon, dietitian, specialist endocrine laboratory and endocrine specialist nurse. This has obvious benefits in terms of receiving 'state of the art' treatment, but it may also have several inconveniences (eg lengthy travel, admission to hospital far from home) and these issues will need to be thought through and discussed.

It is important to explain to the patient the nature of his condition. Carcinoid tumours can fall anywhere along a spectrum from indolent to highly malignant. This degree of uncertainty is difficult for both patients and doctors to deal with, but one can be cautiously optimistic as survival for 10–15 years is not uncommon. It remains unclear as to whether any of the treatment options outlined below significantly affect life expectancy.

- Lifestyle and simple remedies: patients may be able to identify precipitating factors that they can avoid, such as alcohol, spicy food or strenuous exercise. Symptomatic treatment of diarrhoea with loperamide is worthwhile. Nicotinic acid supplements should be recommended. Antihistamines with antiserotoninergic activity (eg cyproheptadine) may be useful. Asthma (if present) can be treated with inhaled β-agonists.

- Surgery: symptomatic primaries and occasionally single hepatic metastases (depending on their size and position) may be amenable to resection.

- Somatostatin analogues: octreotide and the longer-acting somatostatin analogues frequently relieve symptoms of flushing and diarrhoea, although there is little evidence that they inhibit tumour growth. Unfortunately they have to be given by injection and side effects may include steatorrhoea (which can be treated with Creon), nausea/vomiting and gallstones. Intravenous octreotide is useful in the event of a carcinoid crisis (see below).

- Selective embolisation via the hepatic artery: the premise for hepatic artery embolisation is that tumours receive most of their blood supply from the hepatic artery, whilst hepatocytes are also able to derive blood from the portal venous circulation. Selective embolisation should be undertaken in specialist centres only. The patient is likely to experience fever, pain and nausea. Treatment carries a risk of massive hepatic necrosis and may precipitate a carcinoid crisis (hypotension, tachycardia and bronchoconstriction). The risk of carcinoid crisis can be minimised with careful hydration, oral cyproheptadine and intravenous octreotide infusion.

- Chemotherapy (eg 5-fluorouracil, interferon alfa): this has a limited role in the treatment of patients with carcinoid syndrome as the benefits are often outweighed by the side effects. Local transcatheter arterial 'chemoembolisation' (TACE) therapy has been tried, when an emulsion of the chemotherapeutic agent (doxorubicin or streptozotocin) is injected into the hepatic artery branches, followed by embolisation using gelatin sponge particles or microspheres. It is difficult to assess how much benefit accrues from the chemotherapy and how much from the embolisation as outcomes thus far appear similar to conventional embolisation.

- Response to treatment: can be assessed clinically, radiologically and by monitoring levels of 24-hour urinary 5-HIAA and fasting gut hormones.

1.1.15 Avoiding another coronary

Letter of referral to general medicine outpatient clinic

Dear Doctor,

Re: Mr John Smith, aged 55 years

This man works as a manager in our local supermarket. He suffered a heart attack 6 months ago but has made a good recovery. He has not had any angina since the event, and the cardiologists are not planning any further intervention at this stage as his post-infarct exercise test was reassuring. Not surprisingly, however, Mr Smith is worried about the possibility that he might have another coronary, and is keen to seek further advice as to what can be done to help him prevent this. He stopped smoking at the time of his admission, but is struggling to follow a healthy diet and lifestyle, due to what he says are 'pressures of the job'.

Currently, he is overweight (BMI 34 kg/m²) and his BP is 150/90 mmHg. There are no signs of heart failure. His most recent lipid profile has shown a total cholesterol of 4.5 mmol/L,

```
high-density lipoprotein
cholesterol (HDL-C) 0.8 mmol/L,
low-density lipoprotein
cholesterol (LDL-C) 3.0 mmol/L
and triglycerides 2.5 mmol/L.
He is taking aspirin, simvastatin,
atenolol and ramipril.

I would be grateful for your
advice as to how we can further
help him to reduce his risk of
another cardiovascular event.

Yours sincerely,
```

Introduction

The aim is clearly to identify all modifiable risk factors and then decide how best to address them in discussion with the patient.

History of the presenting problem

In taking the history you will obviously discuss symptoms of vascular disease and enquire about further episodes of chest pain, evidence of cardiac failure (has he had shortness of breath, orthopnoea or swelling of his ankles?) and any symptoms of cerebrovascular or peripheral vascular disease. After any positive replies have been explored, attention then moves to risk factors.

Diet

Is he on any sort of diet? What did he have to eat yesterday? Was this a typical day? Note consumption of saturated fat and also ask specifically about dietary/vitamin supplements, eg antioxidant vitamins, folic acid, ω-3 unsaturated fatty acids (fish oil). Is there a problem with total calorie intake? Eating healthier options but in copious amounts is unlikely to help with weight management.

Ask about his average weekly alcohol intake: is it within recommended 'safe' limits?

Exercise

Does he take regular exercise? If yes, how much and how often? The GP's letter mentions that he is 'struggling to follow a healthy diet and lifestyle'. Aside from formal exercise, what does his typical working day involve? As manager of the supermarket he may not be involved in physical tasks, but may spend much of the time sitting at his desk.

Smoking

It is important to confirm that he has completely given up smoking, and that he is not still having the occasional cigarette at work 'during stressful moments' or to 'help him relax' at home.

Hypertension

When was he first noted to be hypertensive? If this is long-standing, was he already overweight at the time of diagnosis and have other secondary causes been excluded? Is there a family history of hypertension?

Diabetes/impaired glucose tolerance

Has he ever been tested for diabetes mellitus (DM) or impaired glucose tolerance? Is there a family history of DM?

Dyslipidaemia

Had he ever had his cholesterol level checked prior to his heart attack? If so, does he know what the levels were and was he advised to alter his diet or that he needed to take tablets to help lower it? Is there a family history of dyslipidaemia?

Overweight/obesity

The GP's letter indicates that his BMI places him in the obese category (>30 kg/m^2). How long has he been overweight/obese? Ask about symptoms that might indicate a secondary cause for his obesity, eg hypothyroidism (see Section 2.3.1) or Cushing's syndrome (see Section 2.1.1).

Other relevant history

Medication

Ensure that you take a careful drug history including current doses: in routine clinical practice and in PACES you cannot rely on the GP's letter giving complete and up-to-date information.

Family history

In addition to checking for a family history of hypertension, diabetes and dyslipidaemia, ask about premature coronary, cerebrovascular or peripheral vascular disease in close relatives.

Plan for investigation and management

Explain to the patient that under normal circumstances you would examine him, paying particular attention to the cardiovascular system and metabolic parameters (eg waist circumference, see below), and then proceed with investigations as follows.

Routine tests

- FBC (anaemia or polycythaemia).

- Electrolytes and renal function (renovascular disease and other secondary causes of hypertension).

- Fasting blood glucose, looking for impaired fasting glucose or frank DM.

- Liver biochemistry (hepatic steatosis).

- Lipid profile (if that reported in the letter from the GP was not from a fasting sample).

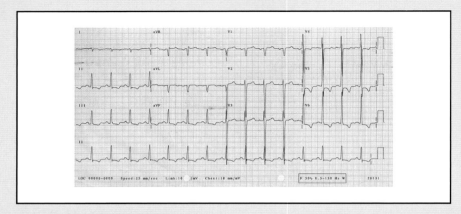

▲**Fig. 8** ECG showing voltage criteria for left ventricular hypertrophy: note the tall R waves in V5–V6, deep S in V2 and inverted T waves in II, III, aVF, V5–V6.

- Thyroid function tests (hypothyroidism).

- Urinalysis, checking specifically for glycosuria and proteinuria.

- CXR, looking for cardiomegaly, left ventricular failure and/or smoking-related lung disease.

- ECG: check for evidence of his previous infarct, ongoing ischaemic changes, left ventricular hypertrophy (Fig. 8).

Further investigations

These will be determined by the history, findings on physical examination and results of initial screening investigations, but may include the following.

- Oral glucose tolerance test: if impaired glucose tolerance is supected (see Section 3.1.7).

- Echocardiogram: if there is evidence of left ventricular hypertrophy or cardiac failure.

- Renal ultrasound: if renovascular or intrinsic renal disease is supected.

- Screening tests for Cushing's syndrome (see Section 2.1.1) and other secondary causes of hypertension (see Section 1.1.16), but these are much less likely to be appropriate.

Management

What can this man do to help himself, and what can be done for him?

Diet Refer to a dietitian to ensure that the diet is low in saturated fat (red meat, dairy products, egg yolks, fried food), low in refined carbohydrates, reduced in calories (to promote weight loss), and high in antioxidant vitamins, folic acid, ω-3 fatty acids (fresh fruit and green vegetables and oily fish).

Exercise Advise moderate exercise (walking, swimming, cycling) for at least 30–40 minutes three to four times per week. If he has not taken exercise for several years, then he should begin gradually and build things up over time.

Smoking Absolute cessation is required.

BP control Target ≤140/80 mmHg. Consider increasing the dose of his angiotensin-converting enzyme inhibitor or introducing another agent (NB although beta-blockers are still important in the secondary prevention of ischaemic heart disease, they are no longer preferred as front-line agents in the management of hypertension).

Diabetes (see Section 2.6) If the patient has impaired fasting glucose or impaired glucose tolerance, then dietary modification and exercise are the mainstay of treatment, but emerging evidence suggests that agents such as metformin may have a role in reducing progression to overt DM (see Section 2.6).

Lipid lowering Aim to achieve total cholesterol <4 mmol/L, LDL-C <2 mmol/L, HDL-C >1 mmol/L and triglycerides <2.0 mmol/L (see Section 2.5.1). In the first instance it would be appropriate to consider adjusting his statin dose in conjunction with dietary review.

Weight reduction This is usually best achieved through a combination of dietary modification and increased exercise. However, it may be necessary to consider the use of pharmacological therapy with an agent such as orlistat or the recently introduced selective cannabinoid (CB)-1 receptor antagonist rimonabant. The centrally acting appetite suppressant sibutramine would not be appropriate in this case, given the patient's ongoing uncontrolled hypertension and history of coronary artery disease.

Antiplatelet therapy Either with aspirin (as in this case) or clopidogrel.

Alcohol Recommend that intake is kept within 'safe' limits.

Further discussion

Metabolic syndrome/syndrome X

Central obesity is recognised to be a major risk factor for cardiovascular disease. This is reflected in the latest recommendations published by the International Diabetes Federation for the diagnosis of the metabolic syndrome (see below), in which central obesity is the only absolute requirement. Indeed, determining BMI alone is no longer considered to be acceptable in the assessment of cardiovascular risk, eg a middle-aged male with a BMI of 27 kg/m^2, but obvious visceral adiposity, is at greater risk of occlusive coronary disease than a younger female with a BMI of 33 kg/m^2 whose fat is predominantly distributed in the gluteal region.

International Diabetes Federation criteria for diagnosis of the metabolic syndrome (2005)

Central obesity (the only core requirement), defined as waist circumference ≥ ethnicity-specific cut-offs (eg ≥94 cm for Europid men and ≥80 cm for Europid women) plus two or more of the following.

- Hyperglycaemia: fasting plasma glucose ≥5.6 mmol/L or previously diagnosed type 2 DM.
- Hypertriglyceridaemia: triglycerides >1.7 mmol/L or treated for this lipid abnormality.
- Reduced HDL-C: <1.03 mmol/L (males) or <1.29 mmol/L (females) or treated for this lipid abnormality.
- Hypertension: BP ≥130/85 mmHg or treated for hypertension.

The clustering of various risk factors for cardiovascular disease with insulin resistance and central obesity has been recognised for more than half a century, but it was only in the early 1990s that these were drawn together under the umbrella term 'metabolic syndrome/syndrome X'. However, it remains a matter of debate as to whether formally diagnosing the disorder confers any additional benefits for patient management over and above identification and correction of individual risk factors.

1.1.16 High blood pressure and low serum potassium

Letter of referral to endocrinology outpatient clinic

Dear Doctor,

Re: Mr Jack Lewis, aged 40 years

Thank you for seeing this 40-year-old man in whom I have recently diagnosed hypertension (BP 160/105 mmHg). He had originally presented to me with generalised weakness and tiredness. Blood tests have shown that he is not anaemic, but his serum potassium is 2.4 mmol/L. I am concerned that he may have Conn's syndrome and would be grateful for your opinion.

Yours sincerely,

Introduction
The history in this case should be directed towards establishing the cause of hypertension and seeking evidence of target organ damage.

Although essential hypertension can strike at any age, a concern in any young patient presenting with high BP is to exclude a secondary cause (Table 15). The tiredness and weakness, although non-specific, are probably related to hypokalaemia in this case and would favour some of the secondary causes, including primary hyperaldosteronism as suggested by the GP.

History of the presenting problem
The history should begin by encouraging the patient to describe his symptoms of tiredness and weakness, also details of how his hypertension was discovered, and whether he has ever had his BP measured previously, before moving on to cover causes and consequences of both hypertension and hypokalaemia.

Causes of hypertension
Ask about the following if the details are not forthcoming.

- Is there a family history of high BP? Does he know if his parents, brothers or sisters are on antihypertensive drugs? If they are, 'essential' hypertension becomes an even more likely diagnosis (although a rare familial

TABLE 15 CAUSES OF SECONDARY HYPERTENSION

Type of condition	Example
Renal	Parenchymal disease, eg glomerulonephritis, chronic pyelonephritis, polycystic kidney disease Renovascular disease, eg atheromatous renal artery stenosis
Endocrine	Primary hyperaldosteronism, eg Conn's syndrome Cushing's syndrome Primary hyperparathyroidism Acromegaly Phaeochromocytoma Diabetes mellitus/insulin resistance (metabolic syndrome/syndrome X)
Drugs	Corticosteroids, oral contraceptive pill
Others	Coarctation of aorta Pregnancy-associated hypertension

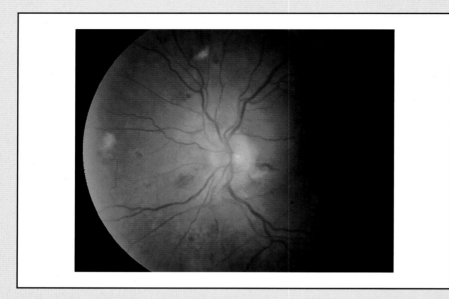

▲ **Fig. 9** Hypertensive retinopathy. Advanced retinal changes (cotton-wool exudates, flame and blot haemorrhages, blurring of the optic disc margins) identified in a 50-year-old man with hypertensive cardiomyopathy.

form of hypertension would be an outside possibility).

- Is there any history of renal disease? Has he had medicals for work or insurance where his urine has been checked in the past? A report of a 'just a bit of protein and/or blood' may indicate that he has long-standing renal disease and hypertension secondary to this.

- Could there be a phaeochromocytoma? Most patients with phaeochromocytoma will have some symptoms suggestive of catecholamine excess, the commonest being headache, sweating, palpitations and episodes of pallor (see Section 2.2.5). This is a very uncommon condition, but if you are not alert to the diagnosis you are unlikely to make it.

- Are there any features to suggest Cushing's syndrome (see Section 2.1.1) or acromegaly (see Section 2.1.2)? These are very unlikely, but again you will never make these diagnoses unless you consider them.

Consequences of hypertension

Enquire about any symptoms related to target organ damage:

- cardiac (chest pain/myocardial infarction, dyspnoea, peripheral oedema);

- cerebrovascular accidents/transient ischaemic attacks;

- retinopathy (Fig. 9).

Causes of hypokalaemia

Given that hypertension is common, it is possible that hypokalaemia in this case is not associated with it and other causes must be considered (Table 16). Ask about the following.

- Diarrhoea or vomiting.

- Diuretics: has he been prescribed these for his hypertension?

- Consumption of laxatives or liquorice.

- Proximal myopathy or other symptoms of steroid excess: hypokalaemia is most prominent in the setting of ectopic adrenocorticotrophic hormone (ACTH) secretion, but can occur

in any form of Cushing's syndrome when circulating cortisol levels are sufficiently high that they 'spill over' to act on the mineralocorticoid receptor. Ectopic ACTH secretion is unlikely to be the diagnosis if there is a long prodromal phase: the usual cause is malignancy and the pace of deterioration rapid (see Section 2.1.1).

- Family history of a 'potassium problem'.

> There are no clinical features beyond hypertension and symptoms related to hypokalaemia that might support the diagnosis of primary hyperaldosteronism: a high index of suspicion is needed to make the diagnosis.

Consequences of hypokalaemia

Enquire about other symptoms that might be due to hypokalaemia, eg thirst, polyuria (nephrogenic diabetes insipidus), paraesthesia (hypokalaemic alkalosis).

Other relevant history

In any patient with hypertension it is clearly important to enquire about other cardiovascular risk factors such as smoking, cholesterol, diabetes mellitus (DM) and family history.

Plan for investigation and management

Investigation of hypertension

In any patient presenting with hypertension it would be appropriate to check the following.

- Dipstick urinalysis: if this shows proteinuria or haematuria, send specimen for microscopy (casts).

- FBC: anaemia of chronic disease, eg renal failure.

TABLE 16 CAUSES OF HYPOKALAEMIA

Total body potassium	Mechanism	Common or important example
Normal	Shift of potassium into cells	β-Adrenergic stimulation Periodic paralysis
Reduced	Renal potassium wasting	Alkalosis, eg due to vomiting[1] Diuretics[1] Hyperaldosteronism Cushing's syndrome Liquorice excess Genetic: Gitelman's, Bartter's syndromes Various renal tubular disorders
	Gastrointestinal potassium loss	Any cause of diarrhoea Intestinal fistulae Colonic villous adenoma

1. The commonest causes of hypokalaemia, which must always be excluded before more exotic diagnoses are considered.

- Electrolytes and renal function: to confirm hypokalaemia and look for renal failure.

- Random glucose, with subsequent fasting sample if abnormal: impaired glucose tolerance/DM is associated with acromegaly and Cushing's syndrome.

- ECG/echocardiography: look for changes of left ventricular hypertrophy seen with long-standing hypertension (see Fig. 8).

- CXR: look for evidence of cardiomegaly, pulmonary oedema or rib notching (coarctation).

Investigation of hypokalaemia

In most cases the cause of hypokalaemia is obvious: in outpatient practice the patient is taking a diuretic and in inpatient practice the patient is (or has been) vomiting. In such cases investigation is not required, but if the cause is not apparent then the following should be considered.

- Electrolytes and renal function: to confirm hypokalaemia.

- Plasma bicarbonate and chloride: to check for metabolic alkalosis, usually a consequence of hyperaldosteronism (primary or secondary). A low plasma chloride would most commonly be explained by vomiting, which may be concealed.

- Urinary chloride: the diagnosis is hypokalaemia due to vomiting if the urinary chloride is very low.

- Urinary assay for diuretics and laxatives (in some cases).

> Always consider concealed vomiting in any case of unexplained hypokalaemia, particularly in young women who are most likely to be affected by anorexia nervosa/bulimia. The finding of a very low urinary chloride is often the crucial diagnostic test.

Specific investigations

These will be guided by the clinical findings and results of routine testing.

- Renal or renovascular disease:

    (a) urinary albumin/creatinine ratio or protein/creatinine ratio to quantitate proteinuria;

    (b) ultrasound to determine renal size and look for parenchymal abnormalities;

    (c) renal artery imaging if renal artery stenosis suspected (angiography using various techniques);

    (d) renal biopsy if renal parenchymal disease is likely.

- Primary hyperaldosteronism, Cushing's syndrome, acromegaly, phaeochromocytoma, primary hyperparathyroidism: see relevant subsections in Section 2.

Management

Treatment is directed where possible at the underlying cause, with correction of hypertension and attention to target organ damage. Specific aspects of management relating to endocrine hypertension are outlined in the relevant sections of this module.

1.1.17 Tiredness, weight loss and amenorrhoea

Letter of referral to endocrinology outpatient clinic

Dear Doctor,

Re: Mrs Mary Pearce, aged 42 years

Thank you for seeing this 42-year-old woman who has a 6-month history of tiredness and lethargy. Although 'routine bloods' were initially unremarkable, subsequent repeat thyroid function tests have shown a slightly elevated thyroid-stimulating hormone (TSH) with a low normal free thyroxine (FT$_4$). She has also lost a 'significant amount' of weight and her periods have stopped. More recently she has been troubled by nausea and vomiting. I wonder if this could be related to hypothyroidism?

Yours sincerely,

Introduction

> ⚠️ If the clinical picture does not fit, do not jump to a diagnosis because a test shows an abnormality.

Although tiredness and lethargy are commonly reported symptoms of hypothyroidism, the relatively mild derangements of thyroid biochemistry reported here seem unlikely to account fully for the clinical picture. In particular, weight loss and oligomenorrhoea/amenorrhoea are more in keeping with thyroid hormone excess than deficiency. It is therefore important to keep an open mind during the clinical assessment. Failure to do so, with treatment given simply on the basis of the biochemical abnormality, could lead to dire consequences.

History of the presenting problem

When did the woman last feel completely well? In retrospect, many patients can identify symptoms or signs in the past which they ignored at the time or failed to associate with their current problem.

Tiredness and lethargy

Tiredness and lethargy are non-specific symptoms seen in the context of many different physical and psychological illnesses as well as in normal individuals, especially when overworked. See Section 1.1.13 and Table 13 for details of the approach to this problem. The most important issue to decide at the beginning is whether the tiredness and lethargy really amount to much more than might be expected given the woman's lifestyle. Does it affect her daily routine, eg is she still able to work/take exercise? Has the tiredness become progressively worse with time? Does she find it necessary to sleep during the day?

In this case a key point to note is the presence of other symptoms: weight loss, nausea and vomiting cannot simply be ascribed to 'overdoing it'.

Weight loss, nausea and vomiting

Important points to ascertain include the following.

- How much weight has she lost and over what time period?

- Has this been associated with deliberate dieting or, alternatively, a loss of appetite?

- Confirm the timing of the onset of nausea and vomiting in relation to the weight loss.

- As a younger woman, did she have trouble with anorexia nervosa or bulimia? Has she ever made herself vomit?

Could a primarily gastrointestinal disease explain all of this woman's problems? Weight loss might be a reflection of reduced calorie intake, malabsorption or an underlying neoplastic process, whilst the development of anaemia could explain the tiredness and lethargy. Ask about appetite/dietary intake, abdominal pain/discomfort,

altered bowel habit, eg frequency/constipation, blood, mucus. Further discussion of the clinical approach to weight loss with gastrointestinal symptoms can be found in *Gastroenterology and Hepatology*, Section 1.1.5.

Oligomenorrhoea/amenorrhoea

> 🔑 Significant weight loss can cause menstrual irregularities.

Take a careful menstrual history. Ask about age at menarche and regularity of cycle thereafter, pregnancies and oral contraceptive use, previous episodes of oligomenorrhoea/amenorrhoea or menorrhagia, and date of her last period and whether it was 'lighter' or 'heavier' than usual. Further discussion on the clinical approach to amenorrhoea can be found in Sections 1.1.6 and 1.1.7.

Other features

This woman does not have symptoms confined to one organ system: how can this all be put together? Consider the following possibilities as you continue the history.

- Malignancy and systemic disorders: weight loss and lethargy are common presenting features of malignancy (including lymphoma) and other systemic conditions (eg hepatitis, HIV-related disease). Ask about night sweats and lymphadenopathy and where appropriate assess risk factors (including sexual partners, intravenous drug use and previous blood transfusions; see *Clinical Skills*, Clinical Skills for PACES).

- Depression/psychological illness: check for other physical manifestations of depression, including early-morning wakening. Ask about mood and social circumstances.

- Thyroid disease: this has been suggested on the basis of the blood tests taken by the GP. Check if there are any other symptoms to suggest thyroid dysfunction (Section 2.3).

- Addison's disease: remember that many of the symptoms of Addison's disease are non-specific, often leading to considerable delay in its diagnosis. Tiredness, weakness, anorexia, weight loss and gastrointestinal disturbances are commonly reported, and menstrual disturbance can be a feature. Has the patient noticed a desire to eat salt? Salt-craving is not uncommon in Addison's disease.

- Pituitary disease: hypogonadotrophic hypogonadism and secondary adrenal insufficiency may complicate primary pituitary disease (eg non-functioning adenomas). Ask about headaches and visual disturbance (suggesting a local mass effect) and galactorrhoea (hyperprolactinaemia due to prolactinoma or stalk disconnection). Bear in mind, however, that the elevated TSH would be unlikely with coexistent central hypothyroidism.

- Diabetes mellitus: enquire about polyuria and polydipsia. Prominent osmotic symptoms might be expected given the duration of illness and degree of systemic upset. Did the initial set of 'routine bloods' include a fasting glucose measurement?

Other relevant history

Is there is a personal or family history of organ-specific autoimmune disease, eg pernicious anaemia, vitiligo, thyroid disease (see Section 2.7.2)? Ask about smoking and alcohol consumption.

Plan for investigation and management

First, explain to the patient that under normal circumstances you would perform a full physical examination to look for signs associated with the conditions outlined above. The differential diagnosis here is very broad and it would be appropriate to begin with some 'routine' tests, although the history may direct you to more specific investigations.

Routine tests

- FBC (anaemia, haematological disorders).

- Electrolytes and renal function (chronic renal impairment, Addison's disease).

- Liver chemistry (malignancy, intrinsic liver disease).

- Fasting glucose (diabetes mellitus).

- Thyroid function tests.

- Erythrocyte sedimentation rate and C-reactive protein (systemic disorders).

- CXR (cardiac disease, intrinsic lung disease, lymphoma, metastases) (Fig. 10).

- With a history of amenorrhoea, pregnancy must always be excluded. Gonadotrophins (luteinising hormone and follicle-stimulating hormone), oestradiol and prolactin should also be measured.

- Dipstick urinalysis (renal disease).

Specific tests

These will depend on the history, physical findings and the results of routine tests described above, but may range from blood cultures and echocardiography if endocarditis is suspected, to testing for Addison's disease or pituitary disease (see specific subsections in Section 2), to psychiatric assessment (if depression/psychological illness is thought likely).

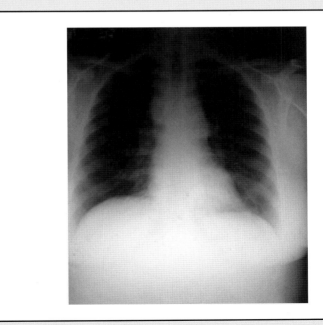

▲ **Fig. 10** Mediastinal lymphadenopathy. CXR demonstrating paratracheal lymphadenopathy in a patient with lymphoma.

Management

As always, management is directed at the underlying cause.

Addison's disease The rules and regulations governing glucocorticoid and mineralocorticoid replacement in both the emergency and routine settings are discussed in detail in Section 2.2.6. Note, as in this case, that minor abnormalities of thyroid function may revert to normal with satisfactory steroid replacement.

> **Treat adrenal insufficiency before hypothyroidism**
>
> In both primary and secondary adrenal insufficiency, glucocorticoid replacement must be initiated before coexisting hypothyroidism is treated in order to avoid the risk of precipitating a hypoadrenal crisis.

Hypopituitarism In addition to treating the underlying cause, appropriate hormone-replacement therapy should be instituted (see Section 2.1.8).

> Mineralocorticoid replacement is not necessary for patients with secondary adrenocortical insufficiency.

Further discussion

> Patient education is extremely important for those with adrenal insufficiency. Patients have to assume responsibility for a life-maintaining therapy that requires adjustment at times of stress and which may cause significant side effects, particularly weight gain.

1.2 Clinical examination

1.2.1 Amenorrhoea and low blood pressure

Instruction

Please examine this woman with secondary amenorrhoea and low blood pressure.

General features

Secondary amenorrhoea may be a consequence of ovarian, pituitary or hypothalamic dysfunction, but the combination with low blood pressure immediately raises the possibility of two scenarios: (i) a pituitary or hypothalamic disorder with malfunction of the hypothalamic–pituitary–adrenal and hypothalamic–pituitary–gonadal axes or (ii) Addison's disease with associated autoimmune ovarian failure. Initial inspection should concentrate on these two possibilities, but looking specifically for:

- general pallor (so called 'alabaster skin');
- vitiligo;
- palmar/buccal/scar pigmentation.

Does the patient appear to be of normal, high or low BMI? For the latter consider possible causes of weight loss, eg anorexia nervosa, malabsorption.

Whilst acromegaly could present with secondary amenorrhoea, low blood pressure is not a common finding. Similarly, in Cushing's syndrome the patient is likely to be hypertensive due to cortisol excess.

Endocrine examination

Specific examination should focus on the likely affected glands, with respect to both anatomical abnormalities caused by mass lesions and hypofunction of the relevant hormonal axes:

Evidence of a pituitary mass lesion

- Bitemporal hemianopia or quadrantanopia.
- Eye movement abnormalities.
- Reduced visual acuity/red extinction/optic disc pallor/relative afferent pupillary defect.

Evidence of dysfunction of hypothalamic–pituitary–target organ axes

Hyperfunction Examine for features of:

- acromegaly (see Sections 1.1.10 and 2.1.2);
- Cushing's syndrome (see Sections 1.2.4 and 2.1.1);
- hyperprolactinaemia (see Section 2.1.3).

Hypofunction Examine for presence of the following.

- Hypothalamic–pituitary–adrenal dysfunction: scanty axillary hair, postural hypotension, but without excess pigmentation.
- Hypothalamic–pituitary–thyroid dysfunction: slow relaxing reflexes, bradycardia, slow mentation, hypothermia.
- Hypothalmic–pituitary–gonadal dysfunction: loss of secondary sexual hair/diminished secondary sexual characteristics.
- Hypothalamic–posterior pituitary dysfunction: evidence of dehydration, although this is not likely to be present in any patient who is well and able to drink freely, such as when assisting in PACES, but may become a significant problem in any situation where the patient is

unable to access or absorb water, eg intercurrent illness/vomiting. May be masked by concomitant glucocorticoid deficiency.

Other disorders

- Addison's disease (see Section 2.2.6).

- Oligomenorrhoea/amenorrhoea/ premature menopause (see Section 2.4.3).

Further discussion

Visual field defects in pituitary disease

The classical visual field abnormality in a patient with a pituitary macroadenoma causing optic chiasmal compression is a bitemporal hemianopia (see Figs 11 and 26). However, it is important to remember that pressure on the optic chiasm from below initially results in a superior quadrantanopia (either unilateral or bilateral) (Fig. 12), before progressing to a complete bitemporal field defect. In contrast, a mass arising in the suprasellar region and primarily compressing the chiasm from above (eg a craniopharyngioma) is likely in the early stages to be associated with an inferior quadrantanopia (Fig. 13).

1.2.2 Young man who has 'not developed'

Instruction

This man presented to his GP concerned that he was 'not developing properly'. Blood tests at the practice have revealed a very low testosterone level. Please examine him and demonstrate relevant physical signs.

General features

The aim of the examination in this case is to (i) demonstrate the findings that suggest hypogonadism

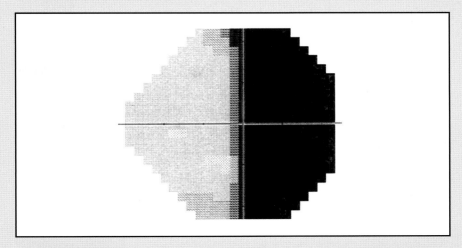

▲**Fig. 11** Dense right temporal hemianopia in a patient with a bitemporal field defect due to chiasmal compression by a large pituitary macroadenoma.

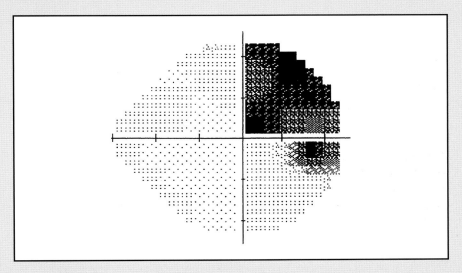

▲**Fig. 12** Right superior quadrantanopia. Note the blind spot just below the horizontal meridian.

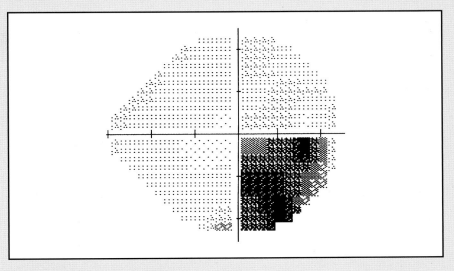

▲**Fig. 13** Right inferior quadrantanopia.

and (ii) to identify features that may point you towards the underlying cause. Long-standing hypogonadism often gives rise to a distinctive facial appearance, especially in older men in whom the poverty of facial hair and lack of temporal recession is most noticeable (Fig. 14).

Endocrine examination

Check for the following.

- An impaired sense of smell (Kallmann's syndrome).

- Eunuchoid habitus (ie span greater than height and heel to pubis distance greater than pubis to crown), which is common in those in whom hypogonadism precedes puberty, eg Klinefelter's syndrome.

- Gynaecomastia: indicates a decrease in the androgen/oestrogen ratio.

Assess pubertal development

The Tanner staging system (see Section 2.4.1) allows objective assessment of sexual maturity. In recognition of the differing actions of adrenal androgens and gonadal steroids, it distinguishes between genital and pubic hair development in boys, and breast and pubic hair development in girls.

In routine clinical practice the presence of bilateral descended testes should be confirmed by palpation and testicular volume assessed with an orchidometer (Fig. 15). In PACES offer to do this, but anticipate that the examiner will not wish you to proceed.

The patient with hypogonadism

Cryptorchidism (unilateral or bilateral absence of the testes from the scrotum) is an important clinical finding since it indicates a significant risk of malignant transformation in the affected gonad(s) and further investigation is mandatory.

▲ **Fig. 14** Hypogonadal male. Note the absence of facial hair and fine wrinkles around the corners of the eyes and mouth.

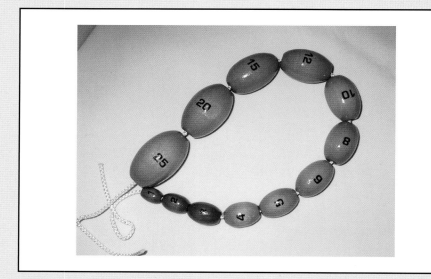

▲ **Fig. 15** Prader orchidometer.

Assess pituitary status

Check for features suggestive of a pituitary tumour, eg bitemporal quadrantanopia/hemianopia, Cushing's syndrome (see Section 2.1.1), galactorrhoea (hyperprolactinaemia; see Section 2.1.3) and hypopituitarism (see Section 2.1.8).

Further discussion

Determining the cause of hypogonadism

Defining whether the patient has hypogonadotrophic or hypergonadotrophic hypogonadism is not always possible clinically, but is important for directing further investigation. Paired measurements of testosterone and gonadotrophins are mandatory. In cases of Klinefelter's syndrome, karyotype analysis will confirm the diagnosis. If there is evidence of a bitemporal hemianopia or hypopituitarism, then a more global assessment of anterior pituitary function is indicated. Pituitary MRI scanning is likely to be required in most cases of hypogonadotrophic hypogonadism.

1.2.3 Depression and diabetes

Instruction

This elderly woman was taken to her GP by her daughters who were concerned that she might be depressed. On direct questioning, she also gives a history of recent weight gain and has noted increasing difficulty rising from her armchair. Urinalysis has revealed glycosuria. Please examine her.

General features

The examination instruction is vague in this case, meaning that the examiner is anticipating that you will base your assessment around your initial clinical observations and the clues provided in the instruction. Thinking about these clues and looking carefully from the end of the bed are critical.

- Cushing's syndrome: the combination of altered mood, weight gain, proximal myopathy (difficulty rising from the chair) and probable diabetes mellitus (glycosuria) strongly suggests this diagnosis.

- Hypothyroidism: may also occasionally present with a proximal myopathy.

If your initial clinical impression supports one or other of these

diagnoses, then direct your examination accordingly, but make sure that you give at least brief consideration to other possibilities.

- Diabetes mellitus: could the difficulty rising from the chair reflect diabetic amyotrophy (see Section 2.6)?

- Thyrotoxicosis: whilst this is very unlikely to present with weight gain, thyrotoxicosis in the elderly can manifest atypical features including apathy and depression (so-called apathetic hyperthyroidism) (see Section 2.3.2).

- Hypercalcaemia: again unlikely, but is there band keratopathy (see Section 2.5.8)?

- Parkinson's disease: check for the classic triad of resting tremor, bradykinesia and cogwheel rigidity (see *Neurology*, Sections 1.1.6 and 2.3.1).

You will also need to decide whether the psychiatric features are sufficiently prominent to merit more formal assessment. For example, consider the following.

- Appearance, general behaviour, speech, thought, abnormal beliefs (see *Psychiatry*, Section 2.5)

- Dementia: assess the mental state if you suspect that this is significantly impaired (see *Medicine for the Elderly*, Section 3.2).

Endocrine examination

- Cushing's syndrome: check for bruises, thin skin, purple striae, proximal myopathy, centripetal obesity, buffalo hump, acne, hirsutism and hypertension (see Section 2.1.1).

- Hypothyroidism: check for goitre, hair/eyebrow loss, dry skin,

bradycardia, carpal tunnel syndrome, slow relaxation of reflexes (see Section 2.3.1).

Further discussion

Cushing's syndrome and pseudo-Cushing's syndrome

Signs that most reliably differentiate Cushing's syndrome from pseudo-Cushing's syndrome are proximal myopathy, easy bruising and thinness and fragility of skin. Centripetal obesity, buffalo hump and hirsutism are also classical clinical features but relatively poor discriminators.

Obesity and Cushing's syndrome

The increase in obesity in the general population means that many more individuals are being referred to endocrine clinics for exclusion of an underlying endocrine cause. It is not necessary or practical to screen all obese individuals for Cushing's syndrome, but additional features such as depression, hypertension, glycosuria, proximal myopathy, easy bruising and thin skin should prompt screening investigations (see Section 2.1.1).

1.2.4 Acromegaly

Instruction

Please examine this man with joint pains and visual problems.

General features

Acromegaly is a classic 'spot diagnosis', and because the morphological features persist even after hormonal cure it is over-represented in examinations. The clinical question posed is unlikely to be particularly clear, and may rely on symptomatic features of acromegaly, such as arthritis, carpal tunnel syndrome, visual problems, sweating or headaches, or on a management problem such as poorly controlled diabetes. Acromegaly should be high on your list of possibilities in Station 5 of PACES when faced with a vague instruction.

Look for the typical facial appearance: greasy skin (seborrhoea), prominent supraorbital ridges, broad nose, thick lips, large tongue and perhaps ears (Fig. 16). Hands are likely to be 'spade-like' (Fig. 17).

Endocrine examination

Check for evidence of prognathism/ malocclusion of the teeth, and a goitre. Then carefully examine the following.

- Hands: as above, and look for signs of carpal tunnel syndrome.

- Eyes: assess visual acuity, examine visual fields to confrontation (looking for evidence of a bitemporal quadrantanopia/ hemianopia; note that supraorbital ridging may also produce a mild altitudinal field defect) and test for ophthalmoplegia (reflecting lateral extension of the pituitary tumour).

- Cardiovascular system: record the BP and look for signs of heart failure.

- Evidence of fingerprick testing suggests a diagnosis of diabetes, while skin tags and acanthosis nigricans are signs of insulin resistance.

- Gynaecomastia and galactorrhoea: may be present if the causative pituitary macroadenoma is co-secreting prolactin and growth hormone (see Section 2.1.3).

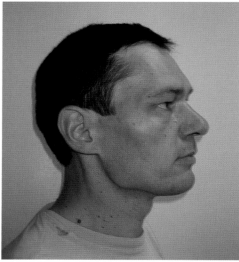

▲**Fig. 16** Acromegalic facies, showing the typical coarse facial features with prominent supraorbital ridges, prognathism and multiple skin tags.

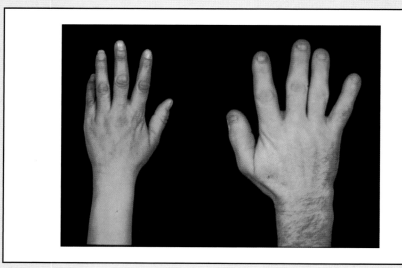

►**Fig. 17** Acromegalic hands. Soft tissue growth leads to marked enlargement and thickening of the digits, such that the hand takes on a 'spade-like' appearance when compared with that of an unaffected subject.

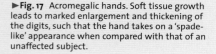

- Signs of hypopituitarism: look for evidence of pituitary hormone deficiencies (see Section 2.1.8)

Further discussion

Active versus inactive disease

It is useful to appreciate the difference between evidence of active growth hormone hypersecretion (such as headaches, poorly controlled diabetes despite significant insulin doses, pronounced seborrhoea, progressive enlargement of hands/feet) and evidence of past disease (the morphological features described above).

1.2.5 Weight loss and gritty eyes

Instruction
This woman has recently lost 10 kg in weight. She also complains of dry eyes with a sensation of 'grittiness', especially first thing in the morning. Please examine her.

General features

Although the differential diagnosis of weight loss is extremely broad (see Table 12), the combination with dry/gritty eyes strongly points to a thyroid disorder, and more specifically Graves' disease. The classical eye signs and goitre may be immediately evident from the end of the bed, but you need to be systematic in your approach to the examination if you are to efficiently demonstrate all the relevant signs in the available time.

Endocrine examination

Eyes

- Lid retraction: can you see the sclera (white of the eye) above the cornea (Fig. 18)?

- Lid lag: does the eyelid lag behind the globe as it turns down?

- Proptosis: forward movement of the globes due to increased volume of orbital connective tissue, muscle and fat. This is often best appreciated by looking either from the side or from above and behind with the head held in the neutral position. The degree of proptosis can be more accurately 'quantified' using an exophthalmometer. Check to see whether the patient can actually fully close the eye; if not, then he or she is at risk of developing an exposure keratitis.

- Periorbital oedema: this is typically non-pitting and boggy and more noticeable in the lower eyelid due to the effects of gravity (Fig. 18).

- Chemosis: excessive redness and watering of the eye (especially the conjunctiva).

- Ophthalmoplegia: tethering of the extraocular muscles may lead to diplopia, particularly on upward or lateral gaze (see Section 2.3.2, Fig. 41).

> ⚠ In any patient with suspected Graves' ophthalmopathy it is important to formally assess visual acuity, examine the fundi and to consider checking for loss of colour vision. If there is any concern, or if the patient has evidence of ophthalmoplegia or complains of pain, then urgent referral to an ophthlamologist is required.

Thyroid gland

Examine for a goitre and bruit and check for a scar of previous thyroid surgery.

Thyroid status

- Hands: are they warm and moist, and is there evidence of a fine resting tremor? Look carefully for the rare but important sign of thyroid acropachy (similar to clubbing).

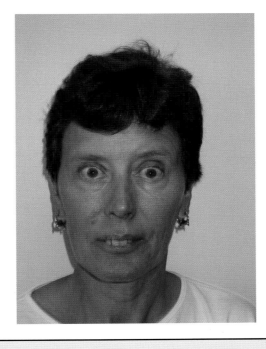

▲ **Fig. 18** Graves' disease. Note the typical 'staring eyes' with evidence of lid retraction and mild periorbital oedema.

- Pulse: check for sinus tachycardia or atrial fibrillation.

- Shins: does the patient have pretibial myxoedema (see Section 2.3.2, Fig. 42)?

- Shoulder/pelvic girdle: is there any evidence of a proximal myopathy?

Further discussion

Specific manifestations of Graves' disease

The specific manifestations of Graves' ophthalmopathy (proptosis, ophthalmoplegia, periorbital oedema and chemosis) are distinct from the more general eye signs of hyperthyroidism/thyrotoxicosis (lid retraction and lid lag), although both may coexist.

> ⚠️ Occasionally proptosis may be asymmetric or even unilateral, and it can occur in the absence of clinical or biochemical evidence of thyrotoxicosis, but always consider other possible diagnoses in this context, eg retro-orbital tumour/lymphoma.

Pretibial myxoedema (sometimes referred to as Graves' dermopathy) and thyroid acropachy are only found in the context of Graves' disease.

1.2.6 Tiredness and lethargy

Instruction

This middle-aged man presented to his GP with profound tiredness and lethargy. His past medical history is notable only for palpitations, which are now well controlled on treatment. His family history includes two maternal aunts with thyroid disease, and a younger sister with type 1 diabetes mellitus. Please examine him.

General features

In routine clinical practice a broad differential diagnosis would need to be considered for this patient, but in Station 5 of PACES and with clear clues to endocrine disorder in the instruction you should tailor your examination accordingly.

Endocrine examination

Specifically consider those endocrine disorders listed in Table 13.

- Thyroid disease: assess thyroid status, looking for evidence of a goitre and for signs of hypothyroidism (lethargy, husky voice, puffy face and hands, cold dry skin and slow relaxing relexes) or hyperthyroidism (sweating, tachycardia, tremor, thyroid eye disease) (see Sections 1.4.4, 2.3.1 and 2.3.2).

- Diabetes mellitus: examine specifically for evidence of complications (see Section 2.6).

- Hypoadrenalism: is the patient pigmented? Examine the buccal mucosa and palmar creases. Check for a postural fall in BP (see Section 2.2.6).

- Primary hyperparathyroidism: hypercalcaemia rarely produces signs, but band keratopathy may be evident (see Section 2.5.7).

- Hypopituitarism: check for features suggestive of a pituitary tumour with local mass effect, eg bitemporal quadrantanopia/hemianopia, galactorrhoea (hyperprolactinaemia; see Section 2.1.3) and hypopituitarism (see Section 2.1.8).

Further discussion

Thyroid dysfunction is a strong possibility here given the family history of thyroid disease, and this becomes even more likely if the patient is taking amiodarone for his palpitations (see Fig. 6).

However, other conditions associated with the type 2 autoimmune polyglandular syndrome (hypoadrenalism, diabetes mellitus, gonadal failure, vitamin B_{12} deficiency; see Section 2.7.2) must be considered, but are less likely given the age and gender of the patient.

1.2.7 Hypertension and a lump in the neck

Instruction

This young man has noted a lump in the left side of his neck following a recent sore throat. His past medical history includes recently diagnosed hypertension, which is controlled with doxazosin and bisoprolol. Please examine his neck and any other relevant features.

General features

You have been asked to examine the neck, which probably means that the patient has a thyroidal problem. However, the instruction mentions that the patient has a history of hypertension, treated with combined α- and β-adrenoceptor blockade. You should therefore consider the possibility that the patient has multiple endocrine neoplasia type 2 (MEN-2) syndrome, and that the abnormality in his neck is due to medullary thyroid carcinoma.

Endocrine examination

Neck

> 🔑 **Examination of a neck lump**
>
> Determine the following 'S' features:
>
> - Site
> - Shape

- Size
- Surface
- Smoothness
- Solid/cyStic
- Surroundings
- pulSatility
- tranSilluminability

Examination of the thyroid gland

- Inspect from the front. Does the lump move on swallowing (helped by giving the patient a glass of water to drink) or with tongue protrusion? The latter is suggestive of a thyroglossal cyst.
- Stand behind the patient and palpate the gland assessing size, texture, mobility and smoothness. Is the lump solitary? Are there multiple nodules?
- Check for tracheal displacement, tracheal narrowing (ask patient to open the mouth and breathe in and out as fast as possible, while you listen for stridor), retrosternal extension (percuss over upper sternum), or a thyroid bruit.
- Assess thyroid status (see Section 2.3).
- If you have not already done so, check for lymphadenopathy.

A lump due to a carotid body tumour/paraganglioma is classically non-tender, found at the level of the carotid bifurcation, fixed vertically but not horizontally, and associated with a bruit/thrill.

If the lump appears to be a lymph node or has associated lymphadenopathy, then in routine clinical practice it would be essential to perform a full physical examination looking for signs of systemic illness associated with lymphadenopathy (eg lymphoma, disseminated malignancy). There will not be time to do this in Station 5 of PACES, but the matter will almost certainly need to be discussed with the examiners.

Hypertension

Again, time pressure will prevent full examination in Station 5 of PACES, but it would be important in routine practice to thoroughly examine any patient presenting with hypertension for features to suggest a secondary cause (especially bearing in mind the possibility of phaeochromocytoma in this case) and check for evidence of end-organ damage.

Further discussion

Causes of a lump in the neck

Causes of a lump in the neck

- Lipoma/sebaceous cyst.
- Lymphadenopathy.
- Thyroid pathology/thyroglossal cyst.
- Pharyngeal pouch.
- Muscle tumour/neuroma.
- Aneurysm.
- Carotid body tumour/ paraganglioma.

Investigation of a neck lump

Initial tests These will be dictated by your clinical impression, but may include the following.

- Blood tests: FBC (± film) and erythrocyte sedimentation rate, electrolytes, renal/liver/bone chemistry, thyroid function tests (hypothyroidism and hyperthyroidism), calcium and parathyroid hormone (hyperparathyroidism).
- CXR: look very carefully for lymphadenopathy (see Fig. 10), masses or retrosternal goitre; if the latter is clinically suspected, request a flow–volume loop to look for evidence of extrathoracic airway obstruction.
- Ultrasound scan: solid or cystic? Within the thyroid or outside it? Relationship to blood vessels?

Paragangliomas have a characteristic appearance on Doppler ultrasound as hypervascular lesions, usually in the region of the carotid bifurcation.

Specific investigations These will be determined by clinical findings and results of the screening tests.

- Lymphadenopathy: consider biopsy of an accessible node (ultrasound guided or surgical) if the cause is unclear.
- Thyroid: check thyroid autoantibodies and fasting calcitonin (medullary thyroid carcinoma); consider thyroid scintigraphy looking for hot or cold nodules; consider fine-needle aspiration (FNA); a CT or MRI scan of the neck will help to delineate thyroid size, tumour extent and lymph node involvement (Fig. 19).

FNA of neck lumps

Do not stick a needle into something that may be highly vascular (aneurysm or paraganglioma/ chemodectoma). If there is clinical suspicion (bruit/thrill/family history), get an ultrasound first!

- Pharyngeal pouch: cine swallow.
- Phaeochromocytoma (see Section 2.2.4).

Imaging in phaeochromocytoma

Combined α- and β-adrenoceptor blockade is recommended prior to imaging with certain types of contrast agent if phaeochromocytoma has not been excluded (see Section 2.2.4).

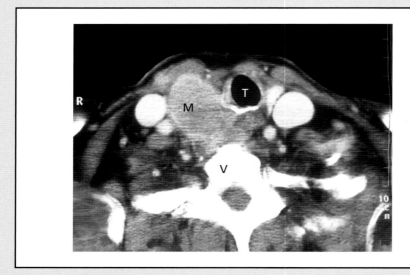

▲ **Fig. 19** Thyroid carcinoma. CT scan of the neck showing a large right-sided thyroid mass (M) displacing the trachea (T) to the left and extending posteriorly to the vertebral body (V).

Multiple endocrine neoplasia

In this particular case there must be the concern that the patient may have medullary thyroid carcinoma in the context of MEN-2 or a familial paraganglioma syndrome (see Sections 2.2.4 and 2.7.1 for further discussion).

1.3 Communication skills and ethics

1.3.1 Explaining an uncertain outcome

Scenario

Role: you are a junior doctor on the admitting medical team.

Mrs Agnes Smith, a 72-year-old woman, previously well apart from mild hypertension, has been admitted comatose to the Emergency Department. A CT scan of her head has shown no abnormality, but her serum sodium is 112 mmol/L. This is almost certainly caused by the thiazide diuretic that she takes for her high BP, although other possible causes have not been excluded, and is the only obvious cause for her coma. The management plan is to give her a controlled infusion of hypertonic saline, with frequent monitoring of the serum sodium concentration until this is corrected into the mildly hyponatraemic range. Her son arrives and is very worried about his mother's condition. The staff nurse asks you to explain the situation to him.

Your task: to explain the management plan and the uncertainty of the prognosis to Mrs Smith's son.

Key issues to explore

Although the son will understandably be concerned for the health of his mother, are there any specific worries or questions that he would like you to address? Is there a hidden agenda or worry? For example, is he concerned that she has been confused or depressed and may have accidentally or deliberately taken an overdose of tablets that has contributed to her condition?

Is he the next of kin, and are there other close relatives or friends who would be appropriate to speak to?

Key points to establish

Outline the basis and prognosis of his mother's condition by explaining the following in simple language.

- Cause of the problem: a 'low level of salt (or sodium) in the blood', which can have many causes; and that the low salt level can itself cause loss of consciousness, but that you are also excluding other causes of coma.

- Treatment: that the low salt level can be corrected with a drip and by restricting water intake.

- Outlook: uncertain. The very low level of sodium can cause irreversible brain damage or death, and the longer-term outlook depends on the underlying cause of the condition.

Appropriate responses to likely questions

Son: *So she is going to get better then doctor?*

Doctor: I'm not hiding anything when I say I don't know. Unfortunately it is very early days and I cannot give a guarantee that she will get better. We're trying to rule out other causes, but we think the reason for her being unconscious is the very low level of salt in her blood and we're trying to correct this. However, this has to be done slowly and carefully: doing it too rapidly can itself cause or worsen damage to the brain.

Son: Is she going to die, or end up like a vegetable?

Doctor: I'm afraid that I don't know. As you can see, she is unconscious now, which means that her brain has been badly affected by the problem. It is possible for people to make a complete recovery from this situation, but that isn't certain. She could die, or could be left with some permanent brain damage. I'm afraid that we just can't tell at the moment.

Son: So why is the salt in her blood so low?

Doctor: Again we're not 100% sure. The most likely reason for it is a reaction to a tablet that she was taking for her high blood pressure, but there are other causes that we need to check for. It's not a common problem, but sometimes some sorts of infection or some sorts of cancer can cause it.

Son: So is it cancer then?

Doctor: As I've said before, we're not absolutely sure what's causing the problem. The most likely thing is a reaction to one of her tablets, so I think that cancer is unlikely, but at the moment I can't rule it out and it is one of the things we need to consider. Is there something that makes you suspect that your mother may have cancer?

Son: Why was she put on a tablet that can cause this sort of problem?

Doctor: The tablet that she was on is one of the drugs that is most widely used to treat high blood pressure, and it normally doesn't cause any serious side effects at all. However, very rarely it can cause the salt in the blood to drop very low, and that's what we think is most likely to have happened in your mother's case.

1.3.2 The possibility of cancer

Scenario

Role: you are the admitting doctor working on an acute medical ward.

Mrs Harriet Claremont, a 64-year-old woman, has presented with with severe but non-specific lethargy and fatigue, and is found to have a serum calcium of 3.2 mmol/L. The initial history and examination fail to provide a clear diagnosis for this. There are no features to suggest malignancy, but the possibility cannot be excluded. The patient's daughter visits the ward wanting to discuss the possible causes of her mother's condition with you, and Mrs Claremont gives you permission to talk with her. She is particularly worried because of the recent demise of her aunt (the patient's sister) from lung cancer.

Your task: to explain what is meant by hypercalcaemia, and to discuss likely investigation and possible diagnoses.

Key issues to explore

What does the daughter already know, and what are her main concerns? Ask her to tell you about these before embarking on explanations.

Key points to establish

Explain the following in simple terms:

* the diagnosis and possible causes of hypercalcaemia;

* that the underlying diagnosis is not certain and that it will not be possible to give a reliable prognosis until it is, but there is

a range of possibilities from the benign to the malignant.

Appropriate responses to likely questions

Daughter: What is the abnormality in the blood tests?

Doctor: There is an abnormally high level of calcium in the blood, which can cause the tiredness and fatigue that your mother is suffering from.

Daughter: What's causing the high calcium?

Doctor: I don't know at the moment, but there are many possible causes that we need to check for. One of the most common is overactivity of the glands which normally control the blood calcium level, called parathyroid glands, and this is usually caused by a small benign tumour that can be removed with a simple operation. But there are some more worrying possible causes, including some types of cancer.

Daughter: Cancer is the most likely thing, isn't it?

Doctor: No, I'm not sure that it is. As I've said, it's certainly a possibility that we need to look for, but I'm not hiding anything when I say that we don't know what the cause of the problem is at the moment. It could turn out to be a cancer, but it could turn out to be something much more straightforward.

Daughter: If it is cancer, you won't tell her, will you?

Doctor: I won't force any information on her that she doesn't want to know, but I won't keep things from her if she does want to talk about them.

Daughter: But she won't cope at all if you tell her. Her sister has just died from lung cancer and she couldn't cope with that.

Doctor: I hear what you say and I understand it. As I've said, I won't force anything on to her that she doesn't want to hear, but I will ask her if she's got any questions about things, and if she has I will answer them as simply, honestly and kindly as I can. But if she doesn't ask, then I certainly won't force information on her.

1.3.3 No medical cause for hirsutism

> #### Scenario
>
> **Role:** you are a junior doctor working in the Endocrine Outpatient Clinic.
>
> Miss Irene Harris has come back to the clinic to discuss the results of investigations for hirsutism. She is 21 years old and has been troubled by mild to moderate hirsutism since menarche: she has been bleaching or shaving her upper lip weekly and waxing her abdomen and thighs monthly. She has regular periods. Her blood tests, including luteinising hormone, follicle-stimulating hormone and testosterone, are all normal.
>
> **Your task:** to explain to the patient that she has idiopathic hirsutism, and that treatment options include cosmetic hair removal and various tablets, eg Dianette (an oral contraceptive pill, with limited efficacy for hirsutism, that typically reduces hair growth by one-third).

Key issues to explore

What is the patient's main worry? Ask her if she is concerned that she has a serious underlying disorder, in which case the diagnosis will be a relief, or if she simply wants you to give her a tablet to make things better for her forthcoming summer holiday, in which case she is likely to be disappointed!

Does she have other concerns? For example, is she worried about fertility? This is unlikely to be a problem in view of her regular periods and normal blood tests.

Key points to establish

Explain the following in simple terms.

- Reassure her that there is no sinister underlying pathology: the diagnosis of idiopathic hirsutism is good news, and no further investigations are needed. But at the same time remember to be sensitive and ensure that you do not sound as if you are dismissing any concerns that she might have as no longer being important.

- Explain the basis for her condition: she may find it helpful to learn that some of the hair follicles on her body are simply a little more sensitive to the normal levels of circulating androgens (which all women have), leading to a coarsening of these hairs. This is a very common problem, and indeed can be viewed as one end of the normal spectrum for hair distribution in women. Emphasise that she is not becoming 'masculinised' in any way. If appropriate, mention that there are significant racial differences in hair biology and that hirsutism can run in families: she may know relatives who have had similar problems.

- Address the patient's expectations: while it is important not to minimise symptoms that are troubling a patient, it may be appropriate to discuss the difference between the ideal woman portrayed by the media and the biological norm (in terms of body fat and hair distribution).

Appropriate responses to likely questions

Patient: People will think I'm turning into a man.

Doctor: I can understand why you say that, but it's not the case. You have normal periods and you're not going to turn into a man at all, but your body is more sensitive to the normal levels of male hormones that you and all other women have, and this shows itself in the way that the hair grows.

Patient: Is this going to get worse?

Doctor: No, that's unlikely. This condition most often causes a reasonably stable level of unwanted excess hair throughout life, although weight gain can make the situation worse. However, it can become more pronounced at the menopause with the change in balance between male and female sex hormones.

Patient: You said earlier on that this problem can run in families, so why isn't my sister affected?

Doctor: It is true that the condition tends to run in families, but different individuals are affected to varying degrees, and some not at all, just as some people with the same parents are taller or shorter or have different hair or eye colour.

Patient: Why can't you give me a tablet to cure this illness?

Doctor: It is important to appreciate that this is not an illness, but rather one end of the spectrum of body hair growth that is normal for women. Many women have to use cosmetic hair removal to achieve an appearance that they are happy with and these remain the mainstay of treatment for you. It is important to understand that no tablets are without side effects. We can give you a tablet that is likely to reduce the hair growth by about a third, but you are still likely to need local hair removal treatments. The tablet has a contraceptive action (Dianette), so is not suitable if you want to get pregnant and has risks associated with other oral contraceptives, including an increased risk of developing blood clots in the veins.

1.3.4 A short girl with no periods

Scenario

Role: you are a junior doctor working in the Endocrine Outpatient Clinic.

Miss Alison Jackson, aged 17 years, presented to her GP with short stature and primary amenorrhoea. Your initial clinical assessment has revealed numerous features (webbed neck and cubitus valgus) that are suggestive of an underlying diagnosis of Turner's syndrome. The GP had already mentioned this as a possibility, and the patient has read up about the condition on the Internet.

Your task: to explain the meaning of 'karyotype analysis' and to ensure that the patient has an appropriate understanding of Turner's syndrome.

Key issues to explore

What does the patient already know and what are her main concerns? Has she heard or read about 'karyotyping' or 'chromosome analysis'? What has she learnt about Turner's syndrome from discussions with her GP and her reading on the Internet? Explore these matters before embarking on explanations.

Key points to establish

- Explain why you (and the GP) believe that the patient might have Turner's syndrome. Recap the salient features from the history and examination (and any relevant available investigations).

- Emphasise the importance of confirming the diagnosis through biochemical testing and karyotype (chromosome) analysis.

- Explain how studying the chromosome pattern helps to establish the diagnosis.

- Briefly mention the associated features of the condition, but try to avoid an over-detailed discussion at this stage when confirmation of the diagnosis is still awaited. It is important to point out that not all patients manifest all features of the condition.

Appropriate responses to likely questions

Patient: Why do you want to check my chromosomes?

Doctor: Because I think it's likely that you have a condition called Turner's syndrome, and checking your chromosomes is the best way of making this diagnosis. The chromosomes contain the genetic information that governs how all the cells and tissues in the body develop. In Turner's syndrome there is a distinctive alteration in the chromosome arrangement – one of the chromosomes called the X chromosome is missing in some or all of the cells of the body – and this can be easily detected in most patients by looking at the chromosome pattern in a small number of cells taken from a simple blood sample. This test is called chromosome analysis or karyotyping/karyotype analysis.

Patient: Do I have to have the test done?

Doctor: No, you don't have to have any test done that you don't want, but I think it would be a good idea to do it. You went to your doctor because you were worried that you hadn't grown as much as your friends and that your periods hadn't started. If we can find out why this is, then we should be able to help; but if we don't do any tests and don't find out what's causing the problem, then I'm afraid that we're not going to be able do anything about it.

Patient: If you find that I have Turner's syndrome, does it mean that I'm not a proper woman?

Doctor: No, it doesn't mean that at all. The absence of one of the X chromosomes, and the impact that this has on some of the tissues of the body such as the ovaries, is the reason why you haven't grown as tall as your friends and have not yet developed fully. But with the correct hormone replacement treatment we will be able to help you grow and develop.

Patient: Would the treatment make me absolutely normal?

Doctor: You might not finish up quite as tall as other girls of your age, but remember that there's a lot of variation in the population as a whole, as I'm sure you're aware from looking at your friends – some are shorter and some are taller. Many women with Turner's syndrome have similar thoughts/questions about their femininity, and this has led to the formation of the Turner's Society, a patient support group. I can give you their details if you like. The society's view is that women with Turner's syndrome should have no doubt about their femininity: physically, behaviourally and sexually.

Patient: Do I have lots wrong with my body? On the Internet I read about possible heart, thyroid and kidney problems with Turner's syndrome.

Doctor: I think we need to do the chromosome analysis before we say that we're sure that you have Turner's syndrome, so at this stage I don't think we should get into very detailed discussion about other conditions that may be associated with the syndrome. But if the diagnosis is confirmed then we will need to talk things through thoroughly. However, do remember that although it is true that Turner's syndrome can be associated with a variety of conditions that can affect the heart, thyroid and kidneys, not all patients with Turner's syndrome are affected by these.

1.3.5 Simple obesity, not a problem with 'the glands'

Scenario

Role: you are a junior doctor working in the Endocrine Outpatient Clinic.

Miss Manju Patel, aged 26 years, was referred by her GP because of concern that there may be an endocrine cause for her obesity (weight 90 kg, BMI 38 kg/m²). Her periods are regular. She is mildly hirsute and has faint striae over her lower abdomen. Examination is otherwise unremarkable. Investigations have excluded polycystic ovarian syndrome, hypothyroidism and Cushing's syndrome, and the diagnosis is one of 'simple obesity'. Both her parents are also obese. Miss Patel remains convinced that 'her glands are to blame' and states that she 'wants something done about it.'

Your task: to explain to the patient that no underlying endocrine cause for her obesity has been identified and to provide advice on weight loss management.

Key issues to explore

In this common scenario, as in others, it is important to allow the patient time to explain her view of things before launching in with explanations. Why does she continue to believe that her 'glands' are at fault, and which 'glands' does she believe are not working properly? What is she hoping/expecting the doctor to offer her in terms of treatment?

Key points to establish

- Explain that there are many different reasons why somebody might become overweight or obese (see Table 10), but that in most cases it is due to an imbalance between energy intake and expenditure. An individual's genetic make-up can affect their predisposition to weight gain, but environmental and behavioural factors are equally important in determining whether or not this occurs.

- Emphasise that endocrine causes of weight gain/obesity (eg polycystic ovarian syndrome, hypothyroidism and Cushing's syndrome) have been looked for and excluded.

- Explain that further medical tests are not required and that attention must now focus on helping her to lose weight through dietary and lifestyle modifications, supplemented with pharmacological/surgical interventions where necessary/ appropriate.

Appropriate responses to likely questions

Patient: How can you be sure that I don't have a problem with my glands? Have you checked all of them?

Doctor: No, we haven't checked all your glands, but we have checked the ones that can be relevant to problems with body weight. In particular we've done tests on the thyroid, the ovaries and the adrenal glands, and we've not found any evidence to indicate a specific problem with any of these. Are there any other glands that you are worried about specifically?

Patient: Does this mean that you think that I'm fat just because I eat too much, because that can't be the case as I hardly eat anything?

Doctor: How heavy a person is depends on the balance between how much energy is taken in – how much they eat and drink – and how much energy they burn – how much exercise they do. But people are variable: we all know some people who can eat what they like and stay thin; and we know other people who put on a lot of weight without eating an enormous amount, just more than their body can burn off. I know that life's unfair, and you may not be eating more than some thin people do, but you are clearly eating more than your body can burn off.

Patient: So are you telling me that I just have to go on a diet and join a gym?

Doctor: Those are easy things to say and they might do some good, but as I'm sure you know it's often not as straightforward as that. I'd like to offer some help if you'd like to have some: I would like to refer you to a dietitian who will be able to provide you with information on the calorie content of different foods and how to achieve a healthy-balanced diet that will help you to lose weight; and I think that it would also be very important for you to undertake regular exercise. This could begin with taking a brisk walk each day or swimming, and doesn't mean that you have to join a gym! But if you would like to take up regular supervised exercise, then many gyms can help out with this. It is also important to alter your day-to-day routine, for example use the stairs rather than taking the lift, walk or cycle to work rather than using the car, all these things can help.

Patient: What if I still do not lose weight despite doing everything that you are saying. Would you check my glands again?

Doctor: I am confident that if you do manage to alter your diet and lifestyle to achieve a situation where you are expending more calories than you are taking in, then you will lose weight. If this is proving difficult to achieve, then we could consider prescribing one or other tablets to try to help with this, but I don't think we will need to reinvestigate your 'glands' unless there are some new symptoms or changes to indicate that we should do so. The glands aren't the problem, and I don't think it's going to be helpful to keep focusing on them.

Patient: Why can't you give me a tablet now or just send me for an operation?

Doctor: There are three reasons for not racing into tablets or operations straight away. Firstly, adjusting your diet and exercise are the most appropriate and logical first steps to tackle weight gain in this situation because they directly address the underlying cause of the problem. Secondly, tablets or surgery rarely work in isolation, and lifestyle adaptation is an important component if these are to succeed.

Thirdly, tablets and surgery can both have side effects and complications, so we should start with the simple things: diet and exercise.

1.3.6 I don't want to take the tablets

Key issues to explore

Patient education is extremely important for those with adrenal insufficiency: this woman will have to assume responsibility for a life-maintaining therapy that requires adjustment at times of stress. But before embarking on a worthy lecture, encourage her to express her concerns. Why is she worried about taking steroids? Has she ever taken them in the past, or known anyone else who has? And did they have problems?

Key points to establish

Explain the following in straightforward terms.

- Physiological versus pharmacological steroid treatment: it is important for the patient to realise that steroid treatment in this setting is to replace what is normally produced by the body and not to administer a pharmacological dose, as would be required for treating inflammatory conditions such as rheumatoid arthritis or asthma. A physiological dose is most unlikely to have side effects.

- The importance of compliance: she requires lifelong steroid replacement therapy. Failure to take an appropriate dose leaves her vulnerable to adrenal crises, which are potentially life-threatening. It is also important to carry a steroid card or bracelet so that in the event of being unable to communicate (eg if involved in a car accident) appropriate medical treatment can be given without delay.

Appropriate responses to likely questions

Patient: Why do I need steroids anyway?

Doctor: Steroids are essential for life: everyone's body produces steroids, and the most important one is cortisol. The condition that you have destroys the glands that make this – the adrenal glands that sit just above the kidney and release cortisol into the bloodstream. This process is important for controlling many systems in the body, including those that regulate blood pressure and response to stress. Without cortisol your body cannot respond properly to stress: your blood pressure can fall, you may suddenly become very unwell and in rare cases the problem can be fatal. So steroids are important, they're not something that you or I could just decide to do without.

Patient: Some of my friends have been on steroids and have put on a huge amount of weight. Will this happen to me?

Doctor: No, it won't. They were almost certainly being given steroids as a drug to treat an illness: asthma, arthritis – do you know what it was? The aim of treating you with steroid is quite different. Everyone's body normally makes some steroid, but in you this doesn't happen because the adrenal glands are damaged. So what we're aiming to do is to give you back only the amount of steroid that your body would produce naturally: we're not intending to give you any extra. Therefore, we don't think that you should suffer excess weight gain as a result of this steroid treatment.

Patient: I don't like the idea of wearing a Medic-Alert bracelet. I don't want to advertise that I've got a problem. I don't have to wear one, do I?

Doctor: I can understand what you're saying. The important thing is that, if you were to become unwell you might not be able to tell a doctor looking after you about the fact that you had Addison's disease and needed steroids. So you need to carry something on you at all times that would give the doctor this information. Some people carry a steroid card in their purse or handbag, some people wear a Medic-Alert bracelet or necklace, but it's important that you carry something.

Patient: I'm confused about this business of increasing the dose when I'm ill. What's all that about?

Doctor: When someone gets ill their body naturally makes more steroid. However, yours can't do that, so the simple rule is that you take double the normal dose if you feel unwell and go back to the normal dose as soon as you feel better. There are no side effects from a few days of double-dose steroid, so if in doubt just increase the dose. If you're back to normal the following day, then cut back the dose to normal.

1.4 Acute scenarios

1.4.1 Coma with hyponatraemia

Scenario

A 72-year-old woman, previously well apart from mild hypertension, has been admitted comatose to the Emergency Department. A CT scan of her head has shown no abnormality, but her plasma sodium is 112 mmol/L.

Introduction

The unconscious patient

1. The first priority in dealing with the unconscious patient is to check and initiate management for problems with airway, breathing and circulation.
2. Consider rapidly reversible causes.
   (a) Hypoglycaemia: check fingerprick blood glucose. If <2.5 mmol/L, give 25–50 mL of 25% dextrose intravenously.
   (b) Opioid overdose: look for pinpoint pupils and slow respiratory rate. If present, give 0.4 mg naloxone intravenously.
3. Check Glasgow Coma Scale score, noting in particular whether there are lateralising neurological signs, which suggest a focal cause (eg stroke).

For further details of the approach to the unconscious patient, see *Acute Medicine*, Section 1.2.31.

The priority in this case is clearly to ensure safe management of the unconscious patient, as described above. This will include consideration of the possibility that the patient's coma and hyponatraemia are not connected, although it is likely that they are.

There are many causes of hyponatraemia (Fig. 20). When considering the differential diagnosis, consider the following.

- Is the patient hypovolaemic, euvolaemic or hypervolaemic? (See Fig. 20.)

- Are there clues to any of the diagnoses listed in Fig. 20 or Table 17?

History of the presenting problem
This woman is unconscious, so any history will need to be obtained from others. Has anyone accompanied her to the hospital? Extract as much information as you can from the GP's letter (if any) and the notes of ambulance/ paramedical staff.

General circumstances
The approach to the patient who is comatose is described in *Acute Medicine*, Section 1.2.31, but it is essential to get the following information.

- Who found her?

- What were the circumstances?

- When was she last seen before that, and did she appear to be well?

- Is there any possibility that she has taken an overdose?

- If anyone who knows anything about the woman is available, then ask for details that might give a clue as to why she is hyponatraemic and why she might be comatose (if the two are different).

TABLE 17 CAUSES OF INAPPROPRIATE SECRETION OF ANTIDIURETIC HORMONE (ADH)

Source of ADH	Type of problem	Example
Ectopic ADH production	Malignancy	Small-cell lung cancer
Inappropriate pituitary ADH secretion	Malignancy	Lung cancer, lymphoma, prostate cancer, pancreatic cancer
	Inflammatory lung disease	Pneumonia, lung abscess
	Neurological disease	Meningitis, head injury, subdural haematoma, tumours, post surgery
	Drugs	Antidepressants (tricyclics, SSRIs), carbamazepine, chlorpropamide, phenothiazines, (eg chlorpromazine), vincristine, cyclophosphamide, ecstasy
	Postoperative[1]	–
	Others	Nausea, pain, porphyria

1. Secretion of ADH is inappropriate to plasma tonicity, being driven by anaesthesia, nausea, pain and intravascular volume depletion, all of which are more powerful stimuli than plasma osmolality.
SSRIs, selective serotonin reuptake inhibitors.

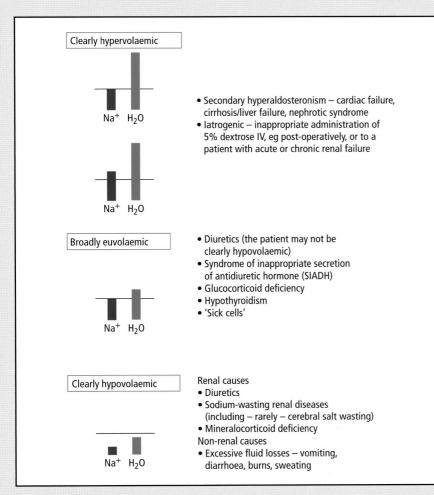

Clearly hypervolaemic

Na^+ H_2O

Na^+ H_2O

- Secondary hyperaldosteronism – cardiac failure, cirrhosis/liver failure, nephrotic syndrome
- Iatrogenic – inappropriate administration of 5% dextrose IV, eg post-operatively, or to a patient with acute or chronic renal failure

Broadly euvolaemic

Na^+ H_2O

- Diuretics (the patient may not be clearly hypovolaemic)
- Syndrome of inappropriate secretion of antidiuretic hormone (SIADH)
- Glucocorticoid deficiency
- Hypothyroidism
- 'Sick cells'

Clearly hypovolaemic

Na^+ H_2O

Renal causes
- Diuretics
- Sodium-wasting renal diseases (including – rarely – cerebral salt wasting)
- Mineralocorticoid deficiency
Non-renal causes
- Excessive fluid losses – vomiting, diarrhoea, burns, sweating

▲ **Fig. 20** Hyponatraemia and volume status.

Clues to other neurological problems

The neurological history is clearly of prime importance in someone who is comatose, since a neurological problem could cause coma in its own right, or in this case via hyponatraemia induced by the syndrome of inappropriate antidiuretic hormone secretion (SIADH). Try to ascertain whether there is a history of:

- head injury;
- epileptic fits;
- fluctuating consciousness (suggestive of subdural haematoma);
- headaches, especially with features of raised intracranial pressure;
- symptoms suggestive of meningeal irritation (neck stiffness, photophobia).

Clues to the cause of hyponatraemia

Think of the conditions listed in Fig. 20 and Table 17 as you seek information about the following.

Drug history Diuretics are a very common cause of hyponatraemia and this woman has hypertension. Is she taking a diuretic? Enquire also about drugs associated with SIADH (Table 17), exogenous steroids and nephrotoxins. Check with the patient's GP, and if possible ask a relative or friend to bring all her bottles of pills into the hospital for you to check.

 Diuretics are the commonest cause of hyponatraemia.

Fluid loss and fluid intake Has the woman had diarrhoea or vomiting? What has she been drinking and how much? Psychogenic polydipsia is extremely unlikely in a woman of this age, most commonly being seen in young psychiatric patients when excessive intake is frequently concealed.

Features of malignancy Has there been weight loss, unexplained fever, night sweats or pruritus? Could this woman have lung cancer complicated by SIADH? What are her current or past smoking habits? Have there been features of lung cancer (eg cough, haemoptysis, dyspnoea, pleuritic chest pain) or symptoms of pulmonary inflammation (eg purulent cough, dyspnoea)?

Other aspects Is there a history of cardiac, renal or liver failure, or of nephrotic syndrome? Is it possible that there is an endocrine or metabolic cause of hyponatraemia? Consider the following.

- Hypothyroidism: ask about weight gain, cold intolerance, constipation (see Section 2.3.1).

- Hypopituitarism: enquire specifically about symptoms of hypocortisolism, hypothyroidism and hypogonadism (see Section 2.1.8).

- Addison's disease: unexplained hyponatraemia in a comatose patient should prompt immediate consideration of primary hypoadrenalism (see Section 2.2.6).

- Porphyria: abdominal pain, neuropathy and preceding psychiatric illness in a younger patient are important clues to the diagnosis (see Section 2.5.2).

Examination

In any comatose patient the immediate priorities are as follows.

- Check airway, breathing, circulation; insert oropharyngeal airway if tolerated.

- Check Glasgow Coma Scale score.

See *Acute Medicine*, Section 1.2.31 for further details, but in this case pursue the cause of hyponatraemia as follows.

Assessment of fluid volume status

Accurate assessment of fluid volume status is vital in diagnosis of the cause of hyponatraemia. Check carefully for the following.

- Hypovolaemia: the most reliable signs are low JVP and postural hypotension.
- Hypervolaemia: look for a raised JVP, gallop rhythm, pulmonary oedema, peripheral oedema.

Look specifically for evidence of the following.

- Infection/inflammation as a cause of SIADH: pyrexia.

- Malignancy/other chest pathology as a cause of SIADH: clubbing (malignancy or pyogenic lung disease), lymphadenopathy (malignancy), Horner's syndrome (Pancoast's tumour).

- Features suggesting an endocrine cause of hyponatraemia: buccal/palmar/generalised pigmentation (Addison's disease), myxoedematous features (hypothyroidism), diminished body hair (hypopituitarism).

A full physical examination is required.

- Cardiac: is there evidence of heart failure?

- Respiratory: many chest pathologies can be associated with SIADH.

- Abdominal: in particular look for signs of chronic liver disease.

- Neurological: check for neck stiffness, photophobia, papilloedema or any focal neurological deficits.

Investigation

In any comatose patient immediate investigations should exclude hypoglycaemia, opioid toxicity and significant head injury. See *Acute Medicine*, Section 1.2.31 for further information. This woman has already had a CT scan, which is normal, and attention is clearly focused on her hyponatraemia.

Beware factitious hyponatraemia

Although highly unlikely in this case, factitious hyponatraemia (eg sampling from a 'drip' arm) and pseudo-hyponatraemia (eg in the context of gross hyperlipidaemia) should be excluded before embarking on more detailed investigations, particularly if the serum sodium is extremely low and yet the patient seems well.

Routine tests

- FBC (anaemia, leucocytosis, low haematocrit).

- Creatinine, urea and electrolytes (dehydration, hypoadrenalism).

- Glucose.

- Liver biochemistry (intrinsic liver disease, malignancy).

- Calcium (malignancy).

- Phosphate (renal tubular defects).

- Free thyroxine (FT_4) and thyroid-stimulating hormone (TSH) (primary or secondary hypothyroidism).

- CXR (lung pathology, including malignancy; aspiration).

Paired plasma (or serum) and urine osmolalities

This is a key investigation in the diagnosis of SIADH, but must be supplemented by measurement of a 'spot' urinary sodium concentration, since SIADH cannot be diagnosed in the face of a low urinary sodium concentration. The latter indicates that the kidney is conserving sodium because of 'real' or 'perceived' intravascular volume depletion, which will stimulate ADH release and water retention that is appropriate for the defence of intravascular volume but which is inappropriate for regulation of osmolality. With reference to Fig. 20, note the following.

- Urinary sodium concentration is generally low (<10 mmol/L) in non-renal causes of hyponatraemia, eg when the kidney is responding appropriately to real (eg vomiting) or perceived (eg hyperaldosteronism of cardiac failure) intravascular volume depletion.

- Urinary sodium concentration is generally high (>30 mmol/L) in renal causes of hyponatraemia (eg diuretics, sodium-losing renal disease).

- Intermediate urinary sodium concentrations (10–30 mmol/L) are difficult to interpret but should probably be regarded as indicating non-renal causes of hyponatraemia.

Criteria for the diagnosis of SIADH

- Clinically euvolaemic.
- Decreased plasma sodium and osmolality.
- Inappropriately high urinary sodium concentration (>20 mmol/L) and osmolality.
- Normal adrenal, renal and thyroid function.

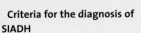

SIADH should never be diagnosed if the urinary sodium concentration is low (<20 mmol/L).

Calculation of plasma osmolality

The measured plasma osmolality can be compared with a calculated value to exclude the presence of other osmotically active substance(s) in plasma:

Calculated osmolality = $\{([Na^+] + [K^+]) \times 2\} + [urea] + [glucose]$

This is most often useful in the context of poisoning, eg ethylene glycol (antifreeze) overdose.

Other investigations

These will be determined by your clinical findings: CT head scan is normal in this case; lumbar puncture may be appropriate.

Management

In any comatose patient the immediate priorities are:

- ensure protection of the airway;
- give high-flow oxygen by face mask.

See *Acute Medicine*, Section 1.2.31 for further information.

Treatment of acute adrenal insufficiency in an emergency

If there is any suggestion of acute adrenal insufficiency, treatment with hydrocortisone (100 mg iv stat) must not be delayed. A serum sample should be saved for subsequent cortisol estimation (see Section 2.2.6), and the patient established on regular hydrocortisone replacement until biochemical testing has excluded hypocortisolism.

Specific management will depend on the underlying condition, and this should be treated vigorously whenever possible.

Acute symptomatic hyponatraemia

Urgent treatment is required if there are neurological complications attributable to hyponatraemia, as in this case, but even here it is important not to undertake too rapid a correction, which has been associated with irreversible and sometimes fatal central pontine myelinolysis. Treatment is as follows.

No formula can accurately predict the patient's response to giving hypertonic saline: all assume a 'closed system' and take no account of the patient's ongoing water losses, which are not predictable.

- 1.8% saline infused at a rate of (1.7 × weight in kg) mL/hour or 3% saline infused at a rate of (1.0 × weight in kg) mL/hour: this is likely to increase the serum sodium concentration by 1 mmol/L per hour.

- Aim to raise the serum sodium concentration in the early stages of correction by about 1 mmol/L per hour and by no more than 15–20 mmol/L over 48 hours.

- Monitor the serum sodium concentration every 2 hours whilst infusing hypertonic saline and replace hypertonic saline with 0.9% saline if the serum sodium is rising more quickly than desired.

Treatment of severe hyponatraemia

Correction of symptomatic hyponatraemia with hypertonic saline requires very close monitoring: check serum sodium every 2 hours.

- Stop infusion of hypertonic saline when serum sodium >125 mmol/L (possibly sooner if neurological symptoms have improved) and, where appropriate, institute water restriction. Remember that the aim is to return the plasma sodium to a 'safe level' and not 'back to normal': do not allow rapid correction into the normal range.

Giving hypertonic saline in hyponatraemia

- Infusion of hypertonic saline is potentially dangerous and should be restricted to those cases where hyponatraemia is causing neurological sequelae such as altered conscious level or fits. In these circumstances the plasma sodium will almost always be <120 mmol/L. If not, consider other causes of coma.
- Administration of hypertonic saline must only be undertaken in a high-dependency or intensive-care setting, via a pump and with regular monitoring of plasma sodium levels (every 2 hours).
- Hypertonic saline should not be given where there is an increase in total body sodium with oedema, eg in advanced liver disease.

Further comments

Chronic asymptomatic hyponatraemia

Chronic hyponatraemia is much commoner than acute hyponatraemia and is usually well tolerated, producing no clear-cut symptoms or symptoms that are rather vague. In this situation plasma sodium should always be corrected over days rather than hours, and there is no indication whatsoever for attempting to raise the plasma sodium rapidly.

- If hypovolaemic with no major symptoms from hyponatraemia, give intravenous 0.9% saline

replacement cautiously until volume is restored.

- If euvolaemic or hypervolaemic with no major symptoms from hyponatraemia, restrict water to 1000 mL per day or less, giving this as ice in aliquots through the day and ensuring that swabs are available to moisten the mouth. In those cases where the underlying cause cannot be corrected (eg lung cancer), demeclocycline may be useful, inducing a partial nephrogenic diabetes insipidus and reversing the inappropriate antidiuresis.

- Deal with precipitant, eg stop diuretics; diagnose and treat cause of vomiting.

⚠ **Chronic asymptomatic hyponatraemia should never be treated with hypertonic saline.**

1.4.2 Hypercalcaemic and confused

Scenario

A 73-year-old woman is admitted from home. She is confused and dehydrated with a Glasgow Coma Scale score of 11/15. Initial blood tests sent on arrival show a serum calcium of 4.0 mmol/L.

Introduction

Hypercalcaemia typically gives rise to insidious symptoms and may go undetected for a considerable period of time before presenting acutely. Patients with hypercalcaemia who become confused tend not to drink, which conspires to produce a vicious circle of worsening dehydration and hypercalcaemia. This is a medical emergency: immediate treatment is

required before investigation aimed at establishing the underlying cause (see Table 1).

History of the presenting problem

As described in Section 1.1.1, enquire about the following.

- Symptoms of acute hypercalcaemia: fatigue, lethargy, constipation, polyuria and polydipsia.

- Symptoms suggesting chronic hypercalcaemia: renal stones, abdominal pain, bone pain/fracture.

- Causes of hypercalcaemia: known malignancy, or symptoms suggestive of malignancy (eg weight loss, night sweats, change in bowel habit, haemoptysis or breathlessness); drug history, with particular reference to calcium- and vitamin D-containing preparations, antacids, and thiazide diuretics.

Although it seems very likely that this woman's confusion is caused by hypercalcaemia, do not neglect to consider, even if only briefly, other possible diagnoses such as sepsis.

Examination

🔑 **How unwell is the woman? Is she well, ill, very ill or nearly dead? If very ill or nearly dead, get help immediately.**

Check vital signs: temperature, pulse, respiratory rate, BP and pulse oximetry.

Conduct a thorough physical examination, looking in particular for signs of the following related to hypercalcaemia.

- Intravascular volume depletion: postural tachycardia, postural hypotension, low JVP.

- Dehydration: reduced skin turgor, dry axillae, dry mucous membranes.

- Possible malignancy, eg cachexia, anaemia, digital clubbing, lymphadenopathy, breast lumps, chest signs, abdominal/rectal masses.

- Chronic hypercalcaemia: there are few signs, but band keratopathy (calcium deposition at the edge of the cornea at 3 and 9 o'clock) may be seen in chronic severe cases.

With regard to other causes of confusion, note in particular:

- any evidence of sepsis;

- focal neurological signs, which would raise the possibility of cerebral metastases in this context.

Investigation

> The higher the serum calcium, the more likely that there is a malignant cause.

As described in Section 1.1.1, but noting that this degree of hypercalcaemia is likely to be associated with the following.

- Acute renal failure: electrolytes, creatinine and urea will require close monitoring.

- A malignant cause: hyperparathyroidism is unlikely to cause a serum calcium of 4.0 mmol/L. Look very carefully at the CXR; make sure that all elements of a myeloma screen are pursued (immunoglobulins, serum electrophoresis, urinary Bence Jones proteins); and have a low threshold for pursuing further investigations if the history, examination or routine screening tests raise suspicions.

A CT brain scan should be organised urgently to look for cerebral metastases if the patient has any focal neurological signs.

Management

The aim must be to reduce the serum calcium level whilst a diagnosis is made and appropriate definitive treatment initiated.

> The most important measures in treating severe hypercalcaemia are:
> - saline diuresis;
> - intravenous bisphosphonate, eg pamidronate.

Immediate treatment

The first aspect of emergency management should be rehydration with intravenous saline.

- Correct intravascular volume depletion: if this is present (postural tachycardia, postural hypotension, low JVP), give 0.9% (normal) saline rapidly until replete (as judged by correction of postural tachycardia/postural hypotension and elevation of JVP to normal).

- When intravascular volume depletion is corrected, insert urinary catheter to monitor urine output and give 0.9% (normal) saline intravenously at a rate of 3–6 L in 24 hours if urine output is satisfactory. Consider giving furosemide 40–80 mg iv to encourage diuresis. Examine the patient regularly for signs of fluid overload or deficit, ensure accurate fluid charts are kept and adjust fluid input accordingly.

- Monitor the calcium level, and also levels of potassium and magnesium which may fall rapidly with rehydration. Replace as necessary.

Other calcium-lowering measures

- Bisphosphonates: following initial rehydration, the drug of first choice for most patients is disodium pamidronate. A dose of 30–90 mg, depending on the magnitude of hypercalcaemia, is administered by intravenous infusion over 4–6 hours. Calcium levels typically fall over the next few days. The hypocalcaemic effect may persist for up to 6 weeks; further doses can be given as required.

- Calcitonin (initially 5–10 units/kg per day, in divided doses): a useful alternative antiresorptive agent that is suitable for acutely lowering serum calcium levels in severe hypercalcaemia. However, its beneficial effects are short-lived, with most patients becoming refractory to treatment within a few days.

- Glucocorticoids (eg prednisolone 40–60 mg/day): limited use except in hypercalcaemia associated with haematological malignancy (eg multiple myeloma or lymphoma), sarcoidosis or vitamin D toxicity.

1.4.3 Thyrotoxic crisis

Scenario

You are called urgently to the Emergency Department to review a 38-year-old woman who has been brought in with palpitations and a high fever. She had undergone treatment for a dental abscess just 24 hours prior to admission. On examination she is restless and tremulous, with 'staring eyes' and an obvious goitre. Her temperature is 40°C, she is in fast atrial fibrillation (ventricular rate 180 bpm) and hypotensive (BP 95/60 mmHg recumbent). Her friend who brought her to hospital mentions that she has not been well for several months and seems to have lost a significant amount of weight, but has refused to see her GP.

Introduction

Thyrotoxic crisis (thyroid storm) is a rare but life-threatening complication of thyrotoxicosis/hyperthyroidism that is typically seen in previously undiagnosed or inadequately treated patients.

> ⚠️ Even with appropriate management the mortality rate of thyrotoxic crisis (storm) approaches 20%.

History of the presenting problem

A brief history should be taken, focusing on features that would support the clinical suspicion of thyrotoxicosis (see Section 2.3.2) but ensuring that an open mind is kept with regard to other potential causes of this presentation, although none apart from thyrotoxic crisis would explain all features of the presentation (eg primary cardiac disease, septicaemia following treatment of dental abscess). Enquire specifically about the following.

- Symptoms of thyrotoxic crisis: weight loss, heat intolerance, sweating, palpitations, diarrhoea, tremor, and anxiety/agitation/irritability.

- Factors that can precipitate a thyrotoxic crisis: intercurrent illness (eg sepsis, surgery), radioiodine therapy, pregnancy (eg toxaemia) and drugs (eg thyroxine, amiodarone, iodine-containing radiographic contrast media).

> ⚠️ Thyrotoxic crisis (storm) leads to apathy, hypotension, seizures, coma and death if not treated appropriately.

Examination

The approach to the examination of the very ill patient is described in *Acute Medicine*, Section 1.2.2, but in this case you would obviously look for features that would be consistent with a diagnosis of thyrotoxic crisis.

- General: agitation, anxiety, restlessness; tremor; skin usually warm and moist. Hyperpyrexia is a feature of thyrotoxic crisis but does not necessarily indicate infection, although this should always be looked for.

- Cardiovascular compromise: sinus tachycardia is usually greater than 140/min in thyroid crisis (storm); fast atrial fibrillation or supraventricular tachycardia are common, as found in this case. Establish whether cardiac failure is present: raised JVP, gallop rhythm, pulmonary oedema and peripheral oedema.

- Neurological/psychological: altered consciousness, frank psychosis, delirium, seizures and coma can all be seen in thyrotoxic crisis.

Findings that might indicate the likely cause of the thyroid pathology include the following.

- Signs of Graves' disease: exophthalmos, lid retraction and lid lag.

- Goitre (as in this case): if present, what are its characteristics (smooth, nodular, painful) and is there an associated bruit?

- Vitiligo: associated with autoimmune thyroid disease.

Investigation

> ⚠️ **Thyrotoxic crisis is a clinical diagnosis**
>
> There are no laboratory criteria to diagnose thyrotoxic crisis: the levels of thyroid hormones are the same as in uncomplicated hyperthyroidism. Start treatment immediately if the clinical diagnosis is thyrotoxic crisis: do not delay while waiting for laboratory confirmation.

Check the following immediately.

- FBC (anaemia, leucocytosis or leucopenia).

- Electrolytes, creatinine and urea (dehydration, electrolyte imbalance, renal failure).

- Glucose (hypoglycaemia or hyperglycaemia).

- Liver and bone biochemistry (abnormalities of liver function, hypercalcaemia).

- Thyroid function tests: free thyroxine (T_4), free triiodothyronine (T_3) and thyroid-stimulating hormone (TSH).

- ECG: to confirm rhythm and check for evidence of ischaemia.

- CXR: look for evidence of pulmonary oedema or consolidation.

- Blood and urine cultures, urinalysis: to identify potential sites of infection.

- Arterial blood gases: to look for hypoxia and metabolic acidosis.

Further investigations will be determined by the findings on clinical examination and the results of initial investigations. If and when the diagnosis of thyrotoxicosis is confirmed biochemically, then attention should turn to identifying its cause (see Section 2.3.2).

Management

> Your threshold for admission to a high-dependency unit/intensive care unit should be low: patients with thyrotoxic crisis (storm) are at risk of cardiovascular collapse and may require sedation to facilitate effective management.

Immediate and acute management

General supportive measures

Emergency resuscitation is the priority.

- Check airway, breathing, circulation.

- Administer high-flow oxygen via reservoir bag.

- Establish intravenous access and take bloods as indicated above.

- Begin active cooling and give paracetamol (not aspirin, which may displace thyroid hormones from thyroid-binding globulin and exacerbate the situation).

- Commence appropriate antibiotics where there is suspicion/evidence of an infective precipitant (as is likely in this case given the recent history of a dental abscess).

- Consider sedation if the patient is particularly anxious/confused: chlorpromazine is the drug of choice.

- Commence strict fluid balance: consider placement of a urinary catheter to help monitor output. If the patient is hypotensive, determine whether this is due to absolute or relative hypovolaemia (eg in a patient with sytemic sepsis), which requires fluid resuscitation, or whether it is secondary to cardiac failure, requiring treatment with diuretics and digoxin (also see below for the role of beta-blockers in this setting).

Specific antithyroid measures

These are described in detail in Section 2.3.2 but in brief include the use of the following.

- Beta-blockers: give propranolol 1 mg iv, repeated every 20 minutes as necessary up to total of 5 mg, or give 40–80 mg po four times daily. Be careful if the patient has cardiac failure. Esmolol, a short-acting beta-blocker, can be used as an infusion for immediate management of sympathetic overactivity.

- Propylthiouracil or carbimazole: propylthiouracil is the preferred drug as it both blocks further synthesis of thyroid hormones and inhibits peripheral conversion of T_4 to T_3, but it is often not immediately available on the wards, whereas carbimazole usually is. If propylthiouracil is available, give a loading dose of 200 mg orally or via a nasogastric tube, then 200 mg every 4–6 hours. If propylthiouracil is not available (you should not wait for the pharmacy to 'get some up to the ward tomorrow'), give carbimazole 20 mg, then 20 mg every 4–6 hours.

- Lugol's iodine (saturated solution of potassium iodide), five drops every 6 hours, or sodium iodide (0.5–1 g every 12 hours by intravenous infusion), beginning 4 hours after starting propylthiouracil/carbimazole (not before as thyroid hormone stores may be increased) to inhibit further release of thyroxine.

> Iodide must *not* be given until organification has been blocked.

- Steroids, eg hydrocortisone 200 mg iv, then 100 mg every 6 hours; or

dexamethasone 2 mg po four times daily.

Consider digitalisation if the patient is in fast atrial fibrillation, but note that higher doses of digoxin than usual may be needed due to relative resistance to the drug.

Further management

Definitive treatment for thyrotoxicosis will be required, eg surgery or radioiodine under antithyroid drug and beta-blocker cover.

1.4.4 Addisonian crisis

Scenario

A 35-year-old woman is brought into the Emergency Department having collapsed in the supermarket. On arrival she is feverish (temperature 38°C), tachycardic (heart rate 115 bpm) and hypotensive (BP 75/50 mmHg). Oxygen saturation is 93% on air, and capillary blood glucose is 2.9 mmol/L. She is unable to give any history, but is carrying a steroid alert card in her purse that states a diagnosis of Addison's disease. Rapid analysis of serum electrolytes has revealed Na^+ 128 mmol/L and K^+ 5.5 mmol/L.

Introduction

> **Acute adrenal insufficiency**
>
> Failure to recognise and treat this condition promptly can lead to death. Fluid resuscitation and administration of parenteral hydrocortisone are life-saving and must be given immediately, before detailed assessment and investigation. If hypoglycaemia is present, then this should be corrected with intravenous dextrose.

History of the presenting problem

A collateral history will be required in this case. Details of the 'collapse' should be sought from any source available: relatives, friends or other witnesses who were present, and from the GP's or paramedics' notes. The differential diagnosis of 'collapse' is wide (see *Acute Medicine*, Section 1.2.8), but in this case a great deal of evidence points towards the diagnosis of Addisonian crisis, in which case important aspects to explore include the following.

- Precipitants for adrenal crisis: most commonly there will be some prodromal illness, eg intercurrent infection; very rarely there may be a history of flank pain attributable to adrenal infarction.

- Drug/medication history: is there any suggestion of non-compliance with steroid replacement therapy? Has there been any recent change to medication, eg introduction of an enzyme-inducing agent (eg phenytoin, carbamazepine or rifampicin), without a corresponding increase in the regular hydrocortisone regimen?

- Symptoms of adrenal crisis: many cases develop non-specific abdominal pain in conjunction with nausea and/or vomiting, also restlessness and confusion, which in some patients can progress to stupor and coma.

Examination

In any comatose or semi-comatose subject, the immediate priorities are:

- check airway, breathing and circulation (insert oropharyngeal airway if tolerated);

- check Glasgow Coma Scale score.

See *Acute Medicine*, Section 1.2.31, for further information.

In the patient with suspected adrenal crisis take particular note of the following.

- Hypotension/postural hypotension: these are expected in all cases.

- Infection: look for evidence of an infective precipitant.

- Features of Addison's disease: look for hyperpigmentation and vitiligo.

Investigation

In any comatose or semi-comatose patient immediate investigations should exclude hypoglycaemia, opioid toxicity and significant head injury (see *Acute Medicine*, Section 1.2.31 for further information).

Routine investigations

The typical findings in acute adrenal insufficiency are hyponatraemia, hyperkalaemia and hypoglycaemia.

- FBC (anaemia, leucocytosis, low haematocrit).

- Electrolytes, creatinine and urea (dehydration, hypoadrenalism).

- Glucose (hypoglycaemia or hyperglycaemia).

- Liver biochemistry (intrinsic liver disease).

- Calcium (may be elevated).

- Thyroid function tests (may be associated hypothyroidism).

- Blood and urine cultures, urinalysis and CXR may identify potential sites/sources of infection.

- Arterial blood gases: to confirm adequate oxygenation and look for acidosis.

- CT scan of the head is indicated if there is focal neurology, or if the cause for the reduced conscious level remains unclear.

Further investigation

This will be determined by the findings on clinical examination and the results of initial investigations. In this case of a patient with known Addison's disease and suspected adrenal crisis, take a serum sample for later cortisol measurement before giving hydrocortisone: an inappropriately low serum cortisol in this setting is diagnostic of acute adrenal insufficiency.

Management

Shoot first, ask questions afterwards

Give steroids immediately if you suspect Addisonian crisis.

Immediate and acute management

Emergency resuscitation must be instigated as a priority.

- Check airway, breathing and circulation.

- Administer high-flow oxygen via reservoir bag.

- Establish intravenous access and take bloods as indicated above.

- Commence fluid resuscitation with 0.9% (normal) saline: infuse 1 L stat and then re-examine. If hypotension/postural hypotension persist, then repeat rapid infusion. Stop rapid infusion when hypotension abolished, JVP normal or signs of fluid overload develop (basal crackles).

- Give hydrocortisone 100 mg iv stat, followed by 50–100 mg iv/im 6-hourly.

- If the patient is hypoglycaemic, give intravenous dextrose (eg 25 mL of 25% given via a large-bore cannula and followed by a flush to minimise damage to the vein). Set up a 10% dextrose drip if necessary and run it at a rate sufficient to keep glucose >5 mmol/L, but do not give more than is needed and avoid using 5% dextrose because this is likely to exacerbate hyponatraemia.

- Consider infection: have a low threshold for starting antibiotics.

Further management

Confirm the reason for the recent collapse. Continue parenteral hydrocortisone until there has been a sustained clinical improvement, at which point a transition back to oral hydrocortisone can be undertaken. Whilst the patient is receiving high-dose hydrocortisone there is no need for additional mineralocorticoid replacement, but fludrocortisone must be re-commenced once the dose of hydrocortisone is lowered.

Before discharge the patient should be seen by an endocrinologist or endocrine nurse specialist to ensure that she is aware of the following.

- 'Sick day rules', ie when and how to increase her hydrocortisone dose at times of illness and stress, and that she should seek medical attention urgently if she is unable to take her medication orally (eg due to recurrent vomiting).
- 'Emergency pack': whenever possible the patient and her next of kin should be provided with an emergency pack and taught how to administer intramuscular hydrocortisone at home in the event of an emergency, whilst stressing that this is not a substitute for seeking medical help.
- How to titrate her dose of hydrocortisone back down to an appropriate maintenance regimen if she is being discharged on an increased dose to cover an intercurrent illness.

Most patients with Addison's disease will already be under long-term endocrine follow-up: an appointment should be made to allow for early review following discharge.

1.4.5 'Off legs'

Scenario

A 72-year-old woman is brought to the Emergency Department by ambulance after one of her carers found that she had not moved from her chair between 9.30 a.m., when the carer left after helping her to get up in the morning, and 8.00 p.m., when the carer returned to help her go to bed. She gives a history of widespread aches and pains and increasing immobility, with particular difficulty in getting to her feet, that has been getting worse over the last 2–3 months. Her past medical history is unremarkable apart from long-standing idiopathic epilepsy that is well controlled on treatment. She is not febrile or confused.

Introduction

The differential diagnosis of immobility in the elderly is broad.

The principal clue in this history is the suggestion of proximal muscle weakness with pain. The history, examination and investigation should be directed at confirming this, whilst excluding other causes of weakness.

The broad differential diagnosis for proximal muscle weakness is provided in Table 18. A possible clue to the diagnosis in this case is the history of epilepsy and long-term anticonvulsant therapy, raising the possibility of osteomalacia exacerbated by hypercatabolism of vitamin D. Polymyalgia rheumatica is a common cause of aches and pains in the elderly, predominantly involving the muscles of the shoulder and pelvic girdle, and clearly needs to be considered, but it does not cause weakness.

History of the presenting problem

Given the wide range of causes of weakness in the elderly, and of proximal myopathy in particular, a full history is required, beginning with careful consideration of the symptoms themselves.

Weakness, aches and pains

The brief details given suggest that weakness might be due to proximal myopathy. The first priority is to

---

TABLE 18 CONDITIONS ASSOCIATED WITH A PROXIMAL MYOPATHY

Type of disorder	Example
Muscle disease	Polymyositis/dermatomyositis Infective myositis Inherited muscular dystrophies
Metabolic and endocrine	Thyrotoxicosis (and occasionally hypothyroidism) Osteomalacia Diabetic amyotrophy (often unilateral) Cushing's syndrome Glycogen and lipid storage diseases
Malignancy	Carcinomatous neuromyopathy
Drug-induced	Alcohol Glucocorticoids

confirm that weakness is indeed present, and that limitation of movement is not simply caused by pain. It would be misleading to probe extensively for causes of proximal myopathy if, in fact, the problem was due to lumbar back pain with nerve root irritation. Ask carefully about the following if the details do not emerge spontaneously.

- Is the problem in one or both legs? If the problem is much worse in one leg than the other, then a myopathic condition is less likely and attention should focus on 'local' disorders, eg spinal pain with nerve root irritation, undeclared hip fracture.

- How did the problem start? Onset after a fall would suggest a traumatic cause of pain, perhaps fracture of a lumbar vertebra or hip.

- Which things are most difficult to do? When is the weakness most noticeable? With proximal myopathy there is particular difficulty when rising from a chair or on climbing stairs. With rheumatic disorders, eg rheumatoid arthritis, there may be diurnal variation, with pain and stiffness worse in the morning and then improving as the patient 'warms up'.

- What is the distribution of aches and pains? Pain in the affected muscles is suggestive of an inflammatory myositis or diabetic amyotrophy. Pain in a radicular distribution suggests nerve root irritation. Generalised aches and pains are in keeping with osteomalacia, and also with the much commoner condition of polymyalgia rheumatica, but polymyalgia rheumatica does not cause weakness, although pain and stiffness in the affected muscle groups may be perceived

as such. Are there any other symptoms to support this diagnosis? Ask about headaches, scalp tenderness, visual symptoms and jaw or tongue claudication.

Polymyalgia rheumatica does not cause weakness.

Neurological symptoms

Weakness could have a primarily neurological cause. Focal symptoms, eg weakness of one leg rather than both as in this case, would imply focal pathology, eg unrecognised stroke. The presence of sensory symptoms, eg numbness and paraesthesia, would suggest neuropathy rather than myopathy.

Other symptoms

A full systems enquiry is needed, particularly bearing in mind the diagnoses listed in Table 18.

- Osteomalacia: a history of long-term anticonvulsant use (eg phenytoin, barbiturates or carbamazepine) but also of renal disease, previous gastric surgery, coeliac disease or other malabsorptive states should prompt consideration of osteomalacia. The elderly and Asian populations are at particular risk, reflecting reduced skin synthesis of vitamin D together with dietary insufficiency (see Section 2.5.5).

- Polymyositis/dermatomyositis: ask about arthralgia/arthritis, especially affecting the small joints of the hand (~50% of cases), and rashes, eg the heliotrope rash of dermatomyositis.

- Diabetic amyotrophy: typically seen in older patients (especially men), who present with asymmetrical weakness and

wasting of the quadriceps muscles. Ask about pain in the thigh, which often keeps the patient awake at night.

- Cushing's syndrome: many of the features of Cushing's syndrome (eg easy bruising, thin skin, weight gain) may be mistaken for part of the normal ageing process (see Section 2.1.1).

- Thyroid disease: ask about the classical symptoms of thyrotoxicosis and hypothyroidism (see Sections 2.3.1 and 2.3.2), but remember that the clinical features may be modified in the elderly.

Other relevant history

Check for a history of asthma, arthritis or other illnesses requiring long-term corticosteroid treatment. Ask about alcohol intake: this could be a pseudo-Cushing's syndrome presentation (see Section 2.1.1).

Examination

A full physical examination will be required, with particular emphasis on the following.

- Hydration state: this woman has been immobile at home and therefore vulnerable to dehydration. Check for postural tachycardia, postural hypotension, low JVP (features of intravascular volume depletion) and reduced skin turgor, dry axillae and dry mucous membranes (features of dehydration).

- General features: is there anything to support any of the diagnoses listed in Table 18?

- Legs: does she have a proximal myopathy (wasting, weakness)? Consider and look for features of stroke/other upper motor neuron lesion, spinal cord compression, radiculopathy/nerve root/peripheral nerve lesion (see *Clinical Skills*, Clinical Skills for PACES). Could she have fractured a hip? Look for shortening and external rotation of a leg.

> ⚠ Always check that the elderly patient admitted 'off legs' has not broken a hip: aside from being bad medicine to miss such a diagnosis, it is embarassing!

Investigation

Investigations will be directed by the findings on careful history and examination, but assuming a proximal myopathy has been confirmed, carry out the following.

Routine tests

Many of the causes of proximal myopathy can be screened for with simple blood tests.

- FBC (anaemia suggestive of chronic disease or iron deficiency).

- Erythrocyte sedimentation rate/C-reactive protein: raised in inflammatory muscle diseases (or polymyalgia rheumatica).

- Electrolytes, creatinine and urea (renal failure, severe hypokalaemia).

- Glucose.

- Creatine kinase: raised in inflammatory muscle disease and hypothyroidism.

- Liver chemistry: low albumin in malabsorption, raised alkaline phosphatase in osteomalacia.

- Calcium, phosphate: low/low normal in osteomalacia.

- Thyroid-stimulating hormone: suppressed in thyrotoxicosis and elevated in hypothyroidism.

- Chest radiograph: look for evidence of malignancy.

Further tests

Other investigations will depend on clinical suspicion and the results of routine tests.

Osteomalacia Perform the following.

- Parathyroid hormone: raised (also in renal osteodystrophy).

- Vitamin D: 25-hydroxyvitamin D_3 typically low, although 1,25-dihydroxyvitamin D_3 may be normal.

- Radiological studies (see Section 2.5.5).

- When malabsorption is suspected as a cause: measure serum folate, vitamin B_{12} and ferritin; prothrombin time to screen for vitamin K malabsorption; anti-tissue transglutaminase antibodies as indicators of coeliac disease.

Cushing's syndrome Perform 24-hour urinary free cortisol estimation and/or dexamethasone suppression test (see Section 2.1.1).

Further tests including electromyography and/or muscle biopsy will be required if these investigations fail to identify a cause for the proximal myopathy.

Management

Osteomalacia

Treatment is with vitamin D supplementation (see Section 2.5.5). The most commonly used daily regimen of combined calcium and 400–800 units of vitamin D will not be sufficient, and high-dose oral therapy (eg ergocalciferol 10,000 units on alternate days) or parenteral therapy (eg ergocalciferol 300,000 units im) may well be required. In cases of renal failure or malabsorption, the vitamin D metabolites alfacalcidol (1α-hydroxycholecalciferol) or calcitriol (1,25-dihydroxycholecalciferol) are usually required, often with dietary calcium supplements.

Other diagnoses

Other causes of proximal myopathy will require specific treatment: for thyroid disease, see Section 2.3; for Cushing's syndrome, see Section 2.1.1; for diabetes mellitus, see Section 2.6; for polymyositis/dermatomyositis see *Rheumatology and Clinical Immunology*, Section 2.3.5.

2.1 Hypothalamic and pituitary diseases

2.1.1 Cushing's syndrome
The clinical disorder resulting from prolonged exposure to circulating supraphysiological levels of glucocorticoid.

Aetiology

> This is most easily thought of in terms of adrenocorticotrophic hormone (ACTH)-dependent and ACTH-independent causes (Table 19). The term 'Cushing's disease' refers exclusively to those cases arising as a consequence of ACTH-secreting corticotroph adenomas of the pituitary gland, as described in 1932 by Harvey Cushing, an American neurosurgeon.

Clinical presentation
The clinical features of Cushing's syndrome have often been present for some time before the diagnosis is made. Patients may have been treated for individual components of the condition, eg obesity, hypertension or diabetes before the 'penny drops' and the diagnosis is considered. Women may present with oligomenorrhoea and infertility, whilst children can exhibit isolated growth failure.

Physical signs
Patients often exhibit many, if not all, of the classical signs (Fig. 21) of Cushing's syndrome, including:

- moon-like facies and plethora;

- central (truncal) obesity ('orange on match-sticks');

- prominent supraclavicular fat pads and 'buffalo hump' (interscapular);

- acne, thin skin with easy bruising and purple striae (abdomen, thighs);

- hypertension;

- muscle wasting and proximal myopathy;

- hirsutism (due to excess adrenal androgen production in ACTH-dependent disease or adrenal carcinoma);

- kyphoscoliosis due to osteoporosis;

- psychiatric features, eg emotional lability, depression, psychosis.

> It is worth noting that in cases arising as a consequence of ectopic ACTH secretion, the clinical picture is often modified with wasting, cachexia and pigmentation more prominent, the latter reflecting very high circulating levels of ACTH.

Investigation
This should be approached in two stages:

- confirmation of the diagnosis;

- definition of the aetiology.

Confirming the diagnosis
Most centres use one or more of the following for screening purposes, with confirmation/further investigation of positive results.

Estimation of 24-hour urinary free cortisol (UFC) Ideally at least three collections should be performed. Reference ranges vary between laboratories, but in general levels >270 nmol per 24 hours merit further investigation.

Overnight dexamethasone suppression test See Section 3.2.1.

TABLE 19 AETIOLOGY OF CUSHING'S SYNDROME

Type	Example
ACTH dependent	Pituitary adenoma (Cushing's disease) Ectopic ACTH secretion Ectopic CRH secretion (very rare)
ACTH independent	Exogenous glucocorticoid administration Adrenal adenoma Adrenal carcinoma AIMAH PPNAD (sporadic or associated with Carney complex)

ACTH, adrenocorticotrophic hormone; AIMAH, ACTH-independent bilateral macronodular adrenal hyperplasia; CRH, corticotrophin-releasing hormone; PPNAD, primary pigmented nodular adrenal disease.

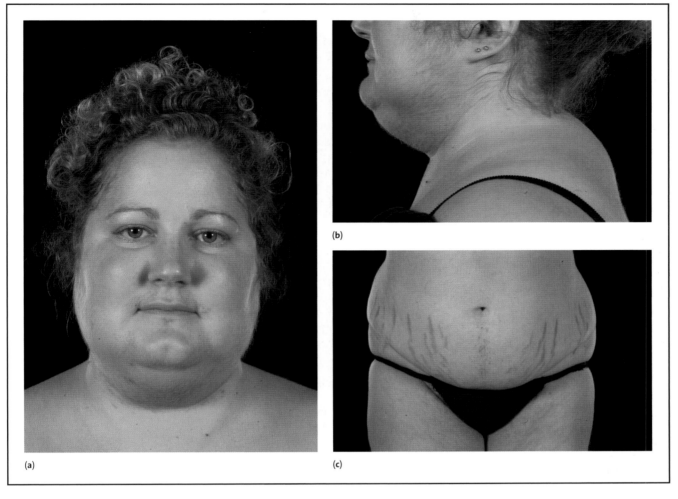

▲ **Fig. 21** Clinical features in Cushing's syndrome: **(a)** moon-like facies and plethora, **(b)** buffalo hump and hirsutism, and **(c)** purple striae.

***Low-dose dexamethasone
suppression test*** See Section 3.2.2.

Loss of diurnal cortisol variation
Measure cortisol at 9 a.m. and
midnight: normal midnight
serum/plasma cortisol, asleep,
is <100 nmol/L (and in many
instances <50 nmol/L). For subjects
who are awake, a higher cut-off is
used (~200 nmol/L). Alternatively,
salivary cortisol measurement
offers an excellent reflection
of the plasma free cortisol
concentration and, due to the
simple non-invasive collection
procedure, can be conveniently
performed at home.

Pseudo-Cushing's syndrome

A disorder that mimics Cushing's
syndrome, sometimes seen in the
setting of excess alcohol consumption
or severe endogenous depression, in
which the overnight and low-dose
dexamethasone suppression tests
and UFC estimation can be
abnormal. However, other indices
(eg mean corpuscular volume, γ-
glutamyltransferase) may suggest
the underlying cause, and the
cortisol response to insulin-induced
hypoglycaemia (see Section 3.1.5)
is preserved, contrasting with the
subnormal response typically seen in
Cushing's syndrome. In addition, the
low-dose dexamethasone suppression

test, followed at its conclusion by a
corticotrophin-releasing hormone
(CRH) test (see Section 3.1.2), has been
proposed as a means of discriminating
pseudo-Cushing's from Cushing's
disease.

Cyclical Cushing's syndrome

A rare variant in which
hypercortisolism occurs periodically.
Serial UFC collections, timed to when
the patient is symptomatic, may
help to establish the diagnosis. All
subsequent testing must be completed
when the patient is in an active phase
of the disease.

Defining the aetiology

Once the diagnosis has been confirmed, tests are undertaken to establish the cause. Measurement of plasma ACTH distinguishes between ACTH-dependent and ACTH-independent causes.

ACTH-dependent cause If an ACTH-dependent cause is suspected, consider the following.

1. High-dose dexamethasone suppression test (see Section 3.2.3).

2. CRH test (see Section 3.1.2).

3. Selective venous sampling for ACTH: inferior petrosal sinus sampling, measuring ACTH before and after CRH stimulation, provides a sensitive and specific means of discriminating Cushing's disease from the ectopic ACTH syndrome. An ACTH ratio of >2 (pre-CRH) or >3 (post-CRH) between inferior petrosal and peripheral samples is indicative of a pituitary source of ACTH. Furthermore, an inter-sinus gradient (between left and right or vice versa) of >1.4 aids lateralisation of an adenoma within the pituitary fossa in approximately two-thirds of cases.

4. Imaging

   (a) MRI of the pituitary: an adenoma can be identified in approximately 60–65% of patients with Cushing's disease, but MRI findings must be interpreted with care, since corticotroph adenomas may be too small to be detected, whilst pituitary incidentalomas (which are not clinically significant) are increasingly reported (up to 10% of normal individuals).

   (b) CT/MRI of neck, chest and abdomen: although a good-quality CXR may identify a bronchial carcinoma or carcinoid tumour as the source of ectopic ACTH production, in virtually all cases detailed cross-sectional imaging is required.

   (c) Other: octreotide scintigraphy and positron emission tomography (PET) may help identify small tumours within the thorax or abdomen that are not visible with CT/MRI.

5. Urea and electrolytes: unprovoked hypokalaemia (ie in the absence of diuretics or other confounding factors) favours an ectopic source, reflecting the tendency for ACTH (and hence cortisol) levels to be higher in this setting.

ACTH-independent cause If an ACTH-independent cause is suspected, consider CT/MRI of the adrenal glands. Providing the patient is not receiving exogenous steroids, the main objective is to differentiate the possible adrenal causes, in particular adenoma (Fig. 22) and carcinoma.

Treatment

Initial treatment should aim to reduce circulating cortisol levels using drugs that block steroid biosynthesis, eg metyrapone or ketoconazole. Use of these agents should be restricted to clinicians with experience of dose titration and monitoring for adverse events (including rendering the patient hypoadrenal). Attention must also be paid to correcting hyperglycaemia and hypertension. Thereafter, specific treatment is directed at the source of hypercortisolism.

- Pituitary adenoma: trans-sphenoidal adenomectomy or hemi-hypophysectomy. Radiotherapy may be required where surgical removal is incomplete or in patients judged unsuitable for surgery.

- Ectopic ACTH: surgical resection of tumour where possible.

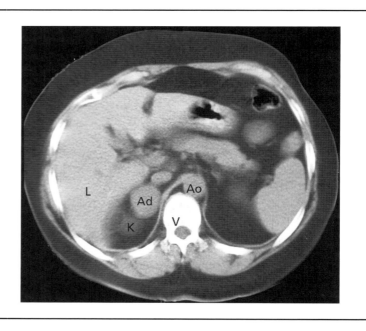

▲**Fig. 22** Adrenal adenoma. CT scan showing a right-sided adrenal adenoma (Ad) in a patient with Cushing's syndrome. K, kidney; L, liver; Ao, aorta; V, vertebral body.

- Adrenal tumour: surgical resection/debulking. For malignant tumours adjunctive medical treatment is often necessary in the form of the adrenolytic agent 1-chloro-2-(2,2-dichloro)-1-(4-chlorophenyl) ethylbenzene (mitotane), a derivative of the insecticide DDT, with or without systemic chemotherapy. Radiotherapy may also be useful in some instances.

- Exogenous corticosteroids: reduce dose or substitute steroid-sparing agents.

> Bilateral adrenalectomy is reserved for those patients in whom the primary source cannot be localised or when conventional treatment measures have failed. In Cushing's disease, however, this can be complicated by expansion of the corticotroph adenoma, leading to enhanced ACTH secretion, pigmentation and local problems due to tumour growth (so-called Nelson's syndrome). Pituitary irradiation may help to prevent/limit this.

Prognosis

Untreated Cushing's syndrome is often fatal, predominantly as a consequence of the complications of sustained hypercortisolism, including hypertension, cardiovascular disease and susceptibility to infection. However, with modern surgical techniques, benign pituitary and adrenal tumours can often be removed in their entirety, thereby curing the patient.

FURTHER READING

Newell-Price J, Bertagna X, Grossman AB and Nieman LK. Cushing's syndrome. *Lancet* 2006; 367: 1605–17.

- - - - - - - - - - - - - - - - - -

Trainer PJ and Besser M. *The Bart's Endocrine Protocols.* Edinburgh: Churchill Livingstone, 1995.

2.1.2 Acromegaly

Acromegaly is the clinical disorder resulting from hypersecretion of growth hormone (GH).

Aetiology/pathophysiology

The majority of cases are caused by a pituitary adenoma. Of these, 70–75% are macroadenomas (>1 cm in diameter) and 25–30% are microadenomas (<1 cm in diameter). A small number of cases have been reported in which acromegaly results from ectopic growth hormone-releasing hormone (GHRH) secretion. Many of the growth-related aspects of this disorder are mediated by insulin-like growth factor (IGF)-1, which is produced by the liver in response to GH, whilst GH itself has direct metabolic effects, eg induction of insulin resistance (see *Scientific Background to Medicine 1*, Physiology – Section 5.1).

Epidemiology

The incidence of acromegaly is estimated at approximately 3–5 per million per year, with a prevalence of 40–70 per million. Patients are typically diagnosed in early middle age, although the onset of disease, and hence symptoms, often pre-dates the diagnosis by 5–15 years.

Clinical presentation

The diagnosis of acromegaly is often first raised by a clinician, dentist or optometrist, who encourages the patient to seek advice for changes that they had attributed to 'ageing'. Commonly reported symptoms include:

- an increase in the size of the hands and feet (often noted as changes in ring and shoe size respectively);

- coarsened facial features, altered bite and prominence of the jaw (prognathism);

- features of carpal tunnel syndrome;

- snoring, reflecting sleep apnoea (which may be central or obstructive in aetiology);

- arthralgia;

- sweating/oily skin;

- thirst and polyuria (diabetes mellitus);

- local symptoms due to the space-occupying effects of a pituitary tumour, eg headache and visual disturbance;

- amenorrhoea, loss of libido or erectile dysfunction secondary to hypogonadotrophic hypogonadism.

Physical signs

Many of the symptoms reported by the patient correlate with specific signs on examination, including evidence of large 'spade-like' hands and feet, prognathism and coarsened facial features (see Section 1.2.4). Hypertension is a common finding and long-standing untreated disease may lead to concentric myocardial hypertrophy and ultimately cardiac failure.

> Careful examination of the visual fields is essential to check for evidence of bitemporal quadrantanopia/hemianopia.

Investigation

Biochemical confirmation of the diagnosis is usually made using an oral glucose tolerance test (see Section 3.2.4) in which GH levels show a paradoxical rise or failure to suppress in response to a glucose challenge. In addition, the IGF-1 concentration is typically elevated above the age-related normal range.

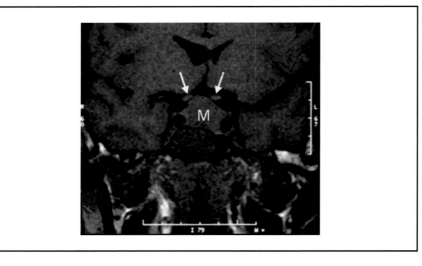

▲ **Fig. 23** Pituitary macroadenoma in acromegaly. Coronal pituitary MRI scan demonstrating a macroadenoma (M) with suprasellar extension abutting the optic chiasm/nerves (arrows).

Once the diagnosis has been established, imaging of the pituitary fossa should be carried out (preferably by MRI; Fig. 23), and visual acuity and visual fields formally assessed (see Figs 11, 12 and 26). A full appraisal of anterior pituitary function is also necessary (see Section 2.1.8). Remember that 20–25% of GH-producing tumours also co-secrete prolactin.

Treatment

> The goals of treatment in acromegaly are to effect a cure, preserve/restore remaining pituitary function and reverse/control complications. Evidence suggests that even if a cure cannot be achieved, then providing that the mean GH level throughout the day can be reduced to <5 mU/L, the life expectancy of patients with acromegaly approximates that of the general population.

Surgery

The first-line treatment for acromegaly is usually surgery. In experienced hands, trans-sphenoidal adenomectomy offers a surgical cure rate of approximately 80%
for microadenomas, although this drops to less than 50% for macroadenomas. Recurrence rates are estimated at 2–7% over 5 years in patients originally considered to be 'cured' postoperatively.

Radiotherapy

Radiotherapy may be given if there is residual tumour postoperatively with persistent elevation of GH or if the patient is medically unfit for surgery. Note that although beneficial effects of radiotherapy are usually evident within 12–24 months of treatment, it can take much longer for GH to fall to 'safe' levels (approximately 50% of patients achieve adequate suppression at 10 years). A similar proportion of patients at the same time point have hypopituitarism involving one or more trophic axes.

Medical therapy

The role of medical therapy in the management of acromegaly is evolving. Traditionally it has been used to supplement surgical treatment, as a 'holding exercise' in patients who have had radiotherapy, or as first-line treatment in patients who are unfit for surgery.

Somatostatin analogues (somatostatin receptor ligands) Somatostatin analogues (octreotide or longer-acting preparations) produce excellent control of symptoms in the majority of patients, reduce GH concentrations to <5 mU/L in up to 80%, and constrain growth or induce tumour shrinkage in approximately 50% of cases. However, they are only available as injections, are expensive and have gastrointestinal side effects, including nausea and diarrhoea in the acute phase and an increased tendency to gallstone formation in the longer term.

Dopamine agonists Dopamine agonists (eg bromocriptine, cabergoline) only suppress GH levels to acceptable 'safe' levels in <15% of patients, athough they may be useful if the tumour co-secretes prolactin, or when combined with a somatostatin analogue.

Growth hormone receptor antagonists Pegvisomant, a growth hormone receptor antagonist, lowers circulating IGF-1 levels into the normal range in >90% of patients, thereby improving many of the clinical features of acromegaly. However, it does not reduce pituitary tumour size nor lower GH secretion, and indeed during treatment GH levels can rise by up to 70% over baseline, which is probably caused by a loss of negative feedback due to the reduction in IGF-1. The drug is also expensive, and is given by daily subcutaneous injection. Currently, its use is limited to those patients who still have uncontrolled disease despite surgery, radiotherapy and somatostatin analogue therapy. Liver function tests must be monitored during treatment and MRI repeated at 6-monthly intervals or sooner if there are any concerns regarding tumour growth.

Other risk factors

Aggressive treatment of other risk factors is essential, including hypertension, diabetes mellitus, dyslipidaemia and sleep apnoea. Most centres also offer screening colonoscopy once the patient is of an appropriate age, as available evidence suggests that the risk of colon cancer in acromegalic subjects is about twice that of the general population. Those with a family history of colon cancer are likely to be at particular risk.

A holistic approach

Other causes of morbidity should not be overlooked, with patients frequently requiring rheumatological/orthopaedic assessments, dental/maxillofacial opinions and psychological input or support to address problems of body image. They may find contact with the Pituitary Foundation (http://www.pituitary.org.uk/) helpful.

Follow-up

Following treatment, periodic MRI scans are required, together with assessment of visual fields, the GH–IGF-1 axis, and anterior pituitary function.

Prognosis

The mortality of subjects with acromegaly has been estimated to be 1.5–4 times that of the general population, mainly due to an excess of cardiovascular, cerebrovascular and respiratory disease. Remember that the mortality rate approaches that of the general population if mean post-treatment GH levels are <5 mU/L.

Disease associations

Acromegaly may be associated with parathyroid and pancreatic tumours as part of multiple endocrine neoplasia type 1 syndrome (see Section 2.7.1), or with cutaneous and cardiac myxomas, primary pigmented nodular adrenal disease and testicular tumours in the Carney complex.

FURTHER READING

Melmed S. Medical progress: acromegaly. *N. Engl. J. Med.* 2006; 355: 2558–73.

2.1.3 Hyperprolactinaemia

Aetiology and pathophysiology

Varying degrees of hyperprolactinaemia are found in an array of physiological and pathological states (Table 20). Prolactin inhibits hypothalamic gonadotrophin-releasing hormone (GnRH) secretion and hence gonadal steroid production.

Epidemiology

The incidence of prolactinoma has been estimated at 25–30 per million per year, with a prevalence of 500 per million. Microprolactinomas are diagnosed much more commonly in females (typically in the age range 20–30 years) and account for approximately one-third of all cases of secondary amenorrhoea in young women. Macroprolactinomas show no major gender difference.

Clinical presentation

- Females typically present with oligomenorrhoea/amenorrhoea and/or galactorrhoea. Some are referred with infertility. On questioning, they may report symptoms of reduced libido and vaginal dryness with dyspareunia.

- Males commonly present with larger tumours (macroadenomas) causing local pressure effects (eg headache or visual disturbance), although reduced libido/potency, subfertility and galactorrhoea may occur.

Physical signs

Always examine for visual field defects (bitemporal hemianopia) and check for galactorrhoea. Signs of other underlying disorders (eg chronic liver or renal disease) may be present.

TABLE 20 CAUSES OF HYPERPROLACTINAEMIA

Condition	Examples
Physiological	Pregnancy, lactation, post partum, physical activity
Idiopathic	–
Stress	Venepuncture (up to two-fold rise)
Drugs	Dopamine antagonists, eg phenothiazines, metoclopramide
Liver/renal disease	Cirrhosis, chronic renal impairment
Hypothalamic–pituitary disorders	Microprolactinoma/macroprolactinoma, stalk disconnection syndrome (eg non-functioning tumour, infiltration)
Other endocrine disorders	Primary hypothyroidism (TRH is a trophic stimulus for prolactin release), polycystic ovarian syndrome

TRH, thyrotrophin-releasing hormone.

Investigation

Prolactin

The finding of an elevated prolactin level should be confirmed on at least one separate occasion.

> A prolactin concentration in excess of 5,000 mU/L usually indicates the presence of a prolactinoma, whilst values up to this level may be seen with many of the other conditions shown in Table 20, including pituitary stalk compression. Prolactin levels in excess of 10,000 mU/L are usually indicative of a macroprolactinoma.

Routine blood tests

Check renal, liver and thyroid function and carry out a pregnancy test if applicable. Follicle-stimulating hormone, luteinising hormone and estradiol may be useful in the differential diagnosis of oligomenorrhoea/amenorrhoea (see Section 2.4.2).

Radiological imaging

Unless there is an obvious explanation for mild hyperprolactinaemia, an MRI (or CT) scan of the pituitary fossa is indicated in virtually all cases (Fig. 24). With modest hyperprolactinaemia, although a microadenoma may be identified, the principal objective of the scan is to exclude tumour/infiltration causing disconnection hyperprolactinaemia.

Visual fields/pituitary function

Formal assessment of visual fields (see Figs 11, 12 and 26) and anterior pituitary function (see Section 2.1.8) may be indicated, depending on the clinical and MRI findings.

Differential diagnosis

The differential diagnosis of oligomenorrhoea/amenorrhoea is discussed in detail in Section 2.4.2.

Treatment

Hyperprolactinaemia not associated with a pituitary tumour

- Drug treatment causing hyperprolactinaemia is sometimes amenable to change, in liaison with the original prescriber (often a psychiatrist). Some of the newer antipsychotic agents (eg quetiapine) are much less prone to inducing hyperprolactinaemia.

- Women with unwanted postpartum galactorrhoea (and their partners) need to be advised to avoid nipple stimulation completely for a while, including 'checking to see if it is still happening'. Bromocriptine can be tried (see below), although some women find the benefit/side-effect profile unfavourable and discontinue treatment.

- Underlying renal or liver disease requires appropriate treatment.

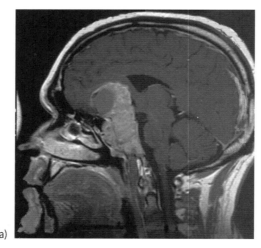

(a)

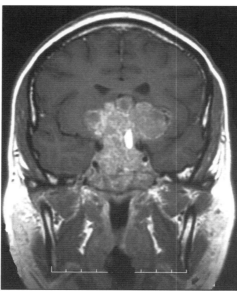

(b)

◄**Fig. 24** Macroprolactinoma: (**a**) sagittal and (**b**) coronal MRI scans demonstrating a massive macroprolactinoma. Note the heterogeneous appearance suggesting cystic components and areas of haemorrhage (high signal).

- Idiopathic hyperprolactinaemia: dopaminergic agonists are often effective in restoring prolactin levels to normal in symptomatic patients.

Hyperprolactinaemia caused by a pituitary tumour

Prolactinomas are unusual amongst pituitary tumours in that the primary treatment for both microadenomas and macroadenomas is medical (providing there is no immediate threat to vision). Dopaminergic agonists (eg bromocriptine, cabergoline) are often highly effective in shrinking tumours, relieving symptoms and preserving/restoring anterior pituitary function.

> The side effects of bromocriptine (including nausea, hypotension, nasal congestion and fatigue) can be minimised if the patient is started on a very low dose and advised to take the tablet with a snack at bedtime. Unfortunately, due to its short duration of action, bromocriptine requires bd or tds dosing. Longer-acting preparations (eg cabergoline and quinagolide) are therefore preferred in most cases, although again it is best to start with a low dose and gradually titrate up according to the serum prolactin level and tolerability. Even if the patient experiences significant side effects on starting treatment, it is worth encouraging him/her to persist with therapy if possible, as tolerance usually develops over a relatively short period of time.

Microprolactinomas Following normalisation of prolactin, follow-up is on an annual basis unless there is evidence of progression. Treatment may be withdrawn every 2–3 years to check for remission.

Macroprolactinomas For those with macroprolactinomas, serial prolactin

concentrations should be checked during the early stages of treatment and a repeat MRI scan performed to monitor the response to medical therapy. Additional bone protection measures (eg bisphosphonate and/or calcium/vitamin D therapy) may be necessary in patients whose prolactin concentration does not drop sufficiently to permit restoration of gonadal function. Remember that exogenous oestrogens should generally be avoided because of their potential trophic effect on the tumour, although some clinicians will permit oestrogen at hormone-replacement therapy (HRT) doses once the tumour has shrunk in response to dopamine agonist therapy, and providing that there is no clinical, biochemical or radiological evidence to suggest tumour regrowth after commencing HRT. Surgical intervention (trans-sphenoidal adenomectomy) is generally preferred as second-line treatment in the UK. Radiotherapy is usually held in reserve for refractory tumours as it takes time to have an effect and often leads to hypopituitarism.

Non-functioning adenomas
Surgery is generally considered to be the treatment of choice (see Section 2.1.4). For mid-range prolactin concentrations (4,000–5,000 mU/L), when it is difficult to distinguish between a prolactinoma and a non-functioning adenoma, a trial of bromocriptine or cabergoline may be considered to see if the tumour shrinks in response to medical therapy.

> The prolactin concentration is likely to fall with dopamine agonist therapy in either case and therefore the size of the tumour must be monitored.

Contraception and pregnancy

> - Women must be warned that they may get pregnant on starting treatment, even before they have a menstrual period. If they wish to defer pregnancy they should use barrier contraception, although the combined oral contraceptive pill is also safe for use in women with microadenomas. Those with microprolactinomas who do not wish to conceive do not need to take bromocriptine or cabergoline but may require HRT or other agents such as a bisphosphonate to prevent osteoporosis. Again, contraceptive advice should be given. For those who elect for no treatment at all, then close surveillance of bone status with periodic dual energy X-ray absoptiometry scanning is mandatory if the patient is oligomenorrhoeic or amenorrhoeic.
> - Bromocriptine is safe in pregnancy (there is less experience with cabergoline although reassuringly there is no evidence that it is detrimental to the pregnant woman or fetus; in contrast, concerns have been raised regarding higher rates of miscarriage and fetal malformation in females taking quinagolide and pergolide, although the number of cases reported to date is small. In general, patients with microadenomas are usually advised to discontinue treatment once pregnancy is confirmed, as there is very little risk of clinically relevant tumour expansion during the remainder of the pregnancy. Most endocrinologists recommend clinical review during each trimester, but it is extremely rare for intervention to be required. Patients should be reassessed following cessation of breast-feeding. With macroadenomas many physicians recommend continuing bromocriptine throughout pregnancy, with avoidance of breast-feeding post partum, in view of the risk of clinically significant tumour expansion. In other cases (eg those with small tumour remnants) bromocriptine may be withdrawn but patients should be warned to present immediately should they develop visual symptoms or a severe headache. Close follow-up is required in either setting.

Complications

Prolonged oligomenorrhoea/
amenorrhoea is associated with an
increased risk of osteopenia and
osteoporosis.

Disease associations

Prolactinomas may rarely be
associated with parathyroid and
pancreatic tumours in the context
of multiple endocrine neoplasia
type 1 syndrome (see Section 2.7.1)

FURTHER READING

Gillam M, Molitch M, Lombardi G and
Colao A. Advances in the treatment of
prolactinomas. *Endocr. Rev.* 2006; 27:
485–534.

2.1.4 Non-functioning pituitary tumours

Aetiology/pathophysiology

Non-functioning pituitary tumours
('chromophobe adenomas') are
usually benign macroadenomas
(>1 cm diameter).

Epidemiology

The incidence of non-functioning
pituitary tumours is estimated at
5–10 per million per year.

Clinical presentation

Local pressure effects often
result in headache and visual
disturbances. The patient
may present with symptoms
of hypopituitarism or
hyperprolactinaemia due to
pituitary stalk compression
(fatigue, lack of well-being and
hypogonadism). Alternatively, it may
be an incidental finding following
routine eye testing or a head scan
for unrelated purposes.

Physical signs

It is important to check carefully
for evidence of bitemporal

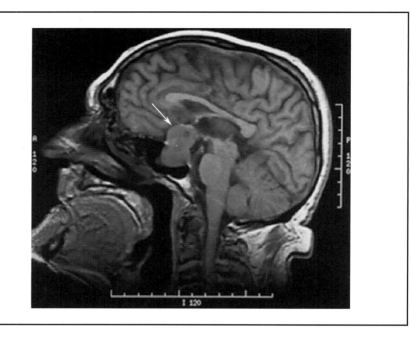

▲**Fig. 25** Non-functioning tumour. Sagittal MRI scan showing a large non-functioning tumour arising from
the pituitary fossa with suprasellar extension (arrow) in a 45-year-old man presenting with a bitemporal
visual field defect.

(sometimes only upper quandrantic)
hemianopia. Features of
hyperprolactinaemia may also be
present (see Section 2.1.3).

Investigation

A full assessment should
include tests of anterior pituitary
function (see Section 2.1.8), an
MRI scan of the pituitary fossa
(Fig. 25), and formal tests of the
patient's visual fields (see Figs 11,
12 and 26) and visual acuity.

> The serum prolactin result
> must be seen before surgery
> is considered in any patient with a
> suspected non-functioning tumour
> to exclude the possibility of a
> prolactinoma that would be amenable
> to medical therapy (see Section 2.1.3).

Differential diagnosis

The differential diagnosis includes
other sellar or parasellar masses,

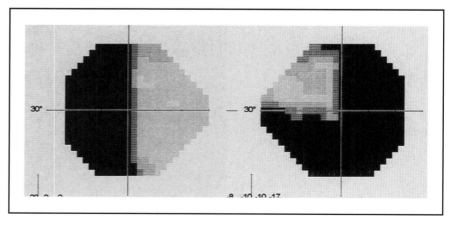

▲**Fig. 26** Bitemporal visual field defect. Computerised perimetry provides accurate details regarding visual
field loss. In this particular patient there was also loss of the right inferior nasal field.

including cysts, craniopharyngioma, meningioma, metastatic, infiltrative or granulomatous disease, and lymphocytic hypophysitis.

Treatment

A non-functioning macroadenoma in a patient with pressure symptoms or signs, particularly loss of visual fields, requires urgent surgical debulking (trans-sphenoidal or occasionally transcranial hypophysectomy). Surgery may lead to partial recovery of anterior pituitary function. Postoperative radiotherapy should be considered if tumour removal is incomplete or subsequently if the tumour recurs.

If there are no pressure symptoms or signs, it may be acceptable in some cases (eg frail elderly patients) to adopt an expectant approach. Either way, patients require serial MRI scans together with assessment of visual fields, visual acuity and anterior pituitary function.

Complications

Operative complications include transient diabetes insipidus in 10–20% of patients, which may persist in 2–5%. Pituitary radiotherapy results in some degree of hypopituitarism in about 50% of patients after 10 years.

Prognosis

Hypopituitarism is associated with an increased mortality rate of at least twice that of the general population (see Section 2.1.8).

FURTHER READING

Clayton RN and Wass JAH. Pituitary tumours: recommendations for service provision and guidelines for management of patients. Summary of a consensus statement of a working party from the Endocrinology and Diabetes Committee of the Royal College of Physicians and the Society for Endocrinology in conjunction with the Research Unit of the Royal College of Physicians. *J. R. Coll. Physicians Lond.* 1997; 31: 628–36.

Freda PU and Wardlaw SL. Diagnosis and treatment of pituitary tumours. *J. Clin. Endocrinol. Metab.* 1999; 84: 3859–66.

2.1.5 Pituitary apoplexy

Aetiology/pathophysiology

Clinically apparent pituitary apoplexy usually results from extensive infarction of a pituitary adenoma with haemorrhage. In about 50% of cases the event is spontaneous and the pathogenesis is not known. One-quarter of all cases are associated with arterial hypertension and occasionally it is also seen following head trauma or dynamic testing of pituitary function. Patients on anticoagulation are at increased risk, and prolactinomas treated with dopamine agonists often show signs of haemorrhage on follow-up MRI, although many of these episodes are clinically silent.

Epidemiology

The incidence of clinical apoplexy in surgically treated pituitary adenomas has been reported to range from 0.6 to 9.0%. Although it can occur at any age, the mean age at presentation is 45 years.

Clinical presentation

Common

The classical presentation is with sudden-onset retro-orbital headache and visual disturbances, including reduced visual acuity, visual field defects, photophobia and ophthalmoplegia (most commonly due to a unilateral third nerve palsy). Symptoms may evolve over hours to days and may be mistaken for those due to subarachnoid haemorrhage.

Uncommon

Occasionally the onset is more insidious, with nausea and vomiting, meningism and an altered level of consciousness. Symptoms of hypopituitarism or hyperprolactinaemia, including chronic lethargy, reduced libido, oligomenorrhoea or amenorrhoea, impotence and galactorrhoea may also be present.

Physical signs

Common

Visual field defects and reduced visual acuity, together with ophthalmoplegia (third, fourth or sixth nerve palsies) are common. The conscious level may be reduced.

Uncommon

Signs of underlying pituitary disease (eg acromegaly) are occasionally present.

Investigation

An urgent MRI (or CT) scan of the pituitary fossa should be performed (Fig. 27). If this fails to demonstrate a pituitary haemorrhage, angiography may be necessary to exclude an intracranial aneurysm. There may be elevated numbers of red blood cells in the cerebrospinal fluid or even a frank aseptic meningitic picture. Blood samples for basic tests of anterior pituitary function should be taken, including cortisol, thyroid function tests, prolactin, luteinising hormone and follicle-stimulating hormone, and oestrogen or testosterone.

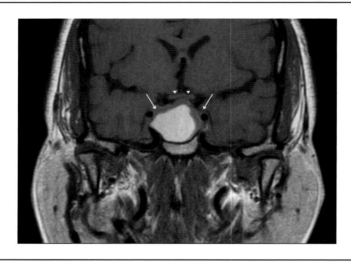

▲ **Fig. 27** Pituitary apoplexy. Coronal MRI scan demonstrating extensive haemorrhage (high signal) within a pituitary adenoma in a patient who presented with acute onset of a severe headache and right third and sixth cranial nerve palsies. Note the splaying of the cavernous sinuses (arrows) particularly on the right side. The apex of the tumour abuts the optic chiasm (arrowheads).

Treatment

Emergency

> ⚠️ Once the diagnosis has been considered, anterior pituitary dysfunction must be assumed. Establish venous access (taking bloods for urea and electrolytes, glucose and cortisol) and give intravenous hydrocortisone (100 mg) immediately prior to establishing on regular replacement (see Section 2.1.8). Fluid and electrolyte balance should be maintained.

Surgery

Urgent decompression is indicated if there is compression of the optic chiasm with visual loss or in patients with reduced consciousness or hemiparesis. In other circumstances a conservative approach may be adopted, particularly if there is no progressive neuro-ophthalmic deficit. Unlike the optic chiasm, the third, fourth and sixth cranial nerves are surprisingly resistant to compression, and spontaneous recovery of function is common even in cases managed conservatively.

Hormone replacement

A full endocrine evaluation should be made postoperatively, and appropriate hormone-replacement therapies instituted with long-term follow-up (see Section 2.1.8).

Complications

Transient postoperative diabetes insipidus is common. Overall mortality rates are not known.

FURTHER READING

Ayuk J, McGregor EJ, Mitchell RD and Gittoes NJ. Acute management of pituitary apoplexy: surgery or conservative management? *Clin. Endocrinol.* 2004; 61: 747–52.

– – – – – – – – – – – – – – – –

Randeva HS, Schoebel J, Byrne J, *et al.* Classical pituitary apoplexy: clinical features, management and outcome. *Clin. Endocrinol.* 1999; 51: 181–8.

2.1.6 Craniopharyngioma

This tumour, typically comprising both solid and cystic components, arises between the pituitary and hypothalamus.

Aetiology/pathophysiology

The exact origin remains uncertain, but the tumour most probably arises from Rathke's pouch. Although histologically benign, local invasion is a frequent finding and many recur after surgery.

Epidemiology

Craniopharyngiomas are estimated to account for 5–12% of all intracranial tumours in childhood and about 1% of brain tumours in adults. The peak incidence is distributed bimodally, with the majority of cases occurring between 5 and 14 years of age, but with a second smaller peak after 50 years of age.

Clinical presentation

Childhood

Although endocrine deficiencies are common, most go unrecognised for years and only come to attention when the child presents with symptoms of raised intracranial pressure (eg headache, nausea and vomiting) or visual disturbance due to the mass effect of an expanding tumour. Growth hormone deficiency (leading to growth retardation) and diabetes insipidus are the most commonly encountered endocrine disturbances.

In older children, there may be pubertal delay or arrest as a consequence of gonadotrophin deficiency. Features of hypothalamic dysfunction, including disturbance of appetite or thirst, somnolence and abnormal temperature regulation, are sometimes seen.

Adulthood

Endocrine manifestations (including diabetes insipidus) are a more common presenting feature in adulthood, although many cases exhibit symptoms of raised intracranial pressure.

Physical signs

Reduced visual acuity, and visual field defects as a consequence of chiasmal compression, together with papilloedema or optic atrophy (reflecting raised intracranial pressure) may be evident. Careful examination for evidence of pituitary insufficiency should be undertaken.

Investigation

Where possible, initial investigation of suspected cases should include the following.

MRI (or CT) scan of the pituitary fossa and hypothalamus

Craniopharyngiomas exhibit a distinctive appearance with mixed solid and cystic components, and heterogeneity of enhancement (Fig. 28). Intrasellar or suprasellar calcification is often evident on plain skull radiographs.

Ophthalmological review

To provide a baseline for monitoring the effects of treatment. Remember that suprasellar cranipharyngiomas often compress the optic chiasm from above, leading to a bilateral inferior quadrantanopia in the first instance, before progressing to a full-blown hemianopia. This is the opposite of the situation with a pituitary macroadenoma, which compresses the chiasm from below thus leading to a superior quadrantanopia (see Figs 12, 13 and 26).

Assessment of hypothalamic–pituitary function

Anterior pituitary function tests and paired urine and plasma osmolalities with serum urea

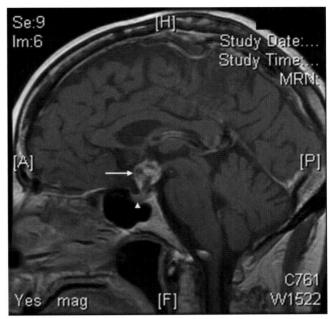

(a)

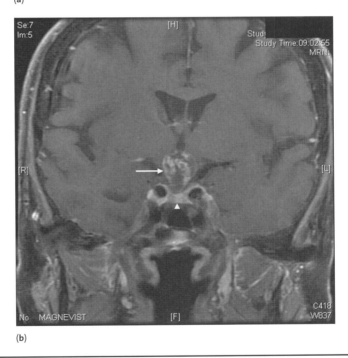

(b)

▲**Fig. 28** Craniopharyngioma: (**a**) sagittal and (**b**) coronal MRI scans showing the typical appearances of a craniopharyngioma (arrow) with mixed solid and cystic components. Note the normal pituitary gland (arrowhead), which can be identified separately from the suprasellar mass.

and electrolytes (to look for evidence of diabetes insipidus). Approximately 80% of patients will have pituitary dysfunction at diagnosis.

Treatment

This is a rare condition and ideally patients should be referred to a centre with expertise in pituitary surgery.

Surgery

Up to 50% of cases have evidence of hydrocephalus on initial imaging and one-third require urgent surgical decompression. Transcranial subfrontal surgery may be required to allow full access to the tumour, although complete excision is frequently not possible. The cyst contents are classically said to have the appearance of 'engine/machine oil'.

> Unless there is clear biochemical evidence to the contrary, assume that all cases have pituitary insufficiency and ensure that adequate steroid cover is given perioperatively (see Section 2.1.8).

Postoperative

Short term Postoperative care will require combined endocrine, neurological, psychological and ophthalmological input. Since complete surgical resection is usually not feasible, adjunctive radiotherapy is often necessary and has been reported to reduce recurrence rates from 80% to 20%.

Long term Long-term follow-up is required to detect and treat regrowth of the tumour and any hypothalamic–pituitary dysfunction. Patients and their carers may find contact with the Child Growth Foundation (http://www.childgrowthfoundation. org/) and the Pituitary Foundation (http://www.pituitary.org.uk/) useful.

Prognosis

Poor prognostic features include young age and presentation with hydrocephalus. Although non-malignant, craniopharyngiomas often have a worse outcome in childhood than other malignant cerebral tumours.

FURTHER READING

Clayton RN and Wass JAH. Pituitary tumours: recommendations for service provision and guidelines for management of patients. Summary of a consensus statement of a working party from the Endocrinology and Diabetes Committee of the Royal College of Physicians and the Society for Endocrinology in conjunction with the Research Unit of the Royal College of Physicians. *J. R. Coll. Physicians Lond.* 1997; 31: 628–36.

- - - - - - - - - - - - - - - - -

Lafferty AR and Chrousos GP. Pituitary tumours in children and adolescents. *J. Clin. Endocrinol. Metab.* 1999; 84: 4317–23.

2.1.7 Diabetes insipidus

Diabetes insipidus (DI) can be defined as the excretion of excessive or 'copious' volumes of urine (traditionally >3 L per 24 hours).

Aetiology/pathophysiology

Classically three types of DI are recognised.

1. Hypothalamic (cranial) DI, in which there is an absolute deficiency of antidiuretic hormone (ADH, also called vasopressin).

2. Nephrogenic DI, which is caused by resistance to the action of ADH in the collecting ducts.

3. Dipsogenic DI, due to excessive inappropriate fluid intake, ie primary polydipsia. Dipsogenic DI is sometimes referred to as psychogenic DI, although this term is not appropriate in all cases and is therefore best avoided.

The most common causes of each of these subtypes are shown in Table 21.

> Pituitary adenomas are very rarely associated with DI prior to surgical intervention. Hence, it is important to keep in mind the other conditions listed in Table 21 when faced with a patient who presents with a pituitary mass and DI.

Epidemiology

Varies according to the underlying cause.

Clinical presentation

Polyuria and polydipsia are the most common presenting symptoms. Nocturia on several occasions is typical; indeed if the patient is able to sleep solidly for 8 hours without needing to get up to the toilet, then it is unlikely that he or she has hypothalamic or nephrogenic DI. Symptoms of anterior pituitary dysfunction and the underlying disorder may also be present.

Physical signs

Reduced visual acuity, and visual field defects due to chiasmal compression, together with papilloedema or optic atrophy (reflecting raised intracranial pressure) may be evident in cases of hypothalamic DI. Examine carefully for evidence of pituitary insufficiency. Other clinical signs will be determined by the underlying disorder.

Investigation

Confirming the diagnosis of DI

Having established that the patient is polyuric, an assessment of renal concentrating ability should be undertaken.

Plasma and urine osmolalities
Measurement of paired early-morning plasma and urine osmolalities, together with

TABLE 21 CAUSES OF DIABETES INSIPIDUS

Condition	Type	Subtype	Examples
Hypothalamic DI	Primary	Idiopathic	–
		Genetic	AD, AR, DIDMOAD
		Developmental	Lawrence–Moon–Biedl syndrome, septo-optic dysplasia
	Secondary	Trauma	Post surgery (TSS, TCS), head injury
		Tumour	Craniopharyngioma, metastasis (especially breast, lung), germinoma. (Very rarely pituitary macroadenoma)
		Inflammatory	Granulomas (eg sarcoidosis, TB, histiocytosis), meningitis, encephalitis, autoimmune
		Vascular	Aneurysm, infarction, Sheehan's syndrome
Nephrogenic DI	Primary	Idiopathic	–
		Genetic	XR, AR, AD
	Secondary	Chronic renal disease	Obstructive uropathy, tubulointerstitial disease
		Metabolic disease	Hypercalcaemia, hypokalaemia
		Osmotic diuretics	Glucose, mannitol
		Drug induced	Lithium, demeclocycline
		Systemic disorders	Amyloidosis
		Pregnancy	–
Dipsogenic DI	Habitual or compulsive water drinking	Occasionally associated with structural/organic hypothalamic disease	Sarcoid, tumours involving the hypothalamus

AD, autosomal dominant; AR, autosomal recessive; DIDMOAD, diabetes insipidus, diabetes mellitus, optic atrophy, deafness; TCS, transcranial surgery; TSS, trans-sphenoidal surgery; XR, X-linked recessive.

urea and electrolytes, following abstention from/limitation of fluid intake overnight may help to exclude cases in which the index of clinical suspicion is low. The finding of a concentrated early-morning urine sample (>750 mosmol/kg) together with normal plasma osmolality and electrolytes effectively excludes DI. Note, however, that given the unsupervised nature of this test, it should not be used in cases where genuine DI is suspected.

Water deprivation test For those in whom the overnight test fails to resolve the issue, or in cases with a higher index of suspicion, a formal water deprivation test can be performed, with subsequent assessment of renal concentrating ability in response to exogenous vasopressin (see Section 3.3.2).

Hypertonic saline infusion test Occasionally, difficulties arise in establishing the diagnosis with fluid

deprivation; moreover, milder forms of hypothalamic, nephrogenic and dipsogenic DI cannot always be differentiated with this type of test. In these circumstances, direct measurement of plasma ADH (AVP) concentration, together with plasma and urine osmolalities, during graded osmotic stimulation (by infusion of hypertonic saline) can accurately diagnose DI and differentiate the various causes. This investigation should only be performed in centres with experience of the test, and must not be undertaken in subjects with cardiac, renal or hepatic impairment, who are likely to become significantly salt overloaded.

Assessment of cause and associated complications in hypothalamic DI

Assessment of hypothalamic–pituitary function Evidence of

anterior pituitary dysfunction must be sought in all cases of hypothalamic DI (see Section 2.1.8).

> Remember that cortisol has a permissive effect on free water excretion. Accordingly, DI may be masked in states of cortisol deficiency and only become evident once glucocorticoid replacement has been commenced.

MRI (or CT) scan of the pituitary fossa and hypothalamus Mandatory in any patient found to have hypothalamic DI. The high signal normally seen at the site of the posterior pituitary gland is likely to be absent even in the absence of a mass lesion (Fig. 29).

Ophthalmological review To provide a baseline for monitoring the effects of treatment.

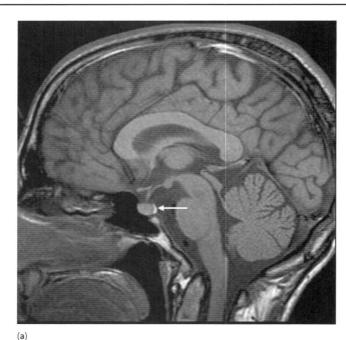

(a)

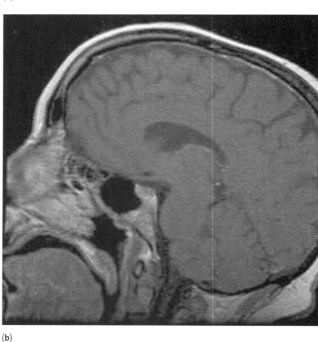

(b)

▲ **Fig. 29** Absent posterior pituitary signal in hypothalamic DI. Saggital MRI scans showing (**a**) the normal high signal from the posterior pituitary gland (arrow) and (**b**) loss of signal in a patient with hypothalamic DI due to pituitary infiltration.

Treatment
Wherever possible, treatment should be directed at the underlying disorder.

Hypothalamic (cranial) DI
Desmopressin (DDAVP), a synthetic long-acting vasopressin analogue, is the treatment of choice for patients with hypothalamic DI. It can be administered via several routes (subcutaneously, intramuscularly, intravenously, intranasally or orally). Patients should be treated with the lowest dose necessary to control their polyuria/nocturia and advised of the potential symptoms of over-replacement, especially if they have pre-existing cardiac or renal impairment. Daily weight measurement may help to alert the patient to cumulative over-treatment. In these circumstances, adjustment to the dose/regimen and omission of desmopressin for a short period at regular intervals, perhaps once weekly (to allow breakthrough polyuria), usually helps to prevent fluid overload. It is important to monitor plasma electrolytes at regular intervals after commencing treatment and following any dose adjustments.

Nephrogenic DI
Nephrogenic DI due to an acquired metabolic problem is best managed by addressing the underlying cause and maintaining adequate hydration while function recovers. For those patients with congenital nephrogenic DI or an acquired irreversible defect, various additional measures can be tried, including high-dose desmopressin in cases of partial nephrogenic DI, thiazide diuretics/amiloride, NSAIDs or dietary salt restriction.

Dipsogenic DI
This is often an extremely challenging condition to manage, especially if the cause is not acknowledged by the patient. Reduction in fluid intake is the only rational treatment. Individuals with persistent dipsogenic DI are at significant risk of hyponatraemia if given desmopressin.

Prognosis

Prognosis is largely dependent on the underlying disorder.

2.1.8 Hypopituitarism and hormone replacement

Hypopituitarism denotes an insufficiency of one or more of the pituitary hormones.

Aetiology and pathophysiology

Destruction/compression of normal pituitary tissue or reduction in the blood supply (including the hypothalamic–pituitary portal circulation) accounts for the majority of cases (Table 22).

> **With pituitary tumours, the usual sequence in which pituitary hormone function is lost is:**
>
> - growth hormone (GH);
> - luteinising hormone (LH) and follicle-stimulating hormone (FSH);
> - adrenocorticotrophic hormone (ACTH);
> - thyroid-stimulating hormone (TSH).

Incidence

The incidence in adults is 8–10 per million per year.

Clinical presentation

This depends on the aetiology, the degree of deficiency and the rapidity of onset. Examples are shown below.

- Chronic hypopituitarism (eg after pituitary radiotherapy) may present with general fatigue and lack of well-being, symptoms of hypogonadism (sexual dysfunction, loss of libido, oligomenorrhoea/amenorrhoea) and possibly symptoms of hypothyroidism and hypoadrenalism.

- GH deficiency may manifest as reduced exercise performance and quality of life.

TABLE 22 AETIOLOGY OF HYPOPITUITARISM

Frequency	Cause
Common	Pituitary/peripituitary tumours (or as a complication of treatment, including surgery and radiotherapy)
Rare	Vascular (eg pituitary apoplexy, Sheehan's syndrome, intrasellar carotid artery aneurysm)
	Pituitary infiltration (eg metastasis, haemochromatosis, sarcoidosis, histiocytosis, Wegener's granulomatosis)
	Infection (eg tuberculosis, pituitary abscess)
	Autoimmune (lymphocytic hypophysitis)
	Traumatic (eg post head injury)
	Congenital (eg isolated or combined pituitary hormone deficiencies)
	Idiopathic

- Pituitary apoplexy (see Section 2.1.5).

Physical signs

The physical signs will generally be those of the primary hormone deficiency syndromes (eg hypogonadism, hypothyroidism). Secondary hypoadrenalism may result in postural hypotension and loss of secondary sexual hair, but as the aetiology of the problem is pituitary hormone deficiency, it is not associated with hyperpigmentation. GH deficiency is associated with a reduction in lean body mass and an increase in fat mass (with an increased waist/hip ratio).

Investigation

Once hypopituitarism is suspected:

- complete biochemical assessment of pituitary function;

- MRI (or CT) scan of the pituitary fossa;

- formal testing of the patient's visual fields and acuity.

Anterior pituitary function

Growth hormone The 'gold standard' investigation for possible GH deficiency is the insulin tolerance test (ITT)

(see Section 3.1.5). Random measurements of GH and serum insulin-like growth factor (IGF)-1 are not reliable means of diagnosing GH deficiency. The glucagon stimulation test and the arginine stimulation test provide alternative provocative tests especially in cases where the ITT is contraindicated.

Gonadotrophins In women with regular menses, who are not on the combined oral contraceptive pill, further tests are probably not necessary. Otherwise, LH, FSH and oestradiol concentrations should be measured. In men, testosterone concentration should be checked in conjunction with LH and FSH. Ideally blood samples should be taken at 9 a.m. to exclude effects of diurnal variation.

Adrenocorticotrophic hormone Although measurement of cortisol at 9 a.m. may be informative (eg if the value is very low), random measurements of ACTH and cortisol should not be used to screen for ACTH deficiency. Dynamic assessment of the hypothalamic–pituitary–adrenal axis with an ITT (Section 3.1.5) is the 'gold standard' in this setting. However, in cases where the ITT is contraindicated, the short Synacthen test (SST) can be used, providing that the results are interpreted with caution. For example, the SST may fail to identify incipient secondary adrenal failure in the first few weeks after trans-sphenoidal surgery. If used, the SST should ideally be undertaken at 9 a.m., thereby allowing both the basal and post-Synacthen cortisol values to be used in assessment of the axis.

Thyroid-stimulating hormone

Measurement of thyroxine (ideally free thyroxine) with or without triiodothyronine (ideally free triiodothyronine) levels provides the most reliable means of assessing thyroid status in patients with hypothalamic–pituitary disease. TSH levels alone should not be used to screen for secondary/tertiary hypothyroidism.

Prolactin Deficiency of prolactin is not clinically evident, except post partum when it is associated with a failure of lactation. Hyperprolactinaemia is a more common finding in the setting of pituitary hormone deficiencies, reflecting stalk compression by an intrasellar mass/infiltration.

Posterior pituitary function
See Section 2.1.7.

Treatment

Hydrocortisone

> ⚠ It is important to avoid the adverse side effects of long-term treatment with supraphysiological doses of glucocorticoids. For most patients, hydrocortisone 20 mg daily is sufficient, divided into 10 mg on waking, 5 mg at lunchtime and 5 mg in the late afternoon, or 15 mg on waking and 5 mg in the late afternoon. The adequacy of replacement can be assessed with a cortisol day curve.

> Patients must be given written advice about doubling their hydrocortisone dose if they are ill, and seeking medical help for parenteral therapy if they are unable to take their tablets. They should be given a steroid card and advised to purchase a Medic-Alert bracelet.

Thyroxine
The thyroxine dose should be titrated to the free thyroxine concentration (not the TSH level).

> ⚠ Hydrocortisone replacement therapy, if indicated, must be instituted before thyroxine in order to avoid the risk of precipitating a life-threatening hypoadrenal crisis.

Sex hormone replacement therapy
Both men and women require sex steroid replacement therapy for normal sexual function, to prevent osteoporosis and to maintain body composition.

- Women should be given cyclical oestrogen and progestogen (eg in the form of the combined oral contraceptive pill) or lower-dose hormone-replacement therapy (HRT), especially if over the age of 35, until the time at which a natural menopause would be expected to occur (typically around 50 years). Fertility treatment requires ovulation induction with gonadotrophins.

- Testosterone can be effectively replaced using intramuscular injections, implants, topical gel/patches or a buccal delivery system. Liver function tests and FBC (haematocrit) should be checked prior to and periodically after starting treatment. Men of an appropriate age should be counselled regarding the pros and cons of prostate surveillance (with periodic digital rectal examination and measurement of serum prostate-specific antigen). In men with oligospermia/azoospermia who desire fertility, induction of spermatogenesis with gonadotrophin therapy may be necessary.

> ⚠ Restoration of normal serum testosterone levels may not be welcomed by long-term hypogonadal males (or their partners!). In these circumstances, or if testosterone replacement is contraindicated for other reasons (eg in men with prostate carcinoma), consider alternative bone prophylaxis, eg with a bisphosphonate.

Growth hormone
GH replacement therapy is relatively expensive and its use in the UK is currently subject to National Institute for Health and Clinical Excellence (NICE) guidelines.

Recombinant human GH is self-administered by subcutaneous injection once a day. The dose is titrated to IGF-1 levels, against the age- and gender-related reference range.

Treatment may increase the patient's lean body mass, bone mineral density, exercise capacity and quality of life, and improve lipid profile and insulin sensitivity. The most common side effects of treatment are oedema and arthralgia, which respond to a reduction in dose. There is no evidence to suggest an increase in the risk of new tumour formation or recurrence of a previously treated pituitary tumour in patients receiving GH therapy.

Antidiuretic hormone
See Section 2.1.7.

Prognosis

Hypopituitarism is often associated with reduced psychological well-being and affected subjects have a mortality rate at least twice the standardised mortality rate. Both may be related to periods of untreated hypogonadism, excessive glucocorticoid or thyroxine therapy, or inadequate glucocorticoid treatment in times of stress or GH deficiency.

FURTHER READING

Jostel A, Lissett CA and Shalet SM. Hypopituitarism. In: DeGroot LJ and Jameson JL, eds. *Endocrinology*, 5th edn. Philadelphia: Elsevier, 2006.

Lamberts SWJ, de Herder WW and van der Lely AJ. Pituitary insufficiency. *Lancet* 1998; 352: 127–34.

2.2 Adrenal disease

2.2.1 Cushing's syndrome

See Section 2.1.1.

2.2.2 Primary hyperaldosteronism

Primary hyperaldosteronism is an important treatable cause of hypertension in the young to middle-aged.

Aetiology

The majority of cases are due to benign aldosterone-producing adrenal adenomas, so-called Conn's syndrome. Other rarer causes are shown in Table 23.

Epidemiology

Although primary hyperaldosteronism has traditionally been considered to account for <1% of all cases of hypertension, the prevalence of the condition is clearly

TABLE 23 AETIOLOGY OF PRIMARY HYPERALDOSTERONISM

Subtype	Notes
Aldosterone-secreting benign adrenal adenoma	Classical Conn's syndrome
Idiopathic hyperaldosteronism	Commonly associated with bilateral adrenal hyperplasia
Adrenal carcinoma	–
Familial hyperaldosteronism	Includes glucocorticoid-remediable hyperaldosteronism, an autosomal dominantly inherited disorder in which the 11β-hydroxylase promoter is fused to the aldosterone synthase gene, allowing ACTH-sensitive production of aldosterone in the zona fasciculata
Ectopic aldosterone-producing adenoma/carcinoma	Very rare

ACTH, adrenocorticotrophic hormone.

dependent on the study population, with some authors reporting significantly higher rates (2–12%) in selected patient groups. A slight female preponderance has been noted for adrenal adenomas.

Clinical presentation

Most cases come to light during investigation of hypertension or unexplained hypokalaemia. Non-specific symptoms including weakness, lassitude and polyuria may be reported, reflecting potassium depletion.

Physical signs

Mineralocorticoid excess *per se* is not associated with specific physical signs. The degree of hypertension is variable, ranging from mild to severe, although malignant/accelerated hypertension is exceptionally rare. There may be associated signs of target-organ damage, for example hypertensive retinopathy. Clinical evidence of oedema is rare, except in those with concommitant cardiac disease.

Investigation

Prior to investigation ensure satisfactory dietary sodium intake (>150 mmol/day). Screening tests are traditionally performed having withdrawn agents (eg beta-blockers) that interfere with the renin–angiotensin–aldosterone system (alpha-blockers, eg doxazosin, may be substituted if necessary). However, screening can be undertaken without changes in medication providing that certain precautions are taken when interpreting results (see below).

Screening tests

Urea and electrolytes The classical picture is one of hypokalaemic alkalosis; the accompanying serum sodium level is usually normal to high. However, many patients subsequently diagnosed with primary hyperaldosteronism are normokalaemic at presentation. This is particularly likely to be the case if the patient is not on a potassium-losing diuretic and has a diet with a low sodium content, as urinary potassium excretion is related to the distal nephron sodium load.

Urinary potassium and sodium Hypokalaemia is associated with inappropriate kaliuresis. Urinary sodium estimation ensures satisfactory dietary intake.

Plasma renin and aldosterone

The hallmark of primary hyperaldosteronism is the excessive autonomous production of aldosterone, which occurs in the face of renin suppression. The ratio of plasma aldosterone to plasma renin activity is a valid screening test for primary hyperaldosteronism and may be peformed without changing antihypertensive medication. An elevated ratio is highly suggestive of the diagnosis. However, it is important to note that various factors can affect plasma renin activity and aldosterone, and hence the ratio: for example, renin secretion is stimulated by volume or salt depletion (eg as occurs with diuretic treatment) and is suppressed when β-adrenergic input to the juxtaglomerular apparatus is attenuated (eg with beta-blockade) or if the patient is treated with NSAIDs which promote salt and water retention; hypokalaemia can impede aldosterone secretion and potassium supplements should be given to correct hypokalaemia before measuring aldosterone levels.

Some laboratories now routinely measure plasma renin concentration/mass rather than activity, and it is important therefore to ensure that aldosterone/renin ratios are compared with the relevant reference range.

Salt-loading tests

In normal subjects volume expansion due to salt and water retention will suppress plasma renin and aldosterone, whereas in primary hyperaldosteronism further volume expansion does not have the same suppressive effect on aldosterone secretion. Salt loading can be achieved by increasing dietary sodium intake, infusing saline, administering exogenous mineralocorticoid (eg fludrocortisone) or a combination of these, but should only be undertaken under specialist supervision, and not in patients prone to fluid overload (eg those with cardiac failure, renal impairment).

Determining the cause

Plasma renin activity and aldosterone

Look for the following.

- Plasma renin: in normal subjects, adoption of an upright posture for 4 hours stimulates plasma renin when compared with resting supine levels. In patients with primary hyperaldosteronism, supine plasma renin is undetectable and remains suppressed despite ambulation.

- Aldosterone: adrenal adenomas exhibit sensitivity to ACTH and, accordingly, aldosterone levels fall in parallel with the circadian cortisol rhythm. In contrast, idiopathic hyperaldosteronism is associated with a lack of ACTH sensitivity, with aldosterone levels typically increasing on ambulation. Aldosterone values must therefore be interpreted in the context of the serum cortisol.

CT/MRI of adrenals

Both techniques can be used to identify the cause of primary hyperaldosteronism (Fig. 30).

Labelled cholesterol scanning/selective venous sampling

Radionuclide scanning and/or selective venous sampling may be helpful in localising adenomas that have not been clearly visualised with CT/MRI.

Treatment

Spironolactone is the medical treatment of choice because of its ability to block the action of aldosterone at the mineralocorticoid receptor. Treatment is titrated to normalise BP and restore normokalaemia.

Amiloride offers an alternative if spironolactone is poorly tolerated, and in some cases additional antihypertensive agents are required to control BP.

Thereafter, specific therapy is directed at the underlying cause.

- Adrenal adenoma: unilateral adrenalectomy (many centres

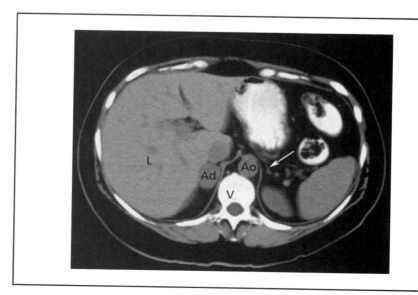

▲ **Fig. 30** Adrenal adenoma (Ad) in Conn's syndrome. Abdominal CT scan showing a right-sided adrenal adenoma in a patient with Conn's syndrome. The normal left adrenal gland (arrow) is just visible adjacent to the crus of the diaphragm. Ao, aorta; L, liver; V, vertebral body.

now routinely offer laparoscopic surgery).

- Idiopathic hyperaldosteronism: long-term spironolactone or amiloride.

Prognosis

Varies according to the underlying cause. For the majority of individuals in whom an adenoma can be identified, excision removes the source of aldosterone but hypertensive end-organ damage may be irreversible. Importantly, hypertension may not be cured by removal of the adenoma.

FURTHER READING

Edwards CRW and Stowasser M. Primary mineralocorticoid excess syndromes. In: DeGroot LJ and Jameson JL, eds. *Endocrinology*, 5th edn. Philadelphia: Elsevier, 2006.

Mckenna TJ, Sequeira SJ, Heffernan A, Chambers J and Cunningham S. Diagnosis under random conditions of all disorders of the renin–angiotensin–aldosterone axis, including primary hyperaldosteronism. *J. Clin. Endocrinol. Metab.* 1991; 73: 952–7.

2.2.3 Virilising tumours

Pathophysiology

Virilising tumours may be either adrenal or ovarian in origin. Both are likely to present in middle age, and the greater the tumour size the higher the likelihood of malignancy.

Epidemiology

Very rare, accounting for less than 1% of all causes of androgen excess. However, because of the potential for underlying malignancy, they must be considered in the differential diagnosis of the hirsute/virilised woman.

Causes of androgen excess in women

- Polycystic ovarian syndrome (>95% of cases).
- Obesity (and associated insulin resistance).
- Androgen-secreting tumours (adrenal or ovarian, benign or malignant).
- Congenital adrenal hyperplasia.
- Cushing's syndrome (ACTH-dependent or adrenocortical carcinoma).
- Acromegaly.

⚠️ With large adrenal tumours (>5 cm diameter) the possibility of adrenocortical carcinoma must be considered.

Clinical presentation/physical signs

Presentation is generally later in life compared with polycystic ovarian syndrome. Clinical manifestations typically include menstrual irregularity (which can be associated with anovulatory cycles), hirsutism, acne, deepening of the voice, frontal balding (androgenic alopecia), muscle hypertrophy and clitoromegaly. Importantly, a rapid onset of severe symptoms should alert the clinician to the possibility of an underlying androgen-secreting neoplasm.

Abdominal pain with a palpable mass and/or ascites may be present, especially if the underlying cause is an adrenocortical carcinoma. Features of Cushing's syndrome should also be sought as some malignant adrenal tumours co-secrete androgens and cortisol.

Childhood presentations include precocious puberty and/or virilisation.

Investigation

Androgen profiles

One or more serum androgens [dehydroepiandrosterone sulphate (DHEAS), androstenedione, testosterone] are typically raised. DHEAS is synthesised exclusively by the adrenal gland, and thus an elevated level indicates an adrenal origin for hyperandrogenism. In contrast, a markedly elevated serum testosterone in a postmenopausal woman with normal DHEAS and androstenedione strongly suggests an ovarian source.

Mildly elevated adrenal androgen levels may be seen in a variety of non-neoplastic conditions. Measurement of DHEAS and androstenedione after the administration of dexamethasone can help to determine which cases require further investigation. Adrenal androgen production is ACTH-dependent and failure of exogenous glucocorticoid to suppress circulating levels suggests an autonomous basis for hyperandrogenism. Similarly, gonadotrophin-releasing hormone analogues can be used to 'switch off' non-tumoral ovarian androgen production.

Other endocrine tests

Gonadotrophins In women with regular menses, who are not on the combined oral contraceptive pill, further tests are probably not necessary. Otherwise, luteinising hormone, follicle-stimulating hormone and estradiol concentrations should be measured.

17α-Hydroxyprogesterone To screen for congenital adrenal hyperplasia (see Section 2.2.5).

Urinary free cortisol and dexamethasone suppression If Cushing's syndrome is suspected (see Section 2.1.1).

Radiological imaging

Adrenal CT and/or MRI An adrenal CT or MRI with contrast should be undertaken if an androgen-secreting adrenal neoplasm is suspected (Fig. 31). If adrenal malignancy is considered a possibility, then more extensive imaging (of the chest, abdomen and pelvis) is required to look for evidence of local and distant spread.

Pelvic ultrasound and/or MRI
Ultrasound (especially transvaginal) provides excellent visualisation of most ovarian neoplasms (Fig. 32). MRI with contrast is reserved for those cases in which the ovaries are not clearly seen or if malignancy is suspected.

Treatment

Surgery is the treatment of choice for both benign and malignant adrenal and ovarian neoplasms.

Adjunctive chemotherapy and radiotherapy can be used for malignant tumours, although response rates are often disappointing. Mitotane is the chemotherapeutic agent of choice for adrenocortical carcinoma.

Prognosis

Although surgery cures the majority of patients with benign tumours, some clincal features such as deepening of the voice may persist. Prognosis for malignant tumours is poor, with overall 5-year survival rates of less than 40%.

FURTHER READING

Allolio B and Fassnacht M. Adrenocortical carcinoma: clinical update. *J. Clin. Endocrinol. Metab.* 2006; 91: 2027–37.

- - - - - - - - - - - - - -

Kaltsas GA, Isidori AM, Kola BP, *et al.* The value of the low-dose dexamethasone suppression test in the differential diagnosis of hyperandrogenism in women. *J. Clin. Endocrinol. Metab.* 2003; 88: 2634–43.

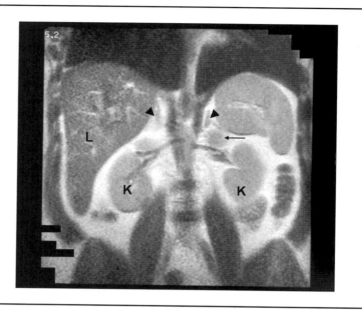

▲**Fig. 31** Virilising adrenal adenoma. Coronally reconstructed abdominal MRI scan showing a left-sided adrenal adenoma in a young female who presented with rapidly progressive virilisation. Although the abnormal mass (arrow) appears to be located just inferior to the left adrenal gland, it was confirmed at surgery to be arising from the tip of the postero-lateral limb. The positions of both adrenal glands are shown by arrowheads. L, liver; K, kidney.

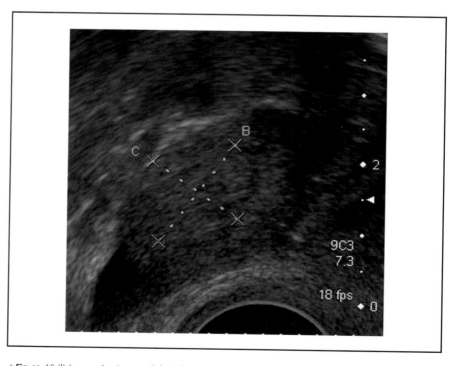

▲**Fig. 32** Virilising ovarian tumour. Pelvic ultrasound reveals a right-sided ovarian mass in a 60-year-old female who presented with androgenic alopecia and deepening of the voice, and who was found to have a markedly elevated serum testosterone level. At surgery, a benign Leydig cell tumour was excised.

2.2.4 Phaeochromocytoma

In adults, phaeochromocytomas were known as the '10% tumour' reflecting approximately:

- 10% extra-adrenal;
- 10% bilateral/multiple;
- 10% malignant;
- 10% familial.

However, this is now considered to be out of date, with up to 25% known to be familial (Table 24). In addition, the prevalence of bilateral tumours is greater than 10% in certain familial syndromes such as multiple endocrine neoplasia type 2 (MEN-2) and von Hippel–Lindau syndrome (VHL), whilst in childhood a higher proportion are extra-adrenal and malignancy is more common.

Aetiology/pathophysiology

Originating from the chromaffin cells of the sympathetic nervous system, the majority of phaeochromocytomas arise within the adrenal medulla, with a smaller number derived from sympathetic ganglia. They commonly secrete noradrenaline (norepinephrine) and adrenaline (epinephrine), but in some cases significant amounts of dopamine may be released. As with many other endocrine tumours, the diagnosis of malignancy depends on evidence of local infiltration or distant spread, since histological appearances do not reliably distinguish benign from malignant tumours.

So far, germline mutations in five genes have been found to cause familial phaeochromocytomas.

- *RET* proto-oncogene: MEN-2a and MEN-2b (see Section 2.7).

- *VHL* gene: von Hippel–Lindau syndrome, comprising renal cysts and carcinomas, pancreatic tumours and cysts, retinal and craniospinal (eg cerebellar) haemangioblastomas, phaeochromocytomas, endolymphatic sac tumours and epididymal cystadenomas.

- *NF1* gene: neurofibromatosis type 1 (von Recklinghausen's disease).

- Mitochondrial *SDHB* and *SDHD*: familial paraganglioma and phaeochromocytoma syndromes.

Succinate dehydrogenase mutations are the most frequent cause of familial phaeochromocytoma and are important, as patients with an *SDHB* mutation typically exhibit more aggressive disease with a high incidence of malignancy (Table 24). They are usually extra-adrenal, mainly occurring as paragangliomas in the head, chest and abdomen. *SDHD* mutations are maternally imprinted; thus only carriers who have inherited the mutation from the father develop the disease.

Epidemiology

Rare, accounting for 0.1–0.6% of all cases of hypertension in general outpatient clinics. Many remain occult and are only diagnosed at post-mortem.

Clinical presentation

Cases may come to light during the investigation of poorly controlled hypertension, when direct questioning reveals an array of other manifestations of catecholamine excess. These are frequently reported to occur in an episodic or paroxysmal fashion. Occasional cases present with pregnancy-associated hypertension, myocardial infarction, cardiac dysrhythmias or a dilated catecholamine cardiomyopathy. The incidence in normotensive asymptomatic subjects is 'rising', due to increased use of high-

---

TABLE 24 FAMILIAL PHAEOCHROMOCYTOMA SYNDROMES[1]

Syndrome	Gene	Protein	Frequency of germline mutations in apparent sporadic phaeochromocytoma	Frequency of malignant disease
VHL	*VHL*	pVHL9 and pVHL30	2–11%	5%
MEN-2a, MEN-2b	*RET*	Tyrosine kinase receptor	<5%	3%
Neurofibromatosis type 1	*NF1*	Neurofibromin	Unknown	11%
Paraganglioma and phaeochromocytoma syndromes	*SDHB*	Catalytic iron—sulphur protein	3–10%	50%
	SDHD	CybS (membrane-spanning unit)	4–7%	<3%

1. Adapted with permission from Lenders JW *et al*. Phaeochromocytoma. *Lancet* 2005; 366: 665–75.
SDHB, succinate dehydrogenase complex, subunit B; SDHD, succinate dehydrogenase complex, subunit D.

resolution imaging and screening for phaeochromocytoma in subjects with predisposing genetic mutations. About 5% of all adrenal 'incidentalomas' are phaeochromocytomas, with about 25% of all phaeochromocytomas now discovered incidentally during imaging for unrelated disorders.

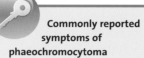

Commonly reported symptoms of phaeochromocytoma

- Headache.
- Sweating.
- Palpitations/forceful heartbeat.
- Anxiety.
- Tremor.
- Nausea and vomiting.
- Chest and abdominal pain/dyspnoea.

Note that the triad of headache, sweating and palpitations is considered to be highly suggestive of a diagnosis of phaeochromocytoma.

Physical signs

Features of increased sympathetic activity are often present during a paroxysm, eg tachycardia, sweating, pallor (not flushing). Hypertension may be sustained or episodic and approximately 50% of cases exhibit orthostatic hypotension (the latter reflecting intravascular depletion in response to long-standing hypertension).

Investigations

This should be approached in two stages:

- confirm catecholamine excess;

- localise the tumour.

Confirm catecholamine excess

Urinary free catecholamines and their metabolites Two 24-hour urine collections for estimation of urinary free catecholamines (adrenaline, noradrenaline and dopamine) are

the most widely used screening method. Assays for urinary catecholamine metabolites, such as total metanephrines and vanillylmandelic acid (VMA), are routinely performed in some centres, although both are associated with a significant false-negative detection rate (lower sensitivity). Measurement of urinary fractionated metanephrines (normetanephrine and metanephrine measured separately) is highly sensitive but less specific and is not routinely available in most centres.

Plasma catecholamines
Measurement of plasma adrenaline and noradrenaline levels can be useful in cases where paroxysms are infrequent and short-lived such that urinary estimations are within normal limits. Normal plasma catecholamine levels measured during an 'attack' make it very unlikely that the underlying disorder is a phaeochromocytoma.

Plasma free metanephrines
Plasma free metanephrines (normetanephrine and metanephrine) afford greater sensitivity than plasma catecholamines due to continuous production of *O*-methylated metabolites in tumours. Although assays for plasma free metanephrines are not yet widely available, their ability to offer a highly sensitive (99%) and specific (89%) mode of screening for phaeochromocytoma means that they are likely to find increasing use.

False positives There are many causes of false-positive biochemical screening. These fall into two groups.

1. True catecholamine excess, due to:

   (a) drugs (tricyclic antidepressants, phenoxybenzamine, monoamine oxidase

   inhibitors, levodopa, α-methyldopa, sympathomimetics, calcium channel blockers);

   (b) stimulants (eg coffee, nicotine);

   (c) anxiety;

   (d) disease states (eg myocardial infarction, heart failure, cardiogenic shock, obstructive sleep apnoea).

2. Interference with analytical method (different depending on assay but including coffee, labetalol, levodopa, α-methyldopa, paracetamol and sympathomimetics).

Most false-positive levels are significantly lower than in phaeochromocytoma. Repeat the test, having stopped any interfering medication, and consider an alternative screening method.

Clonidine suppression test
Clonidine acts via presynaptic α-adrenergic receptors to block catecholamine secretion and can be used to distinguish increased noradrenaline release due to sympathetic activation from autonomous tumoral secretion. Failure to adequately suppress plasma noradrenaline in response to clonidine is highly predictive of phaeochromocytoma (97%), but a normal test result does not exclude phaeochromocytoma (negative predictive value only 75%). Use of plasma normetanephrine increases the positive and negative predictive values to 100 and 96% respectively.

Localise the tumour

CT/MRI CT scans of the abdomen and pelvis are commonly used (Figs 33 and 34). T2-weighted MRI with gadolinium enhancement has similar sensitivity and specificity to CT, but lacks concerns about radiographic contrast. The tumour

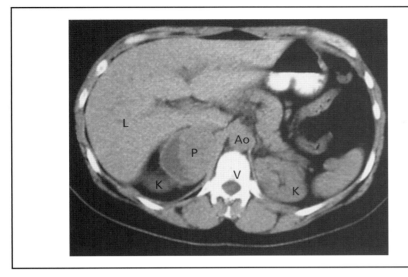

▲ **Fig 33** Phaeochromocytoma. Abdominal CT scan showing a right-sided phaeochromocytoma (P). Ao, aorta; K, kidney; L, liver; V, vertebral body.

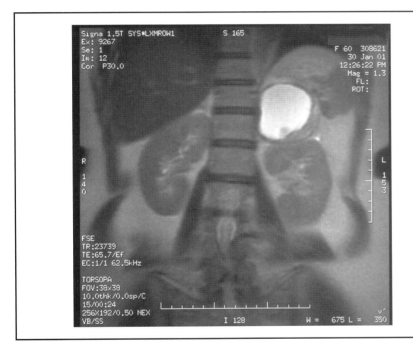

▲ **Fig. 34** Phaeochromocytoma. Abdominal T2-weighted MRI scan showing a large left-sided phaeochromocytoma indenting the upper pole of the adjacent kidney.

typically exhibits a distinctive 'bright white' signal on T2-weighted images.

⚠ Intravenous injection of certain types of contrast media can precipitate pressor crises, and accordingly α- and β-adrenergic blockade is recommended prior to examination with these agents.

Radioiodine-labelled metaiodobenzylguanidine (^{123}I-MIBG) scintigraphy ^{123}I-MIBG, which is taken up by chromaffin cells, is useful in localising both adrenal and extra-adrenal tumours (Fig. 35) and is the first-line nuclear imaging method. Pretreating with potassium iodide blocks thyroidal uptake.

A newer promising localisation technique, ^{18}F-labelled DOPA positron emission tomography (PET), offers the higher spatial resolution of PET scanning and may allow detection of smaller lesions not visualised with ^{123}I-MIBG.

Genetic testing

Sporadic forms of phaeochromocytoma are usually diagnosed in individuals aged 40–50 years, whereas hereditary forms are diagnosed earlier, most before age 40 years. Genetic screening in phaeochromocytoma/paraganglioma syndromes is a 'hot' clinical topic, with recent advances in diagnosis and genetics now challenging the traditional 'rule of 10' for phaeochromocytomas (see above): the prevalence of extra-adrenal tumours is up to 20% and prevalence of bilateral or multiple tumours is higher in some familial syndromes such as MEN-2 and VHL. Up to one-quarter or more are hereditary. It has therefore been suggested that all patients with a phaeochromocytoma should be considered for genetic testing, firstly to allow early diagnosis and treatment of other features of the associated hereditary syndrome; secondly to prompt more stringent, lifelong clinical follow-up, as recurrences are highly probable in familial phaeochromocytoma; and thirdly to prompt appropriate family screening. Presently, cost-effective genetic screening is recommended to those with a positive family history or those aged under 50 years, especially children. Other clues that should be regarded as an indication for genetic testing include bilateral adrenal or multifocal extra-adrenal disease or the association of phaeochromocytoma with other tumours. The clinical picture may direct genetic testing to one of the suspected genes.

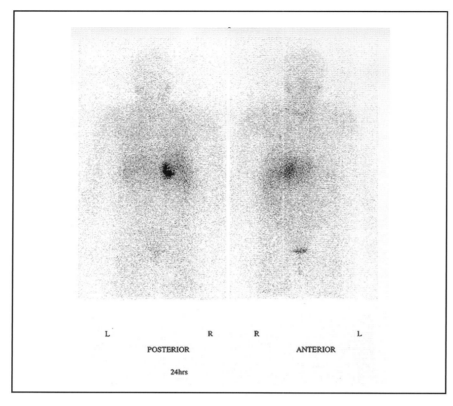

▲ **Fig. 35** Phaeochromocytoma: ¹²³I-MIBG scan. The right-sided phaeochromocytoma shown in Fig. 33 demonstrates avid uptake of MIBG.

Differential diagnosis

Several conditions may present with features of sympathetic overactivity and thus mimic phaeochromocytoma (see Table 3).

Treatment

Medical therapy

Prior to considering surgical removal, medical treatment must be instituted with the aims of:

- ameliorating symptoms;
- normalising BP;
- correcting intravascular depletion.

> ⚠ Beta-blockers must not be given to patients with suspected or proven phaeochromocytoma until alpha-blockade has been established, since there is a significant risk of precipitating a life-threatening hypertensive crisis due to unopposed α-adrenoceptor activity.

Alpha-blockade The non-competitive α-adrenoceptor antagonist phenoxybenzamine is the initial treatment of choice, with escalating dose titration (start with 10 mg twice daily and increase gradually until BP is normalised; most cases require 1–2 mg/kg per day in divided doses). The α_1-adrenoceptor antagonist doxazosin provides an alternative for those intolerant of phenoxybenzamine.

Beta-blockade The non-selective agent propranolol (20–80 mg every 8 hours) is generally preferred.

Surgical excision

Both traditional and laparoscopic approaches can be used for tumour removal.

Adjunctive therapy for malignant tumours

- α-Methylparatyrosine: ameliorates symptoms through inhibition of tyrosine hydroxylase, the rate-limiting enzyme in the biosynthetic process.
- Radioiodine (¹³¹I)-labelled MIBG: large and repeated doses may be necessary.

Prognosis

Even those with malignant tumours frequently survive for many years. The extent of end-organ damage is often a key factor in determining long-term outcome.

FURTHER READING

Lenders JWM, Eisenhofer G, Mannelli M and Pacak K. Phaeochromocytoma. *Lancet* 2005; 366: 665–75.

2.2.5 Congenital adrenal hyperplasia

Congenital adrenal hyperplasia (CAH) is not a single disease entity but encompasses several autosomal recessive disorders (arising as a consequence of inborn errors in adrenal cortical enzyme function) that result in varying degrees of impairment in the synthesis of cortisol and aldosterone.

Pathophysiology

The key stages in the steroid biosynthetic pathway are outlined in Fig. 36. Conversion of cholesterol to pregnenolone is the rate-limiting step and a major site of regulation by adrenocorticotrophic hormone (ACTH). Deficiency of 21-hydroxylase is the most common enzyme defect in CAH (~90–95% of all cases), with 11β-hydroxylase deficiency, 3β-hydroxysteroid dehydrogenase deficiency and other enzyme deficiencies accounting for a relatively small number of cases.

Reduced cortisol synthesis is the common denominator, with

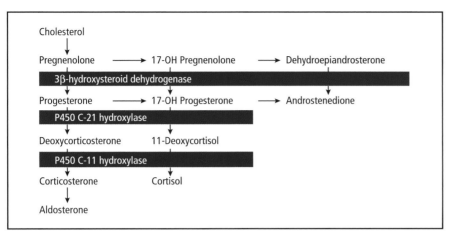

▲**Fig. 36** Adrenal cortical steroid biosynthetic pathways.

consequent elevation of circulating ACTH levels further stimulating steroidogenesis. Precursors that cannot be metabolised by the deficient enzyme are then shunted down adjacent pathways, with the resulting clinical phenotype reflecting both hormone deficiency (eg cortisol and aldosterone) and excess (eg androgens).

Epidemiology
Classical 21-hydroxylase deficiency affects approximately 1 in 14,000 live births in Caucasians. Non-classical 21-hydroxylase deficiency (see below) occurs more frequently (1 in 1,000 live births in the general population).

Clinical presentation/physical signs
Both 'classical' and 'non-classical' variants of CAH are recognised. The former denotes a more severe form, predominantly seen in the neonate or young child, whilst the latter is reserved for milder variants that often only come to light in adulthood. Table 25 indicates typical clinical features according to gender and age at presentation.

Investigation
Depending on the enzyme defect, different steroid precursors/androgens accumulate and can be measured in plasma. In practice most laboratories restrict screening to the following.

- 17α-Hydroxyprogesterone (17-OHP): this precursor accumulates in 21-hydroxylase deficiency. Its ability to discriminate from normal controls in mild non-classical cases is improved following ACTH stimulation with Synacthen (tetracosactide) 250 µg im, which exaggerates the enzyme block (see Section 3.1.1).

- Testosterone, androstenedione and dehydroepiandrosterone sulphate: elevated in most cases.

- Plasma ACTH: elevated, although serum cortisol may be low or normal.

- Plasma renin activity: usually elevated in proportion to mineralocorticoid deficiency.

Screening

Identification of the genes encoding each of the enzymes involved in adrenal steroidogenesis permits screening for mutations using the polymerase chain reaction. For example, the 21-hydroxylase gene lies on chromosome 6 in close proximity to the major histocompatibility complex, and several common mutations have now been identified. One potential application of this technique is for prenatal diagnosis in families where there is already one affected child.

Treatment

Acute adrenal crisis
Episodes of acute adrenal insufficiency should be managed as outlined in Section 2.2.6, with doses adjusted according to body weight/surface area in neonates.

TABLE 25 CLINICAL PRESENTATIONS OF CAH[1]

Type	Age	Female	Male
Classical	Neonatal	Ambiguous genitalia Virilisation Salt wasting	Salt wasting
	Childhood	–	Precocious puberty
Non-classical	Childhood	Virilisation	Precocious puberty
	Adulthood	Hirsutism Menstrual irregularities Infertility	No specific symptoms

1. Symptoms of cortisol deficiency are surprisingly rare, although hypoglycaemia is sometimes seen. However, intercurrent illness is likely to unmask glucocorticoid deficiency and result in a life-threatening adrenal crisis, which is exacerbated by concomitant aldosterone deficiency.

Routine replacement

- Glucocorticoids inhibit ACTH release, restoring androgen levels to the normal range. Dose titration should be performed in relation to 17-OHP and adrenal androgen levels (in particular androstenedione). In childhood this is particularly important as over-treatment is associated with poor growth (through suppression of growth hormone secretion). Hormone levels should be measured at a consistent time in relation to medication dosing, and used in conjunction with other parameters such as growth measurements and bone age to monitor therapy. Standard steroid sick-day rules (see Section 2.1.8) should be observed.
- Mineralocorticoid replacement (fludrocortisone) is indicated in salt-wasting forms.
- Plastic surgery may be required in cases with ambiguous external genitalia.
- Psychological support is an important component of the long-term management of patients with CAH.

Prognosis

Salt-wasting forms are potentially life-threatening if unrecognised. Once diagnosed, however, adequate treatment allows most individuals to lead a normal life and retain fertility.

Prevention

In those families in which there is already one affected child with CAH, it is advisable to treat the mother with dexamethasone (which crosses the placenta) from the beginning of all subsequent pregnancies until chorionic villus sampling or amniocentesis is possible, the principal aim being the prevention of excessive fetal androgen production that would lead to virilisation of an affected female fetus. If the fetus is found to be male or an unaffected female, treatment can be stopped.

FURTHER READING

Merke DP and Bornstein SR. Congenital adrenal hyperplasia. *Lancet* 2005; 365: 2125–36.

Young MC and Hughes IA. Congenital adrenal hyperplasia. In: Grossman A, ed. *Clinical Endocrinology*, 2nd edn. Oxford: Blackwell Science, 1998.

2.2.6 Primary adrenal insufficiency

Adrenocortical insufficiency may be:

- primary, arising as a consequence of destruction or dysfunction of the adrenal cortex, as described by Thomas Addison in 1855;
- secondary, consequent to deficient pituitary adrenocorticotrophic hormone (ACTH) secretion (see Section 2.1.8).

Table 26 outlines the main differences between primary and secondary adrenal insufficiency.

This section focuses on primary adrenal insufficiency and the clinical picture resulting from combined cortisol, aldosterone and adrenal androgen deficiency.

Aetiology

Although tuberculosis (TB) probably remains the commonest cause of primary adrenal insufficiency worldwide, in the UK more than 75% of cases are due to immune-mediated destruction of the adrenal glands, and may be associated with other autoimmune glandular hypofunction (see Section 2.7.2).

Aetiology of primary adrenocortical insufficiency

- Autoimmune: isolated or part of a polyglandular syndrome.
- Infection: TB, histoplasmosis; AIDS (often multifactorial, eg infection with cytomegalovirus, use of drugs such as ketoconazole, adrenal infiltration with Kaposi's sarcoma).
- Infiltration: metastatic malignancy/lymphoma (note, however, that despite adrenal metastases being a relatively common finding on imaging, clinically evident adrenal insufficiency is rare); amyloidosis, sarcoidosis, haemochromatosis.
- Iatrogenic: adrenalectomy, drugs that block adrenal steroidogenesis (eg metyrapone, ketoconazole).
- Adrenal haemorrhage: severe sepsis, meningococcaemia.
- Congenital adrenal hyperplasia.
- Adrenoleukodystrophy (rare X-linked disorder).

TABLE 26 PRIMARY AND SECONDARY ADRENOCORTICAL INSUFFICIENCY

	Primary	Secondary
Cases	80%	20%
Aetiology	75% autoimmune	Hypothalamic–pituitary disease
ACTH	High	Low
Glucocorticoid	Deficient	Deficient
Mineralocorticoid	Deficient	Preserved
Na^+	Low	Low/normal
K^+	High	Normal
Treatment	Hydrocortisone and fludrocortisone	Hydrocortisone
Associations	Autoimmune polyglandular syndrome	Hypopituitarism

ACTH, adrenocorticotrophic hormone.

- Familial glucocorticoid deficiency including Algrove (triple A) syndrome (very rare disorder comprising adrenal insufficiency, achalasia, alacrima and, in some cases, autonomic neuropathy).

Clinical features of acute adrenocortical insufficiency

- Fever.
- Nausea and vomiting.
- Weakness and impaired cognition.
- Hypotension/shock.
- Hypoglycaemia.

intravenous hydrocortisone (100 mg) immediately.
- Set up a normal saline drip.
- Check blood glucose using a fingerprick sample.

Epidemiology

Rare: prevalence <0.01% of the UK population, and with female/male ratio of approximately 3:1.

Clinical presentation

The clinical picture varies widely, from the acutely ill patient in Addisonian crisis to the relatively asymptomatic patient with pigmentation. When present, symptoms are often non-specific and the diagnosis is sometimes only made at post-mortem, leading to its description as 'the unforgiving master of non-specificity and disguise' (Brosnan and Gowing, 1996). Tiredness, weakness, dizziness, anorexia, weight loss and gastrointestinal disturbance are commonly reported. Some patients develop salt craving.

Physical signs

The more common clinical findings include the following.

- Pigmentation: generalised (Fig. 37), palmar creases, scars, buccal mucosa.

- Postural hypotension.

- Loss of axillary and pubic hair in females (due to a lack of adrenal sex steroids).

Investigation

⚠️ In the acutely ill patient in whom you suspect adrenal insufficiency do not delay treatment.

- Establish venous access (taking blood for urea and electrolytes, glucose and cortisol) and give

In non-emergency cases, consider the following investigations.

- Urea, electrolytes and glucose: note that the classical abnormalities (low sodium, high potassium, high urea and low glucose) are only seen in severe cases. Hypercalcaemia is occasionally reported.

- FBC: normochromic normocytic anaemia, neutropenia and eosinophilia are all recognised. The presence of macrocytosis should prompt consideration of possible coexistent pernicious anaemia.

- Synacthen test: short (see Section 3.1.1) and long Synacthen tests. In the short Synacthen test, include a basal 9 a.m. ACTH measurement (high in primary adrenal failure).

- Autoantibodies: check for adrenal, thyroid and intrinsic factor autoantibodies.

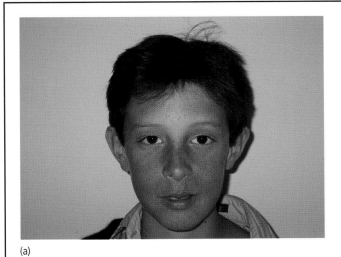

(a)

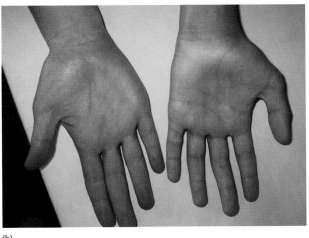

(b)

▲ **Fig. 37** Addison's disease. (**a**) Generalised hyperpigmentation of the skin and mucous membranes is one of the earliest manifestations of Addison's disease and is increased in sun-exposed areas. (**b**) Increased pigmentation of the palmar creases (right) compared with an unaffected control subject (left).

- CXR/abdominal radiograph/CT: look for evidence of TB including adrenal calcification.

- Thyroid-stimulating hormone (TSH) and thyroxine: ideally free thyroxine should be used. There may be concomitant thyroid dysfunction in both primary (autoimmune thyroid disease) and secondary (TSH deficiency) adrenal insufficiency. Note, however, that in Addison's disease, mild thyroid function abnormalities may revert to normal with satisfactory glucocorticoid replacement.

Treatment

Hypoadrenal crisis

Treat as above, and establish on regular 6-hour intramuscular hydrocortisone (50–100 mg). Intravenous hydrocortisone may also be used, although it is important to note that continuous delivery via an infusion produces more stable replacement than intermittent boluses, which are associated with significant peaks and troughs in circulating cortisol levels. Investigate and treat any precipitating cause.

Routine replacement

Hydrocortisone Although most conveniently taken twice daily (eg 15 mg on waking and 5 mg in the late afternoon), thrice-daily dosing (eg 10 mg on waking, 5 mg at midday and 5 mg in the late afternoon) probably achieves more physiological replacement. Adequacy can be checked with a cortisol day curve. Larger patients and those on enzyme-inducing agents (eg phenytoin, carbamazepine, rifampicin) typically require higher doses of steroid replacement therapy. The patient must be advised about steroid sick-day rules and

carry a card/bracelet (see Section 2.1.8) (Fig. 38).

Fludrocortisone Start with 50–100 µg daily and adjust according to clinical status (postural hypotension, oedema, hypokalaemia) and/or plasma renin activity. Usual maintenance is with 50–200 µg daily.

Adrenal androgens Although not routinely given, evidence suggests that dehydroepiandrosterone sulphate may significantly improve well-being in individuals with primary adrenal insufficiency.

> ⚠️ Thyroid hormone replacement should not be given until glucocorticoid replacement has been established due to the risk of precipitating an Addisonian crisis.

Prognosis

Providing hormone deficiency is adequately corrected, the underlying aetiology is often the most important determinant of outcome.

STEROID TREATMENT CARD

I am a patient on STEROID treatment which must not be stopped suddenly

- Always carry this card with you and show it to anyone who treats you (for example a doctor, nurse, pharmacist or dentist). For one year after you stop the treatment, you must mention that you have taken steroids.

- If you become ill, or if you come into contact with anyone who has an infectious disease, consult your doctor promptly. If you have never had chickenpox, you should avoid close contact with people who have chickenpox or shingles. If you do come into contact with chickenpox, see your doctor urgently.

- Make sure that the information on the card is kept up to date.

- If you have been taking this medicine for more than three weeks, the dose should be reduced gradually when you stop taking steroids unless your doctor says otherwise.

- Read the patient information leaflet given with the medicine.

Name	
Address	
Tel No	
GP	
Hospital	
Consultant	
Hospital No	

Date	Drug	Dose

▲**Fig. 38** Steroid treatment card.

Patients with Addison's disease and one or more of the other disorders associated with the autoimmune polyglandular syndrome type 2 (eg insulin-dependent diabetes or Hashimoto's thyroiditis; Section 2.7.2) may be at risk of the particularly devastating complication of premature ovarian failure. Depending on the patient it may be appropriate to discuss this to allow her to make an informed decision about the timing of any attempts that she might wish to make to have a family.

FURTHER READING

Arlt W, Callies F, van Vlijmen JC, *et al*. Dehydroepiandrosterone replacement in women with adrenal insufficiency. *N. Engl. J. Med.* 1999; 341: 1013–20.

Brosnan CM and Gowing NF. Addison's disease. *BMJ* 1996; 312: 1085–7.

Hunt PJ, Gurnell EM, Huppert FA, *et al*. Improvement in mood and fatigue after dehydroepiandrosterone replacement in Addison's disease in a randomized, double blind trial. *J. Clin. Endocrinol. Metab.* 2000; 85: 4650–6.

Oelkers W. Adrenal insufficiency. *N. Engl. J. Med.* 1996; 335: 1206–12.

2.3 Thyroid disease

2.3.1 Hypothyroidism

Hypothyroidism is the clinical syndrome that results from deficiency of the thyroid hormones thyroxine (T_4) and triiodothyronine (T_3).

Aetiology/pathogenesis

The causes of hypothyroidism are listed in Table 27. Iodine deficiency remains an important cause worldwide whilst, in the UK,

TABLE 27 AETIOLOGY OF HYPOTHYROIDISM

Cause	Frequency	Pathology	Clinical condition
Primary	Common	Autoimmune	Hashimoto's thyroiditis Atrophic thyroiditis (primary myxoedema)
		Previous treatment for thyrotoxicosis	Thyroidectomy Radioactive iodine
	Less common	Defects of hormone synthesis	Iodine deficiency (or excess) Drugs, eg antithyroid agents, lithium, amiodarone Inborn errors of thyroid hormone synthesis
		Transient hypothyroidism	Subacute thyroiditis Postpartum thyroiditis
		Infiltration Thyroid hypoplasia/ agenesis	Tumour, amyloidosis
Secondary	–	Hypothalamic or pituitary disease	

autoimmune thyroid disease and previous treatment for thyrotoxicosis account for nearly 90% of cases.

The tendency for autoimmune thyroid disease (autoimmune hypothyroidism and Graves' disease) to run in families is strongly suggestive of a significant genetic component, although the nature of the interplay between genetic and environmental factors in their evolution remains to be elucidated.

Hashimoto's thyroiditis is characterised by lymphocytic infiltration of the gland and the presence of thyroid microsomal antibodies. Atrophic thyroiditis also appears to be immune mediated (with lymphocytic infiltration and microsomal antibodies) and is associated with other organ-specific autoimmune disorders.

Epidemiology

Hypothyroidism is common, with a prevalence of 1–2% in the general population. Females outnumber males by about 10:1. Congenital hypothyroidism occurs in about 1 in 4,000 live births in the UK.

Clinical presentation and physical signs

The classical presenting symptoms and associated physical signs of hypothyroidism are shown in Fig. 39.

Other presentations

Myxoedema coma Patients with unsuspected or inadequately treated hypothyroidism are at risk of developing this rare but life-threatening condition. Coma may complicate an intercurrent illness (eg myocardial infarction, cerebrovascular accident, pneumonia) or be precipitated by certain drugs, particularly sedatives. Hypothermia is accompanied by bradycardia, hypotension, hypoglycaemia, hyponatraemia, hypoxia and hypercapnia.

Congenital hypothyroidism The introduction of routine neonatal

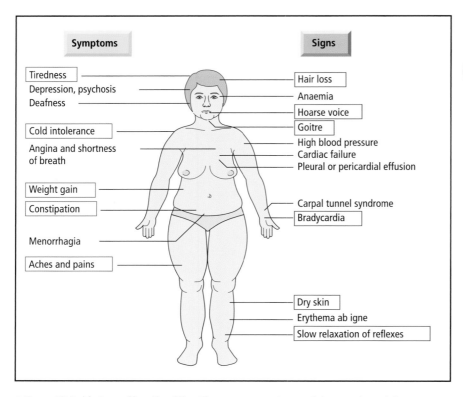

▲ **Fig. 39** Clinical features of hypothyroidism. The common symptoms and signs are shown in boxes.

Investigations

It is important to have a low threshold for actively excluding hypothyroidism in 'at-risk' groups, including those with:

- goitre;
- history of autoimmune disease;
- previously treated thyrotoxicosis;
- family history of thyroid disease.

And:

- in the elderly, in whom the symptoms of hypothyroidism may be mistaken for the normal ageing process.

Thyroid function tests

Table 28 outlines the abnormalities of thyroid function tests typically seen in various hypothyroid states (see Section 3.3.1).

Anti-thyroid peroxidase and anti-thyroglobulin antibodies

Anti-thyroid peroxidase (also known as anti-microsomal) and anti-thyroglobulin antibodies are commonly found in Hashimoto's thyroiditis and in atrophic hypothyroidism.

Full blood count

Hypothyroidism can be associated with anaemia:

screening in the UK and other countries now permits the early diagnosis of this condition which, if untreated, can lead to short stature, mental retardation and a characteristic puffy appearance of the face and hands (cretinism). It may arise in the setting of:

- placental transfer of thyroid-stimulating hormone (TSH) receptor-blocking antibodies from a mother with autoimmune thyroid disease;

- maternal iodine deficiency or treatment with antithyroid agents during pregnancy;

- thyroid hypoplasia/agenesis or inborn errors of thyroid hormone synthesis.

Subclinical hypothyroidism It has been estimated that 10% or more of all females over the age of 50 are affected by this condition, which

is characterised biochemically by normal free $(F)T_4$ and FT_3 levels in the presence of a mildly elevated TSH. Although few report specific symptoms of hypothyroidism, hypercholesterolaemia and subtle cardiac abnormalities are recognised, which resolve following normalisation of TSH with exogenous T_4.

TABLE 28 ABNORMALITIES OF THYROID FUNCTION IN VARIOUS 'HYPOTHYROID' STATES

Condition	TSH	FT_4/FT_3
Primary hypothyroidism	↑↑	↓
Secondary hypothyroidism	↓ or →	↓
Subclinical hypothyroidism	↑	→
Sick euthyroidism	↓ or →	↓ or →
Poor compliance with T_4 replacement	↑ or ↑↑	↓ or → or ↑

- normocytic (impaired erythropoiesis);
- microcytic (menorrhagia, impaired iron absorption);
- macrocytic (vitamin B_{12} or folate deficiency).

Urea and electrolytes

Hyponatraemia may reflect increased antidiuretic hormone activity and reduced free water clearance or, if associated with hyperkalaemia, should prompt consideration of coexistent adrenal insufficiency.

Cholesterol and creatine kinase

Both serum cholesterol (total and low-density lipoprotein) and creatine kinase are typically elevated, indicating tissue hypothyroidism within liver and muscle, respectively.

Anterior pituitary function

A full assessment of pituitary function should be performed if secondary hypothyroidism is suspected (see Section 2.1.8).

Treatment

Myxoedema coma

Myxoedema coma is a medical emergency, with mortality in some series approaching 50%. Circulatory and ventilatory support are frequently required. Hypoglycaemia must be excluded, hypothermia corrected, and potential precipitating events (eg infection) sought and treated appropriately. Ventilatory support is often required.

> In the absence of clear evidence to the contrary, it is advisable to assume coexistent adrenal insufficiency and to give hydrocortisone 100 mg iv immediately. Steroid replacement should be continued until normal adrenal function has been demonstrated.

There is some debate as to the best method of starting thyroid hormone replacement. Levothyroxine (L-T_4) can be given as a single 500-µg bolus followed by a daily maintenance dose of 50–100 µg. Alternatively, it has been argued that liothyronine (L-T_3) should be the preferred mode of replacement due to its rapid onset of action and short half-life, a typical starting dose being 5–10 µg every 6–8 hours. Both can be administered by nasogastric tube. Liothyronine can also be given by intravenous injection. In either case, extreme care must be taken if the patient is supected/known to have ischaemic coronary disease.

Long-term replacement

Although most cases of hypothyroidism require lifelong replacement with levothyroxine, occasionally thyroid dysfunction is transient, requiring only temporary treatment, eg subacute or postpartum thyroiditis. If this is suspected, then subsequent withdrawal of treatment should be considered, with repeat thyroid function tests 4–6 weeks later.

The starting dose for levothyroxine is typically 50 µg daily. Assessment of adequacy of replacement and adjustments to dose are made on the basis of clinical findings together with measurement of TSH and free thyroid hormone levels, initially checked at 6–8 week intervals. Once stabilised, the patient can be followed up by the GP with annual thyroid function tests.

> - The elderly and those with ischaemic heart disease may be particularly sensitive to T_4, and therefore lower starting doses should be used, eg 25 µg levothyroxine daily or on alternate days. If necessary, consider admission to hospital for

> supervision of replacement with ECG monitoring.
> - Always consider the possibility of coexistent adrenal insufficiency, and if in doubt exclude by formal testing (eg short Synacthen test) prior to initiating T_4 replacement.

> - Remember that TSH should not be used to guide levothyroxine dose titration in cases of secondary hypothyroidism.
> - It has been suggested that there may be some benefit in terms of cognitive function from combining liothyronine with levothyroxine replacement to mimic the natural pattern of hormone release by the thyroid gland. However, this is not currently routine practice in the UK.

Subclinical hypothyroidism

Management is mainly a matter of clinical judgement and each case should be dealt with on its own merits. Epidemiological evidence would suggest that there is high risk of progression to overt hypothyroidism in certain situations, eg in the presence of positive microsomal antibody titres. One suggested strategy for managing such cases is shown in Table 29.

Pregnancy

There is a higher incidence of stillbirths, miscarriages and congenital abnormalities in women with untreated hypothyroidism. In addition, evidence suggests that even mild hypothyroidism may have significant consequences for the long-term intellectual development of the unborn child. Maintenance of TSH within normal limits is therefore important. Dose requirements for T_4 may increase by as much as 50–100%, especially during the latter stages of pregnancy. It is important to check thyroid

TABLE 29	STRATEGY FOR MANAGING SUBCLINICAL HYPOTHYROIDISM	
TSH	**Clinical circumstance**	**Management**
>10 mU/L	Asymptomatic or symptomatic	Treat with T_4
5–10 mU/L	Asymptomatic	Observe with repeat TFTs in 6 months
	Symptomatic	Treat with T_4
	Antibodies positive	Treat with T_4
	Abnormalities of lipids	Treat with T_4
	History of radioactive iodine or subtotal thyroidectomy	If asymptomatic, observe with repeat TFTs in 6 months, otherwise treat with T_4

TFTs, thyroid function tests.

function tests in each trimester and adjust the dose of T_4 accordingly.

FURTHER READING

Roberts CG and Ladenson PW. Hypothyroidism. *Lancet* 2004; 363: 793–803.

Weetman AP. Controversy in thyroid disease. *J. R. Coll. Physicians Lond.* 2000; 34: 374–80.

2.3.2 Thyrotoxicosis

Thyrotoxicosis is the clinical syndrome associated with raised levels of thyroid hormone (T_4 and/or T_3). Although usually the result of increased production of thyroid hormones (hyperthyroidism), it can also arise when stored hormone is released from a damaged gland (as in subacute thyroiditis) or when exogenous T_4 is taken in excess. Secondary hyperthyroidism due to increased TSH secretion is very rare and accounts for less than 1% of all cases.

Aetiology/pathophysiology

The causes of thyrotoxicosis are shown in Table 30.

TABLE 30	AETIOLOGY OF THYROTOXICOSIS	
Cause	**Frequency**	**Clinical condition**
Primary	Common	Graves' disease
		Toxic multinodular goitre
	Less common	Toxic adenoma
		Postpartum thyroiditis
		Drug induced, eg amiodarone
		Over-treatment with T_4
		Subacute thyroiditis
		Hyperthyroid phase of Hashimoto's thyroiditis ('Hashitoxicosis')
	Rare	Struma ovarii
		Metastatic differentiated follicular thyroid carcinoma
Secondary	Rare	TSH-secreting pituitary adenomas
		Pituitary resistance to thyroid hormone
		Trophoblastic tumours secreting hCG

hCG, human chorionic gonadotrophin.

Graves' disease

Approximately 15% of patients with Graves' disease have a close relative with the same condition, suggesting a significant genetic component in the aetiology of this autoimmune disorder. Sensitisation of T lymphocytes to antigens within the thyroid gland leads to the production of autoantibodies (from activated B lymphocytes) targeted against these antigens. The development of antibodies, which are capable of binding to and stimulating the TSH receptor, usually correlates with the appearance of thyrotoxic features.

In Graves' ophthalmopathy, infiltration of the extraocular muscles by mononuclear cells is accompanied by an accumulation of glycosaminoglycans (derived from orbital fibroblasts) which promote fluid retention, thereby effectively reducing the available space within the bony orbit. This in turn leads to proptosis, ophthalmoplegia and the other features which typify Graves' eye disease (see below). A similar infiltrative process appears to underlie the skin lesion called pretibial myxoedema.

Epidemiology

The prevalence of hyperthyroidism in the UK has been estimated at 1–2%, with an incidence of 3 per 1,000 per year. Females are more commonly affected, especially in Graves' disease (5–10:1), with a peak age of onset in the fourth decade. In contrast, toxic multinodular goitre typically occurs in older patients (>50 years), often in the context of a long-standing non-toxic goitre.

Clinical presentation and physical signs

Figure 40 illustrates the common clinical features seen in thyrotoxicosis.

Many of the manifestations of thyrotoxicosis reflect increased sensitivity to circulating catecholamines, eg tremor, sweating, anxiety. Included amongst these are the eye signs 'lid lag' and 'lid retraction', which are commonly found in thyrotoxicosis of any cause. In contrast, certain eye signs are specific to Graves' disease: proptosis, ophthalmoplegia, chemosis and periorbital oedema (Fig. 41). Interestingly, the development/progression of Graves' ophthalmopathy is independent of thyroid status, although there is a suggestion that it may be exacerbated if TSH is allowed to rise during treatment. Overall only 3–5% of cases are classified as severe. The condition tends to be more pronounced in smokers.

Similarly, pretibial myxoedema is seen only in Graves' disease (Fig. 42).

Table 31 summarises the important differences between Graves' disease and toxic multinodular goitre.

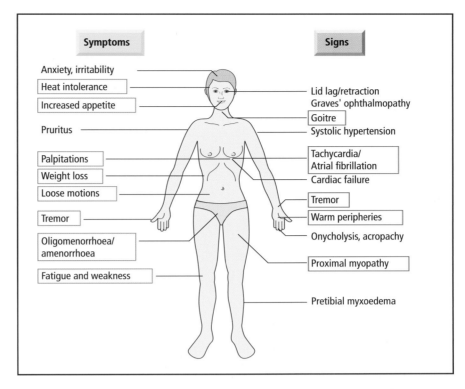

Symptoms

Anxiety, irritability
Heat intolerance
Increased appetite
Pruritus
Palpitations
Weight loss
Loose motions
Tremor
Oligomenorrhoea/amenorrhoea
Fatigue and weakness

Signs

Lid lag/retraction
Graves' ophthalmopathy
Goitre
Systolic hypertension
Tachycardia/Atrial fibrillation
Cardiac failure
Tremor
Warm peripheries
Onycholysis, acropachy
Proximal myopathy
Pretibial myxoedema

▲ **Fig. 40** Clinical features of thyrotoxicosis. The common symptoms and signs are shown in boxes.

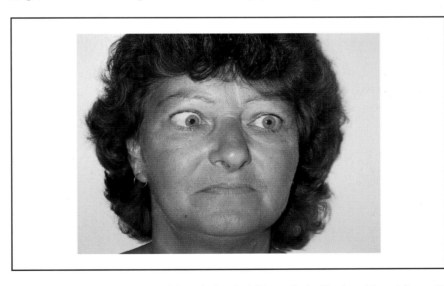

▲ **Fig. 41** Graves' ophthalmoplegia. Inability to look to the left in a patient with relapsed Graves' disease. Lid retraction is also evident.

Other presentations of thyrotoxicosis

The young and the old
Hyperactivity, increased linear growth and weight gain may occur in children with thyrotoxicosis. Older patients may present with apathy and depression or with symptoms of heart failure, angina or dysrhythmias (so-called apathetic hyperthyroidism). It is therefore important to exclude hyperthyroidism in any patient with atrial fibrillation or heart failure of undetermined aetiology.

Thyroid crisis Patients with unrecognised thyrotoxicosis or severe poorly controlled disease are at risk of developing a potentially fatal thyroid crisis/storm. Precipitating factors include intercurrent illness, surgery or ^{131}I therapy. Hyperpyrexia, profuse sweating, extreme restlessness, confusion, psychosis, dysrhythmias and features of heart failure are common manifestations. Left untreated, progression to shock, coma and death may occur within hours or days.

Pregnancy The child of any mother with Graves' thyrotoxicosis during pregnancy, or with a previous history of Graves' thyrotoxicosis, is at risk of developing fetal or neonatal thyrotoxicosis, since thyroid-stimulating antibodies may persist and cross the placenta from 26 weeks onwards.

Close monitoring is essential, especially in those who have

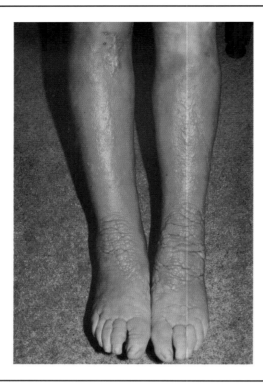

▲ **Fig. 42** Pretibial myxoedema.

TABLE 31 CLINICAL FEATURES OF GRAVES' DISEASE AND TOXIC MULTINODULAR GOITRE		
	Graves' disease	Toxic multinodular goitre
Gender	Female >> male	Female > male
Peak age	20–40 years	>50 years
Goitre	Diffuse, smooth	Multinodular
Eye signs	Lid lag and lid retraction	Lid lag and lid retraction
	Graves' ophthalmopathy	
Skin	Pretibial myxoedema	
Nails and fingers	Acropachy, onycholysis	
Autoantibodies	Usually present	Usually absent

previously received definitive treatment in the form of surgery or ^{131}I, and in whom high antibody titres may go undetected because of the lack of clinical signs in the mother. Monitoring of fetal heart rate and growth, and in some centres for evidence of a fetal goitre, may help to identify potential cases.

Neonatal thyrotoxicosis is more common than intrauterine thyrotoxicosis, often becoming clinically apparent 1–2 weeks after delivery. In either case, measurement of TSH receptor-stimulating antibody titres in the mother and infant may help to predict the likelihood/severity of the disorder.

Thyroiditis Several different forms of thyroiditis are recognised. In some cases there is accompanying thyrotoxicosis, reflecting destruction of thyroid follicles with resultant release of T_4 and T_3 into the bloodstream (eg subacute thyroiditis). This may be followed by a period of transient hypothyroidism, although in the case of postpartum thyroiditis up to 20% become permanently hypothyroid.

Different types of thyroiditis

- Acute (suppurative).
- Subacute (de Quervain's or granulomatous thyroiditis).
- Drug induced (eg amiodarone).
- Autoimmune: chronic lymphocytic (Hashimoto's disease).
- Atrophic (primary myxoedema); postpartum; juvenile.
- Riedel's thyroiditis.
- Painless (non-postpartum).

Investigations

Thyroid function tests

- TSH is suppressed unless the cause is a TSH-secreting pituitary tumour.

- FT_4 and/or FT_3 are raised. T_3 thyrotoxicosis (normal FT_4 in the presence of signs and symptoms, with a raised FT_3 and suppressed TSH) is more commonly associated with toxic adenoma.

Thyroid autoantibodies

- Anti-thyroid peroxidase antibodies are present in some but not all patients with autoimmune hyperthyroidism.

- TSH receptor-stimulating antibodies are usually detectable in Graves' disease. Measurement may be particularly helpful in certain situations, eg pregnancy (see above).

Radioisotope uptake scan

Radioisotope scans (^{99m}Tc or ^{131}I) may be helpful in differentiating between the different causes of thyrotoxicosis (Fig. 43).

- In the absence of ophthalmopathy, uniform increased uptake suggests Graves' disease.

- A patchy and irregular appearance is in keeping with toxic multinodular goitre.

- A toxic adenoma will appear as a localised area of increased uptake

with suppressed activity elsewhere.

- In thyroiditis the uptake is typically low, although one should also keep in mind the possibility of iodine or T_4 ingestion.

Other investigations

- CXR: tracheal narrowing or deviation may be evident (see Fig. 5). Flow–volume loops can help to confirm or exclude extrathoracic obstruction by moderate to large goitres.

- ECG and echocardiography: if there is evidence of associated

cardiac disease, eg atrial fibrillation.

Treatment

Thyroid crisis

This is a serious and potentially fatal disorder, requiring immediate emergency treatment:

Antithyroid drugs Give carbimazole (CBZ) (20 mg orally or via nasogastric tube immediately, then every 4–6 hours) or propylthiouracil (PTU) (200 mg orally or via nasogastric tube, then every 4–6 hours). PTU may confer additional benefits due to its ability to inhibit conversion of T_4 to T_3.

Iodide Sodium iodide (0.5–1 g every 12 hours by intravenous infusion) or saturated solution of potassium iodide (6–8 drops orally every 6 hours) should be added 1 hour later to prevent additional release of stored thyroid hormone.

> ⚠ **Iodide must not be started before organification has been blocked with an antithyroid drug due to the risk of providing further substrate for hormone synthesis.**

The radiographic contrast agents ipodate and iopanoate may also be used to decrease thyroid hormone release, and have additional beneficial effects including inhibition of peripheral conversion of T_4 to T_3.

Beta-blockade Propranolol (0.5–2 mg iv given slowly, followed by 40–80 mg orally every 6–8 hours)

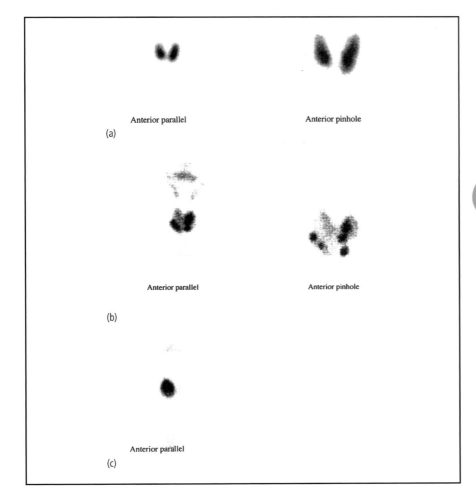

▲ **Fig. 43** Thyroid isotope scans: uptake of ^{99m}Tc in (**a**) Graves' disease, (**b**) toxic multinodular goitre and (**c**) solitary toxic adenoma.

blocks many of the peripheral actions of T_3 and partially impairs conversion of T_4 to T_3. Clinically dramatic improvement in cardiovascular performance may follow effective beta-blockade. However, caution is needed in subjects with intrinsic cardiac disease in whom removal of the remaining sympathetic drive to the myocardium may result in rapid decompensation. In these circumstances, the very short-acting agent esmolol is preferred. Alternatively, verapamil (5–10 mg by slow intravenous injection) may be used if there is a history of asthma or evidence of marked cardiac failure. In either case the patient should be monitored closely in a high-dependency or intensive-care unit.

Dexamethasone A dose of 2 mg orally (or iv) every 6–8 hours helps to reduce peripheral conversion of T_4 to T_3, and may inhibit further hormone release.

Supportive measures Oxygen therapy, intravenous fluids and active cooling (with cooling blankets and antipyretic agents, although avoid aspirin because it displaces thyroid hormone from thyroid-binding globulin) are usually required. Diuretics and digoxin may be indicated for cardiac failure. Chlorpromazine (50–100 mg im) can be used safely as a sedative.

Short- and long-term treatment

Beta-blockers Non-selective beta-blockers (eg propranolol 10–80 mg tds) are useful for symptomatic relief and rapid control of cardiac toxicity. They can usually be discontinued 3–4 weeks after commencing an antithyroid agent.

Antithyroid drugs CBZ (40–60 mg daily in divided doses) will render most patients euthyroid within 3–4 weeks. Thereafter, the dose can be reduced in a stepwise fashion to a maintenance level of 5–15 mg given once daily. Alternatively, after initial blockade, a higher dose of CBZ (40 mg daily) can be maintained and T_4 replacement added in (starting with 50–100 µg daily) as part of a 'block and replace' regimen, with the dose gradually titrated upwards if necessary. In Graves' disease, treatment is normally continued for 6–18 months, depending on the regimen used. Following cessation of therapy, approximately 50% of patients will relapse, although the timing of this is variable.

> 🔑 The effectiveness of treatment should be monitored clinically and biochemically with periodic measurement of FT_4 and/or FT_3. Remember that the TSH level often remains suppressed for several months after restoration of euthyroidism.

> ⚠️ **Carbimazole**
>
> A number of patients are unable to tolerate CBZ, with rashes the most commonly reported adverse event (up to 5%). In a smaller number of cases (~0.5%), life-threatening agranulocytosis and/or thrombocytopenia occur and require immediate cessation of therapy.
>
> All patients placed on antithyroid drugs should be warned of this potentially serious side effect, and given written instructions advising them to immediately discontinue treatment and attend their GP or accident and emergency department for an FBC should they develop a sore throat, mouth ulceration or fever.

PTU represents an alternative to CBZ (with 200 mg of PTU equivalent to 20 mg of CBZ). It has a shorter half-life and therefore must be given in a bd or tds regimen even during the maintenance phase of treatment. In light of this, it is often reserved for those unable to tolerate CBZ, although it must *not* be used in patients who have developed agranulocytosis and/or thrombocytopenia in response to CBZ as there is a high risk of recurrence with PTU. It is also the preferred agent for use in pregnancy (see below).

Radioiodine ^{131}I offers a safe and effective means of treating thyrotoxicosis. [131]I is trapped and organified in the same manner as natural iodine but emits locally destructive β particles that lead to cell damage and death over a period of several months. It is of particular use in the management of toxic multinodular goitre, toxic adenoma and relapsed Graves' disease. In some instances it is also preferred as first-line treatment for Graves' disease, eg in the elderly with cardiac disease.

Patients are normally rendered euthyroid prior to treatment, although younger patients with normal cardiac status and mild to moderate thyrotoxicosis can be treated under beta-blockade alone. It is necessary to stop CBZ 5–7 days before administration to allow uptake of the isotope (if PTU is used, then a longer period of withdrawal is required despite its shorter half-life). These can then be restarted 5–7 days after treatment and continued for a further 3 months, at which point residual thyroid status can be assessed. The advantage of this approach is that stable thyroid function is maintained in the peri-radioiodine period. Alternatively, if antithyroid drugs are not recommenced after radioiodine, then earlier review is required. Long-term follow-up is mandatory in all those treated with ^{131}I because of the high risk of subsequent hypothyroidism. Some centres aim to render patients hypothyroid early and treat with T_4 to minimise the risk of recurrence or missed late hypothyroidism. Many regions operate thyroid registers that facilitate annual recall for thyroid function tests in the community.

- ^{131}I crosses the placenta and is therefore contraindicated in pregnancy, which should also be avoided for at least 6 months after treatment.
- There is ongoing controversy as to whether ^{131}I worsens Graves' ophthalmopathy. Many centres avoid ^{131}I in severe eye disease, but permit treatment in mild to moderate cases under steroid cover (eg prednisolone 30–40 mg daily).

Surgery Subtotal thyroidectomy is rarely the first-line treatment for uncomplicated thyrotoxicosis. However, it may be indicated in the presence of:

- relapsing thyrotoxicosis;
- compressive symptoms;
- multiple allergies to medication or non-compliance with treatment;
- toxic adenoma;
- personal preference.

Patients should be rendered euthyroid prior to surgery to minimise the risks of precipitating dysrhythmias during anaesthesia or of postoperative thyroid storm.

Table 32 outlines the potential complications of thyroid surgery.

TABLE 32 POTENTIAL COMPLICATIONS OF THYROID SURGERY

Time course	Complication
Early	Haemorrhage
	Vocal cord paresis
	Hypoparathyroidism (transient or permanent)
Late	Recurrent thyrotoxicosis
	Hypothyroidism

Pregnancy

Low TSH values are not uncommon in the first trimester (see Section 3.3.1). FT_4 and FT_3 levels at this stage are usually normal, but may be mildly elevated. However, as the pregnancy progresses, FT_4 and FT_3 levels can fall to outside of the 'normal' range. It is likely that specific pregnancy-related reference ranges will be introduced in due course.

- ^{131}I therapy is contraindicated (as are radioisotope scans) and, accordingly, treatment options are limited to antithyroid drugs or, in some cases, surgery during the second trimester.
- PTU is preferred to CBZ during pregnancy and lactation because it crosses the placenta to a lesser extent and very little is found in breast milk. It is administered as a titration regimen.
- Graves' disease often remits during pregnancy and some patients are able to come off antithyroid treatment completely. However, relapse is common during the postnatal period.
- TSH receptor antibody titres should be determined early in the third trimester to assess the risk of neonatal thyroid dysfunction.

Thyroiditis

Subacute, postpartum and painless thyroiditis are characterised by destruction of thyroid follicles with release of stored T_4 and T_3 into the circulation. In the thyrotoxic stage, beta-blockers are the treatment of choice by virtue of their ability to relieve adrenergic symptoms. Antithyroid drugs are of little use. Levothyroxine replacement may be required subsequently during the hypothyroid phase.

FURTHER READING

Cooper DS. Hyperthyroidism. *Lancet* 2003; 362: 459–68.

Kendall-Taylor P. Thyrotoxicosis. In: Grossman A, ed. *Clinical Endocrinology*, 2nd edn. Oxford: Blackwell Science, 1998.

2.3.3 Thyroid nodules and goitre

The term 'goitre' denotes enlargement of the thyroid gland. It may be diffuse or nodular, simple or toxic, benign or malignant and physiological or pathological (Table 33).

Aetiology/pathogenesis

It is likely that an array of different factors interact to stimulate thyroid enlargement/nodule formation. For example, elevated TSH levels in hypothyroid states provide a strong trophic stimulus to the gland; similarly, antibodies directed against the TSH receptor may promote thyroid growth.

Epidemiology

Thyroid nodules and goitre are common; up to 8% of the population

TABLE 33 CLASSIFICATION OF GOITRE AND THYROID NODULES

	Type	Cause
Diffuse goitre	Physiological	Puberty Pregnancy
	Autoimmune	Graves' disease Hashimoto's thyroiditis
	Thyroiditis	Subacute (de Quervain's) Riedel's disease
	Iodine deficiency Dyshormonogenesis Goitrogens	Antithyroid drugs Lithium Iodine excess
Nodular goitre	Multinodular goitre	Toxic Non-toxic
	Solitary nodule	Toxic adenoma Benign nodule Malignant nodule Lymphoma Metastasis
	Infiltration (rare)	Tuberculosis Sarcoidosis

have palpable goitres and post-mortem series report thyroid nodules in about 50% of people over the age of 40. Women are more commonly affected than men.

Clinical presentation
Many cases are noted incidentally, although there may be features of associated hypothyroidism or hyperthyroidism. Occasionally, thyroid enlargement leads to local pressure symptoms, eg difficulty in breathing (with stridor) or swallowing.

Physical signs
An approach to the examination of the thyroid gland is outlined in Section 1.2.7. Remember to check for the presence of lymphadenopathy: enlarged lymph nodes in the cervical chain may be a sinister feature when associated with a thyroid nodule.

Investigations

Blood tests

Thyroid function tests FT$_4$, FT$_3$ and TSH should be checked to exclude overt thyroid dysfunction.

Subclinical hyperthyroidism (normal free thyroid hormone levels in the presence of a suppressed TSH) is a relatively common finding in clinically euthyroid patients with nodule(s) or goitre. It is associated with an increased risk of atrial fibrillation, and some evidence also points to potential deleterious effects on bone status.

Thyroid antibodies The demonstration of positive thyroid antibody titres (anti-thyroid peroxidase, thyroglobulin) may support your suspicions of underlying autoimmune disease. However, it does not exclude coexistent pathology, including malignancy.

Calcitonin Measurement of basal and stimulated calcitonin levels (see Section 3.1.6) is reserved for cases where medullary thyroid carcinoma (MTC) is suspected. This test was previously used to screen family members of probands with multiple endocrine neoplasia (MEN) type 2 or familial MTC, but these individuals should now undergo genetic screening and be offered prophylactic thyroidectomy if they carry the *RET* mutation (see Section 2.7.1). The main clinical indication now for measurement of calcitonin is in monitoring for recurrence or disease progression in individuals with previously resected MTC.

Thyroglobulin Although thyroglobulin estimation serves as a valuable tumour marker in individuals with differentiated thyroid carcinoma who have undergone completion thyroidectomy, it is of little use in the screening of newly presenting nodules/goitre, since levels are also elevated in several benign conditions.

Imaging

Plain radiography/CT Radiographs of the chest and thoracic inlet may demonstrate retrosternal extension of a goitre and/or compression of surrounding structures (see Fig. 5), which can be confirmed on CT examination. Flow–volume loop studies should be considered in such cases.

Ultrasonography Although ultrasound is helpful in distinguishing between solid, cystic or mixed (solid and cystic) nodules, it cannot reliably differentiate between benign and malignant lesions.

99mTc scintigraphy Radioisotope scans are not routinely used in the investigation of thyroid nodules since the identification of a 'cold' or 'hot' lesion does not necessarily correlate with the presence of a malignant or benign lesion, respectively.

> • Less than 20% of cold nodules are malignant. The remainder are benign (colloid nodules, Hashimoto's thyroiditis, haemorrhage).
> • The presence of a 'warm' or 'hot' nodule does not exclude malignancy.
> • On ultrasound, a solid nodule is more likely to be malignant than a cystic lesion. However, the majority of solid nodules are benign, whilst some cystic lesions are malignant.

Fine-needle aspiration biopsy/ultrasound-guided biopsy

Because of the lack of sensitivity and specificity of clinical examination and routine radiology in the differentiation of benign from malignant solitary/dominant thyroid nodules, fine-needle aspiration (FNA) biopsy is the first-line investigation in such cases. Results are typically reported as:

• non-diagnostic (indicating a need for repeat aspiration);

• benign;

• suspicious;

• malignant.

The latter two groups should be referred for surgical management, whilst those with benign cytology can be observed. However, the identification of a follicular lesion merits special mention, since follicular adenomas cannot be distinguished from carcinomas on FNA biopsy and accordingly all require referral for surgery.

Treatment

Wherever possible, the underlying condition should be treated appropriately, eg T_4 replacement in hypothyroidism associated with Hashimoto's thyroiditis; thyroidectomy for suspicious or frankly malignant nodules. Surgery may also be indicated for single benign nodules or non-toxic multinodular goitre associated with local pressure effects, although ^{131}I may be equally as effective in the long term.

FURTHER READING

Franklyn J and Stewart PM. Diagnosis and treatment of thyroid nodules and goitre. *J. R. Coll. Physicians Lond.* 1998; 32: 6–10.

Hermus AR and Huysmans DA. Treatment of benign nodular thyroid disease. *N. Engl. J. Med.* 1998; 338: 1438–47.

2.3.4 Thyroid malignancy

Thyroid malignancy represents the commonest of the endocrine cancers. Although several mutations have been described in various proto-oncogenes (eg the *PTC/RET* mutation in some cases of papillary carcinoma) and tumour-suppressor genes (eg p53 mutations in anaplastic carcinoma), considerable work remains to be done to understand the molecular basis for thyroid carcinoma. Table 34 outlines the important clinical aspects of this disorder.

It is important to remember that the common forms of thyroid cancer often behave in an indolent manner, and in a patient with a clinically static nodule and no other worrying features most centres would accept a repeat negative FNA at 4–6 months as reasonable for exclusion of thyroid malignancy. However,

the only 100% reliable means of exclusion is surgical excision and histology. This may be preferable to some patients for cosmetic reasons or for peace of mind. These considerations should be discussed with a patient before embarking on a management plan involving FNA.

2.4 Reproductive disorders

2.4.1 Delayed growth and puberty

Definition

The average age of onset of puberty is 11.5 years in girls and 12 years in boys. In general, investigations should be initiated if there are no secondary sexual characteristics by 13.5 years in girls and 14.5 years in boys, and/or if the child's height falls below the 3rd centile and is inappropriate for the height of the parents. Remember, however, that up to 3% of children exhibit constitutional pubertal delay.

Assessment of pubertal development

The Tanner staging system (Tables 35 and 36) allows for an objective assessment of sexual maturity. In recognition of the differing actions of gonadal steroids and adrenal androgens, it distinguishes between genital and pubic hair development in boys and breast and pubic hair development in girls.

Aetiology/pathophysiology

Causes of pubertal delay and/or short stature are shown in Table 37.

Clinical presentation

Patients may present with short stature, failure to develop secondary

TABLE 34 CLINICAL ASPECTS OF THYROID MALIGNANCY

Type of thyroid malignancy	Epidemiology	Clinical features/spread/ metastases	Treatment/prognosis
Papillary	About 70% of all cases ♂:♀ ~1:3 Peak incidence during fourth decade of life	Considered to be the slowest growing of the thyroid cancers. Although local spread to cervical lymph nodes is not uncommon at presentation, distant metastases are rare	Total thyroidectomy is recommended for all but the smallest of tumours, and is followed by an ablative dose of radioactive iodine. This in turn is followed by lifelong suppressive T_4 therapy. In these circumstances thyroglobulin acts as a useful tumour marker. Cancer-related death occurs in only about 10% of cases during 20 years' follow-up
Follicular	About 15% of all cases ♂:♀ ~1:2.5 Peak incidence during fifth decade of life	More aggressive than papillary carcinoma. Spread may occur by local invasion of lymph nodes or by blood vessel invasion with distant metastases to lung and bone	Follicular carcinoma is treated along the same lines as papillary carcinoma. However, cancer-related deaths occur in a higher proportion of patients (20–60%) during 20 years' follow-up
Anaplastic	<10% of all cases ♂:♀ ~1:1 Peak incidence at 65–70 years of age	An aggressive form of thyroid cancer, which typically presents with a painful rapidly expanding thyroid mass	Despite combined treatment with surgery, radiotherapy and in some cases chemotherapy, the prognosis is poor, with few patients surviving more than 6–8 months
MTC	<5% of all cases ♂:♀ ~1:1 Sporadic MTC has a peak incidence in the fourth to fifth decades, whilst hereditary MTC is often detected at a much earlier age	More aggressive than papillary or follicular carcinoma, but less so than anaplastic tumours. Locally invasive with distant spread via lymphatics and blood. Associated with MEN-2 syndromes	Total thyroidectomy may be curative in the early stages, hence the rationale for screening relatives of affected individuals in MEN kindreds. Radiotherapy and chemotherapy are usually of little benefit. Long-term survival is variable
Lymphoma	<1% of all cases	May arise as a primary in the thyroid or as part of a generalised lymphoma	Variable prognosis and response to radiotherapy

MEN, multiple endocrine neoplasia; MTC, medullary thyroid carcinoma.

TABLE 35 TANNER PUBERTAL STAGES IN BOYS

Area of development	Stage	Description
Genital	1	Pre-adolescent: testes, scrotum and penis are of about the same size and proportion as in early childhood
	2	Enlargement of scrotum and testes. Skin of scrotum reddens and changes in texture. Little or no enlargement of the penis at this stage
	3	Enlargement of the penis, which occurs at first mainly in length. Further growth of testes and scrotum
	4	Increased size of penis with growth in breadth and development of glans. Testes and scrotum larger; scrotal skin darkened
	5	Genitalia adult in size and shape
Pubic hair	1	Pre-adolescent: the vellus over the pubes is not further developed than that over the abdominal wall, ie no pubic hair
	2	Sparse growth of long, slightly pigmented downy hair, straight or slightly curled, chiefly at the base of the penis
	3	Considerably darker, coarser and more curled. The hair spreads sparsely laterally
	4	Hair now adult in type, but the area covered is still considerably smaller than in the adult. No spread to medial surface of the thighs
	5	Adult in quantity and type

TABLE 36 TANNER PUBERTAL STAGES IN GIRLS

Area of development	Stage	Description
Breast	1	Pre-adolescent: elevation of papilla only
	2	Breast bud stage: elevation of breast and papilla as small mound. Enlargement of areolar diameter
	3	Further enlargement and elevation of breast and areola, with no separation of their contours
	4	Projection of areola and papilla to form a secondary mound above the level of the breast
	5	Mature stage: projection of papilla only, due to recession of the areola to the general contour of the breast
Pubic hair	1	Pre-adolescent: the vellus over the pubes is not further developed than that over the abdominal wall, ie no pubic hair
	2	Sparse growth of long, slightly pigmented downy hair, straight or slightly curled, chiefly along labia
	3	Considerably darker, coarser and more curled. The hair spreads sparsely over the junction of the pubes
	4	Hair now adult in type, but the area covered is still considerably smaller than in the adult. No spread to medial surface of the thighs
	5	Adult in quantity and type

TABLE 37 AETIOLOGY OF DELAYED GROWTH AND PUBERTY

Frequency	Cause
Commonest causes of delayed growth and puberty	'Constitutional delay', a non-pathological condition, commoner in boys, which is often familial. Bone age is typically less than chronological age and the child usually achieves predicted adult height Chronic/severe illness, eg coeliac disease, hypothyroidism, renal tubular acidosis, eating disorders, psychosocial deprivation
Rarer causes of short stature	Chromosomal abnormalities, eg Down's syndrome, Turner's syndrome Single-gene defects, eg the skeletal dysplasias such as achondroplasia Dysmorphic syndromes, eg Prader–Willi syndrome Endocrine disorders, eg growth hormone deficiency or resistance, pituitary disease, glucocorticoid excess
Rarer causes of delayed puberty	Hypogonadotrophic hypogonadism, eg idiopathic, Kallmann's syndrome, pituitary dysfunction Hypergonadotrophic hypogonadism, eg Turner's syndrome, Klinefelter's syndrome, gonadal dysgenesis, previous cytotoxic treatment or radiotherapy, trauma/orchitis in males, androgen insensitivity (testicular feminisation) Androgen excess, eg CAH, adrenal or ovarian tumours, Cushing's syndrome

CAH, congenital adrenal hyperplasia.

sexual characteristics or primary amenorrhoea. It is important to determine whether there is a family history of delayed growth and puberty or a history of other childhood illnesses.

During the initial assessment it is useful to consider the following points.

- Are data showing the time course of growth failure available, eg child health records which include growth charts (see Fig. 4)? Enquire about birth weight and problems at delivery since low birth weight is associated with short stature.

- Is there a history of chronic illness, eg asthma, cystic fibrosis, Crohn's disease or chronic renal disease? Consider also occult coeliac disease. All these conditions can be associated with short stature.

- Is there a family history of short stature or delayed puberty?

- Is there any evidence of nutritional deficiency or disorders such as anorexia nervosa.

- What are the social circumstances? Emotional stress can have adverse effects on growth.

Physical signs

A thorough examination is necessary, looking for signs of systemic illness, eg chronic lung disease. You should also make a note of the following.

- Height, weight and arm span: this will help to determine whether growth failure is uniformly distributed.

- Pubertal stage, using the Tanner staging scheme.

- Presence or absence of testes within the scrotal sac; testicular volume should be assessed with an orchidometer (see Fig. 15).

- Features suggesting a specific diagnosis such as Kallmann's syndrome, Klinefelter's syndrome, Turner's syndrome or other genetic, endocrine (eg hypothyroidism, Cushing's syndrome) or dysmorphic disorders.

Investigation

Initial investigations

Routine blood tests/urinalysis
Initial evaluation should include screening for underlying disorders with the following.

- FBC (anaemia).

- Urea and electrolytes (chronic renal impairment).

- Glucose.

- C-reactive protein and/or erythrocyte sedimentation rate (systemic disorders).

- Thyroid function tests: measure free thyroxine and thyroid-stimulating hormone (TSH).

- Anti-tissue transglutaminase antibodies and IgA (coeliac disease).

- Plasma bicarbonate and urinalysis (renal tubular acidosis).

Gonadotrophins (luteinising hormone, follicle-stimulating hormone) and oestradiol or testosterone Whilst hypergonadotrophic hypogonadism, ie high luteinising hormone (LH) and follicle-stimulating hormone (FSH) with low oestradiol/testosterone, suggests primary gonadal failure, hypogonadotrophic hypogonadism (ie low/normal LH and FSH with low oestradiol/testosterone) does not distinguish between constitutional delay (ie prepubertal levels) and secondary gonadal failure.

Bone age

Bone age (determined by plain radiograph, typically of the wrist) can be compared with chronological age to aid in the diagnosis of pubertal delay and allow predictions regarding potential future growth. For example:

- low gonadotrophins and a more advanced bone age is suggestive of underlying pathology;
- low gonadotrophins and a relatively delayed bone age are more likely in the long term to be associated with normal pubertal development.

Karyotype analysis The karyotype of all girls with delayed puberty and short stature should be checked, as the diagnosis of Turner's syndrome is not always clinically apparent (1 in 1,500–2,500 of live-born females; see Section 2.4.4). Analysis may be necessary using DNA extracted from a second tissue (eg skin fibroblasts) in cases of mosaicism, where lymphocyte DNA is normal.

Males with delayed puberty should be screened for possible Klinefelter's syndrome.

Further investigations
Depending on the results of the initial investigations, more complex tests of pituitary function (eg gonadotrophin-releasing hormone test, see Section 3.1.4; assessment of growth hormone status, see Section 2.1.8) may be indicated, together with structural studies, eg MRI of the pituitary fossa, visual field assessment and pelvic ultrasound.

Treatment
The choice of treatment will be directed by the underlying aetiology. Most children with constitutional delay of puberty, especially if mild, require only simple reassurance (they are normal, but their 'body clock' is starting later than that of their friends). Occasionally, psychological pressures are such that intervention may be indicated to 'start things off'. This typically involves the use of short-term (<6 months) low-dose sex steroids, eg oestrogen treatment in girls (5–10 μg ethinylestradiol daily) or testosterone injections (starting at 50 mg im every 4 weeks) in boys. In both sexes, once treatment is discontinued the child's own pubertal development takes over in cases of constitutional delay.

Complications
The main problems associated with constitutional delay of growth and puberty are psychological and social. It is important to define the worries of the patient, the parents, and you (as their doctor): these may be different. Adolescence is a difficult time anyway, and short stature and sexual infantilism will exacerbate the usual problems. The child's behaviour may become immature or aggressive and antisocial. Parents may not allow children the independence appropriate for their age, and may be inclined to 'baby' them. There may be bullying or teasing at school, with delays in developing social skills if they feel unable to start 'dating' at the same time as their peers. Contact with the Child Growth Foundation may be useful.

FURTHER READING

Buchanan CR. Abnormalities of growth and development in puberty. _J. R. Coll. Physicians Lond._ 2000; 34: 141–6.

Stanhope R and Fry V. *Constitutional Delay of Growth and Puberty: A Guide for Parents and Patients*, 3rd edn. London: The Child Growth Foundation, 2000. Available full text at http://www.childgrowthfoundation.org/

2.4.2 Male hypogonadism

A small proportion of patients presenting with delayed puberty and poor growth and with a prepubertal hormone profile, namely low luteinising hormone (LH) and follicle-stimulating hormone (FSH) and low oestradiol or testosterone, prove on follow-up to have true hypogonadotrophic hypogonadism, ie they fail to enter puberty spontaneously as the years advance or, conversely, fail to progress through puberty after a small priming dose of sex steroids, as outlined in Section 2.4.1. In girls this typically presents with primary amenorrhoea (see Section 2.4.3), whilst in boys there is failure to acquire secondary sexual characteristics.

Men may also present with loss of secondary sexual characteristics later in life and, again, determination of paired gonadotrophins and testosterone is critical in directing further investigation.

Aetiology/pathophysiology

Hypothalmic/pituitary disease, whether due to tumour, inflammation, infiltration or previous surgery/radiotherapy, may present with hypogonadotrophic hypogonadism (indeed, the hypothalamic–pituitary–gonadal axis is among the most sensitive of the hormonal axes to damage), and these disorders must be excluded. In the case of true isolated hypogonadotrophic hypogonadism, the aetiology is often not apparent,

but genetic advances continue to define single-gene defects that produce the phenotype. Traditionally, patients with hyposmia/anosmia were considered to form a separate group defined as Kallmann's syndrome (see below). However, it is now clear that there is considerable overlap between Kallmann's syndrome and other forms of so-called idiopathic hypogonadotrophic hypogonadism, and both entities have even been described in the same family. Identification of specific genetic defects is likely to rationalise this diagnostic classification. Affected genes discovered to date include the *KAL1* gene (see below) and those encoding the gonadotrophin-releasing hormone (GnRH) receptor, the fibroblast growth factor receptor (FGFR) and the G protein-coupled receptor 54 (GPR54). Some of the syndromes produced by these defects have characteristic associated features as outlined in the following section. A retrospective clue to the diagnosis is a history of cryptorchidism, often bilateral, reflecting failure of the perinatal activation of the hypothalamic–pituitary–testicular axis.

In later-onset hypogonadism, the finding of a hypogonadotrophic hormone profile should prompt a careful search for more generalised hypothalamic or pituitary disease.

Moderate to severe obesity and/or severe insulin resistance may also be associated with apparent mild hypogonadism (typically with normal LH and FSH levels), as these conditions are associated with suppression of sex hormone-binding globulin, and hence total testosterone levels, but with relative preservation of free testosterone as gauged by calculation of the free testosterone index.

Where gonadotrophin levels are elevated, primary testicular failure is present, which may be due to a range of infective, traumatic or ischaemic insults or, more rarely, as a consequence of excess iron deposition in the context of haemochromatosis (see Section 2.5.3). Klinefelter's syndrome is an important congenital cause of hypergonadotrophic hypogonadism (see below).

Kallmann's syndrome

Kallman's syndrome is a congenital disorder characterised by isolated gonadotrophin deficiency and hypoplasia of the olfactory lobes with consequent hyposmia/anosmia, the latter due to a range of genetic defects that interfere with normal migration of neurons from the olfactory placode during development. Associated abnormalities in some patients include gynaecomastia, mirror movements, mid-face abnormalities such as cleft lip/palate, renal agenesis, hearing loss and ataxia. Inheritance may be autosomal dominant, X-linked recessive or, rarely, autosomal recessive. Genes implicated to date include *KAL1* on the X chromosome, and those encoding FGFR1 and prokineticin receptors (PROKR1 and 2).

Klinefelter's syndrome

Klinefelter's syndrome is a congenital disorder associated with one or more supernumerary X chromosomes (karyotype 47,XXY in 80–90% of cases). It is the commonest chromosomal abnormality leading to hypogonadism in men. It is characterised by small firm testes, small phallus, eunuchoid proportions and gynaecomastia. Case–control studies have suggested an associated mild degree of learning impairment. The most common presentations are in late teenage or adult life with gynaecomastia or infertility. Azoospermia is the norm, reflecting seminiferous tubule dysgenesis. Testosterone production is variable, leading to differing degrees of sexual development. Psychosocial problems are commonly seen, and there is also an excess incidence of mitral valve prolapse which should be screened for.

Clinical presentation

Androgen status

Ask about:

- frequency of shaving and beard growth;

- axillary and pubic hair development;

- deepening of the voice;

- libido, erectile function (and where appropriate fertility).

Enquire further about:

- problems with sense of smell (hyposmia or anosmia in Kallmann's syndrome);

- colour vision (also sometimes impaired in Kallman's syndrome);

- undescended testes in infancy (and timing of corrective surgery);

- history of cleft palate/lip (a rare feature of FGFR mutations);

- features suggesting other pituitary hormone deficiencies (see Section 2.1.8);

- headaches/visual problems (hypothalamic/pituitary space-occupying lesion);

- galactorrhoea (hyperprolactinaemia);

- testicular trauma or bilateral orchitis in the past (eg due to postpubertal mumps);

- gynaecomastia;

- diabetes, arthritis or liver disease (haemochromatosis; see Section 2.5.3).

Physical signs

Check for the presence of the following.

- The distinctive facial appearance of long-standing hypogonadism, especially in older men, in whom the poverty of facial hair and lack of temporal recession is most noticeable (see Fig. 14).

- Other secondary sexual characteristics.

- Testicular volumes using an orchidometer (see Fig. 15).

- An absent or impaired sense of smell (Kallmann's syndrome).

- Eunuchoid habitus (ie span greater than height and heel to pubis distance greater than pubis to crown), which is common in those in whom hypogonadism precedes puberty, eg Klinefelter's syndrome.

- Mirror movements, eg the tendency of the contralateral side to mimic unilateral hand movements.

- Gynaecomastia: indicates a decrease in the ratio of androgen to oestrogen.

- Features suggestive of a pituitary tumour, eg bitemporal hemianopia, hypopituitarism, galactorrhoea (hyperprolactinaemia).

> ⚠️ **Cryptorchidism**
>
> Cryptorchidism (unilateral or bilateral absence of the testes from the scrotum) is an important clinical finding since it indicates a significant risk of malignant transformation in the affected gonad(s) and further investigation is mandatory (see below).

Investigation

Initial investigations

Routine blood tests Unless the clinical features suggest a specific underlying disorder, some simple screening tests should be performed, including FBC (anaemia), urea and electrolytes (chronic renal impairment), fasting glucose, thyroid function, prolactin, liver biochemistry and serum transferrin saturation/iron studies (haemochromatosis).

Gonadotrophins (LH, FSH) and testosterone To distinguish primary (hypergonadotrophic) and secondary (hypogonadotrophic) hypogonadism.

Specific investigations

These will be guided by clinical impression and preliminary screening tests, but may include the following.

- Karyotype analysis: to exclude Klinefelter's syndrome.

- Assessment of pituitary function/ MRI pituitary fossa: in cases of secondary hypogonadism/ hyperprolactinaemia (see Section 2.1.8).

- Ultrasound of the testes: the clinical finding of cryptorchidism must be investigated further to try to identify the site of the undescended/maldescended tissue.

- Genetic screening for haemochromatosis (see Section 2.5.3).

- Semen analysis: including assessment of number, morphology and motility.

- Human chorionic gonadotrophin (hCG) stimulation: hCG is able to mimic the ability of LH (with which it shares a common α-subunit) to stimulate testosterone synthesis and secretion, and therefore may help to differentiate primary and secondary gonadal failure.

- Bone densitometry (dual energy X-ray absorptiometry): testosterone is required for maintenance of normal bone mineral density in men. Bone densitometry may help to identify those at significant risk of fracture, and is particularly useful in older men who decline testosterone replacement, when alternative prophylaxis should be offered, eg a bisphosphonate.

Management

The general principles governing management of the hypogonadal male include:

- patient and sympathetic explanation;

- treatment of any underlying disorder;

- replacement of hormone deficiency;

- referral for specialist fertility advice if appropriate.

Various formulations of testosterone replacement are available and are discussed in more detail in Section 2.1.8.

FURTHER READING

Belchetz P. Male hypogonadism. In: Grossman A, ed. *Clinical Endocrinology*, 2nd edn. Oxford: Blackwell Science, 1998.

Allan CA and McLachlan RI. Androgen deficiency disorders. In: DeGroot LJ and Jameson JL, eds. *Endocrinology*, 5th edn. Philadelphia: Elsevier, 2006.

2.4.3 Oligomenorrhoea/amenorrhoea and premature menopause

Amenorrhoea is traditionally subdivided into two groups.

- Primary amenorrhoea: lack of menses by the age of 16 years.

- Secondary amenorrhoea: absence of menstrual periods for 6 months or more after cyclical menses have been established.

TABLE 38 CAUSES OF AMENORRHOEA

Cause	Condition
Physiological	Pubertal delay Pregnancy Lactation Post-menopausal
Pathological	Polycystic ovarian syndrome (PCOS) Hypothalamic–pituitary dysfunction (including excessive weight loss or exercise, stress, pituitary tumours/infiltration, hyperprolactinaemia) Turner's syndrome Premature ovarian failure (POF) Congenital adrenal hyperplasia (CAH) Adrenal/ovarian neoplasms Congenital anomalies of the female reproductive tract

Oligomenorrhoea indicates lighter/irregular periods.

Aetiology/pathophysiology

In practice, there is considerable overlap between primary and secondary amenorrhoea, as a number of conditions can give rise to either (Table 38). However, a small number of disorders are specifically associated with primary amenorrhoea, including anatomical defects of the female reproductive tract and Turner's syndrome (see Section 2.4.4).

> Most clinicians agree that 'post-pill amenorrhoea' does not exist, and that an underlying cause should be sought in such cases.

Clinical presentation

Common

- Oligomenorrhoea/amenorrhoea.

- Impaired fertility.

- Hirsutism or acne.

Uncommon

Menopausal symptoms including:

- hot flushes;

- night sweats;

- vaginal dryness with or without dyspareunia.

Rare

If there is a space-occupying pituitary lesion:

- visual symptoms;

- headache;

- features of other pituitary hormone deficiency or excess.

Physical signs

Common

- Extremes of BMI (>30 or <20 kg/m^2).

- Mild hirsutism or acne.

Rare

- Virilisation (marked hirsutism, muscle development in a male pattern, clitoromegaly) (see Section 2.2.3).

- Bitemporal hemianopia (suggestive of a pituitary tumour).

Investigation

Patients should be fully evaluated at initial presentation: subfertility is always an urgent concern, and prolonged low oestrogen levels may lead to osteopenia and osteoporosis. However, before embarking on more complex investigations the possibility of pregnancy must be considered to prevent embarrassment for all concerned at a later date!

TABLE 39 DIFFERENTIAL DIAGNOSIS OF OLIGOMENORRHOEA/ AMENORRHOEA ACCORDING TO GONADOTROPHINS AND PROLACTIN

Cause	Condition
Hypogonadotrophic	Excessive weight loss, exercise or stress, pubertal delay, Kallmann's syndrome, idiopathic hypogonadotrophic hypogonadism, pituitary disease/treatment
Normogonadotrophic	PCOS, CAH, androgen-secreting tumour, anatomical defects, androgen insensitivity
Hypergonadotrophic	Turner's syndrome, POF
Hyperprolactinaemia	Prolactinoma, stalk disconnection syndrome, drugs (eg dopamine antagonists)

CAH, congenital adrenal hyperplasia; PCOS, polycystic ovarian syndrome; POF, premature ovarian failure.

Once pregnancy has been excluded, baseline investigations should include measurement of gonadotrophins (luteinising hormone and follicle-stimulating hormone), oestradiol and prolactin.

Together with the clinical features, these preliminary screening tests will guide subsequent investigations (Table 39), which may include the following.

- Thyroid function tests: ideally free thyroxine and thyroid-stimulating hormone to distinguish primary and secondary thyroid dysfunction.

- Dynamic assessment of pituitary reserve, eg insulin tolerance test (see Section 3.1.5).

- Testosterone and dehydroepiandrosterone sulphate (if there are any signs of androgen excess).

- 17α-Hydroxyprogesterone: late-onset CAH may present in adulthood with oligomenorrhoea (see Section 2.2.5).

- Provera (medroxyprogesterone) withdrawal test: in non-pregnant patients, Provera 10 mg daily is administered for 5 days. If a withdrawal bleed occurs within 10 days, the endometrium must have been exposed to oestrogen, and it is likely that oestrogen levels are sufficient to protect against osteopenia/osteoporosis even if she is amenorrhoeic.

- A mid-luteal phase (day 21) progesterone: in menstruating patients, a level of more than 30 nmol/L suggests that ovulation has occurred during that cycle.

- Karyotype analysis (Turner's syndrome).

- Radiological imaging of the pituitary, adrenals or ovaries, depending on the biochemical pattern of results.

- Bone densitometry.

Treatment

General

Specific treatment should be directed at the underlying disorder. Weight adjustment may be effective in hypogonadotrophic hypogonadism and PCOS but is often very difficult for the patient to achieve.

Prevention/amelioration of osteopenia/osteoporosis

Oestrogen therapy (with a cyclical progestogen unless the patient has had a hysterectomy) is indicated to prevent osteoporosis if the Provera (medroxyprogesterone) test is negative. This can be given in the form of postmenopausal hormone-replacement therapy (which would not prevent conception, however unlikely) or the combined oral contraceptive pill.

Fertility

Hypogonadotrophic hypogonadism may respond to specialist treatment with gonadotrophins or gonadotrophin-releasing hormone. In women with POF, *in vitro* fertilisation using a donated oocyte is the only option (see Section 2.4.8).

Complications

- Osteopenia, with the subsequent risk of osteoporotic fractures, due to oestrogen deficiency.

- Psychological problems linked to impaired fertility or hirsutism.

Disease associations

POF may be associated with other autoimmune endocrine disorders such as type 1 diabetes, hypothyroidism and Addison's disease (see Section 2.7.2).

FURTHER READING

Baird DT. Amenorrhoea. *Lancet* 1997; 350: 275–9.

Master-Hunter T and Heiman DL. Amenorrhea: evaluation and treatment. *Am. Fam. Physician* 2006; 73: 1374–82.

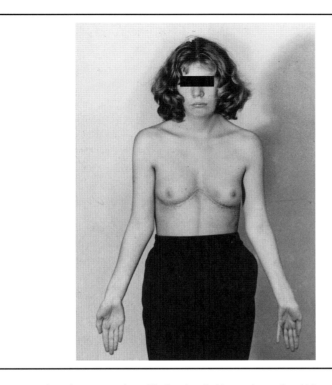

▲**Fig. 44** Turner's syndrome. Note the webbed neck and wide carrying angle, which are typical of classical Turner's syndrome. In addition, there is a visible thoracotomy scar from a previous atrial septal defect repair.

2.4.4 Turner's syndrome

Turner's syndrome commonly presents as primary amenorrhoea in a girl with short stature. The classical stigmata of Turner's syndrome include a webbed neck, low hairline, widely spaced nipples and cubitus valgus (Fig. 44). Remember, however, that the clinical features may be less marked if there is only partial X chromosome deletion or alternatively mosaicism.

Patients with classical Turner's syndrome usually exhibit:

- low/undetectable oestradiol with high levels of luteinising hormone and follicle-stimulating hormone (hypergonadotrophic hypogonadism);

- 45,XO karyotype.

Further investigations in confirmed cases of Turner's syndrome are discussed below.

Specific management

There are many issues, both physical and psychological, that need to be addressed in the management of women with Turner's syndrome.

Hormone-replacement therapy

A natural oestrogen will promote the development of secondary sexual characteristics. Treatment should be started with a low dose of oestrogen alone and gradually increased. After 1–2 years, maintenance treatment with cyclical combined oestrogen and progestogen therapy can be substituted.

Gonadal replacement therapy in Turner's syndrome

The timing and dose of oestrogen replacement is critical. Use of a low dose in the early stages of treatment helps to maximise growth and final height, especially in those receiving concomitant growth hormone (GH) therapy (see below).

Osteoporosis

Women with Turner's syndrome are at increased risk of developing osteoporosis. In addition to oestrogen replacement therapy, their diet should be checked to ensure an adequate supply of calcium, and regular weight-bearing exercise encouraged.

Ischaemic heart disease

A three-fold excess mortality from ischaemic heart disease probably reflects an increased incidence of insulin resistance/type 2 diabetes and hypertension. Both of these conditions should therefore be sought and treated, and the benefits of hormone-replacement therapy, weight control and exercise reiterated.

Structural cardiac and renal abnormalities

Echocardiography, cardiac MRI and renal ultrasonography may reveal structural abnormalities. In addition to any specific management that might be indicated, prompt treatment of urinary tract infections and antibiotic prophylaxis against infective endocarditis should be considered. A bicuspid aortic valve is the commonest cardiac abnormality and may be associated with progressive aortic root dilatation. Good BP control is essential.

Hypothyroidism

Turner's syndrome is associated with an increased incidence of primary autoimmune hypothyroidism (Hashimoto's thyroiditis) and thyroid function tests should be monitored on a regular basis, even in asymptomatic patients.

Cryptic Y chromosome material

Karyotyping may reveal cryptic Y chromosome material (45,XO/46,XY). This predisposes to gonadoblastoma and is an indication for prophylactic gonadectomy (or close observation).

Fertility

Between 2 and 5% of women with Turner's syndrome have spontaneous menstrual periods, although only 0.5% have ovulatory cycles, and an early menopause is likely. Contraceptive advice and genetic counselling are important in this subgroup, since there is an approximately 30% risk that their offspring will have a congenital anomaly. For the majority of cases, however, specialist fertility input is required if they wish to conceive by *in vitro* fertilisation or gamete intrafallopian transfer (GIFT) using a donor ovum. Prepregnancy cardiovascular and renal screening is imperative.

Intelligence

Intelligence is generally normal, although hand–eye coordination and visuospatial skills may be impaired. Lower social competence has also been reported.

Short stature

Although children with Turner's syndrome are not GH deficient, treatment with recombinant human GH (either alone or in combination with anabolic agents such as oxandrolone) may increase their final adult height.

Hearing loss

Recurrent middle-ear infections occur commonly during the first decade of life, and there may be a history of glue ear requiring ventilation tubes. Unfortunately, many adult women with Turner's syndrome are left with a significant hearing loss and, accordingly, all should be referred for formal audiological assessment.

Turner's syndrome: ethical issues and communication

There are many important psychological issues to consider in caring for women with Turner's syndrome. Most importantly, to quote from literature produced by the Turner Syndrome Support Society (http://www.tss.org.uk/), 'women with Turner's syndrome should have no doubt of their femininity: physically, behaviourally and sexually'. A number of the management issues outlined above may be self-evident to a physician, but confusing to the patient unless fully explained:

- the need for gonadectomy if there is cryptic Y material, even though the ovaries are non-functioning;
- the need for 'periods' (rather than unopposed oestrogen therapy);
- that 'periods' are actually withdrawal bleeds and do not represent restored fertility;
- why the patient is prescribed the low-dose combined oral contraceptive pill even though she is infertile.

FURTHER READING

Ranke MB and Saenger P. Turner's syndrome. *Lancet* 2001; 358: 309–14.

- - - - - - - - - - - - - - - - - -

Stanhope R and Fry V. *The Turner Woman: A Patient's Guide*, 2nd edn. London: The Child Growth Foundation, 2000. Available full text at http://www.childgrowthfoundation.org/

2.4.5 Polycystic ovarian syndrome

Polycystic ovarian syndrome (PCOS) describes the association of ovarian hyperandrogenism with chronic anovulatory cycles in females with polycystic ovaries.

Aetiology/pathophysiology

Although the aetiology of PCOS is unclear, there is evidence to suggest that it is a complex disorder reflecting interplay between genetic susceptibility and environmental factors. It is now recognised that decreased peripheral insulin sensitivity with consequent hyperinsulinaemia are key features of the metabolic derangement typical of PCOS. In addition, retention of insulin sensitivity by the ovary has been suggested to contribute to ovarian thecal androgen production (in response to insulin and insulin-like growth factor 1).

The risk of developing type 2 diabetes is approximately six-fold higher in women with PCOS than in the general population, and they frequently exhibit dyslipidaemia typical of the metabolic syndrome.

Epidemiology

PCOS is estimated to affect approximately 5% of women of reproductive age.

Clinical presentation

The symptoms of PCOS usually date from menarche and develop gradually. The most common presentation is with features of hyperandrogenism (hirsutism/acne) and menstrual irregularity (oligomenorrhoea or amenorrhoea).

Physical signs

Obesity and hirsutism (but not virilisation) are common findings. About 5% of women exhibit acanthosis nigricans (Fig. 45), which is a sign of insulin resistance.

Investigations

The choice of investigations should be guided by the clinical presentation.

- Luteinising hormone (LH) and follicle-stimulating hormone (FSH): the ratio of LH to FSH may be increased to >2 (reflecting anovulatory cycles and a lack of

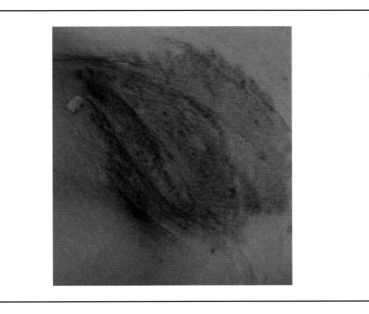

▲ **Fig. 45** Marked acanthosis nigricans in the axilla of a patient with severe insulin resistance.

progesterone to inhibit LH release). However, gonadotrophins are normal in a significant number (30–50%) of women who meet the other diagnostic criteria for PCOS.

- Testosterone: is often slightly increased (although usually <5 nmol/L, thereby distinguishing PCOS from most androgen-secreting tumours).

- Prolactin: 10–20% of cases have mildly elevated prolactin levels.

- Fasting glucose/oral glucose tolerance test/lipid profile: check for evidence of impaired glucose tolerance/frank diabetes mellitus and the dyslipidaemia of the metabolic syndrome.

- Provera (medroxyprogesterone) withdrawal bleed: PCOS is not an oestrogen-deficient state and therefore a withdrawal bleed typically follows progesterone treatment.

- Pelvic ultrasonography: a pelvic ultrasound scan (preferably transvaginal) may reveal the typical ovarian appearance of multiple follicles ('string of pearls') with increased stroma. However, note that the presence of polycystic ovaries does not in itself indicate that the women has PCOS (approximately 20% of all women have polycystic changes on ultrasound, although only one-third of these have PCOS).

Further investigations
Other tests may be considered to help distinguish between PCOS and:

- adult-onset congenital adrenal hyperplasia (17α-hydroxyprogesterone) (see Section 2.2.5);

- ovarian or adrenal tumours (dehydroepiandrosterone sulphate, androstenedione) (see Section 2.2.3);

- Cushing's syndrome (see Section 2.1.1);

- monogenic causes of insulin resistance (especially in slim women: check paired fasting glucose and insulin).

Treatment

Weight loss

> There is good evidence to suggest that if patients manage to lose weight, this will ameliorate many of the features of PCOS.

Hirsutism/infertility
Approaches to the management of hirsutism and infertility are outlined in Sections 2.4.6 and 2.4.8 respectively.

Metformin treatment
Several studies have suggested that metformin (eg 500 mg tds) in obese women with PCOS can regularise menses, reduce the frequency of anovulatory cycles and perhaps improve hirsutism. However, this is not yet a licensed use for metformin, and there remain questions about the optimum dose and safety in early pregnancy. Larger studies are awaited, both with metformin and other insulin sensitisers including the thiazolidinediones (eg rosiglitazone, pioglitazone).

Other cardiovascular risks
In women with the metabolic form of PCOS, risk factors for coronary heart disease should be addressed, including type 2 diabetes, hypertension, hyperlipidaemia and smoking.

Prognosis
Epidemiological data have not confirmed the expected increase in the risk of coronary heart disease or cerebrovascular disease: some speculate that the excess risk conferred by insulin resistance is balanced by the protective effects of oestrogens.

Prevention

It has been suggested that if patients are targeted when they first present with mild hirsutism and oligomenorrhoea, and strongly encouraged to lose weight and engage in regular aerobic exercise using whatever support systems are available, the progression of the syndrome to infertility can be avoided.

FURTHER READING

Barber TM, McCarthy MI, Wass JA and Franks S. Obesity and polycystic ovary syndrome. *Clin. Endocrinol.* 2006; 65: 137–45.

Franks S. Polycystic ovary syndrome. *N. Engl. J. Med.* 1995; 333: 853–61.

2.4.6 Hirsutism

Hirsutism is excessive terminal hair growth in an androgen-dependent (or male pattern) distribution, and is a very common presenting complaint in endocrine practice. It should be discriminated from hypertrichosis, in which hair growth occurs in a non-androgen-dependent distribution. A visual scale developed by Ferriman and Gallwey can be used to make an objective assessment of the extent and severity of hirsutism, using a score of 1 (a few scattered hairs) to 4 (complete cover) for each of 11 body areas (Table 40).

Aetiology/pathophysiology

Excessive androgen-dependent hair growth can reflect high levels of circulating free androgens of adrenal or ovarian origin, or enhanced sensitivity of the hair follicles to androgens due to variations in local androgen metabolism or androgen receptor sensitivity. There is only a relatively poor correlation between levels of total testosterone and degree of hirsutism, although most women with a testosterone level more than twice the upper limit of normal will exhibit some degree of excess hair growth. Other women with high testosterone will show features of hyperandrogenism (seborrhoea, acne, male-pattern alopecia) but without significant hirsutism. Furthermore, some women with apparently normal serum testosterone actually have elevated free testosterone: this is generally a consequence of reduced levels of sex hormone-binding globulin (SHBG), the main binding protein, which is very hormonally responsive, being suppressed by the hyperinsulinaemia of insulin

TABLE 40 THE FERRIMAN–GALLWEY SCORING SYSTEM[1]

Site	Grade	Definition
Upper lip	1	Few hairs at outer margin
	2	Small moustache at outer margin
	3	Moustache extending halfway from outer margin
	4	Moustache extending to midline
Chin	1	Few scattered hairs
	2	Scattered hairs with small concentrations
	3	Light complete cover
	4	Heavy complete cover
Chest	1	Circumareolar hairs
	2	Additional midline hairs
	3	Fusion of these areas with three-quarter cover
	4	Complete cover
Upper back	1	Few scattered hairs
	2	Rather more, but still scattered
	3	Light complete cover
	4	Heavy complete cover
Lower back	1	Sacral tuft of hair
	2	With some lateral extension
	3	Three-quarter cover
	4	Complete cover
Upper abdomen	1	Few midline hairs
	2	Rather more, but still midline
	3	Half cover
	4	Full cover
Lower abdomen	1	Few midline hairs
	2	Midline streak of hair
	3	Midline band of hair
	4	Inverted V-shaped growth
Upper arm	1	Sparse growth affecting not more than one-quarter of limb surfaces
	2	More than this, but cover still incomplete
	3	Light complete cover
	4	Heavy complete cover
Forearm	1–4	Complete cover of dorsal surface, two grades of light and two grades of heavy growth
Thigh	1–4	As for arm
Leg	1–4	As for arm

1. Adapted with permission from Ferriman D and Gallwey JD. Clinical assessment of body hair growth in women. *J. Clin. Endocrinol. Metab.* 1961; 21: 1440–7.

TABLE 41 CAUSES OF HIRSUTISM

Frequency	Condition
Common	Idiopathic
	Racial/familial
	Polycystic ovarian syndrome (PCOS)
Less common	Congenital adrenal hyperplasia (CAH) (non-classical)
	Adrenal or ovarian androgen-secreting tumours
	Cushing's syndrome
	Hypothyroidism
	Other severe insulin resistance states
	Drugs, eg glucocorticoids, anabolic steroids

resistance, by androgens themselves and by hypothyroidism. However a significant number of women with hirsutism have no elevation of androgens, and their condition is often called idiopathic hirsutism. This is believed to be due to genetic variation in genes encoding the androgen receptor and in enzymes such as 5α-reductase which is responsible for local activation of testosterone to the more potent dihydrotestosterone (DHT). Causes of hirsutism are shown in Table 41.

Epidemiology

Using a cut-off score of 8 on the Ferriman–Gallwey scale, a prevalence of hirsutism of around 5% is estimated in women of reproductive age, although there is significant ethnic and familial variation.

Clinical presentation and history

The presentation is almost always with cosmetically distressing hirsutism, often in association with oligomenorrhoea. Assessment of the patient should be strongly guided by (i) the need to identify the small proportion of patients with an underlying virilising tumour and (ii) an appreciation of the importance of the subjective distress caused by the excess hair growth. Thus the time course of the development of

hirsutism should be established: onset and gradual progression after puberty, often with progressive weight gain, is most common. A short history of rapid hair growth or sudden onset in adulthood are important clues to a possible underlying tumour. The extent and frequency of cosmetic measures taken to control hair growth also give a useful idea of the extent of the problem. Deepening of the voice in association with hair growth is sinister as it implies very high levels of androgens, with virilisation due to their action on androgen-responsive tissues other than hair follicles. The history should also be directed towards eliciting symptoms suggestive of diabetes (see Section 2.6) or Cushing's syndrome (see Section 2.1.1), and should document the presence and degree of menstrual disturbance. The drug history should concentrate on any preparations with androgenic activity, and the desire for fertility and use of contraception are important in deciding upon the therapeutic strategy.

Because in most cases anxiety caused by the cosmetic appearance of hirsutism is the main problem, it is also important to pay attention to the degree of psychological distress and extent of lifestyle disturbance

produced by the excessive hair growth.

Physical signs

Using the Ferriman–Gallwey visual scale, hirsutism may be graded and given a numerical score for future comparative purposes. Signs of virilisation (deep voice, masculine body habitus and muscularity, clitoromegaly) should be sought, as well as alopecia, acne and seborrhoea. Features suggestive of insulin resistance (obesity, acanthosis nigricans), Cushing's syndrome or other endocrinopathy should also be noted, and the abdomen palpated for masses.

Investigation

Opinions differ as to the extent to which women with hirsutism should be investigated. A practical approach based on clinical findings is shown in Table 42.

The presence of obesity or clinical features of PCOS/insulin resistance should prompt measurement of fasting glucose and lipids. Clinical suspicion of endocrinopathy such as hypothyroidism or Cushing's syndrome necessitates appropriate investigation.

Treatment

In general, the evidence base for the treatment of hirsutism is fragmented, and individual physicians' experience and preferences still inform treatment advice significantly. Specific causes of hirsutism should be treated appropriately, eg using glucocorticoids to suppress adrenal hyperandrogenism in non-classical CAH. Because of the long hair growth cycle, it is important to emphasise to patients that effective systemic therapies may not show clinical benefit until they have been used for 6–9 months.

TABLE 42 STRATEGY FOR THE INVESTIGATION OF HIRSUTISM

Clinical presentation	Likely diagnosis	Investigation
Mild long-standing hirsutism with regular menses	Idiopathic	None (if the patient is concerned, LH, FSH and testosterone can be checked for reassurance)
Moderate hirsutism with long-standing irregular menses	Idiopathic, PCOS, CAH	LH, FSH, testosterone, SHBG, DHEAS, 17α-hydroxyprogesterone (± ACTH stimulation) ± ovarian ultrasound
Severe hirsutism/rapid onset of symptoms/ virilisation/testosterone >5 nmol/L	CAH, adrenal/ovarian tumour	LH, FSH, testosterone, SHBG, DHEAS, 17α-hydroxyprogesterone (± ACTH stimulation), ultrasound/CT/MRI of adrenals and/or ovaries

ACTH, adrenocorticotrophic hormone; CAH, congenital adrenal hyperplasia; DHEAS, dehydroepiandrosterone sulphate; FSH, follicle-stimulating hormone; LH, luteinising hormone; PCOS, polycystic ovarian syndrome; SHBG, sex hormone-binding globulin.

Reassurance and lifestyle advice

Reassurance that there is no sinister underlying problem (in most cases) and explanation of the cause of the excess hair growth is a very important part of management. In the large proportion of patients with PCOS or features of insulin resistance, dietary advice should be given, and aerobic exercise and weight loss, where relevant, encouraged.

Cosmetic and topical measures

After reassurance and explanation of the condition, mild or moderate hirsutism may often be managed to the satisfaction of the patient with local cosmetic measures including waxing, plucking, bleaching, depilatory creams or shaving. A more recent advance has been the development of a topical preparation of the cell cycle inhibitor eflornithine, which has been shown to improve facial hirsutism in some patients. Laser therapy and electrolysis to individual hair follicles may also be very effective in selected patients, although they are uncomfortable, repetitive and costly to patients,

with a paucity of large-scale clinical evidence to support their use.

Suppression of ovarian function

As the most common cause of elevated circulating androgens is ovarian hyperproduction, approaches aimed at suppressing ovarian function are logical. Most commonly prescribed combined oral contraceptive preparations can be used, in particular those with low androgenic activity. Particularly popular is Dianette (co-cyprindiol), containing cyproterone acetate, which has some antagonistic activity at the androgen receptor. A common limitation of the combined oral contraceptive pill is exacerbation of weight gain, as well as other common complications of exogenous oestrogens including migraines and increased thromboembolic risk. In intractable cases of ovarian hyperandrogenism, chemical ablation of ovarian function is achieved with potent gonadotrophin-releasing hormone agonists such as leuprorelin, although this renders the patient oestrogen deficient and at increased risk of unduly rapid bone loss.

Antiandrogens

Androgen receptor antagonists (eg spironolactone, cyproterone acetate, flutamide) have been used successfully to treat hirsutism in small-scale clinical trials. However, none of these agents are licensed for this clinical indication and flutamide is generally avoided due to rare but occasionally fatal hepatotoxicity. Because of their antiandrogenic activity, all of these agents are potentially teratogenic and should not be prescribed without reliable contraception or sterilisation. 'Additional' cyproterone acetate is commonly given during the first 10 days of each menstrual cycle, often in conjunction with the low-dose cyproterone-containing preparation Dianette (co-cyprindiol). Spironolactone is used at doses of 50–200 mg daily, except in the presence of liver or kidney disease. The 5α-reductase inhibitor finasteride (which blocks the conversion of testosterone to DHT) may also be tried (5 mg daily), although again it is unlicensed in this setting.

FURTHER READING

Rosenfield RL. Clinical practice: hirsutism. *N. Engl. J. Med.* 2005; 353: 2578–88.

2.4.7 Erectile dysfunction

Aetiology and pathophysiology

Erectile dysfunction can be conveniently classified according to pathophysiology (Table 43).

Several different factors (eg diabetes, medication and anxiety) may contribute to erectile dysfunction in any one patient. Furthermore, the psychological response to 'organic' impotence can be difficult to distinguish from primary psychogenic erectile dysfunction.

TABLE 43 CLASSIFICATION OF ERECTILE DYSFUNCTION

Category	Examples
Psychogenic	Anxiety, depression, relationship problems
Drug-induced	Beta-blockers, thiazides, many recreational drugs, alcohol
Neurogenic	Post-CVA, Parkinson's disease, spinal cord injury, pelvic surgery
Vascular	Hypertension, atherosclerosis, diabetes mellitus
Hormonal	Hypogonadism, hyperprolactinaemia
Chronic/systemic illness	Chronic renal failure, diabetes mellitus

CVA, cerebrovascular accident.

Epidemiology

General population

Impotence is estimated to affect 5% of men aged 40–50 years, 15% aged 50–60 years, 25% aged 60–70 years and 40% aged 70–80 years.

Men with diabetes

For men who were less than 30 years old when their diabetes was diagnosed, 45–50% will be impotent by 50 years of age and 60–70% will be impotent by 60 years of age.

Clinical presentation and physical signs

Erectile dysfunction should be distinguished from premature ejaculation or reduced libido. Penile curvature suggests Peyronie's disease. If the patient experiences masturbatory or early-morning erections, this effectively excludes organic pathology and suggests a psychogenic basis.

In all other cases, take a detailed history and perform a careful clinical examination bearing in mind those conditions listed in Table 43. Check femoral pulses, examine for evidence of a peripheral neuropathy and consider performing a digital rectal examination of the prostate in men of an appropriate age.

> Men may not volunteer the symptom of impotence. It is therefore important to ask 'at-risk' groups, including those with diabetes, hypertension, atherosclerotic disease and hypopituitarism.

Investigation

The availability of the phosphodiesterase (PD) inhibitors, the prototype of which is sildenafil (Viagra), has changed the investigation and management of erectile dysfunction.

Where applicable, a psychological evaluation should be arranged, and medication that could be causally related changed. It may then be appropriate to institute a therapeutic trial of sildenafil (see below) without further investigation, when the aetiology of the problem is clear (eg in a man with long-standing diabetes mellitus). Otherwise, a screen for systemic disease should be carried out, including FBC, urea and electrolytes, glucose, cholesterol and possibly prostate-specific antigen. Prolactin and testosterone levels should also be checked.

If the testosterone level is below the normal range, it should be repeated (at 9 a.m.), together with measurement of sex hormone-binding globulin (SHBG), luteinising hormone (LH) and follicle-stimulating hormone (FSH) concentrations.

- If the testosterone concentration remains low (<10 nmol/L) with an appropriately raised LH and FSH, a trial of androgen replacement therapy may be instituted for primary gonadal failure.

- If the pattern is that of hypogonadotrophic hypogonadism (low testosterone with low LH and FSH), assessment of anterior pituitary function together with imaging of the pituitary fossa is necessary (see Section 2.1.8).

Treatment

An approach to the management of erectile dysfunction is shown in Fig. 46.

Phosphodiesterase inhibitors

Inhibitors of phosphodiesterase type 5 such as sildenafil produce increased cyclic guanosine monophosphate (cGMP) concentrations in the glans penis, corpus cavernosum and corpus spongiosum, mimicking the effect of parasympathetically induced nitric oxide (NO) release and leading to increased smooth muscle relaxation and an improved erection. During clinical trials, 60% of attempts at intercourse were successful following sildenafil compared with 20% following placebo. Tadalafil and vardenafil have subsequently followed sildenafil into clinical use, with the same mechanism of action, but variations in pharmacokinetics.

> PD inhibitors augment the erectile response to sexual stimulation, but do not cause an erection to occur by itself. It is important that the patient understands that sexual activity must be attempted before the treatment is considered a failure.

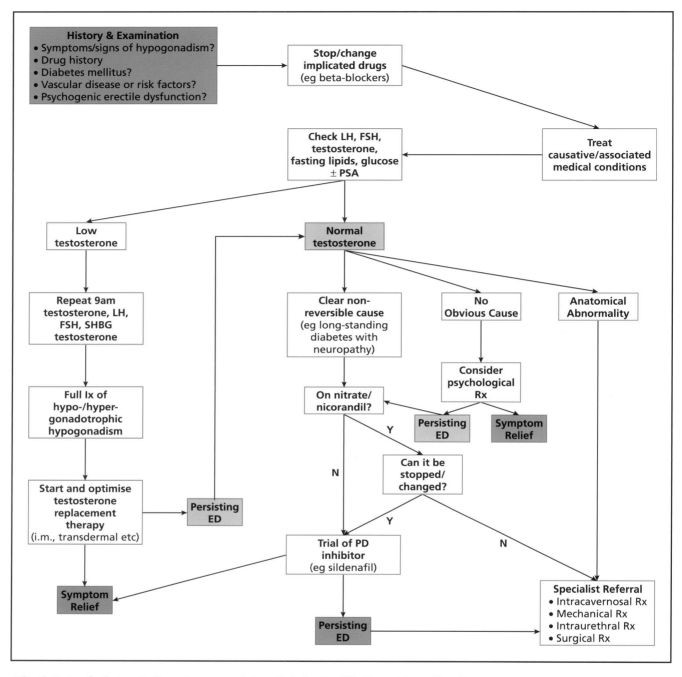

▲**Fig. 46** Strategy for the investigation and management of erectile dysfunction (ED). PSA, prostate-specific antigen.

Headache and flushing are the most commonly experienced side effects. Contraindications to the use of PD inhibitors include nitrate therapy (risk of severe hypotension), significant cardiovascular disease and retinitis pigmentosa, the latter because of the strong expression of phosphodiesterase type 6 in the retina, and some inhibitory activity of sildenafil and other current PD inhibitors also against that enzyme. PD inhibitors should also be used with care in those with Peyronie's disease and in subjects with a predisposition to prolonged erection (eg in sickle cell disease, leukaemia).

Urological treatment

Urologists may institute treatment with alprostadil (a synthetic form of prostaglandin E_1) either by intracavernosal injection or intraurethral application. Papaverine (a non-specific PD inhibitor) and phentolamine (α-adrenoceptor antagonist) may also be given by intracavernosal injection, often in combination or with alprostadil. Some men prefer the use of mechanical devices, such as vacuum constrictors. Various surgical treatments are available including penile prostheses and attempts at revascularisation.

Androgen replacement

Where indicated, testosterone replacement should be instituted (see Section 2.1.8).

Prognosis

Erectile dysfunction can have a considerable impact on a patient's quality of life, although one should not assume that all men (or all relationships) require sexual activity. Importantly, it may also be an important surrogate marker of cardiovascular risk, and overall risk of cardiovascular disease should be carefully assessed and managed as appropriate.

Prevention

Prevention of erectile dysfunction, particularly in patients with diabetes mellitus, is dependent on achieving optimal hypertensive and glycaemic control, correction of dyslipidaemia, cessation of smoking and avoidance of excessive alcohol consumption.

FURTHER READING

Lue TF. Erectile dysfunction. *N. Engl. J. Med.* 2000; 342: 1802–13.

- - - - - - - - - - - - - - - - - - -

Rees J and Patel B. Erectile dysfunction. *BMJ* 2006; 332: 593.

2.4.8 Infertility

Infertility is defined as a failure to conceive despite regular unprotected sexual intercourse for 2 years, in the absence of known reproductive pathology. The cumulative probability of conception in the general population under these circumstances is 84% after 1 year and 92% after 2 years. It is estimated that around one in six couples seek medical advice at some stage due to failure to conceive. In part because of the expensive technology involved in some forms of assisted conception, and because of its high media and political profile, there is an extensive evidence base for many aspects of assisted conception, a subject covered by extensive guidelines from the National Insitute for Health and Clinical Excellence (NICE) in 2004. Much of the management of infertility occurs in specialist reproductive medicine clinics, but because many endocrine disorders can compromise fertility, there is close liaison with endocrinologists and often an integrated multidisciplinary approach involving both specialties.

Aetiology/pathophysiology

Infertility may be due to dysfunction at any level of the hypothalamic–pituitary–gonadal axis in either men or women, as well as to anatomical, infective or inflammatory disorders affecting the reproductive tracts. Among the most common endocrine causes for reduced fertility are polycystic ovarian syndrome (PCOS) with reduced or absent ovulation, hypogonadotrophic hypogonadism in either male or female, and primary gonadal failure, whether acquired or due to underlying genetic disorders (eg Turner's syndrome, Klinefelter's syndrome). In a significant proportion of cases, no clear cause for impaired fertility is discovered.

Clinical assessment

A key principle of the assessment and management of infertility is that it is couple-centred. Assessment often begins after 1 year with no conception despite regular unprotected sexual intercourse. The history should concentrate on identifying predisposing factors for infertility, including woman's age >35 years, amenorrhoea, oligomenorrhoea, pelvic inflammatory disease, or undescended testes. Prior treatment for cancer or infection with HIV or hepatitis B or C should also be documented. Clinical examination should note body weight, signs of PCOS (see Section 2.4.5) or hypogonadism (see Section 2.4.2), and features of syndromes such as Klinefelter's syndrome.

Investigation

Initial investigations should include the following.

- Semen analysis should be carried out with reference to World Health Organisation (WHO) standards. Repeat at 3 months if abnormal, or immediately if grossly abnormal.

- Day 21 progesterone (assuming a 28-day cycle) to look for evidence of ovulation.

Guided by these results, further investigation may include:

- luteinising hormone (LH), follicle-stimulating hormone (FSH), testosterone/oestradiol;

- prolactin;

- screening for *Chlamydia trachomatis*;

- hysterosalpingogram or pelvic ultrasound (if no history of pelvic disease);

- laparoscopy and dye (if history of pelvic disease).

These investigations will allow identification of several types of problem, which may be grouped as follows:

- hypogonadotrophic hypogonadism (male or female);

- gonadal failure;

- ovarian dysfunction due to PCOS;

- obstructive azoospermia;

- tubal occlusion;

- no clear explanation.

Treatment

At first assessment of couples concerned by delays in conception, care should be taken to explain the cumulative probability of conception over 2 years, and the marked decline in female fertility in women from 35 years onwards. Simple lifestyle advice should be given:

- sexual intercourse every 2–3 days;

- cut down alcohol consumption to less than 2 units per week for women and less than 4 units per day for men;

- smoking cessation;

- aim for a BMI between 19 and 29.

Advice about drugs (both prescribed and recreational) should be given, and appropriate preconception measures such as folic acid, rubella and cervical screening recommended.

Medical management will be guided by the nature of any underlying problem, and should be undertaken under specialist supervision. Options include the following.

- Ovulation induction: using agents such as clomifene, a non-steroidal oestrogen analogue that enhances gonadotrophin release among other actions. Treatment with clomifene should be supervised using ovarian ultrasound to assess follicular development. Where ovulation is not achieved, adjunctive therapy with metformin, FSH or ovarian drilling may be used.

- Intrauterine insemination: may enhance chances of conception with clomifene by overcoming the hostile cervix produced by the antioestrogenic action of clomifene. It may also be used in mild male factor infertility, after treatment of tubal disease and in unexplained infertility.

- Gonadotrophin or pulsatile gonadotrophin-releasing hormone (GnRH) therapy (for hypogonadotrophic hypogonadism).

In cases of bilateral tubal occlusion, azoospermia or persisting infertility despite the above measures (NICE suggests a duration of 3 years), various different techniques using *in vitro* fertilisation (IVF) may be tried.

- Sperm recovery: may be used in cases of obstructive azoospermia, with recovered cells subsequently used for IVF.

- Ovulation induction/oocyte maturation/oocyte retrieval: produces oocytes for fertilisation.

- Intracytoplasmic sperm injection (ICSI): may be required to achieve IVF in cases with severe semen quality defects or azoospermia.

- Donor insemination or oocyte donation: may be required where defects in spermatogenesis or oogenesis are irremediable (eg premature ovarian failure, Klinefelter's syndrome).

- Ultrasound-guided embryo transfer: used to introduce no more than two embryos to the uterus.

- Luteal support with exogenous progesterone may additionally be required.

Complications

The main complications of ovulation induction therapy are the occurrence of multiple pregnancy and ovarian hyperstimulation syndrome (OHSS). Both these risks should be explained prior to treatment.

The clinical symptoms and signs of OHSS may range from transient lower abdominal discomfort, mild nausea, vomiting, diarrhoea and abdominal distension through to rapid weight gain with tense ascites, postural hypotension, tachycardia, tachypnoea and oliguria. These features result from extravasation of protein-rich fluid and contraction of the vascular volume, compounded by mechanical effects of tense ascites. Complications of OHSS which may be life-threatening include renal failure, acute respiratory distress syndrome, haemorrhage from ovarian rupture, and thromboembolism.

Mild OHSS can be managed as an outpatient using only oral analgesia and counselling regarding the signs and symptoms of progressing illness. Treatment of more severe OHSS requires antiemetics and more potent analgesics, with careful evaluation including frequent physical and ultrasound examinations (to detect increasing ascites), daily weight measurements, and serial determinations of haematocrit, electrolytes and serum creatinine. Hospitalisation may be required based on severity of symptoms, analgesic requirements and social considerations. Such patients may require intravenous volume expansion with careful monitoring of electrolytes and clinical state, diuretics and sometimes ultrasound-guided paracentesis. Thrombo-embolic deterrent stocking (TEDS) and prophylactic heparin are important. Surgery is occasionally required for ovarian rupture or ectopic pregnancy.

Units that offer assisted reproduction technologies should have protocols in place for management of OHSS, but occasionally patients do present to hospital in the context of unselected medical takes.

FURTHER READING

National Collaborating Centre for Women's and Children's Health. *Fertility: Assessment and Treatment for People with Fertility Problems.* London: Royal College of Obstetricians and Gynaecologists, 2004 (commissioned by the National Institute for Health and Clinical Excellence). Available full text at http://www.nice.org.uk/

2.5 Metabolic and bone diseases

2.5.1 Hyperlipidaemia/ dyslipidaemia

As with osteoporosis there is no easy definition of hyperlipidaemia/ dyslipidaemia. Instead attention focuses on how best to define those at high risk of developing cardiovascular disease, based on the lipid profile and other risk factors.

Physiology/pathophysiology

Lipoproteins

The majority of lipids in plasma are contained within lipoproteins, which comprise a core of cholesterol, cholesterol esters and triglycerides, surrounded by a coat of proteins (principally apolipoproteins A, B, C and E) and phospholipids.

Lipoproteins can be divided into six major classes by ultracentrifugation or electrophoresis:

- chylomicrons (CM);
- very low density lipoproteins (VLDL);

- intermediate-density lipoproteins (IDL);
- low-density lipoproteins (LDL);
- high-density lipoproteins (HDL);
- lipoprotein(a) or Lp(a).

Exogenous lipid pathway

CM are formed in the intestine from absorbed cholesterol and fatty acids and released into the circulation via the thoracic duct. As they pass through the circulation, the majority of their triglyceride content is hydrolysed by the action of endothelial lipoprotein lipase in a process dependent on the presence of apoprotein (apo)-CII. The fatty acids released are taken up by skeletal muscle and adipose tissue and stored as re-esterified triglyceride or used as a source of energy. The modified chylomicron remnants are taken up by the liver by a putative remnant receptor recognising apo-E.

Thus, the basic role of this exogenous lipid pathway is to deliver dietary cholesterol to the liver and fatty acids to the liver, skeletal muscle and adipose tissue.

Endogenous lipid pathway

VLDL are produced by the liver and form the starting point of the endogenous lipid pathway. Like CM they are rich in triglycerides and are modified by lipoprotein lipase to form VLDL remnants and subsequently IDL. IDL can be taken up by the liver and peripheral cells via the LDL receptor, or they can undergo further conversion to LDL. The majority of LDL are removed by LDL receptor-mediated endocytosis in the liver, with a small amount taken up by peripheral cells such as monocytes/macrophages.

LDL metabolism

LDL receptor-mediated endocytosis is subject to negative feedback (ie as intracellular cholesterol increases, LDL receptor expression diminishes). In contrast, oxidatively modified LDL are taken up by scavenger receptors that exhibit no such feedback regulation. It is thought that this unregulated scavenger receptor-mediated uptake of oxidised LDL contributes to the formation of the lipid-laden foam cells that are a characteristic feature of atherosclerotic plaques.

HDL metabolism

In general HDL tends to be antiatherogenic, removing cholesterol from peripheral tissues (via reverse cholesterol transport) and acting as antioxidants.

Lipoprotein(a)

Lp(a) forms the final lipoprotein class, differing from LDL only by the additional presence of apo(a).

Classification

The most accurate (Fredrickson) classification defines hyperlipidaemia by the lipoprotein classes present in increased concentration. However, most laboratories do not perform ultracentrifugation or electrophoresis routinely, measuring instead total cholesterol, triglycerides and HDL cholesterol, with calculation of LDL cholesterol by the Friedewald formula. Hence, often only a working division into hypercholesterolaemia, hypertriglyceridaemia or mixed hyperlipidaemia is possible. However classified, all dyslipidaemias may be either primary (monogenic or polygenic) or secondary (Table 44).

Two of the monogenic hyperlipidaemias warrant brief mention.

TABLE 44 **CLASSIFICATION OF DYSLIPIDAEMIA ACCORDING TO CLINICAL PHENOTYPE, LIPOPROTEIN ABNORMALITY AND FREDRICKSON CLASS**

	Lipoprotein class	Fredrickson	Primary causes	Secondary causes
Hypercholesterolaemia	↑ LDL	IIa	Familial hypercholesterolaemia Polygenic hypercholesterolaemia	Hypothyroidism Obstructive jaundice Corticosteroids Anorexia nervosa
Hypertriglyceridaemia	↑ CM	I	Lipoprotein lipase deficiency Apo-CII deficiency	Diabetes
	↑ VLDL	IV	Familial combined hyperlipidaemia Familial hypertriglyceridaemia	Oral contraceptive pill Alcohol excess
	↑ CM + ↑ VLDL	V	Lipoprotein lipase deficiency Apo-CII deficiency	Thiazide diuretics
Mixed dyslipidaemia	↑ Remnants	III	Familial dysbetalipoproteinaemia	Diabetes Obesity
	↑ VLDL + ↑ LDL	IIb	Familial combined hyperlipidaemia	Nephrotic syndrome Renal failure Glycogen storage disease Paraproteinaemia

- The molecular defect in familial hypercholesterolaemia involves the LDL receptor. In homozygotes there is minimal LDL uptake, with high (~20 mmol/L) levels of total and LDL cholesterol and a greatly increased risk of atherosclerosis. Heterozygotes have an intermediate phenotype.

- Type III hyperlipoproteinaemia is a classic example of gene–environment interaction: apo-E_2 homozygosity is required but in combination with some 'environmental' factor (such as diabetes, obesity, hypothyroidism) to produce the characteristic lipid profile and clinical features.

Epidemiology

Several large-scale studies, such as the Multiple Risk Factor Intervention Trial (MRFIT), Framingham study, and Prospective Cardiovascular Münster Study (PROCAM), have examined the potential links between dyslipidaemia and ischaemic heart disease (IHD).

Epidemiological evidence suggests:

- an association between high levels of total and LDL cholesterol and risk of IHD;
- the relationship between cholesterol and risk of IHD is curvilinear, a 10% increase in cholesterol conferring a 20% increase in risk;
- an inverse relationship between HDL cholesterol and IHD risk;
- a weak relationship between hypertriglyceridaemia and IHD risk, which has not been confirmed in all studies, although high triglycerides do seem to confer an increased risk in the presence of hypercholesterolaemia.

Clinical presentation

Hyperlipidaemia may present with IHD (myocardial infarction or angina) or other vascular disease. Alternatively, it may be uncovered in an asymptomatic patient screened because of a positive family history of premature IHD, the presence of other risk factors for IHD, the existence of a known secondary cause of hyperlipidaemia, or because he or she exhibits the characteristic stigmata of one of these disorders (see below).

Relevant points in taking the history from a hyperlipidaemic patient include:

- past history of vascular disease;

- assessment of lifestyle factors (diet, exercise, smoking, alcohol consumption);

- family history of hyperlipidaemia, hypertension, premature IHD;

- drug history;

- past history or symptoms of diabetes, thyroid disease, liver or renal failure, myeloma.

Physical signs

Some of the stigmata of hyperlipidaemia (Fig. 47) are given in Table 45.

The examination of the hyperlipidaemic patient should include a search for evidence of

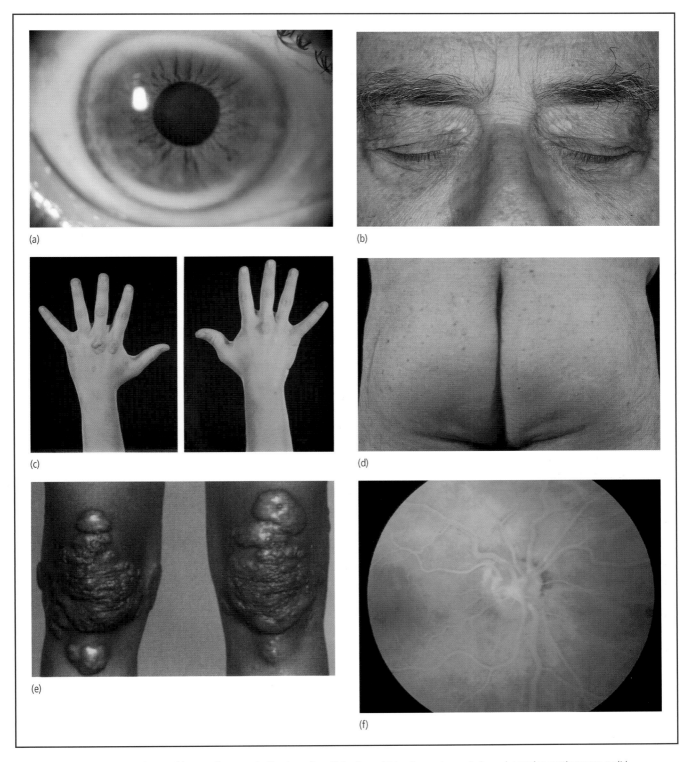

▲ **Fig. 47** Stigmata of hyperlipidaemia. (**a**) Corneal arcus: note the circumferential nature of this advanced arcus; in less advanced cases the upper eyelid may need to be retracted to expose the arcus. (**b**) Xanthelasmata. (**c**) Tendon xanthomata over the extensor tendons of a patient with homozygous familial hypercholesterolaemia. (**d**) Eruptive xanthomata: these appear classically over the buttocks, but can be more widespread. (**e**) Tuberous xanthomata over the knees of a patient with mixed hyperlipidaemia. (**f**) Lipaemia retinalis: note the lipaemic appearance of all the retinal vessels, both arteries and veins.

TABLE 45 STIGMATA OF HYPERLIPIDAEMIA

Type of hyperlipidaemia	Stigmata
↑ LDL cholesterol	Corneal arcus Tendon xanthomata, eg of the Achilles' tendons Xanthelasmata
Mixed hyperlipidaemia	Tuberous xanthomata Eruptive xanthomata Lipaemia retinalis
Type III hyperlipidaemia	Linear xanthomata of the palmar creases

> In general, statins should be given where the predominant problem is elevated total and LDL cholesterol and fibrates where there is significant hypertriglyceridaemia or low HDL cholesterol.

vascular disease (eg carotid or femoral bruits, diminished peripheral pulses), features of other disorders associated with secondary hyperlipidaemia (eg diabetes mellitus, hypothyroidism, liver or renal failure) and an assessment of other risk factors (eg obesity or hypertension).

Investigation

Initial laboratory assessment should include FBC and erythrocyte sedimentation rate (with or without serum electrophoresis to exclude myeloma), tests of renal, liver and thyroid function, fasting glucose and a baseline creatine kinase. A resting ECG may not be as useful as an exercise test. In all cases a full fasting lipid profile (with measurement of total and HDL cholesterol and triglycerides and calculation of LDL cholesterol) should be obtained.

Treatment

Given the high prevalence of IHD and the fact that many people who develop IHD appear to be at a relatively low risk, it is sensible to offer lifestyle advice to all (see Section 1.1.15).

Secondary causes of hyperlipidaemia and other risk factors must be managed appropriately and subjects at high risk of IHD should be started on aspirin.

There is now abundant evidence that lipid-lowering drug therapy (with statins or fibrates) reduces IHD risk and overall mortality in patients with IHD (secondary prevention) or in subjects at high risk of developing IHD (primary prevention). The current Joint British Societies' guidelines recommend that people with established cardiovascular disease, people with diabetes and those asymptomatic individuals at high cardiovascular risk (10-year IHD risk >20%) aim for a total and LDL cholesterol of <4.0 mmol/L and <2.0 mmol/L respectively, or a 25% reduction in total cholesterol and a 30% reduction in LDL cholesterol, whichever achieves the lowest absolute value. Note that these targets are more stringent than previous recommendations (total cholesterol <5.0 mmol/L, LDL cholesterol <3.0 mmol/L) which are still in use in some areas of practice. Convenient tables or computer programs for estimating 10-year risk based on age, sex, total cholesterol/HDL cholesterol ratio, BP, diabetes and smoking status are now widely available.

Failure to achieve target (LDL cholesterol <2.0 mmol/L, HDL cholesterol >1.0 mmol/L and triglycerides <2.0 mmol/L) with monotherapy is an indication for referral to a lipid clinic.

Complications

Both statins and fibrates are generally well tolerated, but patients should be monitored for the rare side effects of myalgia, raised creatine kinase and the development of abnormal liver function tests.

FURTHER READING

British Cardiac Society, British Hypertension Society, Diabetes UK, *et al.* JBS2: Joint British Societies' guidelines on prevention of cardiovascular disease in clinical practice. *Heart* 2005; 91: 1–52.

- - - - - - - - - - - - - - - - - -

Durrington P. Dyslipidaemia. *Lancet* 2003; 362: 717–31.

2.5.2 Porphyria

The porphyrias are a group of metabolic disorders resulting from defects in the enzymes of the haem synthetic pathway with consequent accumulation of various precursors. Clinically they may be divided into the acute and non-acute porphyrias (Table 46).

Pathophysiology

The haem synthetic pathway is shown in outline in Fig. 48.

- In both acute and non-acute porphyrias the reduced production of haem results in increased activity of δ-aminolaevulinic acid (δ-ALA) synthetase as a consequence of impaired negative feedback.

TABLE 46 CLASSIFICATION OF THE PORPHYRIAS

Type	Conditions
Acute porphyrias	Acute intermittent porphyria Variegate porphyria Hereditary coproporphyria
Non-acute porphyrias	Porphyria cutanea tarda Congenital porphyria Erythropoietic protoporphyria

- In the acute porphyrias there is accumulation of δ-ALA and porphobilinogen.

- In the non-acute porphyrias, however, increased porphobilinogen deaminase activity means there is no accumulation of δ-ALA or porphobilinogen.

The acute porphyrias are all dominantly inherited.

Clinical presentation

Acute porphyrias
Presentation is typically in early adult life with intermittent episodes characterised by:

- acute abdominal pain and vomiting;

- sensorimotor neuropathy, respiratory muscle weakness, coma, seizures;

- psychiatric disturbance;

- sinus tachycardia, hypertension and occasionally left ventricular failure.

Attacks may be precipitated by alcohol, sex steroids and a wide variety of drugs, especially barbiturates and other enzyme inducers. In variegate porphyria and hereditary coproporphyria (but not acute intermittent porphyria) these features are accompanied by the cutaneous features of porphyria cutanea tarda.

Non-acute porphyrias
The clinical features of each disorder are as follows.

- Porphyria cutanea tarda: a bullous photosensitive rash that heals by scarring, hepatomegaly, haemochromatosis.

- Congenital porphyria: a scarring bullous photosensitive rash, dystrophic nails, tooth discoloration, anaemia, splenomegaly.

- Protoporphyria: presentation in childhood, photosensitivity, peripheral paraesthesiae, hepatic dysfunction.

Investigation
During an attack of acute porphyria, porphyrin can usually be detected in fresh urine (red/brown on standing). Porphobilinogen in fresh urine can be detected by the development of a characteristic pink/red colour on mixing with Ehrlich's reagent, which is not absorbed out by chloroform or other organic solvents.

Elevated bilirubin and alanine aminotransferase levels are also often present during an acute episode. Family members should be offered screening (ideally genetic, but failing that biochemical) to detect latent cases.

Treatment
Acute attacks are treated with supportive measures, a high carbohydrate intake, with or without parenteral haem administration. Beta-blockers (eg propranolol), chlorpromazine, certain opiates (eg codeine, morphine, diamorphine) and diazepam are safe treatments.

- Following recovery, patients should be advised to abstain from alcohol, and given a list of drugs to be avoided (including oral contraceptives). An up-to-date list of agents to avoid can be found on several websites including http://www.uq.edu.au/porphyria and http://www.porphyriafoundation.com
- Porphyria cutanea tarda is treated by venesection to reduce iron overload. Again alcohol should be avoided.
- Congenital porphyria may be helped by low-dose chloroquine.
- Protoporphyria can be helped by β-carotene and bile acid sequestrants.

FURTHER READING

Scientific Background to Medicine 1,
Biochemistry and Metabolism – Haem.

Cox TM. The porphyrias. In: Warrell DA, Cox TM, Firth JD and Benz EJ, eds. *Oxford Textbook of Medicine*, 4th edn, Vol. 2. Oxford: Oxford University Press, 2003.

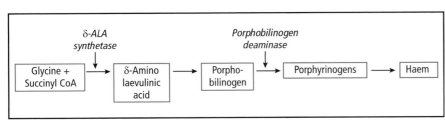

▲ **Fig. 48** Key steps in the haem synthetic pathway.

2.5.3 Haemochromatosis

Aetiology
The term 'haemochromatosis' was introduced by von Recklinghausen in 1889 to describe the pathological accumulation of iron in a wide range of tissues producing organ dysfunction. It is most frequently due to a recessively inherited genetic disorder (adult, juvenile and neonatal forms), but may also complicate repeated blood transfusion, chronic iron ingestion and some forms of anaemia (thalassaemia, chronic haemolytic and dyserythropoietic anaemias).

Pathophysiology
Adult hereditary haemochromatosis (HH) is usually due to mutations in a novel major histocompatibility complex (MHC) class 1-type gene, originally called *HLA-H* and now termed *HFE*, on chromosome 6 (which is close to, and in linkage disequilibrium with, the gene for HLA-A3). Approximately 90% of cases are homozygous for the C282Y mutation (tyrosine replacing cysteine at residue 282). The mutated protein, unlike wild-type HFE, cannot bind β_2-microglobulin and hence is unable to bind to the transferrin receptor. Another mutation, H63D (aspartate substituting for histidine at codon 63), has been identified and approximately 4–7% of patients with HH are C282Y/H63D compound heterozygotes. How these mutations lead to pathological iron accumulation is incompletely understood, but the current model proposes that mutations in *HFE* may impair transferrin receptor-mediated uptake of transferrin-bound iron into crypt cells, providing a false signal that iron stores are low.

Iron is involved in oxygen transport and redox reactions, but the mechanism of its cellular toxicity is not known. In haemochromatosis excess iron is found in almost all tissues, accompanied by cell loss and marked fibrosis, with the liver, pancreas, spleen, heart and several endocrine organs (anterior pituitary, testes and parathyroids) particularly affected. A similar pattern is seen in the other (secondary) causes of haemochromatosis.

Epidemiology
HH is the commonest known inherited disease amongst Caucasians of northern European descent, with a homozygote prevalence of 0.1–0.5% (giving a gene frequency of 3–7%). Penetrance is incomplete, with one large series reporting an incidence of clinical disease of less than 1% in patients with homozygous C282Y *HFE* mutations identified by population screening. This might be due to the need for a concomitant mutation in a second gene (eg the transferrin receptor 2 gene) for full disease expression. Males are more likely to develop disease than females, presumably reflecting protection by menstrual losses. Accumulation of iron and associated tissue damage takes years to develop, with 70% of cases presenting between 40 and 70 years of age.

Clinical presentation
The classical triad of diabetes mellitus (DM), cirrhosis and skin hyperpigmentation (bronze diabetes) occurs relatively late, usually when total body iron stores exceed 20 g. A variety of other organ systems may be involved, as described below. However, increasingly patients are detected prior to clinical presentation with evidence of iron overload on routine biochemistry or when screening is performed because a relative has HH.

Liver disease
- Cirrhosis: abdominal pain, fatigue, bruising.

Endocrine disease
- DM: polyuria, polydipsia, weight loss.
- Hypogonadism: hair loss, diminished libido, impotence.
- Hypoparathyroidism: weakness, tetany.

Cardiac disease
- Dilated cardiomyopathy: fatigue, breathlessness.

Arthritis
- Large joints with chondrocalcinosis.
- Small joints resembling rheumatoid arthritis (particularly second and third metacarpophalangeal joints).

Arthritis occurs in about half of all cases, as does hypogonadism (usually hypogonadotrophic, but sometimes hypergonadotrophic), while cardiac disease occurs in approximately one-third.

Physical signs
The clinical signs of haemochromatosis include:

- hyperpigmentation (due to a combination of iron and melanin);
- hepatomegaly with other stigmata of chronic liver disease;
- testicular atrophy;
- diminished body hair;
- arthritis, especially second and third metacarpophalangeal joints and wrists;
- splenomegaly;
- cardiac disease (cardiomegaly, signs of biventricular failure).

Investigation

Who to screen?

1. Symptomatic patients with:

    (a) liver disease;

    (b) DM, particularly with hepatomegaly/stigmata of chronic liver disease, atypical cardiac disease or early-onset sexual dysfunction;

    (c) early-onset atypical arthropathy, cardiac disease and male sexual dysfunction.

2. Asymptomatic patients:

    (a) first-degree relatives of a confirmed case of HH;

    (b) individuals with unexplained elevation of liver enzymes or incidental finding of asymptomatic hepatomegaly or radiological detection of enhanced attenuation of the liver on CT.

As treatment is more effective the earlier it is initiated, the aim is to identify subjects before they become symptomatic. Most centres recommend concurrent measurement of iron status and genetic screening for relatives of HH probands. Whilst population screening is probably not currently cost-effective, some centres make a case for biochemical screening of all patients with DM, in whom a prevalence of approximately five times that in the general population has been described.

Basic blood tests and radiology

Routine haematology and biochemistry should be sent, including liver function tests, clotting screen, and alpha-fetoprotein if hepatocellular carcinoma is suspected. Radiology may show deposition of calcium pyrophosphate (chondrocalcinosis) in large joints such as the knee.

Iron status

Iron overload can be assessed by transferrin saturation, plasma (or serum) iron concentration and plasma ferritin. A fasting transferrin saturation ≥60% in men or ≥50% in women detects about 90% of patients with homozygous HH. However, many centres use a 'cut-off' value of 45% for both sexes, leading to fewer missed diagnoses at the expense of an increased false-positive rate. Increased plasma ferritin provides supporting evidence but, compared with transferrin saturation, it is generally less specific (as it is also an acute-phase reactant) and less sensitive (as higher levels of iron overload are required to increase ferritin concentration). The definitive test for iron overload is liver biopsy.

In a patient where plasma indices indicate iron overload and genetic analysis demonstrates a homozygous C282Y *HFE* mutation, the diagnosis of HH is secure. If the patient is under 40 years with normal liver enzymes, cirrhosis is unlikely and therefore liver biopsy is not always necessary. Non-invasive imaging studies such as CT and MRI have become increasingly accurate for determining both hepatic and cardiac iron deposition.

Treatment

Genetic haemochromatosis is best treated by venesection on a weekly basis until iron depletion is demonstrated by normalisation of serum ferritin and transferrin saturation and the development of a mild anaemia. Thereafter, the frequency of venesection can be reduced to 1–2 monthly to prevent reaccumulation of iron stores.

Venesection has been shown to reduce the early mortality associated with untreated haemochromatosis, particularly cardiac or hepatic failure, but does not appear to reduce the risk of hepatocellular carcinoma or the severity of diabetes or arthritis. Given the efficacy of venesection, especially when instituted early in the course of the disease, identification of a case of haemochromatosis should be followed by screening of the relatives.

Diabetes (see Section 2.6), hypogonadism (see Sections 2.4.2 and 2.4.3) and hypoparathyroidism (see Section 2.5.9) are managed according to standard guidelines.

The iron-chelating agent desferrioxamine may be used in the prevention/treatment of secondary haemochromatosis.

Complications

Haemochromatosis carries an approximately three-fold increased risk of premature death due to hepatocellular carcinoma (32%), other malignancy (14%), cirrhosis (20%), DM (6%) or cardiomyopathy (6%). Patients must be kept under regular surveillance to allow early detection and treatment of these complications.

FURTHER READING

Pietrangelo A. Hereditary hemochromatosis: a new look at an old disease. *N. Engl. J. Med.* 2004; 350: 2383–97.

Tavill AS (in collaboration with the Practice Guideline Committee of the American Association for the Study of Liver Diseases). Diagnosis and management of hemochromatosis. *Hepatology* 2001; 33: 1321 8. Available full text at http://www.aasld.org/

2.5.4 Osteoporosis

Osteoporosis has been defined as 'a disease characterised by low bone mass and microarchitectural deterioration of the tissue, leading to enhanced bone fragility and a consequent increase in fracture risk'.

More pragmatic definitions of osteoporosis rely on measurement of bone mineral density (BMD), as it has been shown that a bone mass 1 SD below the mean peak bone mass of young adults carries a 1.5–2.5-fold increased risk of fracture. There is continuing debate as to whether the BMD should be compared with peak bone mass (the T score) or the age-adjusted bone mass (the Z score). In fact, just as for hyperlipidaemia, the issue is not the definition of the disease but the identification of which patients should be treated.

Pathophysiology

Bone mass increases during growth and adolescence, peaks in the third decade and declines with age thereafter, with an increased rate of loss after the menopause in women. A number of factors influence bone mass.

- Genetic/racial, eg Afro-Caribbeans are much less likely to develop osteoporosis than white people.

- Sex hormones: risk factors for osteoporosis include early menopause in women and hypogonadism in men.

- Environmental: inadequate calcium intake, physical inactivity, cigarette smoking and alcohol abuse.

- Drugs: especially corticosteroids and long-term heparin.

In addition, osteoporosis may arise secondary to a large number of other medical conditions (Table 47).

> **Bone mass is not the only determinant of fracture risk, which also depends on the quality and geometry of the bone, previous history of fracture and frequency of falls.**

TABLE 47 SECONDARY CAUSES OF OSTEOPOROSIS

Cause	Conditions
Gastrointestinal disease	Coeliac disease, Crohn's disease, ulcerative colititis, gastrectomy, primary biliary cirrhosis
Endocrine disease	Cushing's syndrome, hyperparathyroidism, hypogonadism, hyperthyroidism, hypopituitarism, diabetes mellitus
Psychiatric disease	Anorexia nervosa, exercise-induced amenorrhoea
Others	Myeloma, mastocytosis, osteogenesis imperfecta, Gaucher's disease

Epidemiology

It has been estimated that half of women and one-third of men in the UK will suffer an osteoporotic fracture in their lifetime, and that 22.5% of women and 5.8% of men aged over 50 years in the UK have a BMD greater than 2.5 SD below the sex-adjusted mean peak BMD.

Clinical presentation

Osteoporosis typically presents with a low trauma fracture. Although any bone may be affected, the hip, vertebrae and distal forearms are classically involved. Relevant features to note in the history include:

- past medical history of major illness or any secondary cause of osteoporosis (including low BMI, ie <19 kg/m²);

- timing of puberty and menopause in females, history of prolonged oligomenorrhoea or amenorrhoea;

- average calcium intake;

- exercise level;

- current and previous drug treatment;

- family history of osteoporotic fractures;

- symptoms of gastrointestinal disease or malabsorption.

Physical signs

If left untreated, osteoporosis leads to progressive loss of height with increased kyphosis as a result of successive vertebral fractures.

Investigation

The principal objectives of investigation are to determine the overall risk of fracture and to identify any treatable cause of secondary osteoporosis.

Blood tests

> **Osteoporosis is not a disorder of calcium metabolism, and therefore serum calcium, phosphate and alkaline phosphatase are usually normal. Following fracture, alkaline phosphatase may be elevated.**

Radiology

- Plain radiographs may demonstrate a fracture or vertebral collapse (Fig. 49).

- BMD, measured by dual-energy X-ray absorptiometry (DEXA), is usually determined at the spine and hip (Fig. 50).

Treatment

Reduce fracture risk

The aim of treatment is to reduce the risk of fracture. Several agents are licensed for use in the UK, although not all have proven efficacy in terms of reducing vertebral and/or non-vertebral fractures.

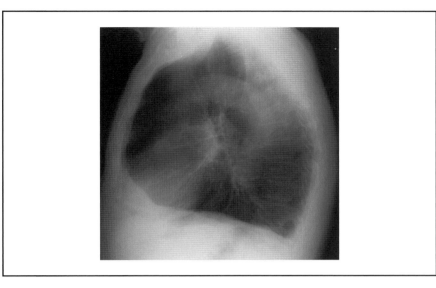

▲ **Fig. 49** Osteoporotic vertebral fractures. Lateral CXR demonstrating loss of vertebral height and anterior wedging at several levels within the thoracic spine, leading to kyphosis. Preferential loss of trabecular over cortical bone gives rise to characteristic 'picture-frame' vertebrae.

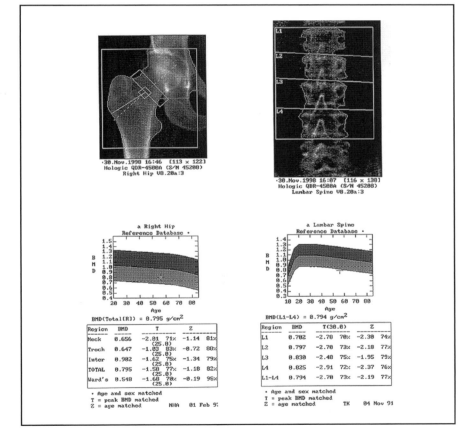

▲ **Fig. 50** Bone densitometry. Dual energy X-ray absorptiometry BMD scan in a man with osteoporosis of the lumbar spine secondary to long-standing hypogonadism. Values for the hip and lumbar spine are shown with both *T* and *Z* scores calculated for each site. The World Health Organisation (WHO) defines osteoporosis as a bone density >2.5 SD below the mean peak bone density in youth.

Females Treatment options include the following.

- Exercise: regular exercise reduces fracture risk, but the magnitude of benefit is relatively small and requires a committed, maintained exercise regime.

- Calcium supplementation: decreases cortical bone loss and rates of fracture. Total calcium intake should be about 1500 mg daily, often requiring supplements of 500–1000 mg, combined with vitamin D (400–800 units daily).

- Selective oestrogen receptor modulators (SERMs), eg raloxifene: exhibit oestrogen-like agonist activity in some tissues, eg bone, whilst acting as antioestrogens in others, eg breast.

- Bisphosphonates: increase BMD and decrease fracture risk, with a magnitude of benefit similar to hormone-replacement therapy (HRT) (see below). They are particularly useful in steroid-induced bone loss. All the bisphosphonates have low bioavailability when taken orally and should be taken on an empty stomach. Oesophageal irritation/ulceration occasionally limits the use of these agents.

- Vitamin D: although not a cause of true osteoporosis, vitamin D deficiency and osteomalacia may compound bone fragility in the elderly.

- Teriparatide (recombinant parathyroid hormone).

- Strontium ranelate: by increasing bone formation and decreasing bone resorption, BMD increases with a decrease in fracture rates.

There are now published guidelines on the management of osteoporosis from the National Institute for

Health and Clinical Excellence (NICE) (http://www.nice.org.uk/). In women presenting with an osteoporotic fracture, first-line treatment is usually a bisphosphonate, having ensured that there is adequate calcium and/or vitamin D supplementation. SERMs are more generally used as second-line treatment. Postmenopausal females without fracture but with low BMD may be managed using bisphosphonates, SERMs and/or strontium ranelate. The use of teriparatide is currently limited to the treatment of osteoporosis in elderly women (>65 years of age) when bisphosphonates have not worked, or if the patient is intolerant of bisphosphonates and has a very high risk of fracture.

> ⚠ HRT has previously been used as a treatment for osteoporosis. However, in light of recent evidence, the risks of treatment (increased breast cancer, thromboembolic and cardiovascular disease; see Further reading below) must be balanced against benefits in relation to BMD. Accordingly, HRT is no longer recommended for the prevention or treatment of osteoporosis in postmenopausal females.

Males Exercise, calcium/vitamin D supplementation and bisphosphonates are also central to the prevention and management of osteoporotic fractures in males. Testosterone replacement is reserved for hypogonadal cases.

Prophylaxis with steroid treatment

Patients who require prolonged treatment with high doses of glucocorticoids (equivalent to ≥7.5 mg of prednisolone per day) should receive calcium/vitamin D supplementation and be considered for treatment with a bisphosphonate

for at least the duration of the steroid therapy.

Secondary osteoporosis

Where possible the underlying cause should be treated appropriately.

FURTHER READING

Rheumatology and Clinical Immunology, Section 1.4.5.

- - - - - - - - - - - - - -

Center J and Eisman J. The epidemiology and pathogenesis of osteoporosis. *Baillière's Clin. Endocrinol. Metab.* 1997; 11: 23–62.

- - - - - - - - - - - - - -

Raisz LG. Screening for osteoporosis. *NEJM* 2005; 353: 164–171.

- - - - - - - - - - - - - -

Rossouw JE, Anderson GL, Prentice RL, *et al*. Risks and benefits of estrogen plus progestin in healthy postmenopausal women: principal results from the Women's Health Initiative randomized controlled trial. *JAMA* 2002; 288: 321–33.

2.5.5 Osteomalacia

Osteomalacia is the result of defective bone mineralisation,

leading to weakness and an increased propensity to fracture with subsequent deformity. If this occurs during childhood before fusion of the epiphyseal plates, it is known as rickets.

Pathophysiology

The formation of bone is a two-stage process involving the deposition of unmineralised matrix and its subsequent mineralisation in a vitamin D-dependent process, requiring normal osteoblast function. The metabolic pathways leading to the synthesis of the active form of vitamin D (1,25-dihydroxyvitamin D_3) are shown in Fig. 51.

Table 48 lists the causes of osteomalacia; by far the commonest is reduced cutaneous production of vitamin D, which declines with age and is often exacerbated by reduced sunlight exposure and poor dietary intake. It is also more frequent following migration to a cooler climate, eg among Asian immigrants in the UK, where dietary consumption of phytates

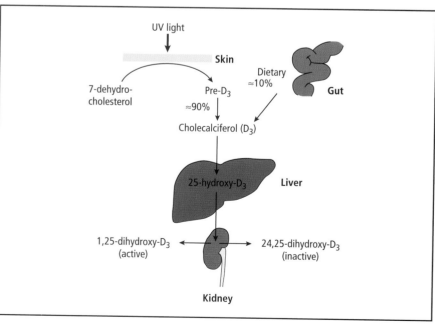

▲ **Fig. 51** Key steps in vitamin D metabolism.

TABLE 48 CAUSES OF OSTEOMALACIA

	Mechanism	Cause
Vitamin D deficiency	↓ Production	↓ Sunlight exposure ↓ Dietary intake Malabsorption, eg coeliac disease, intestinal resection Liver disease, eg primary biliary cirrhosis
	↑ Clearance	Enzyme inducers, eg anticonvulsants
	↓ 1-Hydroxylation	Renal failure Vitamin D-dependent rickets type I (AR)[1]
	↓ Action	Vitamin D-dependent rickets type II (AR)[2]
Hypophosphataemia	↓ Intake	Antacids (phosphate binding)
	↑ Loss	Hypophosphataemic rickets (vitamin D-resistant rickets, XLD) Fanconi syndrome Renal tubular acidosis Oncogenic osteomalacia
Defective mineralisation		Hypophosphatasia High-dose etidronate
Defective bone matrix		Fibrogenesis imperfecta ossium

1. Renal 25-hydroxyvitamin D 1α-hydroxylase deficiency.
2. Absent or defective vitamin D receptor.
AR, autosomal recessive; XLD, X-linked dominant.

- Low or low-normal serum phosphate (except in renal failure).

- Elevated serum alkaline phosphatase.

- Vitamin D levels: if measured, 1,25-dihydroxyvitamin D_3 levels are often normal, albeit inappropriately so in the face of hypocalcaemia, hypophosphataemia and secondary hyperparathyroidism. Vitamin D-dependent rickets type II is an exception to the rule.

> **Many of the biochemical findings are attributable to progressive secondary hyperparathyroidism.**

additionally impairs calcium absorption.

Epidemiology

Definitive diagnosis of osteomalacia depends on bone histology, so an accurate estimate of its prevalence is not readily available. The biochemical features of osteomalacia are present in about 5% of the elderly population and up to 10–20% of patients with hip fractures.

Clinical presentation and physical signs

The presentation of osteomalacia is often vague and insidious with a gradual onset of generalised muscle aches and pains. A history of immigration, long-term anticonvulsant use, gastric surgery, coeliac disease or other malabsorption should prompt consideration of the diagnosis. Proximal myopathy may occur and manifest as difficulty rising out of a chair or in climbing stairs (see Section 1.4.5). Features of hypocalcaemia may be present (see Section 2.5.9). A significant proportion of patients presenting with a pathological fracture have underlying osteomalacia. In childhood the characteristic features are of rickets with short stature, bowed legs and widened metaphyses (seen as 'rickety rosary' of the ribs).

Investigation

Although a definitive diagnosis of osteomalacia can only be made on bone biopsy, this is rarely indicated and most centres rely on biochemical and radiological evidence.

Bone chemistry

- Low or low-normal serum calcium.

Radiography

- Vertebrae: 'cod-fish' appearance due to ballooning of intervertebral disc.

- Pelvis, long bones, ribs: Looser's zones or 'pseudo-fractures', ie areas of low density representing unmineralised osteoid (Fig. 52).

- Rickets produces characteristic widening of the epiphyses with widening and cupping of the metaphyses.

Treatment

Multiple formulations of vitamin D and its metabolites are available. Osteomalacia due to vitamin D deficiency can usually be treated by dietary supplementation. For mild cases of dietary deficiency, replacement doses (800–1000 units daily) may suffice. However, in more severe deficiency and in patients with malabsorption, pharmacological doses are required: the dose, preparation and route of delivery

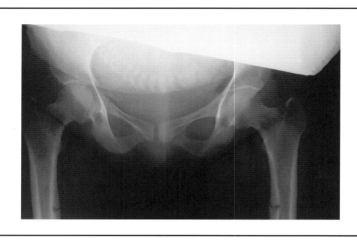

▲**Fig. 52** Looser's zones. Pelvic radiograph showing pseudo-fractures (Looser's zones, ie areas of low density) in a patient with severe osteomalacia.

should be determined in conjunction with a physician with an interest in metabolic bone disorders. Calcium supplementation may also be required, with close monitoring of serum calcium levels to avoid induction of hypercalcaemia. The treatment of rickets secondary to phosphate wasting disorders requires oral supplementation sufficient to balance renal losses. Co-administration of vitamin D is often required to prevent hypocalcaemia. Any underlying disorder, eg coeliac disease, should be managed appropriately.

Prognosis

With treatment, hypocalcaemia, hypophosphataemia and any accompanying symptoms, including proximal myopathy, improve over several weeks. Alkaline phosphatase and parathyroid hormone levels may take up to 6 months to normalise, during which time the bone remains weak and liable to fracture.

FURTHER READING

Francis RM and Selby PL. Osteomalacia. *Baillière's Clin. Endocrinol. Metab.* 1997; 11: 145–63.

2.5.6 Paget's disease

Paget's disease of bone was first described by Sir James Paget in 1879 as 'osteitis deformans'. It is characterised by grossly disordered bone formation giving rise to deformity and pain.

Aetiology/pathophysiology

The cause of Paget's disease remains uncertain. Evidence suggests both genetic and environmental influences. Heterozygous mutations in one or other of two genes have been documented in some cases.

The primary disorder appears to be an increase in the number and activity of osteoclasts, possibly as a consequence of exposure to a viral pathogen (although the latter remains contentious). This is followed by imperfect osteoblast-mediated bone repair. Thus, the normal regulation of bone resorption and new bone formation is lost, with subsequent production of hypertrophied osteosclerotic bone. Bone deformity and pain are common, together with partial and pathological fractures. The disease process mainly affects the axial skeleton, skull and long bones, and frequently results in secondary osteoarthritis and nerve root entrapment.

Epidemiology

Approximately 1% of European and North American Caucasians aged 40 years or over are affected. It is uncommon in other ethnic groups.

Clinical presentation

Paget's disease is not infrequently an incidental radiological finding, or comes to light during the investigation of an elevated alkaline phosphatase noted on routine blood tests in an otherwise asymptomatic individual. Bone pain may reflect disease activity, which is often localised but multicentric, although it can also arise as a result of partial or complete fractures. The deformed bone places abnormal stresses on adjacent joints with subsequent osteoarthritis. The characteristic bony deformities (bowing of long bones and thickening of the skull) may be noticed by the patient. Nerve root entrapment can affect any of the cranial nerves (classically the eighth nerve, resulting in deafness) or spinal nerve roots. Occasionally enlargement of the base of the skull (platybasia) leads to paraplegia or aqueductal stenosis and hydrocephalus.

Physical signs

Bony deformities

- Enlargement of the skull with frontal bossing.

- Bowing of long bones, especially the tibia.

- Kyphosis of the skeleton.

Increased vascularity

- Warmth over affected bones.

- Prominence of superficial temporal arteries.

- High cardiac output (bounding pulse, cardiac failure).

Nerve entrapment

- Deafness.

Investigation

Biochemistry

- Alkaline phosphatase is usually raised, but without abnormalities of serum calcium or phosphate (except following prolonged immobility when hypercalcaemia may occur).

- Other markers of bone resorption (eg urinary deoxypyridinoline) may provide evidence of increased bone turnover, but are not routinely measured.

Radiology

Plain radiographs May show localised enlargement of bone with cortical thickening and localised areas of both sclerosis and osteolysis (Fig. 53).

Radioisotope scanning Bone scintigraphy allows demonstration of the full extent of bone involvement.

Treatment

Bisphosphonates are the mainstay of treatment for symptomatic Paget's disease, and produce a prolonged marked reduction of bone resorption by inhibiting osteoclast activity. Administration is followed by decreased uptake on bone scanning, reduction in alkaline phosphatase, stabilisation of hearing loss and improvement in other neurological dysfunction. The role of bisphosphonates in asymptomatic patients remains unclear, and further trials are awaited. Treatment with salmon calcitonin provides an alternative for those patients who are unable to tolerate bisphosphonates.

Accompanying arthritis requires suitable analgesia and knee or hip replacement as indicated.

Complications

In addition to the neurological (nerve entrapment), rheumatological (osteoarthritis) and cardiac (high-output cardiac failure) complications, osteosarcoma occurs in ≤1% of cases; it is not yet known whether the risk is reduced by bisphosphonates.

> ⚠ **In a patient with Paget's disease, soft tissue swelling, increased pain or a rapidly rising alkaline phosphatase level should alert the clinician to the possibility of a developing osteosarcoma.**

FURTHER READING

Whyte MP. Clinical practice: Paget's disease of bone. *N. Engl. J. Med.* 2006; 355: 593–600.

2.5.7 Hyperparathyroidism

Pathophysiology

There are normally four parathyroid glands, closely related to the thyroid, although occasionally there may be extra glands, eg ectopically sited in the superior mediastinum. Hyperparathyroidism means overproduction of parathyroid hormone (PTH). Conventionally, this is classified as primary, secondary or tertiary, although some clinicians argue that secondary and tertiary should be grouped together.

Primary hyperparathyroidism refers to production of PTH in a physiologically inappropriate manner that is not entrained to serum calcium levels. It is most frequently the result of a single adenoma, but in about 20% of cases there are multiple adenomas or diffuse hyperplasia of all four glands. Parathyroid carcinoma is rare (~1% of cases). *Secondary*

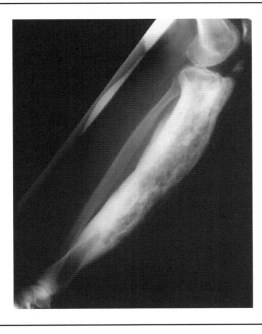

▲ **Fig. 53** Paget's disease of the tibia. Involvement of the weight-bearing long bones leads to bowing, particularly of the femur and, as shown here, the tibia ('sabre' tibia), which bow anteriorly and laterally. Note that the fibula is spared.

hyperparathyroidism refers to hyperplasia and hypersecretion of PTH as part of the homeostatic response to chronically low serum calcium, almost invariably due to renal disease with deficiency of activated vitamin D. This PTH hypersecretion generally restores serum calcium levels to normal, at the expense of bone mineral loss. Screening for this and intervening with activated vitamin D at the appropriate stage of chronic renal disease is important in both preserving bone mineral density and preventing autonomous parathyroid adenomas arising from the hyperplastic parathyroid glands. Once this occurs, with an attendant rise in serum calcium, *tertiary* hyperparathyroidism is said to have developed.

The excess PTH produces hypercalcaemia through three routes:

- increased osteoclastic bone resorption;

- increased renal calcium reabsorption (although note that the increase in serum calcium usually overwhelms the resorptive capacity of the tubules, and hence hypercalciuria is the norm in hyperparathyroidism);

- increased intestinal calcium absorption (mediated through increased vitamin D activity).

Epidemiology
The prevalence is estimated to be approximately 0.1–0.2%, affecting females twice as frequently as males.

Clinical presentation and physical signs
Asymptomatic hypercalcaemia, discovered on routine biochemical testing, is now most commonly the first indication of the diagnosis. A smaller number of cases present with hyperparathyroid renal disease (urolithiasis, nephrocalcinosis) or hyperparathyroid bone disease, leading to bone pain, especially once osteoporosis is established. Other features of hypercalcaemia may also be present (see Section 2.5.8).

Investigation

Routine biochemistry
Hypercalcaemia is an almost universal finding in patients with primary hyperparathyroidism. The serum phosphate level is usually low-normal or low, reflecting the effects of PTH in promoting urinary phosphate excretion. Alkaline phosphatase levels are typically normal or mildly elevated. Urea and electrolytes should be checked and occasionally more formal assessment of renal function, eg determination of glomerular filtration rate, is required. A 24-hour collection for estimation of urinary calcium excretion should be performed; this will also help to discriminate hyperparathyroidism from familial hypocalciuric hypercalcaemia, an asymptomatic trait caused by loss-of-function mutations in the parathyroid calcium-sensing receptor.

PTH levels
Confirmation of the diagnosis can be made by determining the intact PTH level in a two-site assay (using monoclonal antibodies directed against both ends of the full-length PTH molecule), which fails to detect the smaller fragment PTH-related peptide. The finding of an elevated or normal PTH level is inappropriate in the setting of hypercalcaemia.

Radiology

Manifestations of hyperparathyroidism The radiological hallmark of hyperparathyroid bone disease (osteitis fibrosa cystica) is the subperiosteal erosion, most easily seen in the distal phalanges of the fingers. A similar process in the skull results in the so-called 'pepper-pot' appearance. Occasionally osteolytic lesions are seen, suggesting the presence of bone cysts or 'brown tumours'. Long-standing hyperparathyroidism leads to generalised osteoporosis, which may be evident on plain radiographs. Nephrocalcinosis and urolithiasis are sometimes identified on plain abdominal radiographs or ultrasound examination of the renal tract (Fig. 54).

Localisation of tumours It has been argued by many that preoperative imaging is unnecessary prior to initial surgical exploration in an uncomplicated case, and that an experienced surgeon should be able to determine the aetiology and effect the appropriate treatment for primary hyperparathyroidism. However, with the advent of minimally invasive parathyroid surgery (see below) and in cases of surgical re-exploration, localisation studies including ultrasonography, ^{99m}Tc-sestamibi (Fig. 55), CT/MRI and/or venous sampling may be useful.

Treatment

Emergency/short-term
Hypercalcaemia should be treated as outlined in Section 2.5.8.

Long-term
The definitive treatment of primary hyperparathyroidism is parathyroid gland surgery. Whilst it is widely accepted that virtually all symptomatic patients should be offered surgery, there is greater debate as to the appropriate management of apparently 'asymptomatic' individuals.

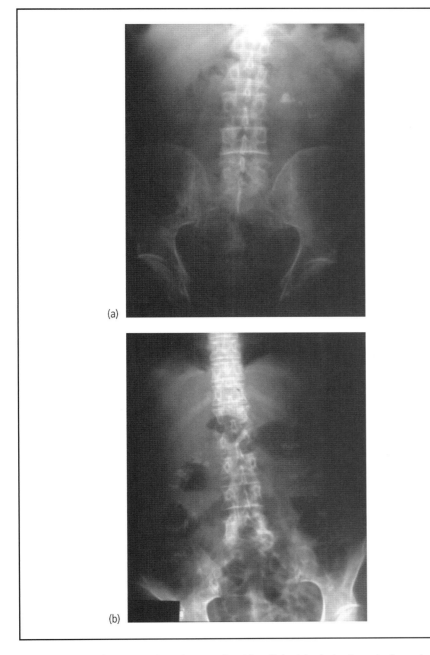

(a)

(b)

▲ **Fig. 54** Renal involvement in primary hyperparathyroidism. Plain abdominal radiographs demonstrating nephrolithiasis (**a**) and nephrocalcinosis (**b**) in the setting of primary hyperparathyroidism.

- symptomatic disease;

- serum calcium >3 mmol/L;

- radiological evidence of urolithiasis or nephrocalcinosis;

- established osteoporosis.

When surgery is not undertaken, regular monitoring is required to check for disease progression/ development of complications.

Some centres now offer minimally invasive parathyroid surgery, in which preoperative localisation is used to guide the surgeon to the site of the adenoma, thus avoiding more formal neck exploration. Intraoperative PTH measurements help to confirm complete excision prior to closure, by virtue of the short half-life of PTH.

Calcimimetics, drugs that mimic the effect of calcium on the parathyroid calcium-sensing receptor and so decrease the synthesis and/or secretion of PTH, may provide an alternative to surgery in some cases. However, currently these agents are not widely available.

Disease associations
Primary hyperparathyroidism occasionally occurs as part of the multiple endocrine neoplasia syndromes (see Section 2.7.1). In such cases there is usually four-gland hyperplasia rather than a single adenoma, and thus conventional rather than minimally invasive surgery is required.

Important information for patients
Where primary hyperparathyrodism is an incidental finding, the indications for, and complications of, surgery must be carefully discussed with the patient. The requirement for follow-up, particularly if surgery is not initially undertaken, should also be stressed, and the patient advised to maintain

For example, in one long-term follow-up study neither the primary hyperparathyroidism nor its associated bone disease progressed over a 10-year period in the majority of cases. However, in approximately 25% significant worsening of osteoporosis was noted, as determined by serial bone densitometry. In addition, parathyroidectomy (when performed) corrected the abnormal biochemistry and produced a sustained increase in lumbar spine and femoral neck bone density in these 'asymptomatic' patients.

In general, parathyroid surgery should at least be offered to young patients (<50 years of age) and also to those with:

adequate hydration (especially in hot weather) and to avoid thiazide diuretics.

FURTHER READING

Silverberg SJ and Bilezikian JP. The diagnosis and management of asymptomatic primary hyperparathyroidism. *Nat. Clin. Pract. Endocrinol. Metab.* 2006; 2: 494–503.

Utiger RD. Treatment of primary hyperparathyroidism. *N. Engl. J. Med.* 1999; 341: 1301–2.

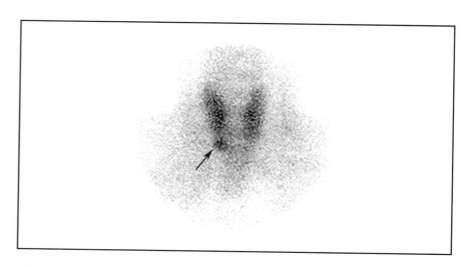

▲**Fig. 55** Parathyroid adenoma. ^{99m}Tc-sestamibi scan showing a parathyroid adenoma (arrow) in close proximity to the inferior pole of the right lobe of the thyroid gland.

2.5.8 Hypercalcaemia

Aetiology/pathophysiology

Regulation of calcium metabolism

The vast majority of body calcium is found in bone and teeth, with only about 1% in extracellular fluid and within cells. Of the extracellular calcium, approximately half is bound to protein (mainly albumin) or complexed to anions (phosphate, citrate and bicarbonate), with the other half existing as free ionised calcium (the bioavailable fraction). Hormonal control of extracellular calcium is exerted mainly by parathyroid hormone (PTH) and vitamin D (Fig. 56). Broadly speaking, the role of PTH is to act rapidly to maintain extracellular free calcium, whilst the actions of vitamin D are directed towards preserving skeletal calcium levels, both to act as structural support and as a reservoir of calcium.

Causes of hypercalcaemia

The major causes of hypercalcaemia are listed in Table 1. The two most important and prevalent groups are hyperparathyroidism and malignancy. Hyperparathyroidism is dealt with in detail in Section 2.5.7. Malignancy can lead to

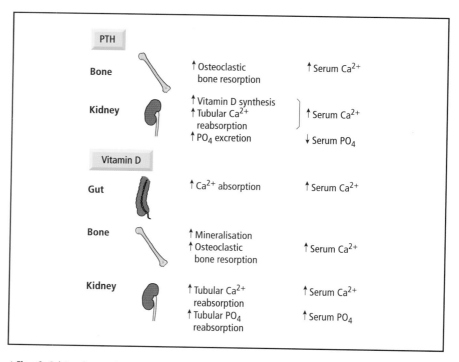

▲**Fig. 56** Calcium homeostasis.

hypercalcaemia via a number of direct and paraneoplastic mechanisms including:

- osteolytic bone metastases (eg breast, bronchus, kidney or thyroid cancer);

- production of PTH-related peptide, which has PTH-like effects (eg squamous cell lung cancer);

- production of cytokines (eg osteoclast activating factor) with bone-resorbing activity, eg multiple myeloma;

- production of vitamin D, eg lymphoma (rare).

The hypercalcaemia associated with some granulomatous disorders, particularly sarcoidosis, is thought to be due to 1α-hydroxylation of vitamin D by granulomas. It is thus classically aggravated by exposure to sunlight, producing summertime rises in the incidence of sarcoidosis-related hypercalcaemia. Vitamin D intoxication is an occasional cause of hypercalcaemia.

Clinical presentation and physical signs

Hypercalcaemia is often an incidental finding in an otherwise apparently asymptomatic individual. In others, symptoms and signs are varied and are often remembered according to the mnemonic 'stones, bones, abdominal groans and psychic moans'.

- Stones: renal colic (urolithiasis), polyuria and polydipsia (nephrogenic diabetes insipidus), nephrocalcinosis.

- Bones: arthritis and bone pain.

- Abdominal groans: nausea and vomiting, anorexia, constipation, peptic ulcer, pancreatitis.

- Psychic moans: lethargy, fatigue, depression, confusion, psychosis.

In addition, chronic hypercalcaemia may be associated with corneal calcification (band keratopathy). In all cases a thorough physical examination should be undertaken, looking for features which suggest an underlying cause, especially malignancy.

Investigation
See Section 1.1.1.

Treatment
Mild hypercalcaemia, detected as the result of routine biochemistry in an otherwise asymptomatic patient, may require no specific treatment. However, such cases should be investigated to establish the underlying cause. The need for adequate hydration, especially

in hot weather, and avoidance of thiazide diuretics should be stressed.

Emergency/short-term
Emergency management of severe hypercalcaemia is described in Section 1.4.2.

Long-term
The long-term management of hypercalcaemia is directed at the underlying condition. Where such treatment fails to control hypercalcaemia, repeated therapy with bisphosphonates may be indicated.

Complications
Long-standing hypercalcaemia can result in ectopic calcification. Renal stones and nephrocalcinosis are both well described, as is widespread calcification of the medial layer of arterial walls. Hypercalcaemia is also a recognised cause of a shortened QT interval on the ECG.

Prognosis
In general, the prognosis is dictated by the underlying disease.

FURTHER READING

Bushinsky DA and Monk RD. Electrolyte quintet: calcium. *Lancet* 1998; 352: 306–11.

2.5.9 Hypocalcaemia

Aetiology/pathophysiology
The causes of hypocalcaemia are listed in Table 49.

Since albumin is the principal calcium-binding protein in blood, hypoalbuminaemic states may be associated with apparent hypocalcaemia by virtue of reducing total calcium levels. Ionised calcium, however, remains unchanged. Accordingly, many laboratories routinely issue a 'corrected' calcium result, which includes an adjustment up or down from the measured level depending on whether the recorded albumin is below or above a defined 'normal' set-point, respectively.

TABLE 49 CAUSES OF HYPOCALCAEMIA

Mechanism	Examples
Hypoparathyroidism	Post surgery Idiopathic/acquired Congenital
'Resistance' to action of PTH	Renal failure Drugs that impair osteoclastic bone resorption, eg bisphosphonates, calcitonin Pseudohypoparathyroidism
Vitamin D deficiency/resistance	
Acute pancreatitis	
Hypomagnesaemia	Alcoholism Gastrointestinal losses
Hyperphosphataemia	Rhabdomyolysis Excessive phosphate administration
Malignant disease	

PTH, parathyroid hormone.

The balance between total and ionised calcium is affected by acid–base balance and occasionally by the presence of anions such as citrate, such that a low ionised calcium, with the clinical features of hypocalcaemia, may occur in alkalosis and following extensive blood transfusion, even though the measured serum level lies within the normal range.

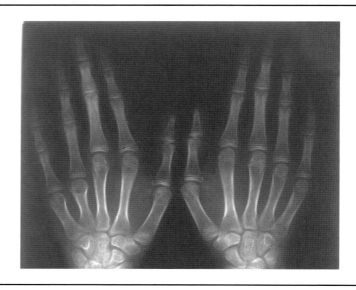

▲ **Fig. 57** Pseudohypoparathyroidism. Plain radiograph demonstrating the classical short fourth and fifth metacarpals of pseudohypoparathyroidism in the left hand compared, in this case, with normal appearances on the right.

Hypoparathyroidism

In hypoparathyroidism PTH deficiency leads to:

- increased renal loss of calcium and retention of phosphate;

- reduced bone resorption;

- reduced calcium absorption (as a consequence of impaired 1-hydroxylation of 25-hydroxyvitamin D_3).

Serum phosphate levels are therefore high and alkaline phosphatase low.

Hypoparathyroidism most commonly arises in the setting of previous neck surgery, eg thyroidectomy. A period of transient hypocalcaemia may follow removal of a parathyroid adenoma, pending restoration of PTH secretion by the remaining intact glands. Occasionally this can be severe, reflecting avid uptake of calcium and phosphate by bone which has been chronically stimulated by PTH ('hungry bone syndrome'). Idiopathic (acquired) hypoparathyroidism may occur as an isolated finding or is sometimes seen in the setting of the polyglandular endocrinopathies (see Section 2.7.2).

Pseudohypoparathyroidism

Pseudohypoparathyroidism is a rare disorder resulting from target organ resistance to the action of PTH. The clinical and biochemical features of hypoparathyroidism are frequently accompanied by a characteristic somatic phenotype including short stature, a rounded face and short fourth and fifth metacarpals (Fig. 57). PTH levels are high. Interestingly, other family members may exhibit the somatic features without evidence of disordered calcium metabolism, so called pseudo-pseudohypoparathyroidism.

Clinical presentation

Hypocalcaemia causes tetany, cramps, paraesthesiae of the extremities and muscle spasms precipitated by exercise or hypoxia. Seizure threshold is reduced and fits may occur. Chronic hypocalcaemia produces lethargy/malaise, and may mimic psychosis.

Physical signs

- In hypocalcaemia, latent tetany can be provoked by inflating a sphygmomanometer cuff to 10–20 mmHg greater than systolic BP for 3 minutes. Carpopedal spasm results in the hand adopting a characteristic posture referred to as *main d'accoucher* (Trousseau's sign).

- Tapping the facial nerve in front of the ear may induce a brief contraction of the facial muscles on that side (Chvostek's sign).

Other manifestations of chronic hypocalcaemia include dystrophic nails, alopecia, subcapsular cataracts, papilloedema and occasionally movement disorders (reflecting basal ganglia calcification). Signs of other autoimmune endocrine failure (eg hypothyroidism, hypoadrenalism) may also be present.

Investigation

Relevant blood tests include urea and electrolytes (checking for renal failure), liver function tests (including albumin and alkaline phosphatase), serum calcium and phosphate. Arterial blood gases may be needed to confirm an underlying alkalosis. Further tests may include determination of 25-hydroxyvitamin D_3 (the most reliable indicator of total body stores of vitamin D) and PTH levels, whilst a failure to increase urinary cAMP in response to infused PTH (Ellsworth–Howard test) may be used to confirm resistance to PTH action in pseudohypoparathyroidism.

Treatment

Emergency

⚠️ In acute, severe, symptomatic hypocalcaemia, intravenous calcium, given as 10 mL of 10% calcium gluconate over 5–10 minutes, should be followed by a maintenance infusion: see the *British National Formulary* (BNF) for guidelines. Oral calcium and vitamin D should be commenced as soon as possible.

🔑 If hypocalcaemia proves refractory to treatment, serum magnesium levels should also be checked.

Long-term

Specific underlying causes require appropriate management. As treatment with PTH is not available, hypoparathyroidism is managed using a combination of alfacalcidol (1α-hydroxycholecalciferol) or calcitriol (1,25-dihydroxycholecalciferol) together with calcium supplements (eg Sandocal) as required. The dose must be carefully titrated, aiming to keep the serum calcium level in the low-normal range (thereby reducing the risk of nephrolithiasis and nephrocalcinosis).

FURTHER READING

Bushinsky DA and Monk RD. Electrolyte quintet: calcium. *Lancet* 1998; 352: 306–11.

TABLE 50 CLASSIFICATION OF DM

Type of diabetes	Condition
Type 1 diabetes (~10%)	Autoimmune or idiopathic
Type 2 diabetes (~85%)	
Specific types of diabetes (<5%)	Endocrine causes, eg Cushing's syndrome, acromegaly, phaeochromocytoma, glucagonoma
	Pancreatic diorders, eg pancreatitis, trauma/neoplasia, pancreatectomy, haemochromatosis, cystic fibrosis
	Genetic defects in β-cell function or insulin action, eg MODY, MELAS syndrome, type A insulin resistance, lipodystrophy
	Drug or chemical induced, eg glucocorticoids, thiazides, pentamidine
	Other genetic syndromes associated with diabetes, eg Down's, Turner's, Klinefelter's, Lawrence–Moon–Biedel, Prader–Willi, and dystrophia myotonica
Gestational diabetes	

MELAS, myopathy, encephalopathy, lactic acidosis, stroke-like episodes; MODY, maturity-onset diabetes of the young.

2.6 Diabetes mellitus

Diabetes mellitus (DM) refers to a group of metabolic disorders characterised by chronic hyperglycaemia and disturbances of carbohydrate, protein and fat metabolism that result from inadequate production and/or impaired action of insulin. Table 50 outlines the current scheme for classification of this disorder.

Aetiology
See Table 51.

Type 1 diabetes
In genetically susceptible individuals, one or more environmental factors trigger immune-mediated destruction of islet β cells (insulinitis) leading to complete deficiency of insulin.

Type 2 diabetes
In the vast majority of type 2 diabetics the principal abnormality is one of insulin resistance. In the very early phase of the disease, euglycaemia may be maintained by increased insulin production. However, if insulin secretion is insufficient to compensate, impaired glucose tolerance or frank diabetes results. This typically occurs as a result of β-cell exhaustion. Occasionally, insulin sensitivity is normal but insulin production is reduced, eg maturity-onset diabetes of the young (MODY); diabetes again results.

Epidemiology

Type 1 diabetes

- Incidence increasing; high prevalence in Caucasians (Europe, North America and Australia).

- Prevalence 0.3% in the UK.

- Typically young age at presentation. Peak incidence: 10–12 years of age.

Type 2 diabetes

- Prevalence varies in different countries but increasing markedly, especially in developing countries. Prevalence in the UK white

TABLE 51 AETIOLOGY AND PATHOGENESIS OF DM

	Type 1	Type 2 and other specific types of diabetes
Genetics	Polygenic. Several susceptibility loci have been identified (*IDDM-1*, *IDDM-2*, etc). *IDDM-1* is the major susceptibility locus, associated with HLA class II genes, situated on chromosome 6p HLA-DR3 and/or -DR4 are found in >90% of type 1 diabetics HLA-DQ (a variant of HLA-DQ β gene) is more closely associated with diabetes *IDDM-2* is the insulin gene locus present on chromosome 11p and is also linked with diabetes	High identical twin concordance (60–100%), familial aggregation and varying prevalence in different ethnic populations suggest a strong genetic component In only about 2% of cases has the genetic mutation been identified, eg MODY types 1 (*HNF4A* gene), 2 (glucokinase gene) and 3 (*HNF1A* gene); MELAS syndrome (mitochondrial DNA mutations)
Environmental factors	Viruses: coxsackie, rubella, mumps, CMV, EBV, etc. Dietary constituents: BSA in cow's milk, especially if infants are fed on it Nitrosamines in certain foods Stress	Strongly associated with obesity BMI >35 kg/m^2 incurs a 40-fold increase in risk compared with BMI <23 kg/m^2 Obesity is present in more than two-thirds of type 2 patients and associated with insulin resistance Malnutrition *in utero* may be linked with increased risk (fetal programming)
Aetiology	Evidence of autoimmunity: HLA genes on chromosome 6 are closely linked to immune modulation; association of type 1 diabetes with other autoimmune diseases; immunosuppressants can prolong β-cell survival	Insulin resistance: whole-body insulin resistance is present in type 2 diabetes. Increased secretion of insulin can limit hyperglycaemia but patients with coexisting β-cell dysfunction are likely to develop diabetes
	Mechanism of autoimmunity: probably T cell-mediated as there is a mononuclear cell infiltrate in the islets (insulinitis) Autoantibodies associated with type 1 diabetes: ICA are present in around 90% of newly diagnosed type 1 diabetics. Other antibodies present include GAD, tyrosine phosphate antibodies and IAA	Defects of insulin secretion: in type 2 diabetics insulin levels are low relative to the degree of hyperglycaemia, with blunting of the acute first phase and other abnormalities of stimulated insulin secretion. Diabetes results if insulin secretion can no longer compensate for the degree of insulin resistance present

BSA, bovine serum albumin; CMV, cytomegalovirus; EBV, Epstein–Barr virus; GAD, glutamic acid decarboxylase; HLA, human leucocyte antigen; IAA, insulin autoantibodies; ICA, islet cell antibodies; IDDM, insulin-dependent diabetes mellitus; MELAS, myopathy, encephalopathy, lactic acidosis, stroke-like episode; MODY, maturity-onset diabetes of the young.

population ~3%, higher in some ethnic groups.

- Strongly linked with the rising prevalence of obesity.

- Predominantly affects older people, with a peak incidence between 50 and 70 years of age.

Clinical presentation

The classic triad of diabetic symptoms consists of:

- polyuria;

- increased thirst (polydipsia);

- weight loss.

These features (Table 52) typically manifest in an acute or subacute fashion in those with type 1

diabetes. Opportunistic infection – such as bacterial (particularly *staphylococcal*) abscess and fungal sepsis – is common. In contrast, patients with type 2 diabetes often give a history of chronic progressive non-specific symptoms, predominantly tiredness. Because of the long interval between disease onset and presentation it is not uncommon for complications to be present at the time of diagnosis or to define the presenting complaint.

Unfortunately, some patients still present as medical emergencies with acute decompensation of their previously unrecognised diabetic state:

- diabetic ketoacidosis (DKA) in those with type 1 diabetes;

- hyperosmolar non-ketotic coma (HONK) in those with type 2 diabetes.

Physical signs

In younger type 1 diabetics there may be clinical evidence of weight loss, dehydration and ketosis, and perhaps opportunistic infection. Older patients with type 2 diabetes not infrequently present with established complications. Those with secondary diabetes may have obvious features of the primary pathology, eg steroid excess, bronzing, acromegaly.

Drowsiness/coma, dehydration and hypotension are common findings in both DKA and HONK. Kussmaul

TABLE 52 CLINICAL FEATURES OF DM: FEATURES OF UNDERLYING CONDITIONS MAY BE PRESENT IN SECONDARY DIABETES

Type 1	Type 2
Usually sudden onset	Mostly gradual onset
Usually lean individuals	Mostly obese individuals
Polyuria (++)	Polyuria (+)
Polydipsia (++)	Polydipsia (+)
Weight loss (+++)	Weight loss (+/−)
Tiredness (++)	Tiredness (+)
Blurred vision (+)	Blurred vision (+/−)
Balanitis, thrush, pruritis vulvae (+)	Balanitis, thrush, pruritis vulvae (++)
Neuritis (++)	Neuritis (+)
Presentation with DKA (not uncommon)	Presentation with HONK (rare)
Presentation with diabetic complications (rare)	Presentation with diabetic complications (common)
Absent C-peptide	C-peptide present
Markers of autoimmunity, eg ICA, usually present	Markers of autoimmunity usually absent

ICA, islet cell antibodies.

respiration (indicating ketosis and acidosis) is usually limited to DKA. It is important to examine for evidence of a precipitating cause, eg infection or myocardial infarction, although this is only found in approximately one-third of cases.

Investigations

Urinalysis

Glycosuria may suggest the presence of diabetes but is not diagnostic and requires confirmation with a blood test. Conversely, absence of glycosuria does not exclude diabetes. It is important to document the presence or absence of ketones. Blood, protein, nitrites and leucocytes should also be noted.

Blood glucose

The World Health Organization (WHO) recommend that the diagnosis of DM should be made on the basis of a fasting venous plasma glucose level of ≥7.0 mmol/L, which should be confirmed on a second occasion. However, the diagnosis can also be made in a symptomatic patient whose random venous plasma glucose is ≥11.1 mmol/L. In those with a random glucose between 5.5 and 11.1 mmol/L, a fasting glucose level should be checked. Subjects with a fasting venous plasma glucose between 6.1 and 6.9 mmol/L are classified as having impaired fasting glycaemia (IFG). Following an oral glucose tolerance test (OGTT) (see Section 3.1.7) they may be reclassified as diabetic if 2-hour venous glucose >11.1 mmol/l, as having impaired glucose tolerance (IGT) if 2-hour venous glucose 7.8–11.1 mmol/L, or remain as IFG if 2-hour venous glucose <7.8 mmol/L.

IFG and IGT are metabolic states between normal glucose homeostasis and diabetes. Both (especially IFG) are predictors of the risk of progression to diabetes and both (particularly IGT) are associated with higher risk of future cardiovascular disease. They incur little or no risk of microvascular complications. Some people with IFG/IGT may revert to normal.

Others

- Routine blood tests: urea and electrolytes, glycosylated haemoglobin (HbA$_{1c}$), lipid profile, thyroid function, liver chemistry.

- ECG and CXR (especially in the older patient).

- Retinal pictures/eye screening.

2.6.1 Management of hyperglycaemic emergencies

Although the basic principles of management for DKA and HONK are similar, there are some important differences reflecting the distinction between absolute and relative insulin deficiency. For example:

- DKA occurs in type 1 diabetics lacking any insulin and is accompanied by ketosis and acidosis;

- HONK arises in type 2 diabetics, with hyperosmolality the predominant biochemical feature.

Both may be precipitated by inadequate treatment (intentional, accidental or misguided) or physical stress such as infection, stroke or myocardial infarction.

Remember that prompt treatment is required. Do not waste time performing unnecessary tests.

Investigations

In all cases check the following.

- Laboratory glucose: to confirm hyperglycaemia.

- Urea and electrolytes: potassium status, renal impairment.

- FBC: for neutrophilia (either as a feature of DKA or as a marker of infection).

- Arterial blood gases/venous bicarbonate: for acidosis.

- Urinalysis: for ketones.

Depending on clinical status consider:

- C-reactive protein and a septic screen (blood cultures, CXR and midstream urine);

- ECG and cardiac enzymes.

Treatment

Both conditions carry a significant mortality (2–5% in DKA and up to 30% in HONK). Treatment must be instituted promptly, beginning with basic supportive measures (to maintain airway, breathing and circulation).

Fluids

Dehydration and severe volume depletion (5–10 L) must be corrected as a matter of priority.

> - Aim to give 5–6 L within the first 24 hours (eg 1 L over 1 hour, followed by 1 L over 2 hours, then 1 L over 4 hours with 1 L every 4–8 hours thereafter), but bear in mind the clinical setting, eg a fit 20 year old is likely to tolerate more aggressive fluid replacement than an elderly patient with a history of cardiac disease. Consider central venous pressure (CVP) monitoring in the latter group.
> - Give an initial 500-mL bolus of colloid if hypotension (systolic BP <100 mmHg) is present, otherwise begin replacement with normal saline. Half-normal saline is preferred if the serum sodium level exceeds 155 mmol/L; however, this must be accompanied by frequent (every 2 hours) monitoring of the serum sodium to prevent a precipitous decline with consequent cerebral oedema. When blood glucose falls below 12 mmol/L, 5% dextrose should be substituted in place of saline.

Potassium

Acidosis often results in transient extracellular hyperkalaemia, and accordingly it is reasonable to omit potassium from the first bag of fluid whilst the results of electrolytes are awaited. However, remember that patients are potassium depleted.

> Thereafter, beware of hypokalaemia, which may develop rapidly. Do not wait for the serum potassium to reach low levels before commencing replacement. Remember, insulin forces potassium inside cells and total body potassium levels are low.
>
> Electrolytes should be measured every 2 hours in the initial stages and potassium added as required.
>
> - Serum [K$^+$] >5.0 mmol/L: none.
> - Serum [K$^+$] 3.5–5.0 mmol/L: 20 mmol KCl per litre.
> - Serum [K$^+$] <3.5 mmol/L: 40 mmol KCl per litre.

Insulin

Add 50 units of soluble insulin to 49.5 mL of normal saline (1 unit/mL) and infuse via a pump at a rate determined by the blood glucose level (Table 53), which should be checked every hour at the bedside. If there is any delay in obtaining a pump, give intravenous soluble insulin at a rate of 6 units/hour.

> Remember, however, that insulin is being given first and foremost to switch off ketosis and normalisation of blood glucose is not the priority. If blood glucose falls to <12 mmol/L, switch to dextrose and maintain the insulin infusion at a rate sufficient to suppress ketosis and therefore acidosis.

Many hospitals have formal guidelines for the management of DKA.

Other considerations

- Broad-spectrum intravenous antibiotics if there is any suspicion of an infectious precipitant.

- Insertion of a nasogastric tube to prevent aspiration if the conscious level is depressed. Remember acidosis delays gastric emptying.

- Systemic anticoagulation in all cases of HONK, which is deemed to be a hypercoagulable state.

- Bicarbonate: should not be given routinely as it may exacerbate intracellular acidosis, and should be reserved for very sick patients with severe acidosis (pH <7.0). Give 200–500 mL of a 1.4%

TABLE 53 SLIDING SCALE FOR INSULIN INFUSION IN DKA AND HONK. DKA MAY REQUIRE HIGHER INFUSION RATES IF THE BLOOD GLUCOSE LEVEL FAILS TO FALL DURING THE FIRST 1–2 HOURS. IN CONTRAST, PATIENTS WITH HONK MAY REQUIRE LOWER INFUSION RATES TO AVOID DRAMATIC FALLS IN BLOOD GLUCOSE WITH ASSOCIATED FLUID SHIFTS

Blood glucose (mmol/L)	Insulin infusion rate [mL(units)/hour]
<5	0.5
5.1–10.0	2.0
10.1–15.0	3.0
>15.0	6.0

solution with additional KCl (20 mmol) over 30 minutes, ideally within the high-dependency/intensive-care setting.

Transition to subcutaneous insulin/oral agents

Continue the insulin infusion until the ketosis/acidosis is controlled, usually reflected by normalisation of blood glucose levels (<12 mmol/L), with no more than 1+ of ketonuria, in a patient tolerating a normal diet. Transition to subcutaneous insulin should ideally take place early in the day so that problems can be promptly dealt with. The intravenous infusion should only be discontinued after the first dose of subcutaneous insulin has been given.

Known type 1 diabetics can often be re-established on their original regimen (unless this contributed to the DKA), whilst newly diagnosed patients should be started on a 'gentle' bd regimen (see below). In some patients with HONK and no evidence of ketonuria, it may be possible to start on oral hypoglycaemic agents.

Patients must be reviewed by a diabetes specialist nurse and dietitian prior to discharge: they provide much needed telephone support. Arrange follow-up in a specialist clinic.

2.6.2 Management of hypoglycaemic emergencies

Hypoglycaemia may occur in diabetics treated with insulin and/or certain oral hypoglycaemic agents. The precipitant is usually a missed or delayed meal, increased activity, excess alcohol or following medication errors (usually non-deliberate). The longer-acting, renally excreted sulphonylureas such as glibenclamide can cause severe prolonged hypoglycaemia.

Those at particular risk are the elderly and patients with renal impairment.

Clinical presentation

- The major features of hypoglycaemia are either autonomic (eg sweating, tremor, palpitations) or neuroglycopenic (eg headache, cognitive impairment, altered conscious state, visual disturbance). The autonomic symptoms usually provide an early warning of hypoglycaemia, but warnings may be reduced in the presence of autonomic neuropathy, adrenergic blocking drugs, recurrent hypoglycaemia, pregnancy or extremely tight control. Occasionally, severe hypoglycaemia may present with seizures/hemiplegia.
- Mild episodes of hypoglycaemia are common and respond to simple measures, eg rapid-acting carbohydrate in the form of a sugary drink (to correct the hypoglycaemia), followed by slow-release carbohydrate, eg a couple of biscuits or two slices of bread (to maintain euglycaemia).
- More severe hypoglycaemia may need third-party assistance, eg application of a glucose gel (GlucoGel) to the buccal mucosa or injection of glucagon (1 mg im).
- If these measures fail, an intravenous bolus of glucose (eg 25 mL of 25% dextrose) should be given, followed if necessary by an infusion of 5 or 10% dextrose.

Re-educate the patient with advice about alcohol, exercise and snacks. Nocturnal hypoglycaemia is much more likely if pre-bedtime glucose levels are below 7 mmol/L. Determine whether there was an obvious precipitant and consider adjustments to the regular regimen.

Consider hospital admission:

- in the elderly or those who live alone;
- when the cause is unclear or symptoms recur despite adequate treatment;
- in the setting of sulphonylurea use or insulin overdose where hypoglycaemia may recur up to several hours later.

2.6.3 Short- and long-term management of diabetes

Principal objectives

- Relieve symptoms and improve quality of life.
- Educate and empower the patient.
- Monitor control, adjust treatment and reduce other risk factors.
- Prevent and treat complications.

General approach

The management of diabetes requires a multidisciplinary team approach, involving doctors (physicians, GPs, orthopaedic and vascular surgeons, ophthalmologists and urologists), nurses (diabetes specialist nurses, practice and district nurses), dietitians, chiropodists, psychologists and, most importantly of all, the patient.

A thorough history and examination should be carried out at the patient's first visit. Record details of presenting symptoms, past medical history (including hypertension and dyslipidaemia), family history and check for features suggestive of vascular disease. Ask about tobacco and alcohol use. Examine the cardiovascular (BP, peripheral pulses, etc.) and peripheral nervous systems, and assess the eyes, feet and skin. Where possible, arrange for the patient to see the diabetes specialist nurse and dietitian at the same visit, and consider referral for chiropody and retinal screening.

Glycaemic control

Several large, prospective, randomised controlled trials have shown that good glycaemic control reduces the risk of developing complications in diabetes (see below). Home monitoring (preferably fingerprick testing) of blood glucose, together with periodic measurement of HbA_{1c} (which reflects glycaemic control over the preceding 8–10 weeks), will indicate the level of diabetic control and the need for adjustment to therapy.

There are varying opinions as to what constitutes good or adequate glycaemic control. In general, blood glucose levels of 4–8 mmol/L are likely to correlate with a satisfactory HbA_{1c} (<7.0%). However, bear in mind the clinical setting, for example whilst it is important to aim for tight control in a young type 1 diabetic, it may be necessary to accept more modest control in an elderly patient with type 2 diabetes who lives alone and in whom it is important to avoid hypoglycaemia.

Landmark trials in diabetes

Diabetes Control and Complications Trial

Tight diabetic control with intensive insulin therapy (mean HbA_{1c} ~7%) reduced diabetic complications over a 7-year period in a cohort of type 1 diabetics. Risk of retinopathy was reduced by 60%, nephropathy by 30% and neuropathy by 20%. However, a two- to three-fold increased risk of severe hypoglycaemia was observed in the intensively treated group.

United Kingdom Prospective Diabetes Study

Good glycaemic control (median HbA_{1c} of 7% over a 10-year period) reduced the risk of microvascular complications in type 2 diabetics, whilst tight BP regulation decreased the risk of both

microvascular and macrovascular complications. These benefits were, for the most part, independent of the agent used, although in obese patients metformin conferred particular advantage.

Diet and lifestyle modifications

Table 54 outlines key dietary and lifestyle issues for patients with diabetes.

Insulin

Candidates for insulin

- All patients with type 1 diabetes.

- Failed oral therapy in type 2 diabetes.

- Type 2 diabetics during pregnancy (other than diet controlled).

- Type 2 diabetics during acute illness/surgery.

- Patients with pancreatic failure/pancreatectomy.

Types of insulin

Table 55 describes the major classes of insulin currently in use.

Which insulin?

Patients who are severely ill at diagnosis should be stabilised on an intravenous insulin infusion (see Section 2.6.1). Less severely ill patients can be started on a twice-daily regimen, often most conveniently given as a biphasic (premixed) insulin. Subsequently, competent/motivated patients are best managed with a 'basal-bolus' regimen with a once-daily injection of an intermediate-acting insulin/long-acting analogue and three meal-time injections of a rapid-onset short-acting monomeric insulin.

Increasingly, short-acting insulin is delivered by continuous subcutaneous insulin infusion (CSII) via a small pump, which may be worn clipped to a belt. However, the current usage of CSII is restricted by National Institute for Health and

TABLE 54 DIET AND LIFESTYLE ADVICE FOR DIABETICS

Category	Advice
Carbohydrates (45–50% of total calories)	Starchy carbohydrates with high fibre content and low glycaemic index, in which release occurs in a slow and uniform fashion
Fats (30–35% of total calories)	Polyunsaturates <10%, saturates <10% and monounsaturates >10% of the total
Proteins (15–20% of total calories)	If urinary albumin normal, 15–20% of total calories; if abnormal, <10% of total calories[1]
Sweeteners	Aspartame and saccharin based are recommended
Diabetic food	Can be high in calories, expensive, and confer no advantage
BMI	Weight reduction: aim for BMI <25 kg/m^2
Alcohol	Moderate consumption (1 unit/day for women and 1–2 units/day for men), especially of wine
Exercise	Regular exercise is important to help reduce and maintain weight, to reduce insulin resistance and to improve BP and lipid control
Smoking	Stop smoking

1. Some clinicians consider protein restriction unnecessary and indeed it may even be deleterious in certain circumstances, eg in adolescence.

TABLE 55 TYPES OF INSULIN FOR SUBCUTANEOUS (AND INHALED) ADMINISTRATION[1]

Type	Action	Onset	Peak	Duration	Examples
Analogue (monomeric)	Very rapid	15–30 minutes	1 hour	5–6 hours	Humalog (insulin lispro) NovoRapid (insulin aspart) Apidra (insulin glulisine)
Soluble (human or animal)	Short	30 minutes	1–2 hours	6–8 hours	Actrapid Humulin S Hypurin
Isophane (human or animal)	Intermediate	2 hours	4–6 hours	8–12 hours	Insulatard Humulin I
Long-acting analogues	Long	1–1.5 hours	Plateau	16–24 hours	Lantus (insulin glargine) Levemir (insulin detemir)
Inhaled insulin	Rapid	10–20 minutes	1–2 hours	4–6 hours	Exubera

1. Mixtures of analogue monomeric insulins and isophane insulins (biphasic) are available, eg Novomix-30, Humalog Mix25 and Humalog Mix50 depending on the percentage of monomeric insulin that they contain. Analogue insulins are now usually the insulin of choice, hence many companies are now beginning to withdraw their soluble insulin products eg Mixtard 10–50.

Clinical Excellence (NICE) guidance to type 1 diabetics who have failed to achieve adequate glycaemic control on multiple (intensive) insulin injection regimens and those in whom hypoglycaemia is frequent and unpredictable irrespective of glycaemic control.

Inhaled insulin, currently Exubera, is licensed for the treatment of (i) type 2 diabetics not controlled with tablets and requiring insulin and (ii) type 1 diabetics when used in conjunction with long/intermediate-acting subcutaneous insulin, and where the potential benefits outweigh the safety concern. NICE have recently reviewed the role for inhaled insulin and recommend that it should not be used routinely and should be initiated and monitored by specialists, and then only in the context of failure of all other treatments to achieve adequate control or in patients with needle phobia confirmed by a diabetes or mental health specialist. Bioavailability appears to be about 10% of subcutaneous insulin; 1 mg inhaled insulin is equivalent to 3 units sc, and 3 mg to 8 units sc. Smoking increases the bioavailability, whereas passive smoking reduces it. Long-term safety data are not yet available. Very common side effects (10%) recorded in trials included coughs and hypoglycaemia. Pulmonary function (forced expiratory volume in 1 second, FEV_1) should be tested at baseline and after 6 months of therapy, and repeated after a further 3 months if FEV_1 falls by 15% or 500 mL. Treatment should be discontinued if there is a reduction of greater than 20%. Containdications include smoking, severe asthma/chronic obstructive pulmonary disease, significant heart failure and pregnancy.

- A phase of transient remission, referred to as the 'honeymoon period', frequently occurs shortly after starting treatment in patients with type 1 diabetes. Stopping insulin in this period is discouraged (although sometimes necessary) as the need for insulin will recur. Educate and empower your patient.
- Whichever regimen is chosen, start cautiously! Aim to avoid hypoglycaemia that adversely affects the patient's confidence and makes your job harder in the long run.

Side effects and complications

These may include the following.

- Transient oedema and changes to lens refraction on starting insulin therapy.

- Lipohypertrophy (fatty lumps) at injection sites, especially if repeated in the same area (Fig. 58).

- Lipoatrophy, although this is less common since the introduction of purified insulins (Fig. 58).

- Hypoglycaemia.

- Weight gain.

Oral therapy in type 2 diabetes

An approach to the management of type 2 diabetes is outlined in Fig. 59. Most patients should undergo an initial trial of diet and lifestyle modification (Table 54), with tablets reserved for those who fail to achieve adequate control. Similarly, insulin can be used if diet and drugs fail to prevent hyperglycaemia.

Oral hypoglycaemic agents

See Table 56.

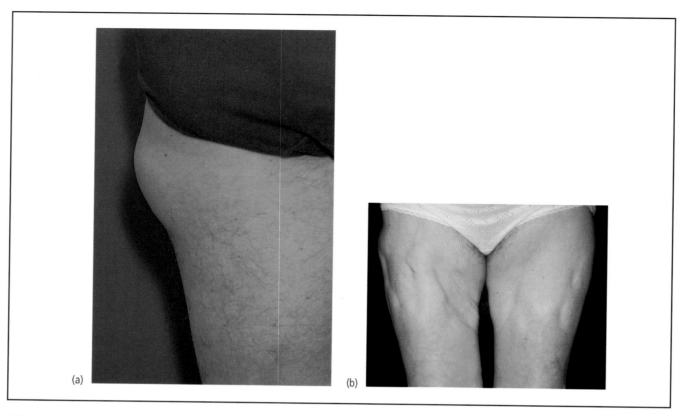

(a)

(b)

▲ **Fig. 58** Insulin-induced lipohypertrophy (**a**) and lipoatrophy (**b**).

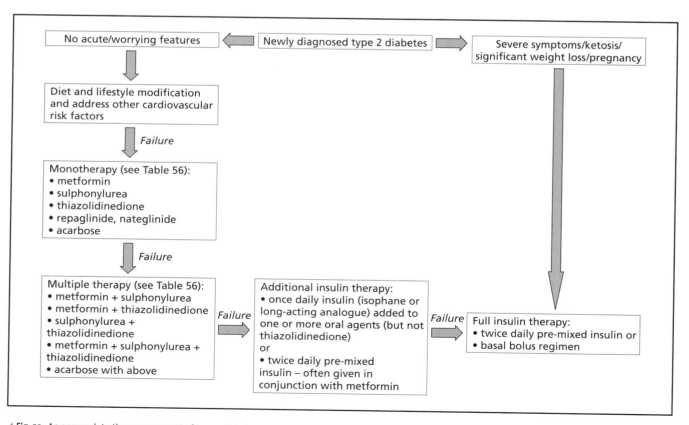

▲ **Fig. 59** An approach to the management of type 2 diabetes.

TABLE 56 ORAL HYPOGLYCAEMIC AGENTS

Agent	Examples	Action	Notes
Sulphonylureas	Gliclazide Glipizide Glibenclamide Glimepiride	Act (via the sulphonylurea receptor) to close β-cell potassium channels, with subsequent calcium channel activation and insulin secretion	Often used as the first-line agent in non-obese type 2 diabetics (reducing HbA_{1c} by up to 2%), although this is becoming an issue for debate In general, shorter-acting agents are preferred (eg gliclazide, glipizide) All can cause weight gain and hypoglycaemia
Biguanides	Metformin is the only biguanide currently licensed for use in the UK	Reduces hepatic glucose production and has beneficial effects on glucose uptake and metabolism	Does not cause weight gain and is the treatment of choice in obese type 2 diabetics (reducing HbA_{1c} by up to 2%) Should be avoided in renal, liver and cardiac failure because of the risk of lactic acidosis Side effects include nausea, vomiting, bloating, diarrhoea and a metallic taste Start with 500 mg once daily and gradually titrate upwards to minimise gastrointestinal adverse effects Slow-release preparations have a less adverse profile
α-Glucosidase inhibitors	Acarbose	Blocks the breakdown of complex carbohydrates in the small intestine, thereby reducing the postprandial rise in blood glucose levels	Use is severely limited by gastrointestinal side effects including flatulence, bloating, diarrhoea and abdominal cramps. It should therefore be started at low dose (50 mg/day) and gradually titrated. When combined with other oral hypoglycaemic agents, it produces a further small reduction in HbA_{1c} of ~0.5%. It does not induce weight gain. Liver function should be monitored during treatment
Thiazolidinediones	Rosiglitazone Pioglitazone	A novel class of antidiabetic agents that act as insulin sensitisers. High-affinity ligands for a member of the nuclear receptor superfamily (PPARγ)	May be used as monotherapy in those intolerant of metformin or sulphonylurea. Mainly used as second-line agents given in combination with metformin and/or sulphonylurea. Contraindicated in heart failure as may cause fluid retention and weight gain. Liver function should be checked prior to and after commencing treatment
Prandial glucose regulators	Repaglinide Nateglinide	New generation of 'prandial glucose regulators'. They act via the sulphonylurea receptor	Principal advantage lies in their rapid onset of action allowing them to be taken with each meal

PPARγ, peroxisome proliferator-activated receptor γ.

Glucagon-like peptide 1 receptor activation

The enteroinsular axis, in which secretion of peptide incretin hormones in response to food intake directly regulates pancreatic islet cell function, offers a novel target for improving glycaemic control in type 2 diabetes. Glucagon-like peptide (GLP)-1 has attracted particular attention, as it regulates blood glucose levels through inhibition of glucagon secretion, gastric emptying and food intake, and stimulation of insulin secretion. Preclinical studies have also demonstrated that GLP-1 stimulates β-cell proliferation and

inhibits apoptosis. The native peptide is rapidly degraded by the enzyme dipeptidyl peptidase IV. Accordingly, current therapeutic approaches to enhance GLP-1 action are based around injectable, degradation-resistant GLP-1 analogues or oral inhibitors of dipeptidyl peptidase IV. Exenatide, a lizard-derived GLP-1 receptor agonist, given by subcutaneous injection twice daily, has been shown in clinical trials to improve glycaemic control but, unlike insulin, does not promote weight gain. However, longer-term randomised studies will be required to help define the true

potential of GLP-1 modulation in the treatment of type 2 diabetes.

Attention to other cardiovascular risk factors

Hypertension

It is now clear that aggressive BP control (≤130/80 mmHg) is an essential part of the strategy to prevent microvascular and macrovascular complications. If hypertension is detected, further investigations may be necessary to exclude secondary causes (see Section 1.1.16). In those with evidence of nephropathy, there is evidence to suggest that the target BP should be even lower (≤125/75 mmHg).

Although angiotensin-converting enzyme (ACE) inhibitors have traditionally been considered the antihypertensive agents of choice, especially in the presence of microalbuminuria/nephropathy, the United Kingdom Prospective Diabetes Study (UKPDS) demonstrated the beta-blocker atenolol to be as efficacious as captopril in reducing microvascular and macrovascular end-points in type 2 diabetes, suggesting that it is the level of BP control that is the most important factor in determining outcome. Note, however, that recent data suggests that beta-blockers should no longer be considered first-choice agents for the treatment of hypertension in the general population. Many patients require two or more agents to achieve their target BP. Calcium channel antagonists, alpha-blockers and diuretics are useful adjuncts. Angiotensin receptor blocker (ARBs), which are often better tolerated than ACE inhibitors, are now considered as efficacious as ACE inhibitors in this setting.

Dyslipidaemia

There is a three-fold excess risk of macrovascular disease associated with diabetes. A number of large trials of lipid-lowering agents suggest that diabetics appear to benefit at least as much as, if not more than, their non-diabetic counterparts from treatment with hydroxymethylglutaryl (HMG)-CoA reductase inhibitors, ie statins.

Current guidelines on prevention of cardiovascular disease, as suggested by the Joint British Societies (also see Section 2.5.1), include the following recommendations.

1. Statin therapy for all those with either type 1 or type 2 diabetes who are aged 40 years or more.

2. Statin therapy for those with either type 1 or 2 diabetes, aged 18–39 years, who have at least one of the following:

   (a) retinopathy (preproliferative, proliferative, maculopathy);

   (b) nephropathy, including persistent microalbuminuria;

   (c) poor glycaemic control (HbA$_{1c}$ >9.0%);

   (d) high BP requiring treatment;

   (e) raised total cholesterol (>6.0 mmol/L);

   (f) features of the metabolic syndrome (see Section 1.1.15);

   (g) family history of premature cardiovascular disease in a first-degree relative.

The most common dyslipidaemia seen in diabetes is low high-density lipoprotein cholesterol (HDL-C) and high triglycerides, although the role(s) of fibrates, nicotinic acid derivatives and other agents in the management of these disorders remains unclear. Accordingly, the Joint British Societies continue to recommend a statin as the agent of first choice.

Aspirin

Aspirin 75 mg daily is recommended for secondary prevention following a cadiovascular event in both diabetic and non-diabetic subjects. Its role in primary prevention in diabetes is outlined in Table 58.

Follow-up

The frequency of follow-up will vary depending on the clinical context. However, even well-controlled patients should be reviewed every 6 months in a diabetic clinic (either at the local hospital or in the community with access to a diabetic centre) to aid early detection and treatment of complications. In addition to assessing glycaemic control, ask about symptoms of vascular disease (ischaemic heart disease, cerebrovascular disease, peripheral vascular disease), check for other macrovascular risk factors (especially smoking, hypertension, dyslipidaemia) and ask about features of neuropathy, including erectile dysfunction in males. Pre-pregnancy counselling should be considered if appropriate. Table 57 details those parameters that should be recorded at each visit and Table 58 outlines targets for management.

TABLE 57 DIABETIC FOLLOW-UP: INTERIM VISITS AND ANNUAL REVIEW

Follow-up	Review and action
Check at each visit	Home-monitoring record, HbA$_{1c}$, BMI, waist circumference, urinalysis, BP. Continue education and assessment. Review and adjust treatment
Check once a year (ie annual review)	Clinical assessment: pulses, BP, feet, visual acuity, fundi, injection sites Biochemical assessment: HbA$_{1c}$, urea and electrolytes, lipid profile, thyroid function, urinalysis, albumin/creatinine ratio (or other indicator of microalbuminuria)

TABLE 58 TARGETS IN THE MANAGEMENT OF DIABETIC PATIENTS: THE 'ALPHABET STRATEGY' AS PER JOINT BRITISH SOCIETIES' GUIDELINES ON PREVENTION OF CARDIOVASCULAR DISEASE IN CLINICAL PRACTICE (2005) (ALSO SEE SECTION 2.5.1)

Domain	Targets
Advice	Education, self-management, compliance with treatment; special focus on smoking cessation, diet, physical activity and weight reduction
Blood pressure	<130/80 mmHg; may require a combination of ACE inhibitor/ARB, diuretics and a calcium channel antagonist
Cholesterol	Total cholesterol <4.0 mmol/L, LDL-C <2.0 mmol/L and preferably triglycerides <1.7 mmol/L, with HDL-C >1.0 mmol/L in men and >1.2 mmol/L in women
Diabetes control	HbA_{1c} <6.5%; metformin is increasingly the agent of first choice for type 2 diabetes. Early escalation to multiple therapies and insulin if targets are not reached; avoidance of hypoglycaemic epsiodes
Eye care	Annual digital photography is recommended with appropriate ophthalmological referral when needed
Foot care	Annual examination with appropriate referral as required
'**G**uardian drugs'	Aspirin is recommended for (i) all who have established atherosclerotic disease, (ii) subjects with diabetes who are over the age of 50 years, (iii) those who are <50 years old but have had diabetes of >10 years' duration and (iv) those who are already receiving treatment for hypertension ACE inhibitor/ARB therapy is indicated when there is microalbuminuria, proteinuria or diabetic nephropathy Therapy with a statin to achieve total and LDL-C targets is appropriate for most patients with diabetes

LDL-C, low-density lipoprotein cholesterol.

2.6.4 Complications

Diabetic complications (Table 59) are more likely with long-standing diabetes and with poor diabetic control.

Macrovascular complications

Diabetes is a major risk factor for the development of atherosclerosis and is associated with a much higher incidence of myocardial infarction, stroke and amputation. The presence of other risk factors such as smoking, dyslipidaemia, hypertension and obesity compound the risk. Management follows the same principles as in non-diabetics, with rigorous control of other risk factors and appropriate use of antiplatelet agents, ACE inhibitors/ARBs and beta-blockers.

Microvascular complications: diabetic eye disease

Retinopathy is the commonest microvascular complication (affecting almost all long-standing type 1 diabetics, and evident in about 20% of type 2 diabetics at presentation). The classification of diabetic eye disease is shown in Table 60.

Routine screening aims to detect eye disease before visual symptoms develop. Every diabetic must therefore undergo yearly examination including:

- visual acuity;

- fundoscopy (through dilated pupils providing that there is no contraindication to tropicamide, eg glaucoma) or preferably with retinal photography.

Background retinopathy

If background retinopathy is present (Table 60 and Fig. 60), assessment should be repeated in 6 months. Review glycaemic control, check for evidence of microalbuminuria and treat hypertension. ACE inhibitors reduce the progression of retinopathy even in normotensive diabetic patients.

> Microaneurysms and haemorrhages are most easily seen with the green lamp of the ophthalmoscope.

TABLE 59 DIABETIC COMPLICATIONS

Complication	Clinical condition
Macrovascular	Coronary artery disease Cerebrovascular disease Peripheral vascular disease
Microvascular	Diabetic eye disease Nephropathy Neuropathy
Specific	Diabetic foot Arthropathy and dermopathy Susceptibility to infections

TABLE 60 DIABETIC EYE DISEASE

Complication	Type	Clinical feature
Retinopathy	Background	Microaneurysms Dot and blot haemorrhages Hard exudates Occasional (<5) cotton-wool spots
	Preproliferative	Venous beading/looping Multiple haemorrhages Multiple cotton-wool spots Intraretinal microvascular abnormalities
	Proliferative	Neovascularisation around the disc Neovascularisation elsewhere
Maculopathy		Exudate within a disc area (DA) of fovea Microaneurysm or haemorrhage within DA of fovea Oedema
Advanced diabetic eye disease		Preretinal or vitreous haemorrhage Retinal detachment
Cataracts		

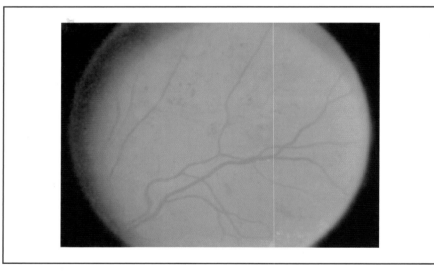

▲**Fig. 60** Background diabetic retinopathy. Note the scattered red 'dots and blots' (microaneurysms and haemorrhages) and hard exudates (inferiorly).

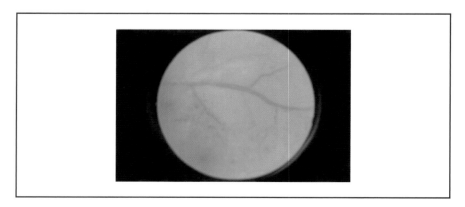

▲**Fig. 61** Preproliferative diabetic retinopathy. Note the venous irregularity and beading.

Preproliferative retinopathy

Multiple cotton-wool spots indicate retinal ischaemia, and together with venous beading/looping and intraretinal microvascular abnormalities (intraretinal new vessels which, unlike 'classical' new vessels, do not lead to haemorrhage) constitute the changes of preproliferative retinopathy (Fig. 61). Prompt referral to an ophthalmologist is necessary for consideration of panretinal photocoagulation. Review glycaemic control and treat associated hypertension/microalbuminuria.

Proliferative retinopathy

If left unchecked, preproliferative changes may progress rapidly with the development of new retinal vessels, which are fragile and prone to haemorrhage, threatening vision (ie proliferative retinopathy; Fig. 62). Urgent referral to an ophthalmologist is necessary for laser treatment. Review glycaemic control; hypertension and microalbuminuria/nephropathy are likely to be present.

Maculopathy

Maculopathy is the commonest threat to vision in type 2 diabetics. It is often difficult to diagnose, although macular ischaemia should be suspected in the presence of circinate macular exudates ('macular star'; Fig. 63). Refer promptly to an ophthalmologist (for consideration for macular grid laser therapy). Again, address poor glycaemic control and hypertension.

Advanced diabetic eye disease

In advanced diabetic eye disease (Fig. 64) widespread neovascularisation and haemorrhage may lead to traction retinal detachment, with preretinal or vitreous haemorrhage, presenting as sudden loss of vision.

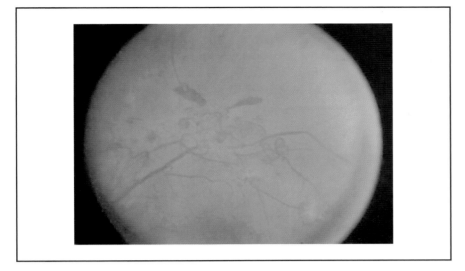

▲ **Fig. 62** Proliferative diabetic retinopathy. Note the leashes of new vessels and multiple haemorrhages.

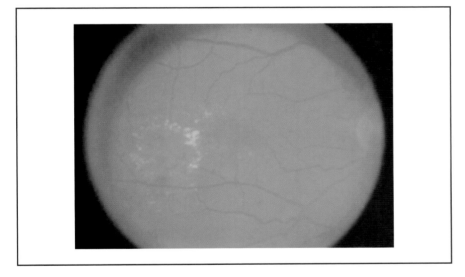

▲ **Fig. 63** Diabetic maculopathy. Note the ring of hard exudates encroaching on the macula.

Cataracts

Cataracts are more common and occur at an earlier age in diabetics. They present with an insidious decline in visual acuity. Occasionally 'snow-flake' cataracts may complicate acute hyperglycaemia, and these transiently worsen with imposition of good glycaemic control.

Microvascular complications: nephropathy

Renal disease is a major cause of morbidity and premature mortality in the diabetic population. 'Nephropathy' is used to denote the presence of macroalbuminuria and a progressive decline in renal function, ie decreasing glomerular filtration rate (GFR) and increasing serum creatinine, often accompanied by hypertension. Its incidence peaks when diabetes has been present for 15–20 years.

Aetiology/pathogenesis

It has been suggested that the elevated GFR seen at the onset of diabetes may predispose to the later development of renal disease, which is characterised by thickening of the glomerular basement membrane (GBM). Microalbuminuria (see above) is the earliest detectable change in the urine and progresses to intermittent and then persistent proteinuria. This is accompanied by mesangial expansion and then nodular sclerosis (Kimmelstiel–Wilson nodules). Eventually, glomeruli are replaced by hyaline material.

Although serum creatinine remains normal during the early stages, once persistent proteinuria develops it takes only 5–10 years to reach end-stage renal failure. Other causes of renal failure are present in approximately 10% of type 1 and 30% of type 2 diabetics.

Epidemiology

Diabetic nephropathy develops in about 30% of type 1 diabetics, around 25% of type 2 diabetics of white origin, but in up to 50% of type 2 diabetics of Asian and Afro-Caribbean origin, reflecting the earlier age of onset of diabetes and increased prevalence of hypertension in these groups. End-stage renal failure now occurs in fewer than 20% of type 1 diabetics, mainly because of aggressive treatment of hypertension.

Clinical presentation/physical signs

Nephropathy is usually detected during routine screening and patients are frequently asymptomatic at the time of presentation. When present, symptoms are those of uraemia. Physical signs may include the pallor of anaemia, oedema from fluid overload, excoriations and associated features such as high BP or retinopathy.

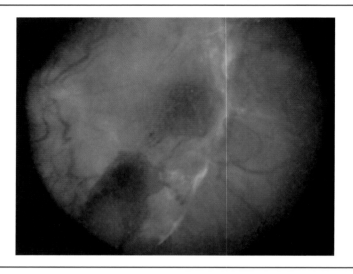

▲ **Fig. 64** Advanced retinopathy. Retinal detachment complicating extensive neovascularisation and haemorrhage.

Investigations

Microalbuminuria is a recognised risk factor for progression to full-blown diabetic nephropathy and macrovascular complications in both type 1 and type 2 diabetes. For example, 20–40% of type 1 diabetics with microalbuminuria will develop renal disease within 5 years. Although it is difficult to estimate its prevalence with certainty, approximately one-quarter of newly diagnosed type 2 diabetics have either microalbuminuria or macroalbuminuria.

> It is important to distinguish between the following.
>
> - Microalbuminuria: albumin excretion 30–300 mg per 24 hours.
> - Macroalbuminuria: albumin excretion >300 mg per 24 hours ('stick positive').
> - Nephrotic syndrome: urinary protein loss >3 g per 24 hours.

> All diabetics should be screened for evidence of microalbuminuria on an annual basis. Methods available include:

> - determination of urinary albumin/creatinine ratio (positive if >2.0 in females and >3.0 in males)'
> - 24-hour collection for measurement of urinary albumin excretion.

A positive result requires confirmation on a second or third occasion, ie two out of three positive.

Diagnosis/initial assessment

Confirmation of macroalbuminuria should prompt assessment of renal function, including:

- serum electrolytes, urea and creatinine (eGFR);

- FBC (for normocytic, normochromic anaemia);

- full lipid profile (for mixed dyslipidaemia).

Exclusion of other causes

Consider investigations to exclude other causes of proteinuria and renal impairment if there is little evidence of retinopathy to suggest microvascular disease elsewhere:

- midstream urine (for red cell casts and signs of infection);

- erythrocyte sedimentation rate, antinuclear factor, antineutrophil cytoplasmic antibodies, anti-GBM antibodies and complement levels;

- calcium, urate, plasma and urinary protein electrophoresis;

- renal tract ultrasound (to assess renal size and symmetry, and check for evidence of obstruction);

- magnetic resonance angiography (if renal artery stenosis suspected);

- renal biopsy (rarely required).

> ⚠ Intravenous urography can precipitate acute renal failure, especially in the presence of dehydration or a serum creatinine >300 mmol/L.

Treatment

- Established nephropathy: once the urinary albumin excretion rate exceeds 300 mg/day, good BP control is the mainstay of treatment, using ACE inhibitors/ARBs and other antihypertensives to keep BP below 125/75 mmHg. Diuretics may be needed for fluid overload and oedema. Drugs that are longer-acting and predominantly renally excreted, eg glibenclamide, should be avoided. Metformin is contraindicated in renal failure (creatinine >150 µmol/L) due to the risk of lactic acidosis.

- End-stage renal failure: patients with nephropathy are best managed in a joint renal/diabetic clinic. Dialysis or renal transplantation is usually required at lower creatinine levels (around 500–550 µmol/L) than in non-diabetics. The preferred option is renal transplantation if comorbidities permit.

Prognosis

With effective renal replacement therapy, the main determinant of prognosis is now the associated vascular disease.

Microvascular complications: neuropathy

Neuropathy is commoner in patients with a long history of diabetes or in those with poor glycaemic control.

Classification of diabetic neuropathy

- Distal symmetrical (predominantly sensory) polyneuropathy.
- Mononeuropathy and multiple mononeuropathy (peripheral or cranial nerve lesions).
- Diabetic amyotrophy (proximal motor neuropathy).
- Acute painful neuropathy.
- Autonomic neuropathy.

Distal symmetrical polyneuropathy (peripheral neuropathy)

This is the most common type of diabetic neuropathy and typically affects long peripheral nerves. There is loss of both myelinated and unmyelinated nerve fibres with segmental demyelination and axonal regeneration.

Clinical presentation Pain (stabbing/burning/shooting), hyperaesthesia and hypoaesthesia may be present, but up to 50% are asymptomatic. Characteristically worse at night.

Physical signs Diminished or absent vibration sense and ankle jerks, together with an inability to feel the 10 g monofilament, are usually the earliest signs, and may be followed by diminished pain and temperature sensation. Muscular weakness and wasting are late features.

Investigations Diagnosis is clinical, confirmed by nerve conduction and vibration perception threshold studies.

Treatment The mainstay of treatment is good diabetic control. Tricyclic antidepressants (eg amitriptyline), anticonvulsants (eg carbamazepine, gabapentin and pregabalin) and topical capsaicin may help with symptom relief. OpSite (a semi-permeable dressing) can provide local relief in hyperaesthetic areas.

Further complications

- Wasting of the small muscles of the hand.

- High arched feet with clawing of toes.

- Neuropathic ulcers leading to sepsis.

- Neuropathic joints (Charcot's joints).

Prevention Good glycaemic control reduces the risk of developing neuropathy. Patients should receive advice regarding foot care and undergo regular review by a chiropodist. Screening for peripheral neuropathy is essential as it is often asymptomatic.

Mononeuropathies, diabetic amyotrophy and acute painful neuropathy

- Cranial mononeuropathies: typically affect the third, fourth or sixth nerves. Pupillary responses are often spared in diabetic third nerve palsy.
- Radiculopathies: may involve any nerve roots, especially those affecting the trunk.
- Diabetic amyotrophy (proximal motor neuropathy): most commonly affects middle-aged men with long-standing type 2 diabetes, who present with asymmetrical painful

wasting of the quadriceps muscles. It is often associated with anorexia and weight loss. Insulin is the mainstay of treatment even in those with apparent satisfactory glycaemic control. Symptoms gradually abate with time, although a significant number are left with residual disability.
- Acute painful neuropathy: pain (stabbing/burning/shooting) is usually severe and may be unremitting. Patients often report hyperaesthesia with marked tenderness of the skin to touch. Simple analgesia can be helpful, although opiates may be required. Tricyclic antidepressants (eg amitriptyline), anticonvulsants (eg carbamazepine, gabapentin, pregabalin) and topical capsaicin can be tried. OpSite may help in hyperaesthesia.

Autonomic neuropathy

Clinical presentation/physical signs Autonomic neuropathy may manifest in a number of different ways (Fig. 65).

Investigations Cardiovascular autonomic reflexes are most easily tested:

- lying and standing BP (a fall in systolic pressure >30 mmHg);

- absence of sinus arrhythmia (variation of <10 bpm with deep breathing).

Erectile dysfunction should be investigated as outlined in Section 2.4.7. Delayed gastric emptying can be documented with a radioisotope-labelled test meal.

Treatment This includes the following therapies.

- Where possible, avoid drugs that cause postural hypotension. Treatment with fludrocortisone (50–100 µg/day) can be helpful in patients who are symptomatic.

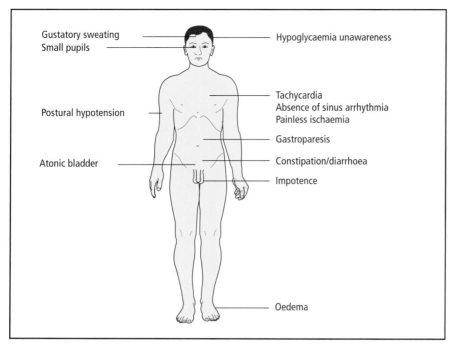

Gustatory sweating
Small pupils

Hypoglycaemia unawareness

Postural hypotension

Tachycardia
Absence of sinus arrhythmia
Painless ischaemia

Gastroparesis

Atonic bladder

Constipation/diarrhoea

Impotence

Oedema

▲ **Fig. 65** Clinical features of diabetic autonomic neuropathy.

- Topical glycopyrrolate cream (0.5%) may be effective in gustatory sweating.

- Consider metoclopramide (10 mg tds) or domperidone (10–20 mg tds) in those with upper gastrointestinal symptoms.

- Codeine phosphate (30 mg qds) and other antidiarrhoeal agents provide symptom relief from diarrhoea. Tetracyclines are preferred for treatment of bacterial overgrowth.

- The management of impotence is described in detail in Section 2.4.7.

- Intermittent self-catheterisation (three to four times daily) or placement of a long-term indwelling catheter is indicated for cases of neurogenic bladder.

Other specific diabetic complications

The diabetic foot

Foot problems are very common and give rise to significant morbidity and mortality, accounting for the majority of hospital admissions in those with diabetes. Proper education and early detection can prevent many of the problems encountered. They are best considered in terms of the underlying pathology:

TABLE 61 CLINICAL FEATURES, INVESTIGATIONS AND MANAGEMENT OF THE DIABETIC FOOT

	Neuropathic foot (Fig. 66)	Neuroischaemic foot (Fig. 67)
Presentation	Numbness, pain, calluses, ulcers, swelling	In addition to the features of neuropathy, patients may complain of intermittent claudication and/or rest pain
Physical signs	Evidence of sensory loss, absent ankle jerk, neuropathic oedema; calluses and ulcers at major pressure points, eg under the first and fifth metatarsal heads. Abscess and cellulitis. Charcot's joint. Good pulses	Cold foot with dependent rubor. Absence of pulses and trophic changes. Ulcers over the heel, dorsum of the foot and toes (often related to ill-fitting shoes). Gangrene or pre-gangrenous changes may be present
Investigations	Ulcer swab, blood cultures, blood glucose, blood count, biochemistry and urine for ketones. Radiograph of the foot/isotope bone scan (for osteomyelitis)	Doppler ultrasound to measure ABPI (normal >1.0; significant arterial occlusive disease is suggested by values <0.7). Arteriography may be indicated with a view to revascularisation. Other investigations are as for neuropathic ulcer
Treatment	Remove callus, clean and débride. Antibiotics for infection. If osteomyelitis, cellulitis, abscess or sepsis present, arrange hospital admission for intravenous antibiotics and review of glycaemic control. Consider surgical/orthopaedic referral for drainage, débridement or amputation	Similar to the management of a neuropathic ulcer, but some patients may be suitable for angioplasty or a bypass graft, whilst others with critical ischaemia will require amputation
Complications	Trauma, infection, gangrene, amputation, Charcot's joint	Similar to those of the neuropathic foot, but with an increased risk of amputation if severe arterial disease is present

ABPI, ankle/brachial pressure index.

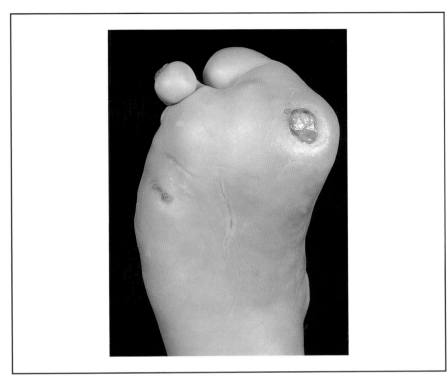

▲ **Fig. 66** Neuropathic ulcer. Typical 'punched-out' neuropathic ulcer in heavily callused skin underlying the first metatarsal head. Note the previous amputations.

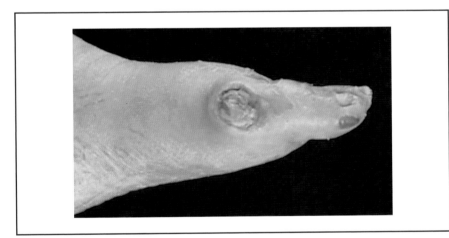

▲ **Fig. 67** Neuroischaemic foot. Classical ulceration reflecting both sensory neuropathy and vascular insufficiency.

- neuropathic foot;

- neuroischaemic foot;

- neuropathic joints.

Table 61 outlines the major clinical features and approach to the investigation and management of the neuropathic and neuroischaemic foot.

Neuropathic joint

- The aetiology of neuropathic or Charcot's joints in diabetes is not fully understood. In the absence of pain, abnormal mechanical stresses may be borne recurrently across joint surfaces. Surgery, even toe amputations, can change the normal weight-bearing axis and precipitate or accelerate the process.

- Clinical presentation is typically with a painful 'hot' joint, especially the mid-foot. Discrimination from an infected joint can be difficult.

- Investigation: radiographs of the foot may be normal in the early stages but soon become abnormal with destruction and disorganisation, particularly of the ankle and tarsometatarsal regions. An isotope bone scan may detect new bone formation and an MRI scan can be helpful, especially in differentiating from infection.

- Management involves bed-rest initially and then mobilisation with crutches or in a well-moulded total contact plaster cast until the swelling and warmth has settled. Improvement usually takes 2–3 months. Bisphosphonates (eg pamidronate 30–90 mg iv) may help to reduce bone resorption.

Arthropathy and skin lesions

In addition to leg ulcers and fungal or bacterial infections of the skin, diabetics may develop the following.

- Granuloma annulare: a cluster of small papules that typically form a ring on the back of hands or feet. Usually recovers spontaneously, but cryotherapy or steroid injections may be used.

- Necrobiosis lipoidica diabeticorum (Fig. 68): a patch of erythematous skin with a central yellow area of atrophy that may ulcerate. The shin is the commonest affected site. The lesions are chronic and rarely resolve. Topical steroids or injection may be used but are not of proven benefit.

- Cheiroarthropathy: predominantly affects the small joints of the

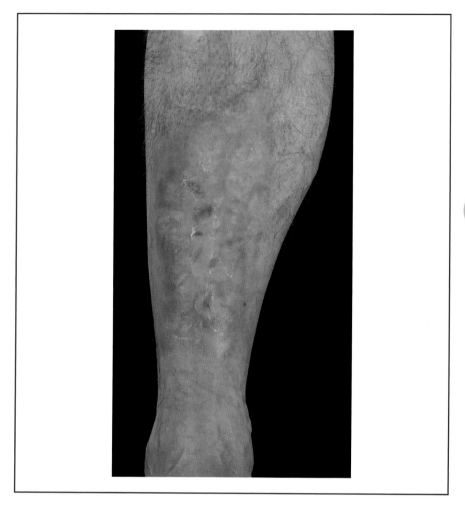

▲ **Fig. 68** Necrobiosis lipoidica diabeticorum.

hands, with inability to flatten the palmar surfaces of the hands together due to collagen thickening.

Susceptibility to infections

Patients with diabetes have impaired neutrophil and lymphocyte function, impaired tissue repair processes and may have poor perfusion of the tissues due to vascular disease. There is a higher incidence of boils, abscesses, cellulitis and fungal skin and mucosal infections (eg balanitis and thrush) amongst diabetics, who are also at risk of developing chest and urinary tract infections and osteomyelitis.

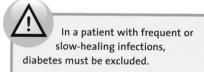

In a patient with frequent or slow-healing infections, diabetes must be excluded.

2.6.5 Important information for patients

Sick-day rules

Stress increases insulin resistance and hepatic glucose production. Accordingly, type 1 diabetics need more insulin, and type 2 diabetics may require short-term insulin, under conditions of severe or acute stress. Patients must be advised never to stop or even reduce their insulin. Indeed, in intercurrent illness the insulin requirement may increase by 10–20%. Meals may be substituted with frequent snacks and drinks, especially in the presence of anorexia or nausea. Frequent monitoring of blood glucose is necessary.

Sick-day rules for diabetic patients

- Never stop or even reduce your insulin; illness usually increases your insulin requirement.
- Seek help if you are unwell, especially with vomiting or diarrhoea and if you cannot keep food or fluid down. If your blood sugar rises above 20 mmol/L or remains above 15 mmol/L for 24 hours, or if your urine test is positive for ketones, seek urgent medical help.

Surgery

Operations on insulin-treated diabetics should be planned for early morning. The preceding day patients should have their usual evening insulin. Omit the morning dose on the day of the operation and commence a sliding-scale insulin infusion (50 units soluble insulin in 49.5 mL of normal saline infused at a rate determined by the blood glucose level; see Table 53) together with an intravenous fluid infusion, typically 1 L of 5% dextrose containing KCl 20 mmol/L every 8 hours. After the operation, change to regular therapy once the patient is stable and tolerating a normal diet.

Patients with tablet-controlled type 2 diabetes undergoing surgery are also best managed by means of a sliding-scale regimen. Diet-controlled type 2 diabetes may be managed by an intravenous fluid infusion and careful monitoring of blood glucose if the planned operation is relatively minor.

Adolescence

Many physiological, behavioural and psychosocial factors complicate the management of diabetes during adolescence. Ideally, patients should attend a specific clinic for adolescent diabetics, where they can experience mutual support away from the delays and obvious complications on view in the adult clinic. Patient-sensitive education and encouragement are vital. Long-term complications and emergencies should be explained in a realistic but non-threatening fashion. Contraceptive advice is essential.

Younger patients may benefit from diabetic camps where informal education is provided and practical techniques are taught.

Pregnancy and diabetes mellitus

Pregnancy should be planned to ensure that diabetic control is optimal prior to the time of conception. Patients taking oral hypoglycaemic agents or inhaled insulin should be switched to subcutaneous insulin, ideally a frequent injection regimen (three or four times daily). Other potentially teratogenic medications should be withdrawn, eg statins, ACE inhibitors. Methyldopa is an acceptable antihypertensive agent. High-dose folic acid (5 mg) should be commenced. Insulin requirements frequently decrease during the first trimester, and hypoglycaemic awareness is often impaired. Patients should be made aware and safety, particularly with respect to driving, discussed. Insulin requirements then significantly increase during pregnancy, especially during the third trimester. Frequent home blood glucose monitoring is encouraged, with the aim of achieving a fasting glucose between 4 and 6 mmol/L and a 2-hour postprandial glucose <8 mmol/L. Patients should preferably attend a joint diabetic and obstetric clinic and have the support of midwives and diabetes specialist nurses throughout. The aim is for a normal vaginal delivery at 38–39 weeks' gestation. Patients are not allowed to proceed to term due to the risk of late stillbirth; however, early induction of primiparas is often unsuccessful, leading to a high Caesarean section rate in this population (~50%).

Where possible every patient should have an indivdualised 'insulin schedule' to cover delivery and the immediate postnatal period. Insulin requirements drop immediately after delivery of the placenta and breast-feeding significantly reduces insulin requirements further.

> ⚠️ Poor diabetic control at conception and in early pregnancy can lead to congenital malformations (twice the background risk) and later in pregnancy to excessive fetal growth (50% risk) and late intrauterine death.

Diabetics with established nephropathy are advised of the significant increased risks of pregnancy in this setting (pre-eclampsia, prematurity, renal failure). The outcome is frequently poor, especially if the serum creatinine level is more than 200 μmol/L.

Patients must be screened for retinopathy in each trimester. Those with retinopathy are seen once a month and referred to an ophthalmologist. Laser therapy is possible during pregnancy.

Diabetics who are hypertensive (with or without nephropathy) are also at increased risk of pre-eclampsia, prematurity, etc.

Gestational diabetes

'Gestational diabetes' comprises gestational impaired glucose tolerance (GIGT) and gestational DM (GDM).

Indications for the OGTT (see Section 3.1.7) in pregnancy include obesity or excessive weight gain, glycosuria in the first trimester, significant glycosuria on two occasions in the second trimester, previous GDM, a previous baby over 4 kg birth weight, early macrosomia on ultrasound or a family history of diabetes.

Try diet alone in mild cases but if fasting blood glucose levels are >6 mmol/L and/or 2-hour postprandial blood glucose levels are >8 mmol/L, treat with insulin throughout pregnancy and labour. The OGTT should be repeated 6–8 weeks after delivery. Half of patients with GDM and GIGT will develop overt diabetes over the next 10–20 years, and it is vital that the patient and her GP are alert to the symptoms that could indicate developing diabetes.

Driving

> 🔑
> - Drivers treated with insulin or oral hypoglycaemic agents are required to notify the UK Driver and Vehicle Licensing Agency (DVLA).
> - If optimal control and the DVLA 'good practice' guidelines are adhered to, a group C1 licence may be retained whilst on insulin therapy, providing that it is supported by the patient's diabetologist.
> - All group 2 [LGV (large goods vehicle) and PCV (passenger-carrying vehicle)] drivers, even if diet controlled, need to notify the DVLA, and the licence must be surrendered if insulin is initiated.

Employment

Prior to October 2004 and the Disability Discrimination Act (DDA) some occupations, eg the fire service, denied entry to those with insulin-treated diabetes. However, the Act has now been extended to cover almost all occupations. The only occupation that is now explicitly excluded from the DDA is the armed forces. Employers such as the fire service and the police will now have to ensure that people with diabetes are medically assessed as to their fitness to work.

Exercise

Regular exercise is helpful in reducing BP, weight and lipid levels, and increases insulin sensitivity. Regular exercise for 20–30 minutes, three to five times a week should be encouraged. Diabetics are advised to carry sugar with them when exercising and to take a snack or meal high in complex carbohydrates afterwards, although those who regularly undertake exercise should be able to reduce their pre-exercise insulin dose in order to avoid further carbohydrate requirement.

FURTHER READING

Diabetes Control and Complications Trial Research Group. The effect of intensive treatment of diabetes on the development and progression of long-term complications in insulin-dependent diabetes mellitus. *N. Engl. J. Med.* 1993; 329: 977–86.

Levy D. *Practical Diabetes*. London: Greenwich Medical Media, 1999.

Reichard P, Nilsson B-Y and Rosenqvist U. The effect of long-term intensified insulin treatment on the development of microvascular complications of diabetes mellitus. *N. Engl. J. Med.* 1993; 329: 304–9.

United Kingdom Prospective Diabetes Study (UKPDS) Group. Effect of intensive blood-glucose control with metformin on complications in overweight patients with type 2 diabetes (UKPDS 34). *Lancet* 1998; 352: 854–65.

United Kingdom Prospective Diabetes Study (UKPDS) Group. Intensive blood-glucose control with sulphonylureas or insulin compared with conventional treatment and risk of complications in patients with type 2 diabetes (UKPDS 33). *Lancet* 1998; 352: 837–53.

United Kingdom Prospective Diabetes Study (UKPDS) Group. Tight blood pressure control and risk of macrovascular and microvascular complications in type 2 diabetics (UKPDS 38). *BMJ* 1998; 317: 703–13.

2.7 Other endocrine disorders

2.7.1 Multiple endocrine neoplasia

Three multiple endocrine neoplasia (MEN) syndromes are recognised: MEN-1, MEN-2a and MEN-2b. Each is characterised by autosomal dominant inheritance. Endocrinopathies develop in several glands which undergo hyperplastic or neoplastic transformation, usually associated with hyperfunction. Table 62 outlines the key features of each syndrome.

TABLE 62 AN OVERVIEW OF MEN

Type	MEN-1 (Wermer's syndrome)	MEN-2a (Sipple's syndrome)	MEN-2b (occasionally denoted MEN-3)
Components	Parathyroid hyperplasia (~80%) Pancreatic tumours (~75%) Pituitary tumours (~65%)	MTC (~100%) Phaeochromocytoma (~50%) Parathyroid hyperplasia (~40%)	Mucosal neuromas (~100%) MTC (~90%) Marfanoid habitus (~65%) Phaeochromocytoma (~45%) (Parathyroid hyperplasia: rare)
Genetic locus	Chromosome 11: loss-of-function mutations of the *MENIN* tumour-suppressor gene	MEN-2a and MEN-2b are both associated with activating mutations in the *RET* proto-oncogene (α-receptor tyrosine kinase) on chromosome 10	
Clinical notes	Hyperparathyroidism is the most common presenting feature Gastrinomas (~50%) and insulinomas (~30%) form the bulk of pancreatic tumours Prolactinomas and non-functioning tumours are the most common pituitary lesions	MTC in the setting of MEN type 2b is particularly aggressive Phaeochromocytoma may be bilateral Hyperparathyroidism is much more common in MEN-2a than MEN-2b	
		Familial MTC without the other features of MEN-2 also occurs with certain mutations in the *RET* proto-oncogene	Mucosal neuromas most commonly affect the oral cavity and gastrointestinal tract

MTC, medullary thyroid carcinoma.

Management

The individual components of the MEN syndromes are managed along standard guidelines, with certain caveats. In contrast to sporadic cases, multiple lesions are common. Four-gland parathyroid hyperplasia is more common than a single adenoma and thus minimally invasive surgery is generally not appropriate. Pancreatic tumours are also often multiple, recurrence is common and surgical cure rates are lower than in sporadic cases. It is particularly important to perform functional localisation using visceral angiography and calcium stimulation, as lesions visible on cross-sectional imaging may not be the functioning lesion causing the patient's symptoms. Additional challenges exist, eg it is clearly important to first exclude/treat a phaeochromocytoma prior to embarking on thyroid or parathyroid surgery. For these reasons, individuals with MEN should be managed at specialist centres.

Screening

Genetic testing has now effectively replaced biochemical screening in the identification of affected members of MEN kindreds. Clearly there are important ethical and legal issues attached to screening in MEN. In MEN-1 genetic screening has clear benefits for unaffected individuals, who can be discharged from further biochemical screening, but has no direct benefit to affected individuals. In MEN-2 and familial MTC kindreds, identification of *RET* proto-oncogene mutations is particularly important as affected individuals should undergo prophylactic thryoidectomy to prevent MTC. There is a well-recognised genotype–phenotype correlation, with some *RET* mutations being associated with

particularly aggressive MTC of very early onset. The timing of thyroidectomy is therefore determined by the mutation, but should in general be performed in childhood (before 5 years of age) and in infancy (before 6 months) for the most aggressive mutations.

FURTHER READING

Association for Multiple Endocrine Neoplasia Disorders (AMEND): patients' association. Available at http://www.amend.org.uk/

Eng C and Ponder BAJ. Multiple endocrine neoplasia type 2 and medullary thyroid carcinoma. In: Grossman A, ed. *Clinical Endocrinology*, 2nd edn. Oxford: Blackwell Science, 1998.

Kouvaraki MA, Shapiro SE, Perrier ND, *et al.* RET proto-oncogene: a review and update of genotype–phenotype correlations in hereditary medullary thyroid cancer and associated endocrine tumors. *Thyroid* 2005; 15: 531–44.

2.7.2 Autoimmune polyglandular endocrinopathies

Two major polyglandular syndromes have been described in which autoimmune-mediated dysfunction of two or more endocrine glands is frequently associated with other non-endocrine autoimmune disorders. Table 63 describes the main features of each condition.

Type I, also referred to as the autoimmune polyendocrinopathy–candidiasis–ectodermal dystrophy (APECED) syndrome, is a rare autosomal recessive disorder due to mutations in the autoimmune regulator (*AIRE*) gene on chromosome 21q22.3, the product of which appears to be a nuclear transcription factor. Hypoparathyroidism or chronic mucocutaneous candidiasis is usually the first manifestation.

Type II is much more prevalent and primary adrenal insufficiency is its principal manifestation. Approximately 50% of cases are

TABLE 63 AUTOIMMUNE POLYGLANDULAR SYNDROMES

Type	Type I	Type II (Schmidt's syndrome)
Epidemiology	Rare, autosomal recessive Childhood onset	Autosomal dominant, recessive or sporadic Young adults: females > males
HLA association	–	DR3, DR4
Common endocrinopathies	Hypoparathyroidism Adrenal insufficiency	Adrenal insufficiency Hypothyroidism or hyperthyroidism Type 1 DM
Less common endocrinopathies	Gonadal failure Hypothyroidism or hyperthyroidism Type 1 DM	Gonadal failure
Non-endocrine manifestations	Mucocutaneous candidiasis Chronic active hepatitis Pernicious anaemia Vitiligo Alopecia	Myasthenia gravis Pernicious anaemia Vitiligo Alopecia

DM, diabetes mellitus.

TABLE 64 ECTOPIC HORMONE SECRETION BY BENIGN AND MALIGNANT TUMOURS AND THEIR ASSOCIATED CLINICAL SYNDROMES

Hormone	Clinical syndrome	Tumours
ACTH	Cushing's syndrome	Small-cell bronchial carcinoma Bronchial carcinoid Pancreatic neuroendocrine tumour Thymic carcinoid
ADH	SIADH	Small-cell bronchial carcinoma
PTHrP	Hypercalcaemia	Squamous cell bronchial carcinoma
OAF	Hypercalcaemia	Multiple myeloma Leukaemia
hCG	Clinical syndromes rare, but may include precocious puberty, gynaecomastia, menstrual irregularity	Testicular germ cell tumour Hepatocellular carcinoma Gastrointestinal tumour Choriocarcinoma
Erythropoietin	Polycythaemia	Renal cell carcinoma Cerebellar haemangioblastoma Uterine fibromas

ACTH, adrenocorticotrophic hormone; ADH, antidiuretic hormone; hCG, human chorionic gonadotrophin; OAF, osteoclast-activating factor; PTHrP, parathyroid hormone-related peptide; SIADH, syndrome of inappropriate antidiuretic hormone.

familial and several modes of inheritance (autosomal recessive, autosomal dominant and polygenic) have been reported. Women are affected up to three times more often than men, with most cases occurring between age 20 and 40 years.

FURTHER READING

Asp AA. Autoimmune polyglandular syndromes. In: McDermott MT, ed. *Endocrine Secrets*, 4th edn. Philadelphia: Elsevier Mosby, 2005.

2.7.3 Ectopic hormone syndromes

A number of tumours (benign and malignant) may be associated with ectopic hormone production and the development of a clinical syndrome due to hormone excess. Several examples are shown in Table 64.

3.1 Stimulation tests

3.1.1 Short Synacthen test

Principle

Administration of tetracosactrin [synthetic adrenocorticotrophic hormone (ACTH) or 'synACTHen'] allows the acute adrenal response to ACTH to be assessed. In addition to promoting cortisol secretion, it also increases the production of other ACTH-dependent steroids (eg androgens) in the biosynthetic pathway and hence can be used to exacerbate the enzyme block in differing types of congenital adrenal hyperplasia (CAH) (see Section 2.2.5), thereby helping to confirm/exclude the diagnosis in patients with equivocal basal values.

Indications

- Diagnosis of primary (and secondary) adrenal insufficiency.

- Diagnosis of CAH (especially non-classical).

Contraindications

Known allergy to Synacthen; poorly controlled asthma.

Practical details

Before investigation

In patients already on hydrocortisone replacement, the morning dose on the day of the test should be withheld until the test has been completed. Some centres also omit the evening dose on the day before the investigation. In subjects taking supraphysiological glucocorticoid therapy (>30 mg hydrocortisone or >7.5 mg prednisolone per day), Synacthen testing should, where possible, be deferred until the dose has been weaned to a more physiological level.

The investigation

1. 9 a.m. Take blood for serum cortisol and plasma ACTH; give Synacthen 250 µg im (or iv).

2. 9.30 a.m. Take blood for serum cortisol.

3. 10 a.m. Take blood for serum cortisol. However, not all centres routinely measure a 60-minute response.

   (a) ACTH samples should be taken on ice to the laboratory for immediate processing.

   (b) Low-dose Synacthen (1 µg) is advocated by some as a more sensitive test of adrenocortical function, especially if the short Synacthen test is being used to screen for secondary adrenal insufficiency. However, there remain problems with accurate dosing (currently the 250-µg vial must be diluted), and the validity of the test remains to be proven.

   (c) For suspected CAH, measurement of 17α-hydroxyprogesterone (17-OHP) is also required.

After investigation: interpretation

Adrenal insufficiency There is variation between laboratories as to the exact cut-off for a normal response. However, a serum cortisol level of >550 nmol/L at 30 minutes is generally taken to exclude primary adrenal failure.

A subnormal response following Synacthen suggests either:

- primary adrenal pathology or

- secondary adrenal insufficiency (eg ACTH deficiency or exogenous steroid therapy) with consequent atrophy of the zonae fasciculata and reticularis.

Paired basal serum cortisol and plasma ACTH levels may help to distinguish between these two possibilities (eg low cortisol with elevated ACTH in primary adrenal failure; low cortisol with inappropriately low/normal ACTH in secondary hypoadrenalism). Alternatively, a long ('depot') Synacthen test can be performed to confirm the persistent lack of responsiveness in primary adrenal failure, which contrasts with a delayed but detectable rise in cortisol in secondary adrenal insufficiency.

> A normal post-Synacthen peak cortisol response in the short Synacthen test does not exclude partial pituitary ACTH deficiency (decreased pituitary reserve) in patients whose basal ACTH production is sufficient to prevent adrenal atrophy but in whom the ACTH response to stress (eg insulin-induced hypoglycaemia) is attenuated.

Congenital adrenal hyperplasia A peak 17-OHP level of >45 nmol/L confirms the diagnosis.

FURTHER READING

Monson JP. How I investigate the hypothalamo-pituitary–adrenal axis and why. *CME Bulletin Endocrinology and Diabetes* 1999; 2(1): 12–15.

3.1.2 Corticotrophin-releasing hormone test

Principle
Unlike pituitary corticotrophs, ectopic ACTH-secreting tumours do not express corticotrophin-releasing hormone (CRH) receptors and are therefore not susceptible to stimulation by CRH. Accordingly, exogenous CRH administration can help to distinguish between pituitary-dependent Cushing's disease and ectopic ACTH secretion, either alone (see below) or in combination with inferior petrosal sinus sampling (see Section 2.1.1).

Indications
To differentiate between Cushing's disease and ectopic ACTH secretion.

Contraindications
Known allergy to CRH.

Practical details

Before investigation
The patient should be fasted from midnight and warned that facial flushing is common following injection of CRH. Occasionally, transient hypotension occurs.

The investigation
1. Insert an intravenous cannula at 8.30 a.m. with the patient recumbent. Take samples for measurement of serum cortisol and plasma ACTH 15 and 30 minutes later (–15 and 0 minute samples respectively).

2. Give synthetic CRH 100 µg iv at 9 a.m.

3. Measure serum cortisol and plasma ACTH at 15, 30, 45, 60, 90 and 120 minutes.

After investigation: interpretation
The majority of patients with Cushing's disease exhibit a normal or exaggerated increment in plasma ACTH and serum cortisol, contrasting with the lack of response from those with ectopic ACTH-secreting tumours. Thresholds for defining a normal response depend on whether human or ovine CRH is used (see Further reading for further details).

Note, however, that up to 15% of pituitary adenomas may fail to respond to CRH.

FURTHER READING

Nieman LK, Oldfield EH, Wesley R, *et al.* A simplified morning ovine corticotrophin-releasing hormone stimulation test for the differential diagnosis of adrenocorticotropin-dependent Cushing's syndrome. *J. Clin. Endocrinol. Metab.* 1993; 77: 1308–12.

- - - - - - - - - - - - - - - - -

Trainer PJ and Besser GM. Corticotrophin releasing hormone test. In: Trainer PJ and Besser M. *The Bart's Endocrine Protocols.* Edinburgh: Churchill Livingstone, 1995.

3.1.3 Thyrotrophin-releasing hormone test

Principle
Administration of thyrotrophin-releasing hormone (TRH) in normal subjects promotes release of pituitary thyroid-stimulating hormone (TSH). This response is blunted in hyperthyroidism and exaggerated in primary hypothyroidism. An abnormal response may also be seen in hypothalamic–pituitary disorders. This test is rarely used now because of the availability of high-precision TSH assays.

Indications
- Borderline cases of thyrotoxicosis, eg normal free thyroxine (FT_4) and free triiodothyronine (FT_3) with suppressed TSH.

- In the investigation of hypothalamic–pituitary disorders, eg as part of a combined pituitary triple test with insulin-induced hypoglycaemia and a gonadotrophin-releasing hormone test.

Contraindications
Known allergy to TRH.

Practical details

Before investigation
Non-fasting unless combined with an insulin tolerance test (see below). The patient should be warned that flushing and a desire to micturate are commonly experienced transient side effects.

The investigation
1. Insert intravenous cannula at 8.45 a.m. (with the patient recumbent). Take blood for basal FT_4 and TSH levels immediately prior to TRH administration (0 min).

2. Give TRH 200 µg iv at 9 a.m.

3. Take samples for TSH measurement at 20 and 60 minutes.

After investigation: interpretation

- In normal controls TSH rises by at least 2 mU/L, with a 20-minute value that is higher than the 60-minute value

- In hyperthyroidism, the basal TSH level is suppressed and fails to respond to TRH.

- Hypothyroidism due to hypothalamic–pituitary disorders may be associated with a subnormal or delayed TSH response.

Complications

Acute pituitary tumour haemorrhage/infarction has been reported following administration of TRH, especially if undertaken as part of a combined pituitary triple test.

3.1.4 Gonadotrophin-releasing hormone test

Principle

Administration of gonadotrophin-releasing hormone (GnRH) in normal subjects leads to a prompt increase in serum luteinising hormone (LH), with a slower and lesser increment in serum follicle-stimulating hormone (FSH). This test is principally used to assess LH and FSH secretory reserves and does not *per se* diagnose gonadotrophin deficiency.

Indications

- As part of a combined triple test in suspected hypopituitarism.

- In the investigation of delayed puberty.

Contraindications

Known allergy to GnRH.

Practical details

Before investigation

Non-fasting unless combined with insulin tolerance test.

The investigation

1. Insert intravenous cannula at 8.45 a.m. Take samples for basal serum LH and FSH immediately prior to GnRH administration (0 min).

2. Give GnRH 100 µg iv at 9 a.m.

3. Obtain further samples for measurement of serum LH and FSH at 20 and 60 minutes.

After investigation: interpretation

- In normal subjects, peak levels of LH are similar in both sexes (10–50 IU/L). Peak levels of FSH are generally lower (1–25 IU/L in females and 1–10 IU/L in males).

- In hypothalamic–pituitary disorders the GnRH response may be subnormal (especially in pituitary disease), normal or enhanced (particularly with hypothalamic dysfunction).

3.1.5 Insulin tolerance test

Principle

Insulin-induced hypoglycaemia is a powerful stimulus to ACTH/cortisol and growth hormone (GH) secretion.

Indications

The 'gold standard' test for the assessment of cortisol and GH reserves in patients with known or suspected hypothalamic–pituitary dysfunction.

Contraindications

> ⚠ • Ischaemic heart disease, dysrhythmias and/or an abnormal resting ECG.
> • Epilepsy.
> • 9 a.m. cortisol <100 nmol/L.

Practical details

Before the investigation

- Check the resting ECG and ensure that 9 a.m. serum cortisol is >100 nmol/L. Serum free thyroxine (FT_4) should also be normal.

> ⚠ If there is any question of adrenal insufficiency, do not commence T_4 replacement to correct hypothyroidism until glucocorticoid replacement has been established as there is a risk of precipitating a hypoadrenal crisis. If in doubt, use an alternative, eg Synacthen test (to assess cortisol reserve), glucagon test (to assess GH and/or cortisol reserve).

- Liaise with the biochemistry laboratory in advance to ensure that glucose samples are assayed rapidly during the test and that the results are phoned through to you as soon as they are available.

- Draw up 25 mL of 25% dextrose and 100 mg of hydrocortisone ready for intravenous use.

- Nil by mouth from midnight.

- Obtain the patient's consent, explaining the test and the symptoms of hypoglycaemia that may be experienced (eg hunger, sweating, tachycardia, tremor). Reassure the patient that you will be present throughout.

- Label the blood bottles.

- Weigh the patient and calculate the dose of soluble insulin required: 0.15 units/kg (0.3 units/kg in those likely to be insulin resistant, eg Cushing's syndrome, acromegaly, marked obesity).

The investigation

1. Insert an intravenous cannula at 8.30 a.m.

2. Take basal blood samples (for glucose, cortisol, ACTH and GH) at 9 a.m.

3. Give the calculated dose of soluble insulin as an intravenous bolus.

4. Take further blood samples at 20, 30, 45, 60, 90 and 120 minutes.

5. Check a blood glucose test strip at each time point, but remember that this only provides an approximate guide to the degree of hypoglycaemia achieved.

6. Blood glucose must fall to less than 2.2 mmol/L (laboratory sample) to provide an adequate stress.

7. By 45 minutes you should expect the patient to experience symptoms of hypoglycaemia. If this does not occur and the blood sugar has not fallen below 2.2 mmol/L, you may need to administer another bolus of insulin and continue sampling for longer.

8. Throughout the test you should record the patient's pulse and BP and note the presence or absence of symptoms of hypoglycaemia.

9. Remember to reassure the patient as the test can be an unpleasant experience.

10. If the patient becomes overwhelmingly hypoglycaemic during the test (especially if there is impending or actual loss of consciousness or a seizure), administer 25 mL of 25% dextrose intravenously (repeated as necessary) and continue sampling, as the hypoglycaemic stimulus will have been sufficient! Consider giving hydrocortisone 100 mg iv if the patient does not recover in response to the dextrose.

After the investigation

- Give oral glucose (eg Lucozade) and lunch, and observe for 2 hours.

- Advise the patient to avoid exercise after the test (including cycling home!).

Interpretation Look for the following.

- Cortisol response: a peak cortisol concentration of >580 nmol/L is generally accepted as a normal response, although some argue that a lower cut-off at 500 nmol/L is acceptable. In addition, an increment of at least 170 nmol/L from the basal level is expected.

- GH response: the definition of GH deficiency is controversial. Most accept that a rise in GH to >20 mU/L denotes an acceptable response, although values in excess of 40 mU/L are seen in many normal control subjects.

Complications

Provided the test is carried out according to these guidelines, it is associated with few serious adverse events.

FURTHER READING

Monson JP. How I investigate the hypothalamo-pituitary–adrenal axis and why. *CME Bulletin Endocrinology and Diabetes* 1999; 2(1): 12–15.

- - - - - - - - - - - - - - - - -

Orme SM, Peacey SR, Barth JH and Belchetz PE. Comparison of tests of stress-released cortisol secretion in pituitary disease. *Clin. Endocrinol.* 1996; 45: 135–40.

3.1.6 Pentagastrin stimulation test

Principle

Although calcitonin is a useful marker for medullary thyroid carcinoma (MTC), levels may lie within the normal range in the early stages of tumour development or if C-cell hyperplasia (a premalignant stage) is present. Provocation with pentagastrin provides a sensitive method for detecting these early cases by inducing calcitonin release from the C-cells, with a correlation between the peak following the stimulus and C-cell mass.

Indications

To screen for MTC in patients with known multiple endocrine neoplasia (MEN)-2/familial MTC or to identify at-risk relatives. However, the latter has been largely superseded by the introduction of genetic testing (see Section 2.7.1).

Contraindications

Hypocalcaemia.

Practical details

Before investigation

- Check that both basal calcium and calcitonin levels are normal.

- Restrict to a light diet with avoidance of alcohol for 12 hours prior to the test.

- Following pentagastrin, patients should be warned that they may experience several unpleasant side effects including flushing, nausea, chest tightness and abdominal cramps.

The investigation

1. With the patient supine, establish intravenous access. Take blood for measurement of basal plasma calcitonin.

2. Give pentagastrin 0.5 μg/kg iv over 10–15 seconds.

3. Repeat samples for calcitonin estimation at 2, 5 and 10 minutes.

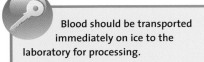

Blood should be transported immediately on ice to the laboratory for processing.

After investigation

Interpretation An increment of two- to three-fold or greater following stimulation is usually taken as a positive result.

Important information for patients It is of paramount importance that relatives understand the implications of this investigation as a screening test for MTC and MEN-2.

FURTHER READING

Eng C and Ponder BAJ. Multiple endocrine neoplasia type 2 and medullary thyroid carcinoma. In: Grossman A, ed. *Clinical Endocrinology*, 2nd edn. Oxford: Blackwell Science, 1998.

3.1.7 Oral glucose tolerance test

Principle
Originally used to confirm/exclude the diagnosis of diabetes mellitus (DM) in individuals with equivocal fasting/random blood glucose levels.

Indications
Currently there is controversy about the role of the oral glucose tolerance test (OGTT) in routine practice (see Section 2.6), although it is still used in pregnancy to diagnose impaired glucose tolerance and gestational DM.

Contraindications
None.

TABLE 65 THE OGTT IN THE DIAGNOSIS OF DM		
Diagnosis	**Fasting glucose**	**2-hour glucose**
Normal	<6.1 mmol/L	<7.8 mmol/L
Impaired glucose tolerance	<7.0 mmol/L	≥7.8 but <11.1 mmol/L
Diabetes	≥7.0 mmol/L	≥11.1 mmol/L

Practical details

Before investigation
Fast from midnight.

The investigation

1. Take a basal venous plasma glucose sample.

2. Give 75 g of oral glucose.

3. Take a further venous plasma glucose sample at 2 hours.

After investigation: interpretation
Values corresponding to a normal response, impaired glucose tolerance and frank DM are shown in Table 65.

3.2 Suppression tests

3.2.1 Overnight dexamethasone suppression test

Principle
Unlike normal subjects, patients with Cushing's syndrome fail to fully suppress endogenous cortisol secretion following administration of dexamethasone.

Indications
Exclusion of diagnosis of Cushing's syndrome.

Contraindications
Although not an absolute contraindication, care should be taken in those with active peptic ulcer disease.

Practical details

Before investigation
No specific preparation is required.

The investigation

1. Day 0: 11 p.m. Give dexamethasone 1 mg orally.

2. Day 1: 9 a.m. Take blood for serum cortisol (ie 10 hours after dose).

After investigation

Interpretation In normal subjects, the serum cortisol suppresses fully to undetectable levels (<50 nmol/L) following dexamethasone, which does not cross-react in the cortisol assay.

Complications Although the procedure itself has few complications, numerous circumstances can complicate interpretation of the results, with an apparent failure to fully suppress serum cortisol, including:

• lack of compliance with dexamethasone;

• pseudo-Cushing's syndrome (see Section 2.1.1);

• hepatic enzyme-inducing drugs (eg rifampicin, phenytoin may facilitate rapid metabolism of dexamethasone to levels such that there is failure to fully suppress a normal hypothalamic–pituitary–adrenal axis);

- cyclical Cushing's syndrome (see Section 2.1.1) with normal dexamethasone suppression in the quiescent phase;

- in addition, a significant number of normal subjects fail to show full suppression in the overnight test.

3.2.2 Low-dose dexamethasone suppression test

Principle

Unlike normal subjects, patients with Cushing's syndrome fail to fully suppress endogenous cortisol secretion following administration of dexamethasone.

Indications

Establishment of diagnosis of Cushing's syndrome.

Contraindications

- Severe intercurrent illness or infection.

- Although not absolute contraindications, care should be taken in those with diabetes mellitus or active peptic ulcer disease.

Practical details

Before investigation

No specific preparation is required.

The investigation

1. Day 0: 9 a.m. Take blood for serum cortisol. A basal ACTH, if not already checked, can be measured on this sample.

2. After venesection, give dexamethasone 0.5 mg orally

every 6 hours (ie at 9 a.m., 3 p.m., 9 p.m. and 3 a.m.) for 48 hours.

3. Day 2: 9 a.m. Take blood for serum cortisol (ie 6 hours after last dose).

After investigation

Interpretation In normal subjects, the basal serum cortisol lies within the reference range (200–700 nmol/L), but suppresses fully to undetectable levels (<50 nmol/L) following 48 hours of dexamethasone, which does not cross-react in the cortisol assay.

Complications Although the procedure itself has few complications, numerous circumstances can complicate interpretation of the results, with an apparent failure to fully suppress serum cortisol, including:

- lack of compliance with dexamethasone (erroneous timing and/or missed doses);

- pseudo-Cushing's syndrome (see Section 2.1.1);

- hepatic enzyme-inducing drugs (eg rifampicin, phenytoin may facilitate rapid metabolism of dexamethasone to levels such that there is failure to fully suppress a normal hypothalamic–pituitary–adrenal axis);

- cyclical Cushing's syndrome (see Section 2.1.1) with normal dexamethasone suppression in the quiescent phase.

Important information for patients

If the test is being performed as an outpatient, it is important to provide the patient with clear instructions as to the timing of doses, and to check for any missed doses.

FURTHER READING

Trainer PJ and Besser M. *The Bart's Endocrine Protocols*. Edinburgh: Churchill Livingstone, 1995.

3.2.3 High-dose dexamethasone suppression test

Principle

Unlike other causes of Cushing's syndrome, pituitary adenomas retain some sensitivity to glucocorticoid feedback such that ACTH release and consequently cortisol levels are reduced in response to high doses of exogenous steroid, eg dexamethasone, which does not cross-react in the cortisol assay.

Indications

To distinguish Cushing's disease from other causes of Cushing's syndrome.

Contraindications

As for the low-dose dexamethasone suppression test, but in addition care should be exercised in patients with psychiatric manifestations of Cushing's syndrome, which may significantly worsen following higher doses of dexamethasone.

Practical details

Before investigation

This test should only be undertaken in individuals in whom the diagnosis of Cushing's syndrome has been confirmed. Ideally it should be performed as an inpatient.

The investigation

1. Day 0: 9 a.m. Take blood for serum cortisol.

2. After venesection, give dexamethasone 2.0 mg orally every 6 hours (ie at 9 a.m., 3 p.m., 9 p.m. and 3 a.m.) for 48 hours.

3. Day 2: 9 a.m. Take blood for serum cortisol (ie 6 hours after last dose).

Note that some centres also routinely check serum cortisol after 24 hours.

After investigation

Interpretation Serum cortisol at completion of the test suppresses to ≤50% of the basal value in the majority of cases of Cushing's disease but not with other causes of Cushing's syndrome.

Complications As with the low-dose test, complications are mainly restricted to the interpretation of results. Just as no single test can reliably confirm or refute the diagnosis of Cushing's syndrome, determination of the aetiology should not be based simply on the result of one investigation. This is important with the high-dose dexamethasone suppression test, since approximately 10% of pituitary adenomas fail to suppress, whilst a smaller number of ectopic ACTH-secreting tumours do so.

FURTHER READING

Trainer PJ and Besser M. *The Bart's Endocrine Protocols*. Edinburgh: Churchill Livingstone, 1995.

3.2.4 Oral glucose tolerance test in acromegaly

Principle

Growth hormone (GH) secretion is pulsatile. As the hormone is rapidly cleared from the circulation, basal GH concentrations are undetectable most of the time. For these reasons, a single random blood sample is not a reliable assessment of GH secretion and dynamic tests are preferred. Normally, glucose suppresses GH secretion. In acromegaly, however, GH levels are paradoxically increased or not suppressed by glucose.

Indications
Patients with suspected acromegaly.

Contraindications
None.

Practical details

Before the investigation
Fast from midnight.

The investigation

1. Site an intravenous cannula.

2. Take a basal blood sample for measurement of glucose and GH.

3. Give 75 g of oral glucose.

4. Take further blood samples for glucose and GH at 30, 60, 90 and 120 minutes.

After investigation: interpretation
Suppression of GH to <2 mU/L (some endocrinologists argue for a lower cut-off of <1 mU/L based on newer more sensitive GH assays) excludes the diagnosis of acromegaly. The glucose results may also show impaired glucose tolerance or diabetes mellitus, which can complicate acromegaly. Other conditions may give rise to non-suppressibility of GH after an oral glucose load, but these are essentially catabolic conditions associated with high GH and low insulin-like growth factor (IGF)-I levels and are unlikely to cause confusion in the clinical context.

FURTHER READING

Duncan E and Wass JA. Investigation protocol: acromegaly and its investigation. *Clin. Endocrinol.* 1999; 50: 285–93.

3.3 Other investigations

3.3.1 Thyroid function tests

Principle
There are a number of tests with which to assess the hypothalamic– pituitary–thyroid axis biochemically. Most laboratories routinely measure thyroid-stimulating hormone (TSH) levels, with many only performing further thyroid function tests if they are specifically requested or indicated on the basis of an abnormal TSH result. Determination of free thyroxine (FT_4) and free triiodothyronine (FT_3) levels avoids many of the problems associated with interpreting the results of total hormone measurements.

Indications
Thyroid function tests are frequently requested, as hyperthyroidism and hypothyroidism are common diseases that may be difficult to diagnose clinically and are relatively easy to treat successfully.

Complications
There are a number of common pitfalls in the interpretation of thyroid function tests.

Non-thyroidal illness or 'sick euthyroid syndrome'
In non-thyroidal illness, concentrations of FT_3, FT_4 and TSH can all 'sag' at various times during the clinical course. In particular, hospitalised patients tend to have lower T_3 and higher reverse T_3 (rT_3) levels than healthy volunteers due to reduced activity of the enzyme responsible for peripheral conversion of T_4 to T_3 and rT_3 to T_2.

> It is best not to test the thyroid function of ill patients unless there is clinical evidence of thyroid disease or concern that hyperthyroidism or hypothyroidism may be contributing to the patient's problems.

During thyrotoxicosis treatment

> **Focus on the FT$_4$ levels shortly after beginning treatment for thyrotoxicosis, as the TSH may remain suppressed for weeks or months.**

Pituitary disease

In clinically hypothyroid patients with a low FT$_4$ whose TSH is not elevated, consider the possibility of pituitary disease causing secondary hypothyroidism. Check remaining anterior pituitary function (hypopituitarism, see Section 2.1.8), and remember that if there is evidence of cortisol deficiency, this must be corrected before thyroid replacement is instituted.

> **In hypopituitary patients on T$_4$ replacement, remember to titrate the dose of T$_4$ against the FT$_4$ concentration: in this context it is probably safest to ignore the TSH.**

Early pregnancy

In the first trimester of pregnancy, human chorionic gonadotrophin (hCG) secretion may result in elevated concentrations of FT$_4$ and FT$_3$, and suppression of TSH (hCG shares a common α-subunit with TSH and the gonadotrophins). This is more marked in patients with hyperemesis gravidarum.

Drugs

Various drugs can interfere with thyroid function through one or more mechanisms.

- High doses of salicylates, furosemide or phenytoin may compete with hormone binding to thyroxine-binding globulin, resulting in increased free (but not total) hormone levels.

- Amiodarone, glucocorticoids, high-dose propranolol and oral cholecystographic agents inhibit peripheral conversion of T$_4$ to T$_3$.

- Dopamine, L-dopa and glucocorticoids may inhibit TSH secretion.

- Heparin increases FT$_4$ ± FT$_3$ levels due to an *in vitro* assay artefact.

> **FURTHER READING**
>
> Chopra IJ. Euthyroid sick syndrome: is it a misnomer? *J. Clin. Endocrinol. Metab.* 1997; 82: 329–34.
>
> ------------------------
>
> Dayan CM. Interpretation of thyroid function tests. *Lancet* 2001; 357: 619–24.

3.3.2 Water deprivation test

Principle

In the presence of diabetes insipidus (DI), water deprivation leads to intravascular depletion with an increase in plasma osmolality; urine osmolality remains inappropriately low due to continued diuresis. In hypothalamic (cranial) DI (ie deficiency of antidiuretic hormone, ADH), administration of synthetic ADH [desmopressin (DDAVP)] corrects the defect to allow concentration of urine; in contrast, the urine remains dilute in nephrogenic DI (ie resistance to the action of ADH).

Indications

Diagnosis of DI and distinction from primary polydipsia.

Contraindications

- Suspected or confirmed thyroid and/or adrenal insufficiency. Ensure adequate hormone replacement prior to test.

- Hypovolaemia.

Practical details

Before the investigation

Although fluid restriction is not necessary prior to the test, ask the patient to avoid excessive intake. It may also be informative to document fluid intake for the 12 hours before the test. Allow a light breakfast but no tea or coffee. Continue normal steroid replacement if the patient is receiving this.

The investigation

1. At 8 a.m. weigh the patient (with an empty bladder) and calculate 97% of this basal level.

2. Under direct supervision, deprive the patient of all fluid and food for 8 hours. Do not allow him/her to smoke.

3. Measure and record all urine volumes on an hourly basis.

4. Measure plasma and urine osmolalities at 0, 2, 4, 6 and 8 hours.

5. Weigh the patient at 2, 4, 6, 7 and 8 hours.

6. At the conclusion of the test, give desmopressin 2 μg im and continue collecting urine samples and measuring urine osmolalities for a further 4 hours. Allow the patient to drink and eat freely during this period.

> ⚠ **If at any point during the test there is a greater than 3% drop in weight compared with the basal level, check plasma osmolality urgently. If this has risen to >295 mosmol/kg, give desmopressin 2 μg im and allow the patient to drink. Otherwise consider continuing the test under close supervision. Abandon if the patient loses ≥5% of body weight.**

After investigation: interpretation

- In normal subjects, plasma osmolality increases but remains below 295 mosmol/kg; urine osmolality rises as urine volume falls.

- With hypothalamic DI, urine osmolality fails to rise and a relative diuresis continues despite the increasing plasma osmolality. Following desmopressin, the urine concentrates normally.

- Nephrogenic DI is similar to hypothalamic DI, except that there is a failure of urine concentration in response to desmopressin.

- With primary polydipsia, excessive fluid intake prior to the test may result in an apparent continued diuresis despite fluid restriction.

Plasma osmolality remains below 295 mosmol/kg.

FURTHER READING

Trainer PJ and Besser M. *The Bart's Endocrine Protocols.* Edinburgh: Churchill Livingstone, 1995.

4.1 Self-assessment questions

Question 1

Clinical scenario

A 45-year-old woman with a long-standing history of schizoaffective disorder is found on routine investigation to be hyponatraemic. Physical examination is unremarkable. Investigations show serum sodium 122 mmol/L (normal range 137–144), serum potassium 4.5 mmol/L (normal range 3.5–4.9), serum urea 2.2 mmol/L (normal range 2.5–7), serum creatinine 55 µmol/L (normal range 60–110), plasma osmolality 262 mosmol/kg (normal range 278–305), plasma thyroid-stimulating hormone 1.8 mU/L (normal range 0.4–5.0), 9 a.m. serum cortisol 510 nmol/L (normal range 200–700) and urine osmolality 420 mosmol/kg (normal range 350–1000).

Question

Which of the following drugs is most likely to cause this biochemical picture?

Answers

A Chlorpromazine
B Lithium carbonate
C Olanzapine
D Sodium valproate
E Venlafaxine

Question 2

Clinical scenario

A 63-year-old woman with a history of hypertension treated with furosemide 40 mg/day and amlodipine 10 mg/day is referred by her GP to the Endocrine Clinic for further investigation of hypercalcaemia. On examination her pulse is 76 bpm in sinus rhythm and BP is 145/85 mmHg. Auscultation of the chest is unremarkable. She has mild peripheral oedema. Investigations show serum sodium 137 mmol/L (normal range 137–144), serum potassium 3.6 mmol/L (normal range 3.5–4.9), serum urea 6.8 mmol/L (normal range 2.5–7), serum creatinine 105 µmol/L (normal range 60–110), serum corrected calcium 2.85 mmol/L (normal range 2.2–2.6), serum phosphate 0.72 mmol/L (normal range 0.8–1.4), plasma parathyroid hormone 7.6 pmol/L (normal range 0.9–5.40) and 24-hour urinary calcium 8.3 mmol/L (normal range 2.5–7.5). Dual energy X-ray absorptiometry (DEXA) scan shows total hip T-score of –0.96 and lumbar spine T-score of –1.65.

Question

What is the most appropriate management?

Answers

A Change furosemide to bendroflumethiazide
B Commence bisphosphonate
C Observation with repeat serum calcium in 3 months
D Parathyroidectomy
E Start low-calcium diet

Question 3

Clinical scenario

A 41-year-old woman is referred by her GP with suspected hypoglycaemic episodes. She has previously been fit and well, but has recently gained weight. Her daughter has well-controlled type 1 diabetes mellitus. On examination she is overweight (BMI 28.0 kg/m^2) and her BP is 120/80 mmHg lying and 110/75 mmHg standing. She is admitted to hospital for a prolonged fast and becomes symptomatic at 18 hours, at which time investigations reveal serum sodium 137 mmol/L (normal range 137–144), serum potassium 4.8 mmol/L (normal range 3.5–4.9), serum creatinine 70 µmol/L (normal range 60–110), serum albumin 40 g/L (normal range 37–49), serum total bilirubin 10 µmol/L (normal range 1–22), serum alanine aminotransferase 25 U/L (normal range 5–35), serum alkaline phosphatase 100 U/L (normal range 45–105), plasma glucose 1.9 mmol/L (normal range 3–6) and plasma insulin 65 pmol/L (normal <21).

Question

Which additional investigation is most likely to help distinguish between the possible causes of her symptoms?

Answers

A Haemoglobin A_{1c}
B Plasma C-peptide
C Plasma pancreatic polypeptide
D Plasma sulphonylurea screen
E Synacthen test

Question 4

Clinical scenario

A 44-year-old man presents to his GP complaining of erectile dysfunction.

He had been fit and well until the age of 39 years when he had been diagnosed with type 2 diabetes mellitus at an insurance medical. He is a non-smoker who consumes no alcohol. On examination he is of normal height but mildly overweight (BMI 28.5 kg/m²), with central adiposity. He appears hypogonadal and has bilateral gynaecomastia. Examination of the external genitalia reveals bilateral testicular volumes of 10–15 mL. Visual fields are full to confrontation. Investigations reveal serum sodium 139 mmol/L (normal range 137–144), serum potassium 4.0 mmol/L (normal range 3.5–4.9), serum creatinine 80 µmol/L (normal range 60–110), serum albumin 42 g/L (normal range 37–49), serum total bilirubin 20 µmol/L (normal range 1–22), serum alanine aminotransferase 150 U/L (normal range 5–35), serum alkaline phosphatase 165 U/L (normal range 45–105), HbA$_{1c}$ 8.0% (normal range 3.8–6.4), plasma luteinising hormone 22 U/L (normal range 1–10), plasma follicle stimulating hormone 31 U/L (normal range 1–7) and serum testosterone 3.1 nmol/L (normal range 9–35).

Question

Which investigation is most likely to help elucidate the cause for his erectile dysfunction?

Answers

A Autonomic function testing

B Karyotype analysis

C Plasma prolactin

D Serum oestradiol

E Serum transferrin saturation

Question 5

Clinical scenario

A 36-year-old man presents to his GP complaining of numbness and tingling in both hands, which is particularly troublesome at night. He had been fit and well until 2 years earlier when he had been diagnosed with hypertension. On examination he has coarse facial features, prognathism and evidence of bilateral carpal tunnel syndrome.

Question

Which of the following would confirm a diagnosis of acromegaly?

Answers

A Blunted growth hormone response to insulin-induced hypoglycaemia

B Detectable midnight growth hormone

C Exaggerated rise in growth hormone levels following glucagon stimulation

D 9 a.m. growth hormone >20 mU/L

E Paradoxical rise in growth hormone levels during oral glucose tolerance test

Question 6

Clinical scenario

A 65-year-old woman with type 2 diabetes mellitus and long-standing hypertension is referred to the Diabetic Clinic by her GP who is concerned about her declining renal function. Her medication includes gliclazide 80 mg bd, metformin 500 mg tds, aspirin 75 mg/day, ramipril 10 mg/day, bendroflumethiazide 2.5 mg/day and atorvastatin 20 mg/day. She is a non-smoker. On examination she is obese (BMI 34 kg/m²), her BP is 130/70 mmHg and she has mild peripheral oedema. Fundoscopy reveals dot and blot haemorrhages, microaneurysms and hard exudates. Investigations show serum sodium 142 mmol/L (normal range 137–144), serum potassium 4.5 mmol/L (normal range 3.5–4.9), serum urea 15 mmol/L (normal range 2.5–7.5), serum creatinine 185 µmol/L (normal range 60–110), serum cholesterol 4.2 mmol/L (normal <5.2), serum high-density lipoprotein cholesterol 0.9 mmol/L (normal >1.55), HbA$_{1c}$ 6.3% (normal range 3.8–6.4) and 24-hour urinary total protein 1.8 g (normal <0.2).

Question

Which management step is most appropriate at this visit?

Answers

A Change bendroflumethiazide to furosemide

B Add ezetimibe

C Start fenofibrate

D Stop metformin

E Stop ramipril

Question 7

Clinical scenario

A 31-year-old woman presents to her GP with recurrent vaginal candidiasis. Her past medical history includes hypothyroidism for which she is on long-term thyroxine replacement. On examination she is mildly overweight (BMI 28 kg/m²) and her BP is 140/85 mmHg. Investigations reveal fasting plasma glucose 12.2 mmol/L (normal range 3–6) and HbA$_{1c}$ 9.8% (normal range 3.8–6.4).

Question

Which of the following would favour a diagnosis of type 2 rather than type 1 diabetes mellitus?

Answers

A Autoimmune aetiology of hypothyroidism

B Detection of islet cell autoantibodies

C Elevated low-density lipoprotein cholesterol level

D Normal urinary albumin/creatinine ratio

E Presence of dot and blot haemorrhages on fundoscopy

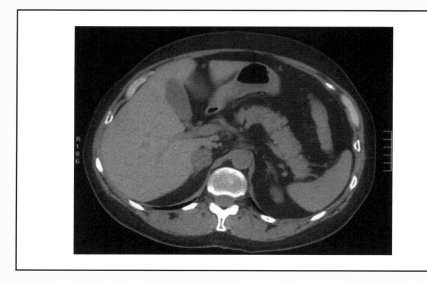

▲**Fig. 69** Question 8.

pyrexial (temperature 37.7°C) but not systemically unwell. The toe is swollen and a small deep ulcer is noted at the tip, with spreading cellulitis over the adjacent foot.

Question

Which of the following investigations would it be most appropriate to organise immediately at this stage?

Answers

A Bone scan

B CT scan of foot

C X-ray of foot

D MRI scan of foot

E White cell scan

Question 8

Clinical scenario

A 45-year-old woman is referred by her GP for further investigation of treatment-resistant hypertension. Her medication includes ramipril 10 mg/day and bendroflumethiazide 2.5 mg/day. On examination her pulse is 72 bpm in sinus rhythm and her BP is 185/95 mmHg. Auscultation of the heart and chest is unremarkable. She has haemorrhages and cotton-wool spots in both fundi. Investigations show serum sodium 144 mmol/L (normal range 137–144), serum potassium 2.6 mmol/L (normal range 3.5–4.9), serum urea 3.6 mmol/L (normal range 2.5–7.5), serum creatinine 135 µmol/L (normal range 60–110) and 24-hour urinary total protein 1.2 g (normal <0.2). A CT scan of her abdomen is shown in Fig. 69.

Question

What is the most likely cause for her hypertension?

Answers

A Conn's syndrome

B Paraganglioma

C Phaeochromocytoma

D Polycystic kidney disease

E Renal artery stenosis

Question 9

Clinical scenario

A 28-year-old woman with gestational diabetes mellitus has required insulin therapy in the form of a basal bolus regimen from 28 weeks' gestation. She is commenced on a sliding-scale intravenous insulin infusion during labour and the delivery proceeds uneventfully.

Question

Following delivery she should be advised to:

Answers

A Restart her basal bolus subcutaneous insulin regimen

B Start gliclazide

C Start metformin

D Start rosiglitazone

E Stop all treatment

Question 10

Clinical scenario

A 54-year-old man with type 2 diabetes mellitus is admitted to hospital with an infected second toe on the right foot. Despite 3 weeks of high-dose oral antibiotics from his GP, the toe has shown no sign of improvement. On examination he is

Question 11

Clinical scenario

A 32-year-old man with long-standing type 1 diabetes mellitus presents to his GP with a 3-month history of tiredness and lethargy. He also reports increasingly frequent hypoglycaemic episodes despite having reduced his total daily insulin dose on three separate occasions during the previous 2 weeks. On examination he is slim (BMI 21.5 kg/m²), his pulse is 68 bpm sinus rhythm and his BP is 100/65 mmHg. Investigations reveal serum sodium 136 mmol/L (normal range 137–144), serum potassium 5.1 mmol/L (normal range 3.5–4.9), serum urea 7.8 mmol/L (normal range 2.5–7), serum creatinine 98 µmol/L (normal range 60–110) and HbA$_{1c}$ 6.4% (normal range 3.8–6.4).

Question

Which of the following investigations is most likely to identify the cause for his symptoms?

Answers

A Anti-tissue transglutaminase antibodies

B Plasma thyroid-stimulating hormone

C Serum vitamin B$_{12}$
D Serum corrected calcium
E Short tetracosactide (Synacthen) test

Question 12

Clinical scenario

A 48-year-old man is reviewed in the Endocrine Clinic with the results of an oral glucose tolerance test (OGTT), which had been carried out to investigate possible acromegaly. Growth hormone levels during the OGTT suppressed appropriately and his insulin-like growth factor (IGF)-1 level was within the age- and gender-matched reference range. He has a strong family history of type 2 diabetes and at his follow-up visit asks whether there was any indication that he was developing diabetes. OGTT results show 0-minute plasma glucose 5.1 mmol/L, 120-minute plasma glucose 7.4 mmol/L.

Question

He should be advised that he has:

Answers

A Diabetes mellitus
B Impaired fasting glycaemia
C Impaired glucose tolerance
D Normal glucose tolerance
E Pre-diabetes

Question 13

Clinical scenario

A 72-year-old woman is referred to the Endocrine Clinic by her GP after she is discovered to have abnormal thyroid function tests while under investigation for tiredness. She reports no other symptoms of thyroid dysfunction, but had been admitted to hospital 4 months earlier with a diagnosis of congestive cardiac failure and atrial fibrillation. She has no family history of thyroid disease. Her medication includes digoxin 125 μg/day, furosemide 80

mg/day and warfarin 3 mg/day. On examination her pulse is 80 bpm atrial fibrillation and her BP 135/85 mmHg. She has a small goitre, no cervical lymphadenopathy and there is no evidence of dysthyroid eye disease. Investigations reveal plasma free T$_4$ 17.5 pmol/L (normal range 10–22), plasma free T$_3$ 9.5 pmol/L (normal range 5–10), plasma thyroid-stimulating hormone <0.1 mU/L (normal range 0.4–5.0) and serum antithyroid peroxidase 35 IU/mL (normal <50).

Question

What is the most likely cause for her abnormal thyroid function tests?

Answers

A Graves' disease
B Hashimoto's thyroiditis
C Non-thyroidal illness (sick euthyroid syndrome)
D Subacute thyroiditis
E Toxic multinodular goitre

Question 14

Clinical scenario

A 56-year-old woman is referred to the hospital by her GP for further investigation of weight loss and palpitations. She has no past medical history of note and is on no regular medications. There is no family history of thyroid disease. On examination her pulse is 110 bpm in sinus rhythm and she has a fine resting tremor. She has a small goitre with no discrete palpable nodules and no cervical lymphadenopathy. There is no evidence of dysthyroid eye disease. Investigations reveal plasma free T$_4$ 55.5 pmol/L (normal range 10–22), plasma free T$_3$ 15.5 pmol/L (normal range 5–10), plasma thyroid-stimulating hormone <0.1 mU/L (normal range 0.4–5.0) and serum antithyroid peroxidase 15 IU/mL (normal <50).

Question

Which investigation is most likely to help determine the cause of this woman's presentation?

Answers

A CT scan of neck and upper thorax
B Fine-needle aspiration biopsy
C Sestamibi scan
D Technetium uptake scan
E Ultrasound neck

Question 15

Clinical scenario

A 26-year-old man is brought to the Emergency Department with a 12-hour history of nausea, vomiting and drowsiness. On examination he has a reduced Glasgow Coma Scale score of 9 (E3, V2, M4). He is apyrexial, with a pulse rate of 120 bpm in sinus rhythm and BP 95/55 mmHg. His heart sounds are normal and his chest is clear to auscultation. There are no focal neurological signs.

Question

Which of the following investigations should take immediate priority?

Answers

A Arterial blood gases
B Blood cultures
C Fingerprick glucose
D Serum cortisol
E Urine toxicology screen

Question 16

Clinical scenario

A 19-year-old man presents to his GP complaining of erectile dysfunction. His past medical history is unremarkable, he is on no regular medication, and he denies excessive alcohol consumption. On examination he appears anxious and embarrassed when asked to undress. He has bilateral gynaecomastia and only sparse pubic hair. Testicular volumes are 5 mL bilaterally, with no identifiable masses. Investigations show plasma luteinising hormone 45 U/L (normal range 1–10), plasma follicle-stimulating hormone 56 U/L (normal range 1–7), serum testosterone 3.1 nmol/L (normal range 9–35), plasma prolactin 555 mU/L (normal <360), plasma free T_4 14.5 pmol/L (normal range 10–22) and plasma thyroid-stimulating hormone 1.5 mU/L (normal range 0.4–5.0).

Question

What is the most likely cause for his hypogonadism?

Answers

A Haemochromatosis
B Kallmann's syndrome
C Klinefelter's syndrome
D Non-functioning pituitary adenoma
E Prolactinoma

Question 17

Clinical scenario

A 57-year-old woman with a long history of depressive illness is referred to the Endocrine Clinic for further investigation of polydipsia and polyuria. Her past medical history includes primary hypothyroidism for which she is on long-term thyroxine replacement. On examination she is mildly overweight (BMI 27.5 kg/m²) and her BP is 140/85 mmHg. Investigations show fasting plasma glucose 5.6 mmol/L (normal range 3–6), serum corrected calcium 2.8 mmol/L (normal range 2.2–2.6), serum phosphate 0.7 mmol/L (normal range 0.8–1.4) and plasma thyroid-stimulating hormone 2.2 mU/L (normal range 0.4–5.0).

Question

Which of the following drugs is most likely to be of relevance to her presentation?

Answers

A Amitriptyline
B Citalopram
C Lithium
D Haloperidol
E Venlafaxine

Question 18

Clinical scenario

A 29-year-old woman complains of excessive weight gain, despite repeated attempts to diet, following the birth of her second child 2 years earlier. Her only regular medication is the combined oral contraceptive pill. Her BMI is 38 kg/m². She has mild facial hirsutism, but the remainder of the physical examination is unremarkable. Investigations reveal fasting plasma glucose 4.6 mmol/L (normal range 3–6), plasma free T_4 10.5 pmol/L (normal range 10–22), plasma thyroid-stimulating hormone 1.2 mU/L (normal range 0.4–5.0), serum antithyroid peroxidase 100 IU/mL (normal <50), overnight dexamethasone suppression test 90 nmol/L (normal <50), midnight serum cortisol 75 nmol/L (normal <100) and 24-hour urinary free

cortisol 240 nmol/L (normal range 55–250).

Question

What is the most likely cause for her weight gain?

Answers

A Cushing's disease
B Cushing's syndrome
C Exogenous oestrogen therapy
D Simple obesity
E Subclinical hypothyroidism

Question 19

Clinical scenario

A 22-year-old woman presents with headaches and galactorrhoea. She is noted to have a prolactin level of 950 mU/L (normal range up to 400). An MRI scan of her pituitary is shown in Fig. 70.

Question

What does the MRI scan show?

Answers

A Normal pituitary gland
B Microprolactinoma
C Macroprolactinoma
D Non-functioning adenoma with compression of pituitary stalk
E Pituitary apoplexy

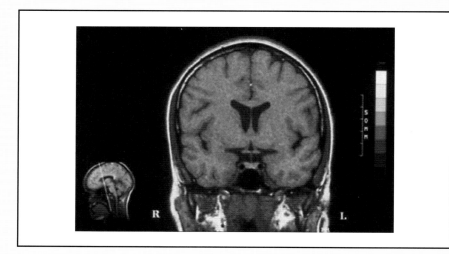

▲ **Fig. 70** Question 19.

Question 20

Clinical scenario

A 65-year-old obese man with type 2 diabetes, who has failed to attend for follow-up for the last 5 years, returns to the diabetic clinic at his daughter's insistence. He is hypertensive (BP 150/110 mmHg) with absent peripheral pulses. The appearance of his left ocular fundus is shown in Fig. 71.

Question

Which of the following best describes the retinal appearance?

Answers

A Background diabetic retinopathy
B Proliferative diabetic retinopathy
C Diabetic maculopathy
D Diabetic maculopathy and background diabetic retinopathy
E Background diabetic retinopathy with accelerated-phase hypertension

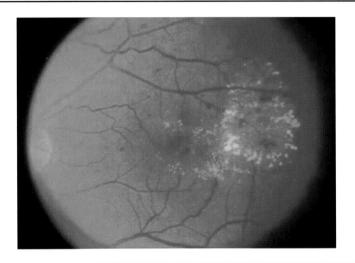

▲ **Fig. 71** Question 20.

Question 21

Clinical scenario

A 37-year-old woman with a 6-month history of tiredness and lethargy is admitted as an emergency complaining of a severe retro-orbital headache and visual disturbance. She is shown in Fig. 72.

Question

What is the clinical diagnosis?

Answers

A Left third nerve palsy
B Left fourth nerve palsy
C Left sixth nerve palsy

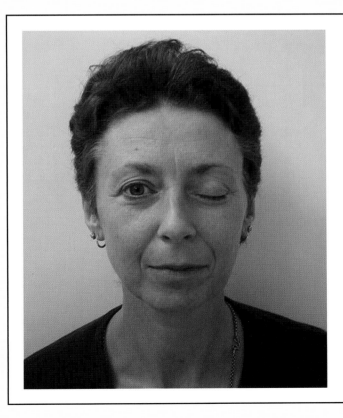
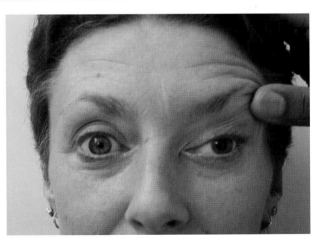

▲ **Fig. 72** Question 21.

D Left seventh nerve (Bell's) palsy
E Left Horner's syndrome

Question 22

Clinical scenario

A 37-year-old woman with a
6-month history of tiredness
and lethargy is admitted as an
emergency complaining of a severe
retro-orbital headache and visual
disturbance. On examination she
has a left third nerve palsy. The
findings of an urgent MRI scan are
shown in Fig. 73.

Question

What is the most likely diagnosis?

Answers

A Subarachnoid haemorrhage due
to a posterior communicating
artery aneurysm
B Haemorrhage into a pituitary
macroadenoma
C Lymphocytic hypophysitis with
suprasellar extension
D Haemorrhagic hypophysitis
E Empty sella syndrome

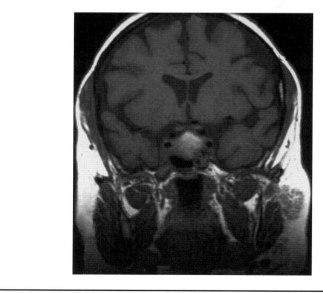

▲ **Fig. 73** Question 22.

4.2 Self-assessment answers

Answer to Question 1

E

In the presence of normal renal,
adrenal and thyroid function
and in a patient who is clinically
euvolaemic, this biochemical profile
is consistent with a diagnosis
of syndrome of inappropriate
antidiuretic hormone (SIADH).
Venlafaxine is a well-recognised
cause of this disorder.

Answer to Question 2

D

This patient has primary
hyperparathyroidism, with the
classical biochemical pattern of
elevated serum calcium, low serum
phosphate and an inappropriately
elevated parathyroid hormone level.
She also has evidence of osteopenia
in the lumbar spine on DEXA

scanning. In these circumstances,
and in the absence of any family
history of inherited endocrinopathy,
it is likely that she has a solitary
parathyroid adenoma. In many
centres preoperative localisation
using ultrasound and/or ^{99m}Tc-
sestamibi facilitates minimally
invasive selective adenomectomy.

Bendroflumethiazide acts to
reduce renal calcium excretion
and is likely therefore to further
elevate the serum calcium level.
Whilst bisphosphonates may be
used to help lower serum calcium
levels in the short term, their use in
the longer term should be reserved
for those in whom surgery is not
possible. In addition, in this case
the patient has only mild osteopenia
at a single site, and this is likely
to respond to correction of the
hyperparathyroidism. Although
long-term surveillance in clinically
asymptomatic subjects has
previously been favoured by
some clinicians, this approach is
no longer recommended in patients
who are suitable for surgery,
especially when there is evidence
of associated complications
(eg nephrolithiasis, osteopenia/
osteoporosis, hypertension).
Low-calcium diets are not
appropriate, and indeed may
exacerbate associated bone disease.

Answer to Question 3

B

The plasma insulin level is
inappropriate for the ambient
glucose concentration and is
consistent with insulin-mediated
hypoglycaemia. The history of
weight gain suggests the possibility
of insulinoma, but other causes
of this biochemical picture must
be excluded before embarking on
a search for a pancreatic lesion.
Exogenous insulin administration

and sulphonylurea use may both lead to hypoglycaemia with inappropriate hyperinsulinaemia. Measurement of plasma C-peptide levels helps to distinguish exogenous insulin administration from other causes because endogenous proinsulin secretion, from which both insulin and C-peptide are derived, is suppressed if hypoglycaemia is driven by exogenous insulin. In contrast, sulphonylureas stimulate endogenous insulin and C-peptide secretion from pancreatic β cells and measurement of plasma or urine sulphonylurea levels when the patient is hypoglycaemic may be necessary to confirm/refute clinical suspicions. In this case the patient's daughter has type 1 diabetes mellitus, so the patient is likely to have access to insulin, making it particularly important to exclude factitious insulin administration.

Answer to Question 4

E

This man has type 2 diabetes mellitus, primary hypogonadism and deranged liver function tests, a combination that raises the possibility of haemochromatosis. Genetic testing for the common mutation in the *HFE* gene is increasingly available, but initial screening with measurement of serum transferrin saturation will identify most cases. Although central obesity *per se* may be associated with hepatic steatosis and borderline low/normal testosterone levels, the gonadotrophins are usually within the normal range, reflecting the fact that these subjects typically have normal free testosterone levels. However, measurements of total testosterone may be borderline low due to a reduction in circulating sex hormone-binding globulin levels.

Answer to Question 5

E

The oral glucose tolerance test remains the gold standard for diagnosing acromegaly, with affected subjects exhibiting failure of suppression of growth hormone levels in response to a glucose challenge; indeed in many cases a paradoxical rise is observed. In most acromegalics, insulin-like growth factor (IGF)-1 levels are also elevated, but this finding should not be used as the sole criterion for diagnosis. In normal physiology, growth hormone is secreted in a pulsatile manner and random measurements should not be used to diagnose growth hormone deficiency or excess. The insulin tolerance test and glucagon stimulation test are used to assess growth hormone reserve in subjects with suspected deficiency.

Answer to Question 6

D

Metformin should not be used in patients with significant renal impairment (eg creatinine >150 μmol/L) due to the risk of associated lactic acidosis. It is also contraindicated in moderate to severe cardiac failure or hepatic impairment. Angiotensin-converting enzyme inhibitors and angiotensin receptor blockers are renoprotective and reduce cardiovascular risk in type 2 diabetes and should be continued unless there is a high index of suspicion that renal artery stenosis is a significant contributor to the patient's renal impairment. No low-density lipoprotein cholesterol level is provided, but even if this was found to be above target, then it is likely that a small increase in the atorvastatin dose would suffice given that the total cholesterol level is only 4.2 mmol/L. Fibrates must be used

with caution in renal impairment as the risk of a myositis-like syndrome is increased, especially if combined with a statin.

Answer to Question 7

E

Subjects with type 2 diabetes mellitus may exhibit microvascular and macrovascular complications at presentation, reflecting the fact that their diabetes has often been present for some time before being diagnosed. This is not typically the case in type 1 diabetes. Low high-density lipoprotein cholesterol levels and high triglycerides are characteristic of type 2 diabetes. Autoimmune hypothyroidism is most commonly associated with type 1 rather than type 2 diabetes, and islet cell antibodies are typical of the former.

Answer to Question 8

A

Significant hypokalaemia in a patient with hypertension should always prompt further investigation. The degree of hypokalaemia in this case is more marked than would normally be expected for a patient on bendroflumethiazide and should prompt consideration of disorders that may be associated with renal potassium wasting, eg primary hyperaldosteronism and Cushing's syndrome. The abdominal CT scan (Fig. 74) is taken at the level of the adrenal glands and shows a right-sided adrenal adenoma (black arrow), suggesting a diagnosis of Conn's syndrome. The normal left adrenal gland is also shown (white arrow).

Answer to Question 9

E

Gestational diabetes mellitus (GDM) is a transient phenomenon. Dietary

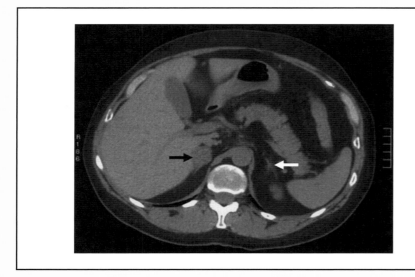

▲**Fig. 74** Answer 8

measures are tried in the first instance, but if blood glucose levels remain above target then insulin therapy is the mainstay of treatment during the remainder of the pregnancy. Most patients with GDM are able to discontinue all therapy following delivery of the placenta. However, women with a history of GDM are at higher risk of developing type 2 diabetes mellitus in later life. Accordingly they should be encouraged to follow a healthy diet and lifestyle. Repeating the oral glucose tolerance test at 6–8 weeks after delivery can help to identify those at higher risk.

Answer to Question 10

C

It is quite likely that this man has underlying osteomyelitis and that the tiny ulcer over the tip of his right second toe extends to the bone. There are several imaging studies that would help in identifying osteomyelitis, but the most readily available and appropriate in the first instance is a plain X-ray. Although plain films may not show bony changes in the early stages of osteomyelitis, there is often some

evidence of soft tissue reaction. This man has had symptoms and signs for a sufficient duration of time (>2 weeks) for X-ray changes of osteomyelitis to be evident (haziness and loss of density of the affected bone, periosteal thickening and/or elevation and focal osteopenia, or the typical lytic changes). However, if plain X-rays are negative and there is sufficient clinical concern of an underlying infection, then further imaging is required, typically an MRI scan or a bone scan, but CT may also be useful.

Answer to Question 11

E

Type 1 diabetes mellitus may be associated with other autoimmune disorders, including Addison's

disease, Graves' disease, Hashimoto's thyroiditis, primary gonadal failure, coeliac disease, pernicious anaemia, vitiligo, alopecia and primary hypoparathyroidism (as part of the type 2 or, less commonly, type 1 polyglandular endocrinopathy syndromes). Tiredness and lethargy are common presenting features of several of these conditions, but the history of recurrent hypoglycaemic episodes despite adjustments to his insulin regimen, low BMI, hypotension and abnormal electrolytes (with low serum sodium and elevated serum potassium and urea) make Addison's disease most likely in this case.

Answer to Question 12

D

The oral glucose tolerance test shows that this man has normal glucose tolerance with both the 0- and 120-minute values clearly falling within the normal range. See Table 66 for interpretation of venous plasma glucose levels.

Answer to Question 13

E

This is a typical presentation of toxic multinodular goitre, which is the commonest cause of hyperthyroidism in the elderly, in whom classical clinical symptoms and signs of thyrotoxicosis are often absent. The diagnosis may be detected incidentally on

TABLE 66 INTERPRETATION OF VENOUS PLASMA GLUCOSE LEVELS		
Diagnosis	Fasting glucose	2-hour glucose
Normal	<6.1 mmol/L	<7.8 mmol/L
Impaired fasting glycaemia	≥6.1 but <7.0 mmol/L	<7.8 mmol/L
Impaired glucose tolerance	<7.0 mmol/L	≥7.8 but <11.1 mmol/L
Diabetes	≥7.0 mmol/L	≥11.1 mmol/L

investigation of tiredness or as part of screening in patients with atrial fibrillation or congestive cardiac failure.

Non-thyroidal illness (sick euthyroid syndrome) manifests most commonly with low TSH, low/normal free T_4 and low free T_3 levels. Hashimoto's thyroiditis is classically associated with hypothyroidism and only rarely with hyperthyroidism, which may occur in the earliest stages of the condition (so-called 'Hashitoxicosis'). Although Graves' disease is the commonest cause of thyrotoxicosis overall, it is typically seen in a younger age group, with goitre, eye signs and a positive family history. Subacute thyroiditis may be associated with preceding pain in the neck or, if painless, typically occurs in a younger age group, particularly when occurring in the postpartum period or when triggered by certain drugs.

Answer to Question 14

D

A technetium uptake scan would help in differentiating between the possible causes of thyrotoxicosis: Graves' disease (diffuse increased uptake), toxic multinodular goitre (patchy increased uptake), toxic adenoma (discrete hot nodule), thyroiditis (absent or reduced uptake). In this case there is no relevant family history, eye signs or other features to allow a clinical diagnosis of Graves' disease to be made. While the patient is older than is classical for a new presentation of Graves' disease, this remains a possibility. The detection of TSH receptor antibodies in the patient's serum would provide an alternative means of diagnosing Graves' disease and in these circumstances a thyroid uptake scan

would not be necessary unless the patient opts for radioactive iodine and it is used to plan the dose. A thyroid ultrasound or CT scan is not helpful in the routine diagnosis or differential diagnosis of thyrotoxicosis. In the absence of a dominant thyroid nodule there is no indication for fine-needle aspiration biopsy to exclude thyroid carcinoma. Sestamibi scanning is used in the investigation of hyperparathyroidism to identify a parathyroid adenoma.

Answer to Question 15

C

In any patient with a reduced conscious level the first investigation should be a fingerprick glucose measurement to exclude hyperglycaemia or hypoglycaemia: this patient could be a new presentation of diabetic ketoacidosis or Addisonian crisis. Remember that it is also important for a sample to be sent to the laboratory for confirmation of the result. The other listed investigations are all potentially important, and depending on the initial assessment of the patient it is likely that they would also be requested at an early stage. If adrenal insufficiency (Addison's disease) is suspected (pigmentation, hypotension, low serum sodium and elevated serum potassium), then blood should be drawn and sent to the laboratory for cortisol and ACTH measurement, and parenteral corticosteroids administered immediately (eg hydrocortisone 50–100 mg stat) and continued thereafter until adrenal insufficiency has been excluded.

Answer to Question 16

C

This man presents with the classical features of Klinefelter's syndrome

(karyotype 47,XXY). Due to the abnormal gonadal development, testosterone levels are low with consequent elevation of gonadotrophins. Patients are usually azoospermic and infertile. Kallmann's syndrome is an inherited form of hypogonadotrophic hypogonadism, typically associated with anosmia. Although the prolactin level is slightly elevated, it is likely that this is a reflection of the patient's anxiety, rather than a consequence of a true microprolactinoma or non-functioning pituitary adenoma with so-called 'stalk disconnection syndrome'. Moreover, both of the latter would predispose to hypogonadotrophic rather than hypergonadotrophic hypogonadism. Given the absence of any significant past medical history, it is extremely unlikely that excessive iron deposition is the cause of hypogonadism in a man of this age.

Answer to Question 17

C

Hypercalcaemia and hyperparathyroidism are recognised side effects of long-term treatment with lithium in patients with chronic affective psychiatric disorders.

Answer to Question 18

D

Although the overnight dexamethasone suppression test is a sensitive test for the exclusion of Cushing's syndrome, false-positive results may occur in patients who are obese, on enzyme-inducing medications, suffering with depressive illness, or consuming excessive alcohol. In addition, the use of exogenous oestrogen therapy raises cortisol-binding globulin levels and thus measured serum total cortisol, which may also yield a false-positive result. In this case, the finding of a normal midnight cortisol level and normal urinary cortisol excretion makes the diagnosis of Cushing's syndrome unlikely. Cushing's disease refers exclusively to cases of Cushing's syndrome arising as a consequence of a corticotroph pituitary adenoma. Weight gain occurs in some patients on the combined oral contraceptive pill, but this is usually modest and unlikely to explain the gross obesity in this case. Although the patient has a mildly elevated antithyroid peroxidase titre and a free T_4 level in the lower part of the reference range, the plasma thyroid-stimulating hormone level, which is the most sensitive indicator of primary thyroid dysfunction, is unequivocally normal.

Answer to Question 19

A

The T1-weighted coronal MRI scan demonstrates a normal-sized pituitary gland with a centrally located stalk. Although this does not exclude the possibility of a microprolactinoma, other causes of mild hyperprolactinaemia should be sought.

Answer to Question 20

D

The retinal appearances are those of diabetic maculopathy (classical circular macular exudates) and background retinopathy (microaneurysms, dot and blot haemorrhages). Maculopathy is the commonest threat to vision in type 2 diabetes. Prompt referral to an ophthalmologist is necessary, in addition to correcting poor glycaemic control and hypertension.

Answer to Question 21

A

The appearances shown in Fig. 72 are typical of a complete left third nerve palsy, with complete ptosis, dilated pupil and abduction of the left eye whilst looking straight ahead.

Answer to Question 22

B

The clinical presentation and scan findings are typical of pituitary apoplexy caused by an area of haemorrhage within a pituitary macroadenoma and complicated by a third nerve palsy (Fig. 73).

THE MEDICAL MASTERCLASS SERIES

Scientific Background to Medicine 1

GENETICS AND MOLECULAR MEDICINE

Nucleic Acids and Chromosomes 3

Techniques in Molecular Biology 11

Molecular Basis of Simple Genetic Traits 17

More Complex Issues 23

Self-assessment 30

BIOCHEMISTRY AND METABOLISM

Requirement for Energy 35

Carbohydrates 41

Fatty Acids and Lipids 45

3.1 Fatty acids 45
3.2 Lipids 48

Cholesterol and Steroid Hormones 51

Amino Acids and Proteins 53

5.1 Amino acids 53
5.2 Proteins 56

Haem 59

Nucleotides 61

Self-assessment 66

CELL BIOLOGY

Ion Transport 71

1.1 Ion channels 72
1.2 Ion carriers 79

Receptors and Intracellular Signalling 82

Cell Cycle and Apoptosis 88

Haematopoiesis 94

Self-assessment 97

IMMUNOLOGY AND IMMUNOSUPPRESSION

Overview of the Immune System 103

The Major Histocompatibility Complex, Antigen Presentation and Transplantation 106

T Cells 109

B Cells 112

Tolerance and Autoimmunity 115

Complement 117

Inflammation 120

Immunosuppressive Therapy 125

Self-assessment 130

ANATOMY

Heart and Major Vessels 135

Lungs 138

Liver and Biliary Tract 140

Spleen 142

Kidney 143

Endocrine Glands 144

Gastrointestinal Tract 147

Eye 150

Nervous System 152

Self-assessment 167

PHYSIOLOGY

Cardiovascular System 171

1.1 The heart as a pump 171
1.2 The systemic and pulmonary circulations 176
1.3 Blood vessels 177
1.4 Endocrine function of the heart 180

Respiratory System 182

2.1 The lungs 182

Gastrointestinal System 187

3.1 The gut 187
3.2 The liver 190
3.3 The exocrine pancreas 193

Brain and Nerves 194

4.1 The action potential 194
4.2 Synaptic transmission 196
4.3 Neuromuscular transmission 199

Endocrine Physiology 200

5.1 The growth hormone–insulin-like growth factor 1 axis 200
5.2 The hypothalamic–pituitary–adrenal axis 200
5.3 Thyroid hormones 201
5.4 The endocrine pancreas 203
5.5 The ovary and testis 204
5.6 The breast 206
5.7 The posterior pituitary 207

Renal Physiology 209

6.1 Blood flow and glomerular filtration 209
6.2 Function of the renal tubules 211
6.3 Endocrine function of the kidney 217

Self-assessment 220

Scientific Background to Medicine 2

CLINICAL PHARMACOLOGY

Introducing Clinical Pharmacology 3

1.1 Risks versus benefits 4
1.2 Safe prescribing 4
1.3 Rational prescribing 5
1.4 The role of clinical pharmacology 5

Pharmacokinetics 7

2.1 Introduction 7
2.2 Drug absorption 7
2.3 Drug distribution 11
2.4 Drug metabolism 12
2.5 Drug elimination 17
2.6 Plasma half-life and steady-state plasma concentrations 19
2.7 Drug monitoring 20

Pharmacodynamics 22

3.1 How drugs exert their effects 22
3.2 Selectivity is the key to the therapeutic utility of an agent 25
3.3 Basic aspects of the interaction of a drug with its target 27
3.4 Heterogeneity of drug responses, pharmacogenetics and pharmacogenomics 31

Prescribing in Special Circumstances 33

4.1 Introduction 33
4.2 Prescribing and liver disease 33
4.3 Prescribing in pregnancy 36
4.4 Prescribing for women of childbearing potential 39
4.5 Prescribing to lactating mothers 39
4.6 Prescribing in renal disease 41
4.7 Prescribing in the elderly 44

Adverse Drug Reactions 46

5.1 Introduction and definition 46
5.2 Classification of adverse drug reactions 46
5.3 Clinical approach to adverse drug reactions 47
5.4 Dose-related adverse drug reactions (type A) 48
5.5 Non-dose-related adverse drug reactions (type B) 51
5.6 Adverse reactions caused by long-term effects of drugs (type C) 56
5.7 Adverse reactions caused by delayed effects of drugs (type D) 57
5.8 Withdrawal reactions (type E) 58
5.9 Drugs in overdose and use of illicit drugs 59

Drug Development and Rational Prescribing 60

6.1 Drug development 60
6.2 Rational prescribing 65
6.3 Clinical governance and rational prescribing 66
6.4 Rational prescribing: evaluating the evidence for yourself 68
6.5 Rational prescribing, irrational patients 68

Self-assessment 70

STATISTICS, EPIDEMIOLOGY, CLINICAL TRIALS AND META-ANALYSES

Statistics 79

Epidemiology 86

2.1 Observational studies 87

Clinical Trials and Meta-Analyses 92

Self-assessment 103

Clinical Skills

CLINICAL SKILLS FOR PACES

Introduction 3

History-taking for PACES (Station 2) 6

Communication Skills and Ethics for PACES (Station 4) 11

Examination for PACES Stations 1, 3 and 5: General Considerations 13

Station 1: Respiratory System 16

Station 1: Abdominal System 21

Station 3: Cardiovascular System 27

Station 3: Central Nervous System 36

Station 5: Skin, Locomotor System, Endocrine System and Eyes 54

PAIN RELIEF AND PALLIATIVE CARE

PACES Stations and Acute Scenarios 61

1.1 **History-taking 61**
   1.1.1 Pain 61
   1.1.2 Constipation/bowel obstruction 63

1.2 **Communication skills and ethics 65**
   1.2.1 Pain 65
   1.2.2 Breathlessness 66
   1.2.3 Nausea and vomiting 67
   1.2.4 Bowel obstruction 69
   1.2.5 End of life 70

1.3 **Acute scenarios 71**
   1.3.1 Pain 71
   1.3.2 Breathlessness 74
   1.3.3 Nausea and vomiting 76
   1.3.4 Bowel obstruction 79

Diseases and Treatments 82

2.1 **Pain 82**
2.2 **Breathlessness 87**
2.3 **Nausea and vomiting 88**
2.4 **Constipation 89**
2.5 **Bowel obstruction 90**
2.6 **Anxiety and depression 91**
2.7 **Confusion 93**
2.8 **End-of-life care: the dying patient 94**
2.9 **Specialist palliative care services 96**

Self-assessment 98

MEDICINE FOR THE ELDERLY

PACES Stations and Acute Scenarios 107

1.1 **History-taking 107**
   1.1.1 Frequent falls 107
   1.1.2 Recent onset of confusion 110
   1.1.3 Urinary incontinence and immobility 114
   1.1.4 Collapse 116
   1.1.5 Vague aches and pains 119
   1.1.6 Swollen legs and back pain 121
   1.1.7 Failure to thrive: gradual decline and weight loss 127

1.2 **Clinical examination 129**
   1.2.1 Confusion (respiratory) 129
   1.2.2 Confusion (abdominal) 130
   1.2.3 Failure to thrive (abdominal) 131
   1.2.4 Frequent falls (cardiovascular) 131
   1.2.5 Confusion (cardiovascular) 132
   1.2.6 Frequent falls (neurological) 132
   1.2.7 Confusion (neurological) 134
   1.2.8 Impaired mobility (neurological) 135
   1.2.9 Confusion (skin) 135
   1.2.10 Frequent falls (locomotor) 136
   1.2.11 Confusion (endocrine) 136
   1.2.12 Confusion (eye) 136

1.3 **Communication skills and ethics 137**
   1.3.1 Frequent falls 137
   1.3.2 Confusion 138
   1.3.3 Collapse 139

1.4 **Acute scenarios 141**
   1.4.1 Sudden onset of confusion 141
   1.4.2 Collapse 143

Diseases and Treatments 147

2.1 **Why elderly patients are different 147**
2.2 **General approach to management 149**
2.3 **Falls 151**
2.4 **Urinary and faecal incontinence 155**
   2.4.1 Urinary incontinence 155
   2.4.2 Faecal incontinence 157
2.5 **Hypothermia 158**
2.6 **Drugs in elderly people 161**
2.7 **Dementia 162**
2.8 **Rehabilitation 165**
2.9 **Aids, appliances and assistive technology 166**
2.10 **Hearing impairment 168**
2.11 **Nutrition 170**

2.12 Benefits 174
2.13 Legal aspects of elderly care 175

Investigations and Practical Procedures 178

3.1 Diagnosis vs common sense 178
3.2 Assessment of cognition, mood and function 178

Self-assessment 181

Acute Medicine

ACUTE MEDICINE

PACES Stations and Acute Scenarios 3

1.1 Communication skills and ethics 3
  1.1.1 Cardiac arrest 3
  1.1.2 Stroke 4
  1.1.3 Congestive cardiac failure 5
  1.1.4 Lumbar back pain 6
  1.1.5 Community-acquired pneumonia 7
  1.1.6 Acute pneumothorax 7
1.2 Acute scenarios 8
  1.2.1 Cardiac arrest 8
  1.2.2 Chest pain and hypotension 12
  1.2.3 Should he be thrombolysed? 15
  1.2.4 Hypotension in acute coronary syndrome 20
  1.2.5 Postoperative breathlessness 21
  1.2.6 Two patients with tachyarrhythmia 23
  1.2.7 Bradyarrhythmia 27
  1.2.8 Collapse of unknown cause 30
  1.2.9 Asthma 33
  1.2.10 Pleurisy 36

1.2.11 Chest infection/ pneumonia 39
1.2.12 Acute-on-chronic airways obstruction 42
1.2.13 Stridor 44
1.2.14 Pneumothorax 46
1.2.15 Upper gastrointestinal haemorrhage 48
1.2.16 Bloody diarrhoea 51
1.2.17 Abdominal pain 54
1.2.18 Hepatic encephalopathy/ alcohol withdrawal 56
1.2.19 Renal failure, fluid overload and hyperkalaemia 59
1.2.20 Diabetic ketoacidosis 62
1.2.21 Hypoglycaemia 65
1.2.22 Hypercalcaemia 67
1.2.23 Hyponatraemia 69
1.2.24 Addisonian crisis 71
1.2.25 Thyrotoxic crisis 74
1.2.26 Sudden onset of severe headache 75
1.2.27 Severe headache with fever 77
1.2.28 Acute spastic paraparesis 79
1.2.29 Status epilepticus 81
1.2.30 Stroke 83
1.2.31 Coma 86
1.2.32 Fever in a returning traveller 89
1.2.33 Anaphylaxis 90
1.2.34 A painful joint 91
1.2.35 Back pain 94
1.2.36 Self-harm 96
1.2.37 Violence and aggression 97

Diseases and Treatments 100

2.1 Overdoses 100
  2.1.1 Prevention of drug absorption from the gut 100
  2.1.2 Management of overdoses of specific drugs 100

Investigations and Practical Procedures 103

3.1 Central venous lines 103
  3.1.1 Indications, contraindications, consent and preparation 103

3.1.2 Specific techniques for insertion of central lines 104
3.1.3 Interpretation of central venous pressure measurements 106
3.2 Lumbar puncture 106
3.3 Cardiac pacing 107
3.4 Elective DC cardioversion 109
3.5 Intercostal chest drain insertion 109
3.6 Arterial blood gases 112
  3.6.1 Measurement of arterial blood gases 112
  3.6.2 Interpretation of arterial blood gases 113
3.7 Airway management 113
  3.7.1 Basic airway management 113
  3.7.2 Tracheostomy 116
3.8 Ventilatory support 117
  3.8.1 Controlled oxygen therapy 117
  3.8.2 Continuous positive airway pressure 117
  3.8.3 Non-invasive ventilation 118
  3.8.4 Invasive ventilation 118

Self-assessment 120

Infectious Diseases and Dermatology

INFECTIOUS DISEASES

PACES Stations and Acute Scenarios 3

1.1 History-taking 3
  1.1.1 A cavitating lung lesion 3
  1.1.2 Fever and lymphadenopathy 5
  1.1.3 Still feverish after 6 weeks 7
  1.1.4 Chronic fatigue 10

1.1.5 A spot on the penis 12

1.1.6 Penile discharge 15

1.1.7 Woman with a genital sore 17

1.2 Communication skills and ethics 20

1.2.1 Fever, hypotension and confusion 20

1.2.2 A swollen red foot 21

1.2.3 Still feverish after 6 weeks 22

1.2.4 Chronic fatigue 23

1.2.5 Malaise, mouth ulcers and fever 24

1.2.6 Don't tell my wife 25

1.3 Acute scenarios 27

1.3.1 Fever 27

1.3.2 Fever, hypotension and confusion 30

1.3.3 A swollen red foot 33

1.3.4 Fever and cough 34

1.3.5 Fever, back pain and weak legs 37

1.3.6 Drug user with fever and a murmur 40

1.3.7 Fever and heart failure 44

1.3.8 Persistent fever in the intensive care unit 47

1.3.9 Pyelonephritis 49

1.3.10 A sore throat 52

1.3.11 Fever and headache 55

1.3.12 Fever with reduced conscious level 60

1.3.13 Fever in the neutropenic patient 62

1.3.14 Fever after renal transplant 65

1.3.15 Varicella in pregnancy 68

1.3.16 Imported fever 70

1.3.17 Eosinophilia 74

1.3.18 Jaundice and fever after travelling 76

1.3.19 A traveller with diarrhoea 78

1.3.20 Malaise, mouth ulcers and fever 81

1.3.21 Breathlessness in a HIV-positive patient 83

1.3.22 HIV positive and blurred vision 86

1.3.23 Abdominal pain and vaginal discharge 88

1.3.24 Penicillin allergy 91

Pathogens and Management 94

2.1 Antimicrobial prophylaxis 94

2.2 Immunisation 95

2.3 Infection control 97

2.4 Travel advice 99

2.5 Bacteria 100

2.5.1 Gram-positive bacteria 101

2.5.2 Gram-negative bacteria 104

2.6 Mycobacteria 108

2.6.1 Mycobacterium tuberculosis 108

2.6.2 Mycobacterium leprae 113

2.6.3 Opportunistic mycobacteria 114

2.7 Spirochaetes 115

2.7.1 Syphilis 115

2.7.2 Lyme disease 117

2.7.3 Relapsing fever 118

2.7.4 Leptospirosis 118

2.8 Miscellaneous bacteria 119

2.8.1 *Mycoplasma* and *Ureaplasma* 119

2.8.2 Rickettsiae 120

2.8.3 *Coxiella burnetii* (Q fever) 120

2.8.4 Chlamydiae 121

2.9 Fungi 121

2.9.1 *Candida* spp. 121

2.9.2 *Aspergillus* 123

2.9.3 *Cryptococcus neoformans* 124

2.9.4 Dimorphic fungi 125

2.9.5 Miscellaneous fungi 126

2.10 Viruses 126

2.10.1 Herpes simplex viruses 127

2.10.2 Varicella-zoster virus 128

2.10.3 Cytomegalovirus 130

2.10.4 Epstein–Barr virus 130

2.10.5 Human herpesviruses 6 and 7 130

2.10.6 Human herpesvirus 8 131

2.10.7 Parvovirus 131

2.10.8 Hepatitis viruses 132

2.10.9 Influenza virus 133

2.10.10 Paramyxoviruses 134

2.10.11 Enteroviruses 134

2.10.12 Coronaviruses and SARS 135

2.11 Human immunodeficiency virus 135

2.11.1 Prevention following sharps injury 140

2.12 Travel-related viruses 142

2.12.1 Rabies 142

2.12.2 Dengue 143

2.12.3 Arbovirus infections 143

2.13 Protozoan parasites 144

2.13.1 Malaria 144

2.13.2 Leishmaniasis 145

2.13.3 Amoebiasis 146

2.13.4 Toxoplasmosis 147

2.14 Metazoan parasites 148

2.14.1 Schistosomiasis 148

2.14.2 Strongyloidiasis 149

2.14.3 Cysticercosis 150

2.14.4 Filariasis 151

2.14.5 Trichinosis 151

2.14.6 Toxocariasis 152

2.14.7 Hydatid disease 152

Investigations and Practical Procedures 154

3.1 Getting the best from the laboratory 154

3.2 Specific investigations 154

Self-assessment 159

DERMATOLOGY

PACES Stations and Acute Scenarios 175

1.1 History taking 175

1.1.1 Blistering disorders 175

1.1.2 Chronic red facial rash 177

1.1.3 Pruritus 178

1.1.4 Alopecia 180

1.1.5 Hyperpigmentation 181

1.1.6 Hypopigmentation 183

1.1.7 Red legs 185

1.1.8 Leg ulcers 187

1.2 Clinical examination 189

1.2.1 Blistering disorder 189

1.2.2 A chronic red facial rash 193

1.2.3 Pruritus 198

1.2.4 Alopecia 200

1.2.5 Hyperpigmentation 202

1.2.6 Hypopigmentation 205

1.2.7 Red legs 207

1.2.8 Lumps and bumps 210

1.2.9 Telangiectases 212

1.2.10 Purpura 214

1.2.11 Lesion on the shin 216

1.2.12 Non-pigmented lesion on the face 217

1.2.13 A pigmented lesion on the face 219

1.2.14 Leg ulcers 221

1.2.15 Examine these hands 223

1.3 Communication skills and ethics 225

1.3.1 Consenting a patient to enter a dermatological trial 225

1.3.2 A steroid-phobic patient 227

1.3.3 An anxious woman with a family history of melanoma who wants all her moles removed 228

1.3.4 Prescribing isotretinoin to a woman of reproductive age 229

1.4 Acute scenarios 231

1.4.1 Acute generalised rashes 231

1.4.2 Erythroderma 238

Diseases and Treatments 243

2.1 Acne vulgaris 243

2.2 Acanthosis nigricans 245

2.3 Alopecia areata 245

2.4 Bullous pemphigoid 246

2.5 Dermatomyositis 248

2.6 Dermatitis herpetiformis 249

2.7 Drug eruptions 249

2.8 Atopic eczema 251

2.9 Contact dermatitis 252

2.10 Erythema multiforme, Stevens–Johnson syndrome and toxic epidermal necrolysis 253

2.11 Erythema nodosum 254

2.12 Fungal infections of skin, hair and nails (superficial fungal infections) 255

2.13 HIV and the skin 257

2.14 Lichen planus 258

2.15 Lymphoma of the skin: mycosis fungoides and Sézary syndrome 260

2.16 Pemphigus vulgaris 261

2.17 Psoriasis 263

2.18 Pyoderma gangrenosum 265

2.19 Scabies 266

2.20 Basal cell carcinoma 268

2.21 Squamous cell carcinoma 270

2.22 Malignant melanoma 271

2.23 Urticaria and angio-oedema 274

2.24 Vitiligo 275

2.25 Cutaneous vasculitis 276

2.26 Topical therapy: corticosteroids and immunosuppressants 277

2.27 Phototherapy 278

2.28 Retinoids 279

Investigations and Practical Procedures 281

3.1 Skin biopsy 281

3.2 Direct and indirect immunofluorescence 282

3.3 Patch tests 282

3.4 Obtaining specimens for mycological analysis 284

Self-assessment 285

Haematology and Oncology

HAEMATOLOGY

PACES Stations and Acute Scenarios 1

1.1 History-taking 3

1.1.1 Microcytic hypochromic anaemia 3

1.1.2 Macrocytic anaemia 5

1.1.3 Lymphocytosis and anaemia 8

1.1.4 Thromboembolism and fetal loss 11

1.1.5 Weight loss and thrombocytosis 12

1.2 Clinical examination 14

1.2.1 Normocytic anaemia 14

1.2.2 Thrombocytopenia and purpura 14

1.2.3 Jaundice and anaemia 16

1.2.4 Polycythaemia 17

1.2.5 Splenomegaly 18

1.3 Communication skills and ethics 19

1.3.1 Persuading a patient to accept HIV testing 19

1.3.2 Talking to a distressed relative 20

1.3.3 Explaining a medical error 22

1.3.4 Breaking bad news 23

1.4 Acute scenarios 25

1.4.1 Chest syndrome in sickle cell disease 25

1.4.2 Neutropenia 27

1.4.3 Leucocytosis 29

1.4.4 Spontaneous bleeding and weight loss 31

1.4.5 Cervical lymphadenopathy and difficulty breathing 32

1.4.6 Swelling of the leg 35

Diseases and Treatments 37

2.1 Causes of anaemia 37
- 2.1.1 Thalassaemia syndromes 38
- 2.1.2 Sickle cell syndromes 39
- 2.1.3 Enzyme defects 41
- 2.1.4 Membrane defects 41
- 2.1.5 Iron metabolism and iron-deficiency anaemia 43
- 2.1.6 Vitamin B_{12} and folate metabolism and deficiency 44
- 2.1.7 Acquired haemolytic anaemia 44
- 2.1.8 Bone-marrow failure and inflitration 46

2.2 Haematological malignancy 46
- 2.2.1 Multiple myeloma 46
- 2.2.2 Acute leukaemia: acute lymphoblastic leukaemia and acute myeloid leukaemia 49
- 2.2.3 Chronic lymphocytic leukaemia 52
- 2.2.4 Chronic myeloid leukaemia 54
- 2.2.5 Malignant lymphomas: non-Hodgkin's lymphoma and Hodgkin's lymphoma 55
- 2.2.6 Myelodysplastic syndromes 58
- 2.2.7 Non-leukaemic myeloproliferative disorders (including polycythaemia vera, essential thrombocythaemia and myelofibrosis) 60
- 2.2.8 Amyloidosis 62

2.3 Bleeding disorders 64
- 2.3.1 Inherited bleeding disorders 64
- 2.3.2 Aquired bleeding disorders 67
- 2.3.3 Idiopathic throbocytopenic purpura 68

2.4 Thrombotic disorders 69
- 2.4.1 Inherited thrombotic disease 69
- 2.4.2 Acquired thrombotic disease 72

2.5 Clinical use of blood products 74

2.6 Haematological features of systemic disease 76

2.7 Haematology of pregnancy 79

2.8 Iron overload 80

2.9 Chemotherapy and related therapies 82

2.10 Principles of bone-marrow and peripheral blood stem-cell transplantation 85

Investigations and Practical Procedures 87

3.1 The full blood count and film 87

3.2 Bone-marrow examination 89

3.3 Clotting screen 91

3.4 Coombs' test (direct antiglobulin test) 91

3.5 Erythrocyte sedimentation rate versus plasma viscosity 92

3.6 Therapeutic anticoagulation 92

Self-assessment 94

ONCOLOGY

PACES Stations and Acute Scenarios 109

1.1 History-taking 109
- 1.1.1 A dark spot 109

1.2 Clinical examination 110
- 1.2.1 A lump in the neck 110

1.3 Communication skills and ethics 111
- 1.3.1 Am I at risk of cancer? 111
- 1.3.2 Consent for chemotherapy (1) 113
- 1.3.3 Consent for chemotherapy (2) 114
- 1.3.4 Don't tell him the diagnosis 116

1.4 Acute scenarios 117
- 1.4.1 Acute deterioration after starting chemotherapy 117
- 1.4.2 Back pain and weak legs 119
- 1.4.3 Breathless, hoarse, dizzy and swollen 121

Diseases and Treatments 124

2.1 Breast cancer 124

2.2 Central nervous system cancers 126

2.3 Digestive tract cancers 129

2.4 Genitourinary cancer 132

2.5 Gynaecological cancer 136

2.6 Head and neck cancer 139

2.7 Skin tumours 140

2.8 Paediatric solid tumours 144

2.9 Lung cancer 146

2.10 Liver and biliary tree cancer 149

2.11 Bone cancer and sarcoma 151

2.12 Endocrine tumours 157

2.13 The causes of cancer 159

2.14 Paraneoplastic conditions 162

Investigations and Practical Procedures 167

3.1 Investigation of unknown primary cancers 167

3.2 Investigation and management of metastatic disease 169

3.3 Tumour markers 171

3.4 Screening 173

3.5 Radiotherapy 175

3.6 Chemotherapy 176

3.7 Immunotherapy 179

3.8 Stem-cell transplantation 180

3.9 Oncological emergencies 180

Self-assessment 185

Cardiology and Respiratory Medicine

CARDIOLOGY

PACES Stations and Acute Scenarios 3

1.1 **History-taking 3**
  1.1.1 Paroxysmal palpitations 3
  1.1.2 Palpitations with dizziness 6
  1.1.3 Breathlessness and ankle swelling 9
  1.1.4 Breathlessness and exertional presyncope 12
  1.1.5 Dyspnoea, ankle oedema and cyanosis 14
  1.1.6 Chest pain and recurrent syncope 16
  1.1.7 Hypertension found at routine screening 19
  1.1.8 Murmur in pregnancy 23
1.2 **Clinical examination 25**
  1.2.1 Irregular pulse 25
  1.2.2 Congestive heart failure 27
  1.2.3 Hypertension 29
  1.2.4 Mechanical valve 29
  1.2.5 Pansystolic murmur 30
  1.2.6 Mitral stenosis 31
  1.2.7 Aortic stenosis 32
  1.2.8 Aortic regurgitation 33
  1.2.9 Tricuspid regurgitation 34
  1.2.10 Eisenmenger's syndrome 35
  1.2.11 Dextrocardia 36
1.3 **Communication skills and ethics 37**
  1.3.1 Advising a patient against unnecessary investigations 37
  1.3.2 Explanation of uncertainty of diagnosis 38
  1.3.3 Discussion of the need to screen relatives for an inherited condition 38
  1.3.4 Communicating news of a patient's death to a spouse 39
  1.3.5 Explanation to a patient of the need for investigations 40
  1.3.6 Explanation to a patient who is reluctant to receive treatment 41
1.4 **Acute scenarios 42**
  1.4.1 Syncope 42
  1.4.2 Stroke and a murmur 46
  1.4.3 Acute chest pain 49
  1.4.4 Hypotension following acute myocardial infarction 52
  1.4.5 Breathlessness and collapse 54
  1.4.6 Pleuritic chest pain 57
  1.4.7 Fever, weight loss and a murmur 60
  1.4.8 Chest pain following a 'flu-like illness 64

Diseases and Treatments 69

2.1 **Coronary artery disease 69**
  2.1.1 Stable angina 69
  2.1.2 Unstable angina and non-ST-elevation myocardial infarction 71
  2.1.3 ST-elevation myocardial infarction 72
2.2 **Cardiac arrhythmia 76**
  2.2.1 Bradycardia 76
  2.2.2 Tachycardia 78
2.3 **Cardiac failure 82**
2.4 **Diseases of heart muscle 86**
  2.4.1 Hypertrophic cardiomyopathy 86
  2.4.2 Dilated cardiomyopathy 89
  2.4.3 Restrictive cardiomyopathy 89
  2.4.4 Arrhythmogenic right ventricular cardiomyopathy 90
  2.4.5 Left ventricular non-compaction 90
2.5 **Valvular heart disease 90**
  2.5.1 Aortic stenosis 90
  2.5.2 Aortic regurgitation 92
  2.5.3 Mitral stenosis 93
  2.5.4 Mitral regurgitation 95
  2.5.5 Tricuspid valve disease 97
  2.5.6 Pulmonary valve disease 98
2.6 **Pericardial disease 98**
  2.6.1 Acute pericarditis 98
  2.6.2 Pericardial effusion 100
  2.6.3 Constrictive pericarditis 102
2.7 **Congenital heart disease 104**
  2.7.1 Acyanotic congenital heart disease 105
    2.7.1.1 Atrial septal defect 105
    2.7.1.2 Isolated ventricular septal defect 107
    2.7.1.3 Patent ductus arteriosus 107
    2.7.1.4 Coarctation of the aorta 108
  2.7.2 Cyanotic congenital heart disease 109
    2.7.2.1 Tetralogy of Fallot 109
    2.7.2.2 Complete transposition of great arteries 111
    2.7.2.3 Ebstein's anomaly 112
  2.7.3 Eisenmenger's syndrome 113
2.8 **Infective diseases of the heart 114**
  2.8.1 Infective endocarditis 114
  2.8.2 Rheumatic fever 119
2.9 **Cardiac tumours 120**
2.10 **Traumatic heart disease 122**

2.11 Disease of systemic arteries 124

2.11.1 Aortic dissection 124

2.12 Diseases of pulmonary arteries 126

2.12.1 Primary pulmonary hypertension 126

2.12.2 Secondary pulmonary hypertension 129

2.13 Cardiac complications of systemic disease 130

2.13.1 Thyroid disease 130

2.13.2 Diabetes 131

2.13.3 Autoimmune rheumatic diseases 131

2.13.4 Renal disease 132

2.14 Systemic complications of cardiac disease 133

2.14.1 Stroke 133

2.15 Pregnancy and the heart 134

2.16 General anaesthesia in heart disease 136

2.17 Hypertension 136

2.17.1 Hypertensive emergencies 140

2.18 Venous thromboembolism 141

2.18.1 Pulmonary embolism 141

2.19 Driving restrictions in cardiology 145

Investigations and Practical Procedures 147

3.1 ECG 147

3.1.1 Exercise ECGs 151

3.2 Basic electrophysiology studies 152

3.3 Ambulatory monitoring 154

3.4 Radiofrequency ablation and implantable cardioverter defibrillators 156

3.4.1 Radiofrequency ablation 156

3.4.2 Implantable cardioverter defibrillator 157

3.4.3 Cardiac resynchronisation therapy 158

3.5 Pacemakers 159

3.6 Chest radiograph in cardiac disease 161

3.7 Cardiac biochemical markers 163

3.8 CT and MRI 164

3.8.1 Multislice spiral CT 164

3.8.2 MRI 165

3.9 Ventilation–perfusion imaging 166

3.10 Echocardiography 167

3.11 Nuclear cardiology 170

3.11.1 Myocardial perfusion imaging 170

3.11.2 Radionuclide ventriculography 170

3.11.3 Positron emission tomography 171

3.12 Cardiac catheterisation 171

3.12.1 Percutaneous coronary intervention 172

3.12.2 Percutaneous valvuloplasty 173

Self-assessment 176

RESPIRATORY MEDICINE

PACES Stations and Acute Scenarios 191

1.1 History-taking 191

1.1.1 New breathlessness 191

1.1.2 Solitary pulmonary nodule 193

1.1.3 Exertional dyspnoea with daily sputum 195

1.1.4 Dyspnoea and fine inspiratory crackles 197

1.1.5 Nocturnal cough 199

1.1.6 Daytime sleepiness and morning headache 202

1.1.7 Lung cancer with asbestos exposure 204

1.1.8 Breathlessness with a normal chest radiograph 206

1.2 Clinical examination 209

1.2.1 Coarse crackles: bronchiectasis 209

1.2.2 Fine crackles: interstitial lung disease 210

1.2.3 Stridor 212

1.2.4 Pleural effusion 213

1.2.5 Wheeze and crackles: chronic obstructive pulmonary disease 215

1.2.6 Cor pulmonale 216

1.2.7 Pneumonectomy/ lobectomy 217

1.2.8 Apical signs: old tuberculosis 218

1.2.9 Cystic fibrosis 219

1.3 Communication skills and ethics 220

1.3.1 Lifestyle modification 220

1.3.2 Possible cancer 221

1.3.3 Potentially life-threatening illness 222

1.3.4 Sudden unexplained death 224

1.3.5 Intubation for ventilation 225

1.3.6 Patient refusing ventilation 226

1.4 Acute scenarios 228

1.4.1 Pleuritic chest pain 228

1.4.2 Unexplained hypoxia 232

1.4.3 Haemoptysis and weight loss 234

1.4.4 Pleural effusion and fever 237

1.4.5 Lobar collapse in non-smoker 239

1.4.6 Upper airway obstruction 241

Diseases and Treatments 243

2.1 Upper airway 243

2.1.1 Sleep apnoea 243

2.2 Atopy and asthma 245

2.2.1 Allergic rhinitis 245

2.2.2 Asthma 246

2.3 Chronic obstructive pulmonary disease 251

2.4 Bronchiectasis 253

2.5   **Cystic fibrosis 256**
2.6   **Occupational lung disease 258**
    2.6.1   Asbestosis and the pneumoconioses 258
2.7   **Diffuse parenchymal lung disease 261**
    2.7.1   Usual interstitial pneumonia 261
    2.7.2   Cryptogenic organising pneumonia 262
    2.7.3   Bronchiolitis obliterans 263
2.8   **Miscellaneous conditions 264**
    2.8.1   Extrinsic allergic alveolitis 264
    2.8.2   Sarcoidosis 265
    2.8.3   Respiratory complications of rheumatoid arthritis 267
    2.8.4   Pulmonary vasculitis 269
    2.8.5   Pulmonary eosinophilia 270
    2.8.6   Iatrogenic lung disease 272
    2.8.7   Smoke inhalation 274
    2.8.8   Sickle cell disease and the lung 276
    2.8.9   Human immunodeficiency virus and the lung 278
2.9   **Malignancy 279**
    2.9.1   Lung cancer 279
    2.9.2   Mesothelioma 283
    2.9.3   Mediastinal tumours 285
2.10 **Disorders of the chest wall and diaphragm 287**
2.11 **Complications of respiratory disease 288**
    2.11.1 Chronic respiratory failure 288
    2.11.2 Cor pulmonale 289
2.12 **Treatments in respiratory disease 290**
    2.12.1 Domiciliary oxygen therapy 290
    2.12.2 Continuous positive airways pressure 292
    2.12.3 Non-invasive ventilation 292
2.13 **Lung transplantation 294**

Investigations and Practical Procedures 297

3.1   **Arterial blood gas sampling 297**
3.2   **Aspiration of pleural effusion or pneumothorax 298**
3.3   **Pleural biopsy 298**
3.4   **Intercostal tube insertion 300**
3.5   **Fibreoptic bronchoscopy and transbronchial biopsy 302**
    3.5.1   Fibreoptic bronchoscopy 302
    3.5.2   Transbronchial biopsy 302
3.6   **Interpretation of clinical data 302**
    3.6.1   Arterial blood gases 302
    3.6.2   Lung function tests 304
    3.6.3   Overnight oximetry 306
    3.6.4   Chest radiograph 306
    3.6.5   Computed tomography scan of the thorax 307

Self-assessment 312

Gastroenterology and Hepatology

GASTROENTEROLOGY AND HEPATOLOGY

PACES Stations and Acute Scenarios 3

1.1   **History-taking 3**
    1.1.1   Heartburn and dyspepsia 3
    1.1.2   Dysphagia and feeding difficulties 5
    1.1.3   Chronic diarrhoea 8
    1.1.4   Rectal bleeding 10
    1.1.5   Weight loss 14
    1.1.6   Chronic abdominal pain 16
    1.1.7   Abnormal liver function tests 18
    1.1.8   Abdominal swelling 21
1.2   **Clinical examination 24**
    1.2.1   Inflammatory bowel disease 24
    1.2.2   Chronic liver disease 24
    1.2.3   Splenomegaly 25
    1.2.4   Abdominal swelling 26
1.3   **Communication skills and ethics 27**
    1.3.1   A decision about feeding 27
    1.3.2   Limitation of management 29
    1.3.3   Limitation of investigation 30
    1.3.4   A patient who does not want to give a history 31
1.4   **Acute scenarios 32**
    1.4.1   Nausea and vomiting 32
    1.4.2   Acute diarrhoea 36
    1.4.3   Haematemesis and melaena 39
    1.4.4   Acute abdominal pain 46
    1.4.5   Jaundice 50
    1.4.6   Acute liver failure 54

Diseases and Treatments 60

2.1   **Oesophageal disease 60**
    2.1.1   Gastro-oesophageal reflux disease 60
    2.1.2   Achalasia and oesophageal dysmotility 62
    2.1.3   Oesophageal cancer and Barrett's oesophagus 63
2.2   **Gastric disease 66**
    2.2.1   Peptic ulceration and *Helicobacter pylori* 66
    2.2.2   Gastric carcinoma 68
    2.2.3   Rare gastric tumours 69
    2.2.4   Rare causes of gastrointestinal haemorrhage 70

2.3 **Small bowel disease 71**
    2.3.1 Malabsorption 71
        2.3.1.1 Bacterial overgrowth 71
        2.3.1.2 Other causes of malabsorption 72
    2.3.2 Coeliac disease 73
2.4 **Pancreatic disease 75**
    2.4.1 Acute pancreatitis 75
    2.4.2 Chronic pancreatitis 78
    2.4.3 Pancreatic cancer 80
    2.4.4 Neuroendocrine tumours 82
2.5 **Biliary disease 83**
    2.5.1 Choledocholithiasis 83
    2.5.2 Primary biliary cirrhosis 85
    2.5.3 Primary sclerosing cholangitis 87
    2.5.4 Intrahepatic cholestasis 89
    2.5.5 Cholangiocarcinoma 89
2.6 **Infectious diseases 92**
    2.6.1 Food poisoning and gastroenteritis 92
    2.6.2 Bacterial dysentery 93
    2.6.3 Antibiotic-associated diarrhoea 94
    2.6.4 Parasitic infestations of the intestine 94
    2.6.5 Intestinal and liver amoebiasis 95
    2.6.6 Intestinal features of HIV infection 95
2.7 **Inflammatory bowel disease 95**
    2.7.1 Crohn's disease 95
    2.7.2 Ulcerative colitis 98
    2.7.3 Microscopic colitis 101
2.8 **Functional bowel disorders 101**
2.9 **Large bowel disorders 103**
    2.9.1 Adenomatous polyps of the colon 103
    2.9.2 Colorectal carcinoma 104
    2.9.3 Diverticular disease 107
    2.9.4 Intestinal ischaemia 108
    2.9.5 Anorectal diseases 109

2.10 **Liver disease 109**
    2.10.1 Acute viral hepatitis 109
        2.10.1.1 Hepatitis A 109
        2.10.1.2 Other acute viral hepatitis 112
    2.10.2 Chronic viral hepatitis 113
        2.10.2.1 Hepatitis B 113
        2.10.2.2 Hepatitis C 114
    2.10.3 Acute liver failure 115
    2.10.4 Alcohol-related liver disease 116
    2.10.5 Drugs and the liver 118
        2.10.5.1 Hepatic drug toxicity 118
        2.10.5.2 Drugs and chronic liver disease 120
    2.10.6 Chronic liver disease and cirrhosis 120
    2.10.7 Focal liver lesion 124
    2.10.8 Liver transplantation 127
2.11 **Nutrition 129**
    2.11.1 Defining nutrition 129
    2.11.2 Protein–calorie malnutrition 133
    2.11.3 Obesity 133
    2.11.4 Enteral and parenteral nutrition and special diets 134

Investigations and Practical Procedures 136

3.1 **General investigations 136**
3.2 **Tests of gastrointestinal and liver function 137**
3.3 **Diagnostic and therapeutic endoscopy 138**
3.4 **Diagnostic and therapeutic radiology 139**
3.5 **Rigid sigmoidoscopy and rectal biopsy 140**
3.6 **Paracentesis 143**
3.7 **Liver biopsy 144**

Self-assessment 147

Neurology, Ophthalmology and Psychiatry

NEUROLOGY

PACES Stations and Acute Scenarios 3

1.1 **History-taking 3**
    1.1.1 Episodic headache 3
    1.1.2 Facial pain 6
    1.1.3 Funny turns/blackouts 8
    1.1.4 Increasing seizure frequency 11
    1.1.5 Numb toes 12
    1.1.6 Tremor 15
    1.1.7 Memory problems 17
    1.1.8 Chorea 19
    1.1.9 Muscle weakness and pain 20
    1.1.10 Sleep disorders 21
    1.1.11 Dysphagia 24
    1.1.12 Visual hallucinations 26
1.2 **Clinical examination 27**
    1.2.1 Numb toes and foot drop 27
    1.2.2 Weakness in one leg 28
    1.2.3 Spastic legs 32
    1.2.4 Gait disturbance 33
    1.2.5 Cerebellar syndrome 36
    1.2.6 Weak arm/hand 37
    1.2.7 Proximal muscle weakness 40
    1.2.8 Muscle wasting 41
    1.2.9 Hemiplegia 42
    1.2.10 Tremor 44
    1.2.11 Visual field defect 45
    1.2.12 Unequal pupils 47
    1.2.13 Ptosis 48
    1.2.14 Abnormal ocular movements 51
    1.2.15 Facial weakness 53
    1.2.16 Lower cranial nerve assessment 55
    1.2.17 Speech disturbance 57
1.3 **Communication skills and ethics 60**

1.3.1 Genetic implications 60

1.3.2 Explanation of the diagnosis of Alzheimer's disease 61

1.3.3 Prognosis after stroke 62

1.3.4 Conversion disorder 63

1.3.5 Explaining the diagnosis of multiple sclerosis 64

1.4 Acute scenarios 65

1.4.1 Acute weakness of legs 65

1.4.2 Acute ischaemic stroke 67

1.4.3 Subarachnoid haemorrhage 71

1.4.4 Status epilepticus 73

1.4.5 Encephalopathy/coma 78

Diseases and Treatments 81

2.1 Peripheral neuropathies and diseases of the lower motor neuron 81

2.1.1 Peripheral neuropathies 81

2.1.2 Guillain–Barré syndrome 85

2.1.3 Motor neuron disease 87

2.2 Diseases of muscle 89

2.2.1 Metabolic muscle disease 89

2.2.2 Inflammatory muscle disease 91

2.2.3 Inherited dystrophies (myopathies) 91

2.2.4 Channelopathies 93

2.2.5 Myasthenia gravis 93

2.3 Extrapyramidal disorders 95

2.3.1 Parkinson's disease 95

2.4 Dementia 99

2.4.1 Alzheimer's disease 99

2.5 Multiple sclerosis 101

2.6 Headache 104

2.6.1 Migraine 104

2.6.2 Trigeminal neuralgia 107

2.6.3 Cluster headache 108

2.6.4 Tension-type headache 109

2.7 Epilepsy 110

2.8 Cerebrovascular disease 116

2.8.1 Stroke 116

2.8.2 Transient ischaemic attacks 120

2.8.3 Intracerebral haemorrhage 122

2.8.4 Subarachnoid haemorrhage 125

2.9 Brain tumours 127

2.10 Neurological complications of infection 131

2.10.1 New variant Creutzfeldt–Jakob disease 131

2.11 Neurological complications of systemic disease 132

2.11.1 Paraneoplastic conditions 132

2.12 Neuropharmacology 133

Investigations and Practical Procedures 139

3.1 Neuropsychometry 139

3.2 Lumbar puncture 140

3.3 Neurophysiology 142

3.3.1 Electroencephalography 142

3.3.2 Evoked potentials 142

3.3.3 Electromyography 142

3.3.4 Nerve conduction studies 143

3.4 Neuroimaging 143

3.4.1 Computed tomography and computed tomography angiography 143

3.4.2 Magnetic resonance imaging and magnetic resonance angiography 144

3.4.3 Angiography 145

3.5 Single-photon emission computed tomography and positron emission tomography 145

3.6 Carotid Dopplers 147

Self-assessment 148

OPHTHALMOLOGY

PACES Stations and Acute Scenarios 161

1.1 Clinical scenarios 161

1.1.1 Examination of the eye 161

1.2 Acute scenarios 164

1.2.1 An acutely painful red eye 164

1.2.2 Two painful red eyes and a systemic disorder 166

1.2.3 Acute painless loss of vision in one eye 168

1.2.4 Acute painful loss of vision in a young woman 170

1.2.5 Acute loss of vision in an elderly man 171

Diseases and Treatments 173

2.1 Iritis 173

2.2 Scleritis 174

2.3 Retinal artery occlusion 175

2.4 Retinal vein occlusion 178

2.5 Optic neuritis 179

2.6 Ischaemic optic neuropathy in giant-cell arteritis 180

2.7 Diabetic retinopathy 181

Investigations and Practical Procedures 186

3.1 Fluorescein angiography 186

3.2 Temporal artery biopsy 186

Self-assessment 188

PSYCHIATRY

PACES Stations and Acute Scenarios 195

1.1 History-taking 195

1.1.1 Eating disorders 195

1.1.2 Medically unexplained symptoms 197

1.2 Communication skills and ethics 199
- **1.2.1** Panic attack and hyperventilation 199
- **1.2.2** Deliberate self-harm 200
- **1.2.3** Medically unexplained symptoms 201

1.3 Acute scenarios 202
- **1.3.1** Acute confusional state 202
- **1.3.2** Panic attack and hyperventilation 205
- **1.3.3** Deliberate self-harm 207
- **1.3.4** The alcoholic in hospital 208
- **1.3.5** Drug abuser in hospital 210
- **1.3.6** The frightening patient 212

Diseases and Treatments 215

2.1 Dissociative disorders 215
2.2 Dementia 215
2.3 Schizophrenia and antipsychotic drugs 217
- **2.3.1** Schizophrenia 217
- **2.3.2** Antipsychotics 218

2.4 Personality disorder 220
2.5 Psychiatric presentation of physical disease 221
2.6 Psychological reactions to physical illness (adjustment disorders) 222
2.7 Anxiety disorders 223
- **2.7.1** Generalised anxiety disorder 225
- **2.7.2** Panic disorder 226
- **2.7.3** Phobic anxiety disorders 228

2.8 Obsessive–compulsive disorder 229
2.9 Acute stress reactions and post-traumatic stress disorder 231
- **2.9.1** Acute stress reaction 231
- **2.9.2** Post-traumatic stress disorder 231

2.10 Puerperal disorders 233
- **2.10.1** Maternity blues 233
- **2.10.2** Postnatal depressive disorder 233
- **2.10.3** Puerperal psychosis 233

2.11 Depression 235
2.12 Bipolar affective disorder 237
2.13 Delusional disorder 238
2.14 The Mental Health Act 1983 239

Self-assessment 241

Endocrinology

ENDOCRINOLOGY

PACES Stations and Acute Scenarios 3

1.1 History-taking 3
- **1.1.1** Hypercalcaemia 3
- **1.1.2** Polyuria 5
- **1.1.3** Faints, sweats and palpitations 8
- **1.1.4** Gynaecomastia 12
- **1.1.5** Hirsutism 14
- **1.1.6** Post-pill amenorrhoea 16
- **1.1.7** A short girl with no periods 17
- **1.1.8** Young man who has 'not developed' 20
- **1.1.9** Depression and diabetes 21
- **1.1.10** Acromegaly 23
- **1.1.11** Relentless weight gain 24
- **1.1.12** Weight loss 26
- **1.1.13** Tiredness and lethargy 29
- **1.1.14** Flushing and diarrhoea 32
- **1.1.15** Avoiding another coronary 34
- **1.1.16** High blood pressure and low serum potassium 37
- **1.1.17** Tiredness, weight loss and amenorrhoea 39

1.2 Clinical examination 42
- **1.2.1** Amenorrhoea and low blood pressure 42
- **1.2.2** Young man who has 'not developed' 43
- **1.2.3** Depression and diabetes 45
- **1.2.4** Acromegaly 45
- **1.2.5** Weight loss and gritty eyes 47
- **1.2.6** Tiredness and lethargy 48
- **1.2.7** Hypertension and a lump in the neck 48

1.3 Communication skills and ethics 50
- **1.3.1** Explaining an uncertain outcome 50
- **1.3.2** The possibility of cancer 51
- **1.3.3** No medical cause for hirsutism 52
- **1.3.4** A short girl with no periods 53
- **1.3.5** Simple obesity, not a problem with 'the glands' 54
- **1.3.6** I don't want to take the tablets 55

1.4 Acute scenarios 56
- **1.4.1** Coma with hyponatraemia 56
- **1.4.2** Hypercalcaemic and confused 60
- **1.4.3** Thyrotoxic crisis 61
- **1.4.4** Addisonian crisis 63
- **1.4.5** 'Off legs' 65

Diseases and Treatments 68

2.1 Hypothalamic and pituitary diseases 68
- **2.1.1** Cushing's syndrome 68
- **2.1.2** Acromegaly 71
- **2.1.3** Hyperprolactinaemia 73
- **2.1.4** Non-functioning pituitary tumours 76
- **2.1.5** Pituitary apoplexy 77
- **2.1.6** Craniopharyngioma 78
- **2.1.7** Diabetes insipidus 80
- **2.1.8** Hypopituitarism and hormone replacement 83

2.2 Adrenal disease 85

2.2.1 Cushing's syndrome 85

2.2.2 Primary hyperaldosteronism 85

2.2.3 Virilising tumours 87

2.2.4 Phaeochromocytoma 89

2.2.5 Congenital adrenal hyperplasia 92

2.2.6 Primary adrenal insufficiency 94

2.3 Thyroid disease 97

2.3.1 Hypothyroidism 97

2.3.2 Thyrotoxicosis 100

2.3.3 Thyroid nodules and goitre 105

2.3.4 Thyroid malignancy 107

2.4 Reproductive disorders 107

2.4.1 Delayed growth and puberty 107

2.4.2 Male hypogonadism 111

2.4.3 Oligomenorrhoea/ amenorrhoea and premature menopause 113

2.4.4 Turner's syndrome 115

2.4.5 Polycystic ovarian syndrome 116

2.4.6 Hirsutism 118

2.4.7 Erectile dysfunction 120

2.4.8 Infertility 123

2.5 Metabolic and bone diseases 125

2.5.1 Hyperlipidaemia/ dyslipidaemia 125

2.5.2 Porphyria 128

2.5.3 Haemochromatosis 130

2.5.4 Osteoporosis 131

2.5.5 Osteomalacia 134

2.5.6 Paget's disease 136

2.5.7 Hyperparathyroidism 137

2.5.8 Hypercalcaemia 140

2.5.9 Hypocalcaemia 141

2.6 Diabetes mellitus 143

2.6.1 Management of hyperglycaemic emergencies 145

2.6.2 Management of hypoglycaemic emergencies 147

2.6.3 Short- and long-term management of diabetes 147

2.6.4 Complications 153

2.6.5 Important information for patients 160

2.7 Other endocrine disorders 162

2.7.1 Multiple endocrine neoplasia 162

2.7.2 Autoimmune polyglandular endocrinopathies 163

2.7.3 Ectopic hormone syndromes 164

Investigations and Practical Procedures 165

3.1 Stimulation tests 165

3.1.1 Short Synacthen test 165

3.1.2 Corticotrophin-releasing hormone test 166

3.1.3 Thyrotrophin-releasing hormone test 166

3.1.4 Gonadotrophin-releasing hormone test 167

3.1.5 Insulin tolerance test 167

3.1.6 Pentagastrin stimulation test 168

3.1.7 Oral glucose tolerance test 169

3.2 Suppression tests 169

3.2.1 Overnight dexamethasone suppression test 169

3.2.2 Low-dose dexamethasone suppression test 170

3.2.3 High-dose dexamethasone suppression test 170

3.2.4 Oral glucose tolerance test in acromegaly 171

3.3 Other investigations 171

3.3.1 Thyroid function tests 171

3.3.2 Water deprivation test 172

Self-assessment 174

Nephrology

NEPHROLOGY

PACES Stations and Acute Scenarios 3

1.1 History-taking 3

1.1.1 Dipstick haematuria 3

1.1.2 Pregnancy with renal disease 5

1.1.3 A swollen young woman 8

1.1.4 Rheumatoid arthritis with swollen legs 11

1.1.5 A blood test shows moderate renal failure 13

1.1.6 Diabetes with impaired renal function 16

1.1.7 Atherosclerosis and renal failure 18

1.1.8 Recurrent loin pain 20

1.2 Clinical examination 22

1.2.1 Polycystic kidneys 22

1.2.2 Transplant kidney 23

1.3 Communication skills and ethics 23

1.3.1 Renal disease in pregnancy 23

1.3.2 A new diagnosis of amyloidosis 24

1.3.3 Is dialysis appropriate? 25

1.4 Acute scenarios 26

1.4.1 A worrying potassium level 26

1.4.2 Postoperative acute renal failure 30

1.4.3 Renal impairment and a multisystem disease 33

1.4.4 Renal impairment and fever 36

1.4.5 Renal failure and haemoptysis 38

1.4.6 Renal colic 41

1.4.7 Backache and renal failure 43

1.4.8 Renal failure and coma 47

Diseases and Treatments 49

2.1 Major renal syndromes 49
   2.1.1 Acute renal failure 49
   2.1.2 Chronic renal failure 51
   2.1.3 End-stage renal failure 58
   2.1.4 Nephrotic syndromes 60
2.2 Renal replacement therapy 64
   2.2.1 Haemodialysis 64
   2.2.2 Peritoneal dialysis 66
   2.2.3 Renal transplantation 69
2.3 Glomerular diseases 72
   2.3.1 Primary glomerular disease 72
   2.3.2 Secondary glomerular disease 79
2.4 Tubulointerstitial diseases 81
   2.4.1 Acute tubular necrosis 81
   2.4.2 Acute interstitial nephritis 82
   2.4.3 Chronic interstitial nephritis 82
   2.4.4 Specific tubulointerstitial disorders 83
2.5 Diseases of renal vessels 86
   2.5.1 Renovascular disease 86
   2.5.2 Cholesterol atheroembolisation 88
2.6 Postrenal problems 89
   2.6.1 Obstructive uropathy 89
   2.6.2 Stones 90
   2.6.3 Retroperitonal fibrosis or periaortitis 91
   2.6.4 Urinary tract infection 92
2.7 The kidney in systemic disease 92
   2.7.1 Myeloma 92
   2.7.2 Amyloidosis 93
   2.7.3 Thrombotic microangiopathy (haemolytic–uraemic syndrome) 94
   2.7.4 Sickle cell disease 95
   2.7.5 Autoimmune rheumatic disorders 95
   2.7.6 Systemic vasculitis 97
   2.7.7 Diabetic nephropathy 99
   2.7.8 Hypertension 101
   2.7.9 Sarcoidosis 102
   2.7.10 Hepatorenal syndrome 102
   2.7.11 Pregnancy and the kidney 103
2.8 Genetic renal conditions 104
   2.8.1 Autosomal dominant polycystic kidney disease 104
   2.8.2 Alport's syndrome 106
   2.8.3 X-linked hypophosphataemic vitamin-D resistant rickets 106

Investigations and Practical Procedures 108

3.1 Examination of the urine 108
   3.1.1 Urinalysis 108
   3.1.2 Urine microscopy 109
3.2 Estimation of glomerular filtration rate 109
3.3 Imaging the renal tract 110
3.4 Renal biopsy 114

Self-assessment 116

Rheumatology and Clinical Immunology

RHEUMATOLOGY AND CLINICAL IMMUNOLOGY

PACES Stations and Acute Scenarios 3

1.1 History-taking 3
   1.1.1 Recurrent chest infections 3
   1.1.2 Recurrent meningitis 5
   1.1.3 Recurrent facial swelling and abdominal pain 7
   1.1.4 Recurrent skin abscesses 9
   1.1.5 Flushing and skin rash 12
   1.1.6 Drug-induced anaphylaxis 14
   1.1.7 Arthralgia, purpuric rash and renal impairment 16
   1.1.8 Arthralgia and photosensitive rash 19
   1.1.9 Cold fingers and difficulty swallowing 23
   1.1.10 Dry eyes and fatigue 25
   1.1.11 Breathlessness and weakness 27
   1.1.12 Low back pain 30
   1.1.13 Chronic back pain 32
   1.1.14 Recurrent joint pain and stiffness 33
   1.1.15 Foot drop and weight loss in a patient with rheumatoid arthritis 35
   1.1.16 Fever, myalgia, arthralgia and elevated acute-phase indices 38
   1.1.17 Non-rheumatoid pain and stiffness 40
   1.1.18 Widespread pain 42
1.2 Clinical examination 44
   1.2.1 Hands (general) 44
   1.2.2 Non-rheumatoid pain and stiffness: generalised osteoarthritis 45
   1.2.3 Rheumatoid arthritis 46
   1.2.4 Psoriatic arthritis 47
   1.2.5 Systemic sclerosis 49
   1.2.6 Chronic tophaceous gout 49
   1.2.7 Ankylosing spondylitis 50
   1.2.8 Deformity of bone: Paget's disease 51
   1.2.9 Marfan's syndrome 51
1.3 Communication skills and ethics 52
   1.3.1 Collapse during a restaurant meal 52
   1.3.2 Cold fingers and difficulty swallowing 54
   1.3.3 Back pain 55
   1.3.4 Widespread pain 56
   1.3.5 Explain a recommendation to start a disease-modifying antirheumatic drug 57

1.4 Acute scenarios 59

1.4.1 Fulminant septicaemia in an asplenic woman 59

1.4.2 Collapse during a restaurant meal 61

1.4.3 Systemic lupus erythematosus and confusion 64

1.4.4 Acute hot joints 66

1.4.5 A crush fracture 69

Diseases and Treatments 72

2.1 Immunodeficiency 72

2.1.1 Primary antibody deficiency 72

2.1.2 Combined T-cell and B-cell defects 75

2.1.3 Chronic granulomatous disease 77

2.1.4 Cytokine and cytokine-receptor deficiencies 78

2.1.5 Terminal pathway complement deficiency 80

2.1.6 Hyposplenism 81

2.2 Allergy 82

2.2.1 Anaphylaxis 82

2.2.2 Mastocytosis 84

2.2.3 Nut allergy 85

2.2.4 Drug allergy 87

2.3 Rheumatology 88

2.3.1 Carpal tunnel syndrome 88

2.3.2 Osteoarthritis 89

2.3.3 Rheumatoid arthritis 91

2.3.4 Seronegative spondyloarthropathies 94

2.3.5 Idiopathic inflammatory myopathies 98

2.3.6 Crystal arthritis: gout 99

2.3.7 Calcium pyrophosphate deposition disease 101

2.3.8 Fibromyalgia 101

2.4 Autoimmune rheumatic diseases 103

2.4.1 Systemic lupus erythematosus 103

2.4.2 Sjögren's syndrome 105

2.4.3 Systemic sclerosis (scleroderma) 106

2.5 Vasculitides 109

2.5.1 Giant-cell arteritis and polymyalgia rheumatica 109

2.5.2 Wegener's granulomatosis 111

2.5.3 Polyarteritis nodosa 113

2.5.4 Cryoglobulinaemic vasculitis 114

2.5.5 Behçet's disease 115

2.5.6 Takayasu's arteritis 117

2.5.7 Systemic Still's disease 119

Investigations and Practical Procedures 121

3.1 Assessment of acute-phase response 121

3.1.1 Erythrocyte sedimentation rate 121

3.1.2 C-reactive protein 121

3.2 Serological investigation of autoimmune rheumatic disease 122

3.2.1 Antibodies to nuclear antigens 122

3.2.2 Antibodies to double-stranded DNA 123

3.2.3 Antibodies to extractable nuclear antigens 124

3.2.4 Rheumatoid factor 125

3.2.5 Antineutrophil cytoplasmic antibody 125

3.2.6 Serum complement concentrations 125

3.3 Suspected immune deficiency in adults 126

3.4 Imaging in rheumatological disease 129

3.4.1 Plain radiology 129

3.4.2 Bone densitometry 130

3.4.3 Magnetic resonance imaging 131

3.4.4 Nuclear medicine 131

3.4.5 Ultrasound 132

3.5 Arthrocentesis 132

3.6 Corticosteroid injection techniques 133

3.7 Immunoglobulin replacement 135

Self-assessment 138

INDEX

Note: page numbers in *italics* refer to figures, those in **bold** refer to tables.

A

acanthosis nigricans 23, 46, *117*
acarbose **151**
ACE inhibitors 152
aches and pains 65–6
acromegaly 23–4, 42, 45–7, 71–3
  active disease 47
  aetiology/pathology 71
  clinical presentation 71
    amenorrhoea 71
    carpal tunnel syndrome 45, 71
    facies *46*
    hands *46*, 71
    obstructive sleep apnoea 23, 71
    prognathism 46, *46*, 71
  complications 24
  disease associations 73
  endocrine examination 46–7
  epidemiology 71
  follow-up 73
  history 23
  inactive disease 47
  investigation 23–4, 71–2
  management 24, 72–3
    holistic approach 73
    medical therapy 72–3
    radiotherapy 72
    surgery 72
  oral glucose tolerance test 171
  physical signs 71
  prognosis 73
  referral letter 23
  risk factors 73
  secondary hypertension **37**
ACTH 83–4
  deficiency 23, **94**
  ectopic 38, 70, 164, **164**
  plasma 93
  sampling for 70
ACTH-dependent Cushing's disease 68, **68**, 70
ACTH-independent Cushing's disease 68, **68**, 70
acute intermittent porphyria **129**
acute painful neuropathy 157
Addisonian crisis 63–4
  examination 64
  history 64
  investigation 64
  management 64–5
  symptoms 64
Addison's disease **10**, 42
  clinical signs *95*

  hyperpigmentation *95*
  hyponatraemia 58
  management 42
  non-compliance with treatment 55–6
  tiredness **30**, 41
  weight loss **27**, 28
adolescents, diabetes mellitus 161
adrenal adenoma *see* Conn's syndrome;
  hyperaldosteronism
adrenal disease
  Cushing's syndrome *see* Cushing's
    syndrome
  hyperaldosteronism **37**, 39, 85–7
adrenal hyperplasia **10**, **85**, 92–4
  acute adrenal crisis 93
  clinical presentation 93, **93**
  congenital **119**
  epidemiology 93
  investigation 93–4
  pathophysiology 92–3, *93*
  physical signs 93
  prevention 94
  prognosis 94
  screening 93
  treatment 93–4
    hormone replacement 94
adrenal insufficiency 63, 94–7
  aetiology 94
  clinical presentation 95
  epidemiology 95
  investigation 95–6
  physical signs 95
    hypoadrenal crisis 96
    tiredness 30, 48
  primary **94**
  prognosis 96
  secondary **94**
  treatment 59, 96, *96*
  see also Addison's disease
adrenal tumours 17
adrenalectomy 71
adrenocorticotrophin *see* ACTH
alabaster skin 42
alcohol abuse
  pseudo-Cushing's syndrome 45, 69
  tiredness **30**
alcohol intake 9
alcohol withdrawal **9**
aldosterone 86
alfacalcidol 143
Algrove syndrome 95
alkaline phosphatase
  hypercalcaemia 4
  hyperparathyroidism 138

  Paget's disease 137
alkalosis 39, **39**
alpha-blockers, phaeochromocytoma 92
alprostadil 122
amenorrhoea 27, 113–14
  acromegaly 71
  aetiology/pathophysiology 113, **113**
  causes 16, **16**
  clinical presentation 113
  differential diagnosis **114**
  history 16–17
  investigation 17
  and low blood pressure 42–3
  management 17
  post-pill 16–17, 113
  premature ovarian failure 16–17
  primary 113
  referral letter 16, 17
  secondary 113
  and short stature 17–20, 53–4
  tiredness and weight loss 39–42
amiloride, hyperaldosteronism 86
δ-aminolaevulinic acid 128
amiodarone, and thyroid function *31*, 48
anaemia
  normochromic normocytic 95
  tiredness 30, **30**
androgen profiles 87
androgen replacement 123
androgen status 112
androstenedione 93
angiotensin receptor blockers 152
anorexia 40
  weight loss **27**
  and osteoporosis **132**
anosmia 20, 112
anterior pituitary function 83
anti-thyroglobulin antibodies 98
anti-thyroid peroxidase 98
antiandrogens 120
  side effects, gynaecomastia **12**
antibodies, thyroid 106
anticonvulsants, side effects,
  osteomalacia 66
antidiuretic hormone
  ectopic **164**
  ectopic production **57**
antihistamines, antiserotoninergic 34
antiplatelet therapy 36
anxiety 9, **9**
  tiredness 30
anxiety attacks 32, **32**
apathetic hyperthyroidism 45
Apo-CII deficiency **126**

appetite 27
arginine stimulation test 83
arrhythmias
    bradycardia 42
    light-headedness 9
    palpitations 8–12, **9**
arthritis
    in haemochromatosis 130
    rheumatoid 66
aspirin 152
atenolol 152
atrophic thyroiditis **97**
autoantibodies
    in adrenal insufficiency 95
    thyroid 49, 102–3
autoimmune polyendocrinopathy-
    candidiasis-ectodermal dystrophy
    syndrome 163
autoimmune polyendocrinopathyûoral
    glucose tolerance test 169, **169**
autoimmune polyglandular
    endocrinopathies 163–4, **163**
azoospermia 124

B

band keratopathy 45, 48, 61, 141
barbiturates, side effects, osteomalacia
    66
Bartter's syndrome **39**
Bence Jones protein 4, 61
beta-blockers
    phaeochromocytoma 92
    porphyria 129
    thyroid crisis 63, 103–4
    thyrotoxicosis 104
biguanides **151**
biliary cirrhosis, and osteoporosis **132**
bisphosphonates 61
    osteoporosis 133
    Paget's disease 137
bitemporal hemianopia *see* hemianopia
blood glucose 145
blood pressure, control of 35, 36
body mass index 37, 42
    and infertility 124
bone age 19, 110
bone densitometry 21, 112–13, *133*
bone mass 132
bone mineral density 132
bony metastases 4
bowel habit 27, 32
bradycardia 42
breast cancer, and diabetes insipidus 7
bromocriptine 17
    acromegaly 72
    hyperprolactinaemia 74
    side effects 75
bronzed diabetes 130
buffalo hump 45, 68
bulimia 40

C

C-peptide 10
C-reactive protein 41, 146
cabergoline
    acromegaly 72
    hyperprolactinaemia 75
caffeine, excess 9, **9**
calcimimetics 139
calcitonin 106
    fasting 49
    hypercalcaemia 61
calcium
    drugs lowering 61
    excess intake **3**
    reduced excretion **3**
calcium channel blockers 152
    side effects, flushing 32
calcium metabolism 140
calcium supplements 133, 136, 143
calorie intake 27
cancer
    bony metastases 4
    pituitary metastasis *8*
    possibility of 51–2
    thyroid 48, *49*, 106, 107
carbamazepine, side effects, osteomalacia
    66
carbimazole 63, 103
carcinoid syndrome 32–4
    management 34
    octreoscan *33*
    referral letter 32
carcinomatous neuromyopathy **65**
cardiomegaly 39
carpal tunnel syndrome, and acromegaly
    45, 71
carpopedal spasm 142
cataracts, diabetes mellitus **154**, 155
catecholamines
    excess *see* phaeochromocytoma
    plasma 90
    urinary 90
Charcot's joints 159
cheiroarthropathy 159–60
chemosis 29, 48
Chlamydia trachomatis 123
chlorpromazine 63
    porphyria 129
chlorpropamide, side effects, flushing 32
cholesterol 99
chondrocalcinosis 130, 131
chronic fatigue syndrome 30, **30**
Chvostek's sign 142
chylomicrons 125
cimetidine, side effects, gynaecomastia
    12
cirrhosis, and hyperprolactinaemia **73**
clomifene 15, 124
clonidine suppression test 90
clubbing, *see also* thyroid acropachy

coeliac disease
    and osteoporosis **132**
    weight loss **27**
collapse
    adrenal insufficiency *see* Addisonian
        crisis
    thyrotoxic crisis *see* thyrotoxic crisis
colonic villous adenoma **39**
coma
    Glasgow Coma Scale 56
    with hyponatraemia 56–60
confusion, hypercalcaemia-related 60–1
congenital adrenal hyperplasia *see*
    adrenal hyperplasia
Conn's syndrome 37, **68**, *70*, 85, **85**, *86*
contraception, hyperprolactinaemia
    75–6
corneal arcus *127*, **128**
corticosteroids
    biosynthesis *93*
    non-compliance 55–6
corticotrophin-releasing hormone test
    166
cortisol 55
    loss of diurnal variation 69
    reduced synthesis 92–3
    24-hour urinary free 68
cranial mononeuropathies 157
craniopharyngioma 78–80
    aetiology/pathophysiology 78
    clinical presentation
        adulthood 78–9
        childhood 78
    and diabetes insipidus **81**
    epidemiology 78
    investigation 79, *79*
    ophthalmological review 79
    physical signs 79
    postoperative care 80
    prognosis 80
    treatment 79–80
creatine kinase 67, 99
cretinism 98
Crohn's disease, and osteoporosis **132**
cryptorchidism 44, 111, 112
cubitus valgus *115*
Cushing's syndrome 15, 22, 68–71
    ACTH-dependent 68, **68**, 70
    ACTH-independent 68, **68**, 70
    aetiology 68, **68**, 70
    clinical signs
        buffalo hump 45, 68
        central obesity 65, 68, *69*
        hirsutism 68
        kyphoscoliosis 68
        moon-like facies 68, *69*
        plethora 68, *69*
        striae *69*
    cyclical 69
    depression 45
    examination 45

Cushing's syndrome (*continued*)
  hypokalaemia **39**
  imaging 70, *70*
  investigation 68–9
  misdiagnosis 66
  and osteoporosis **132**
  physical signs 68
  prognosis 71
  proximal myopathy **65**
  screening for 36
  secondary hypertension **37**, 38
  treatment 70
cyproheptadine 34
cyproterone acetate 53, 120

D

dadalafil 121
de Quervain's thyroiditis **106**
deafness, Turner's syndrome 116
dehydration 61, 66
dehydroepiandrosterone sulphate 87, 93
delayed puberty 17–20, 107–10
  aetiology/pathophysiology **18**, 107, **109**
  clinical presentation 107, 109
  complications 110
  definition 107
  investigation 110
  karyotype analysis 110
  physical signs 109–10
  treatment 110
demeclocycline 60
dementia 22, 45
depression 9, 45
  endocrine examination 45
  history 21–2
  investigation 22
  management 22
  referral letter 21
  tiredness 30
  underlying physical illness 21–2, **22**
dermatomyositis, heliotrope rash 66
desferrioxamine 131
desmopressin, diabetes insipidus 7
dexamethasone, thyroid crisis 104
dexamethasone suppression test 68–9,
    87, 169–70
  high-dose 170–1
  low-dose 170
diabetes insipidus 5, 80–3
  aetiology/pathophysiology 80
  causes **81**
  clinical presentation 80
  craniopharyngioma 78
  dipsogenic 6, 8, 80, **81**
    management 7–8, 82
  epidemiology 80
  hypothalamic 6, 80, **81**
    management 7, 82
  investigation 80–1
    imaging 81, *82*

  nephrogenic 6, 80, **81**
    management 7–8, 82
  physical signs 80
  prognosis 83
  treatment 82
diabetes mellitus 36, 143–7
  aetiology 143, **144**
  cardiovascular risk factors
    dyslipidaemia 152
    hypertension 151–2
  classification **143**
  clinical presentation 144, **145**
  complications 153–60, **153**
    arthropathy and skin lesions 159–60
    diabetic eye disease 153–5, *154*, **154**,
      155
    diabetic foot 148–9
    macrovascular 153
    microvascular 153–4, **154**
    nephropathy 155–7
    neuropathy 157–60
    susceptibility to infections 160
  coping with diagnosis 22–3
  depression 21–3, 45
  driving 161
  employment 162
  environmental factors **144**
  epidemiology 143–4
  erectile dysfunction 121
  exercise 162
  flushing and diarrhoea 32
  follow-up 152–3, **152**
  genetic factors **144**
  gestational 161
  glycosuria 22
  hyperglycaemic emergencies 145–6
    investigation 145–6
    treatment 146
  hyperosmolar non-ketotic coma 144,
    145–6
  hypoglycaemic emergencies 147
  investigation 145
  management 147–53
    Alphabet Strategy **153**
    diet and lifestyle modifications 148,
      148
    glucagon-like peptide 1 receptor
      activation 151
    glycaemic control 148
    insulin 148–9
    oral hypoglycaemic agents 149, **151**
  oral glucose tolerance test 169, **169**
  and osteoporosis **132**
  patient information 160–2
    adolescents 161
    sick-day rules 160
    surgery 160–1
  physical signs 144–5
  polydipsia 144
  polyuria 5, 144
  and pregnancy 161

  secondary hypertension **37**
  testing for 35
  tiredness 30, **30**, 41, 48
  transient remission 149
  type 1
    aetiology 143
    clinical signs **145**
    epidemiology 143
    treatment 148–9
  type 2
    aetiology 143
    clinical signs **145**
    epidemiology 143–4
    treatment 149, *150*, **151**
    weight loss 27, **27**, 144
diabetic amyotrophy 45, **65**, 66
diabetic autonomic neuropathy **32**
diabetic eye disease 153–5, *154*, **154**,
    155
diabetic foot 158–60, **158**
  neuroischaemic **158**, *159*
  neuropathic **158**, *159*
  neuropathic joint 159
diabetic ketoacidosis 144, 145–6
  insulin therapy **146**
diabetic maculopathy 154, **154**, *155*
diabetic nephropathy 155–7
  aetiology/pathogenesis 155
  clinical presentation 155
  epidemiology 155
  investigations 156
  Kimmelstiel-Wilson nodules 155
  microalbuminuria 155, 156
  physical signs 155
  prognosis 157
diabetic neuropathy 157–9
  autonomic 157–8, *158*
  distal symmetrical polyneuropathy 157
diabetic retinopathy 153–4, **154**
  advanced *156*
  background *154*, **154**
  proliferative 154, **154**, *155*
  proproliferative 154, *154*, **154**
Dianette 53, 120
diarrhoea
  conditions associated with **32**
  and flushing 32–4
    investigation 33
    management 33–4
diazepam, porphyria 129
diet 54–5
  diabetes mellitus 148, **148**
  healthy 35, 36
dietary assessment 25–6
digoxin, side effects, gynaecomastia **12**
dipstick urinalysis 38
distal symmetrical polyneuropathy 157
diuretics
  hypokalaemia 38, **39**
  hyponatraemia 57
  thiazide 4

donor insemination 124
dopamine agonists, acromegaly 72
doxorubicin 34
driving, diabetes mellitus 161
dumping syndrome **10**
dyslipidaemia *see*
    hyperlipidaemia/dyslipidaemia
dysphagia, weight loss 27

E

eating habits 25
ectopic hormone syndromes 164, **164**
eflornithine 120
embryo transfer 124
enterochromaffin cells 32
eosinophilia 95
epilepsy 65
erectile dysfunction 120–3
    aetiology and pathophysiology 120–1,
        121
    clinical presentation 121
    drug-induced **121**
    epidemiology 121
    hormonal **121**
    illness-related **121**
    investigation 121
    neurogenic **121**
    physical signs 121
    prevention 123
    prognosis 123
    psychogenic **121**
    treatment 121–3, *122*
        androgen replacement 123
        phosphodiesterase inhibitors
        121–2
        urological 122–3
    vascular **121**
erythrocyte sedimentation rate 41, 67
erythropoietic protoporphyria **129**
erythropoietin, ectopic **164**
ethical issues, Turner's syndrome 116
eunuchoid appearance 44, 112
eurovolaemia 56
euvolaemia 56, *57*, 60
exercise 25, 26, 35, 36, 55
    and amenorrhoea 16
    diabetic patients 162
exophthalmos 29, 47, *48*, 62
exposure keratitis 48
Exubera 149, **149**
eyes
    band keratopathy 45, 48, 61
    chemosis 29, 48
    diabete mellitus 153–4, **154**
    exophthalmos 29, 47, *48*, 62
    gritty 47–8
    lid lag 62
    lid retraction 47, *47*, 62
    ophthalmoplegia 29, 46, 48
    proptosis 47

F

fainting/faints *see* syncope
Fallopian tube, occlusion of 124
familial combined hyperlipidaemia **126**
familial dysbetalipoproteinaemia **126**
familial hypercholesterolaemia **126**
familial hypertriglyceridaemia **126**
familial hypocalciuric hypercalcaemia **3**, 4
female athletic triad **27**
Ferriman-Gallwey scoring system **118**
ferritin 131
fertility 14
    Turner's syndrome 116
fibrates 128
finasteride, hirsutism 120
fine needle aspiration
    neck lump 49
    thyroid nodules 107
fludrocortisone, adrenal insufficiency 96
fluid intake 6, 57–8
fluid loss 57–8
fluid volume status 58
5-fluorouracil 34
flushing
    conditions associated with **32**
    and diarrhoea 32–4
    history 32
flutamide, hirsutism 120
follicle-stimulating hormone 19, 21, 83
    delayed puberty 110
Friedewald formula 125
fructose intolerance **10**

G

galactorrhoea 16, 41, 46, 48, 112
gastrectomy, and osteoporosis **132**
Gaucher's disease, and osteoporosis **132**
gestational diabetes 161
Gitelman's syndrome **39**
Glasgow Coma Scale 56
glibenclamide 147, **151**
gliclazide 15, **151**
glimepiride **151**
glipizide **151**
glucagon stimulation test 83
glucagon-like peptide 1 receptor 151
glucocorticoids
    deficiency **94**
    hypercalcaemia 61
glucose, blood levels 145
α-glucosidase inhibitors **151**
glycaemic control 148
glycogen storage diseases **65**
glycosuria 22, 45
goitre 27, *28*, 29, 47–8, 105–7
    diffuse **106**
    nodular **106**
    retrosternal 49
    toxic multinodular **100**, **102**

gonadotrophin-releasing hormone
    receptor 111
gonadotrophin-releasing hormone test
    167
gonadotrophins 83
    virilising tumours 87
granuloma annulare 159
Graves' dermopathy *see* pretibial
    myxoedema
Graves' disease 29, 47–8, 62, 97, 100,
    100
    clinical features **102**
    endocrine examination 47
Graves' ophthalmoplegia *101*
gritty eyes 47–8
growth
    delayed **18**
    normal 18, *18*
growth hormone 83
    deficiency 78
    excess 23–4
    hypopituitarism 84
growth hormone receptor antagonists,
    acromegaly 72
growth hormone-releasing hormone 71
gynaecomastia 12–14, 20, 46, 112
    causes **12**
    cosmetic surgery 13
    definition 12
    drug history 13
    history 12–13
    investigation 13
    management 13–14
    physiological 12
    pituitary function 13
    psychological impact 13
    referral letter 12
    testicular function 13

H

haem synthetic pathway *129*
haemochromatosis 130–1
    aetiology 130
    clinical presentation 130
        arthritis 130
        cardiac disease 130
        endocrine disease 130
        liver disease 130
    complications 131
    epidemiology 130
    investigation 131
    pathophysiology 130
    physical signs 130
    treatment 131
hair 14
hair loss 42
hands
    in acromegaly 46, *46*
    resting tremor 48
Hashimoto's thyroiditis 97, **97**, **106**

headache, and polyuria 6–7
heat intolerance 27
heliotrope rash 66
hemianopia 42, *43*, 45, 46, 48, 71, 79
hepatic artery embolisation 34
hepatomegaly, haemochromatosis 130
hereditary coproporphyria **129**
high-density lipoproteins 125
  metabolism 125
hirsutism 14–16, 45, 118–20
  aetiology/pathology 118–19, **119**
  clinical presentation 119
  Cushing's syndrome 68
  epidemiology 119
  extent of 14
  family history 14–15
  Ferriman-Gallwey scoring system **118**
  history 14–15, 119
  investigation 15, 119, **120**
  management 15–16, 119–20
    antiandrogens 120
    cosmetic and topical measures 120
    lifestyle advice 120
    suppression of ovarian function 120
  no medical cause 52–3
  polycystic ovarian syndrome 117
  referral letter 114
  underlying disorders 14
hormone replacement
  adrenal hyperplasia 94
  hypopituitarism 84
  Turner's syndrome 115
human chorionic gonadotrophin, ectopic
  164
hungry bone syndrome 142
hydrocortisone
  Addisonian crisis 64–5
  adrenal insufficiency 96
  hypopituitarism 84
  thyrotoxic crisis 63
5-hydroxyindoleacetic acid 33
21-hydroxylase deficiency 92, 93
hydroxymethylglutaryl-CoA reductase
  inhibitors *see* statins
17α-hydroxyprogesterone 87, 93
5-hydroxytryptamine, and carcinoid 32–3
hyperalbuminaemia **3**
hyperaldosteronism **37**, 39, 85–7
  aetiology 85, **85**
  of cardiac failure 59
  clinical presentation 85
  epidemiology 85
  investigation 85
  physical signs 85
  prognosis 87
  screening tests 85–6
    plasma renin and aldosterone 86
    urea and electrolytes 85
    urinary potassium and sodium 85
  treatment 86–7
hyperandrogenism 118

hypercalcaemia 3–5, 22, 51–2, 138,
  140–1
  aetiology/pathophysiology 140, *140*
  artefactual **3**
  asymptomatic 5
  band keratopathy 45, 48, 61, 141
  causes **3**, 60, 140
  clinical presentation 141
  complications 4, 141
  confusion related to 60–1
  differential diagnosis **3**
  drug history 4
  examination 60–1
  familial hypocalciuric **3**, 4, 5
  family history 4
  functional enquiry 3–4
  history 3–4, 60
  investigation 4–5, 61
  management 5, 61, 141
  physical signs 141
  prognosis 141
  referral letter 3
hypercalciuria 3
hypercholesterolaemia 125, **126**
hypercortisolism 71
  see also Cushing's syndrome
hypergammaglobulinaemia **3**
hyperglycaemic emergencies 145–6
  investigation 145–6
  treatment 146
hypergonadotrophic hypogonadism **18**,
  19, 20, 41, 44
hyperinsulinaemia 10
hyperkalaemia, and hyperglycaemia 146
hyperlipidaemia, mixed 125
hyperlipidaemia/dyslipidaemia 35, 125–8
  classification 125–6, **126**
  clinical presentation 126
  complications 128
  diabetes mellitus 152
  endogenous lipid pathway 125
  epidemiology 126
  exogenous lipid pathway 125
  investigation 128
  physical signs 126–8, *127*, **128**
  physiology/pathology 125
  treatment 128
hyperosmolar non-ketotic coma 144,
  145–6
hyperparathyroidism 3, 4, 30, **30**, **37**, 48,
  137–9
  brown tumours 138
  clinical presentation 138
  disease associations 139
  epidemiology 138
  familial 5
  and hypercalcaemia 138
  investigation 138
  nephrocalcinosis 138, *139*
  nephrolithiasis *139*
  osteitis fibrosa cystica 138

  and osteoporosis **132**
  pathophysiology 137–8
  patient information 139–40
  'pepper-pot' skull 138
  physical signs 138
  secondary hypertension **37**
  tiredness 30, **30**, 48
  treatment 138–9
hyperphosphataemia, and hypocalcaemia
  141
hyperpigmentation
  Addison's disease 64, *95*
  haemochromatosis 130
hyperprolactinaemia 12, **12**, 41, 42,
  73–6, 84, **114**
  aetiology and pathophysiology 73, **73**
  clinical presentation 73
  complications 76
  contraception and pregnancy 75–6
  differential diagnosis 74
  disease associations 76
  epidemiology 73
  idiopathic 75
  investigation
    blood tests 74
    imaging 74, *74*
    prolactin 74
    visual fields/pituitary function 74
  macroprolactinoma **73**, *74*, 75
  microprolactinoma **73**, 75
  physical signs 73
  treatment 74–5
hyperpyrexia, thyrotoxic crisis 62
hypertension
  in acromegaly 23
  causes 37–8
  consequences 38, *38*
  diabetes mellitus 151–2
  history 37–8
  investigation 38–9
  management 39
  and myocardial infarction 35
  and neck lump 48–50
  pregnancy-associated **37**
  secondary 37–9, 49
    causes **37**
hypertensive retinopathy *38*
hyperthyroidism
  and osteoporosis **132**
  subclinical 106
hypertonic saline infusion test 60, 81
hypertrichosis 14, 118
hypertriglyceridaemia 125, **126**
hyperventilation 9
hypervolaemia 56, *57*, 60
hypoadrenal crisis 96
hypoadrenalism *see* adrenal insufficiency
hypoalbuminaemia 141
hypocalcaemia 5, 141–3
  aetiology/pathophysiology 141, **141**
  Chvostek's sign 142

hypocalcaemia (*continued*)
  clinical presentation 142
  hypoparathyroidism 142
  investigation 142–3
  physical signs 142
  pseudohypoparathyroidism 142
  treatment 143
  Trousseau's sign 142
hypoglycaemia 9, **9**, 56
  causes **10**
  clinical presentation 147
  emergencies 147
  factitious 10–11
    management 11
  insulinoma 9, 10–11, **10**, *11*
  investigation 10–11
  nocturnal 147
  reactive 11
hypogonadism
  female 17, **18**, 19, 41
  male *see* male hypogonadism
  and osteoporosis **132**
hypogonadotrophic hypogonadism **18**,
    19, 20, 41, 44
  idiopathic 111
hypokalaemia 146
  causes 38, **39**
  consequences 38
  and hypertension 37–9
  investigation 39
  management 39
  nausea and vomiting 39
  referral letter 37
hypomagnesaemia, and hypocalcaemia
    141
hyponatraemia 50–1
  acute symptomatic 59
  cause of 57–8
  chronic asymptomatic 60
  and coma 56–60
  drug history 57
  examination 58
  factitious 58
  history 56–7
  hypertonic saline in 60
  hypothyroidism 99
  routine tests 58
  severe 59
hypoparathyroidism 105, **105**, 131, 141,
    142
  and hypocalcaemia **141**
hypophosphataemia **135**
hypopituitarism **10**, 23, 24, **30**, 42, 48,
    83–5
  aetiology and pathophysiology 83,
    83
  clinical presentation 83
  and hyponatraemia 58
  incidence 83
  investigation 83–4
  management 42

and osteoporosis **132**
  physical signs 83
  prognosis 85
  tiredness **30**
  treatment 84–5
    growth hormone 84
    hydrocortisone 84
    sex hormone replacement therapy 84
    thyroxine 84
hyposmia 20, 112
hypotension, postural **9**, 48
hypothalamic-pituitary function 79, 81
hypothalamic-pituitary-adrenal axis 42,
    83
hypothalamic-pituitary-target organ axis
    dysfunction 42–3
hypothalamic-pituitary-thyroid
    dysfunction 42
hypothalamic-posterior pituitary
    dysfunction 42
hypothalamic/pituitary disorders
  acromegaly *see* acromegaly
  and amenorrhoea 16, 41
  Cushing's syndrome *see* Cushing's
    syndrome
  galactorrhoea *see* galactorrhoea
  hypopituitarism *see* hypopituitarism
  visual field defects 43, *43*
hypothyroidism 15, 22, 40, 45, 97–100
  aetiology/pathogenesis 97, **97**
  clinical presentation 97–8, *98*
  congenital 97–8
  epidemiology 97
  examination 45
  and hyperprolactinaemia **73**
  and hyponatraemia 58
  investigations, urea and electrolytes
    99
  myxoedema coma 97
  physical signs 97–8, *98*
  in pregnancy 99–100
  secondary **98**
  subclinical 98, **98**, 99, **100**
  thyroid function tests 98, **98**
    anterior pituitary function 99
    anti-thyroid peroxidase and anti-
      thyroglobulin antibodies 98
    cholesterol and creatine kinase 99
  tiredness 48
  treatment 99–100
  Turner's syndrome 115
hypovolaemia 56, *57*
hysterosalpingogram 123

I

immobility 65–7
  history 65–6
  investigation 67
  management 67
  neurological symptoms 66

impotence *see* erectile dysfunction
in vitro fertilisation 124
infective myositis **65**
infertility 15, 123–5
  aetiology/pathology 123
  clinical assessment 123
  complications 124–5
  definition of 123
  investigation 123–4
  polycystic ovarian syndrome 117
  treatment 124
insulin 146, 148–9
  candidates for 148
  choice of 148–9
  diabetic ketoacidosis **146**
  infusion 146
  inhaled 149, **149**
  isophane **149**
  long-acting **149**
  side effects and complications 149, *150*
  soluble **149**
  subcutaneous 147
  subcutaneous infusion 148–9
  types of 148, **149**
insulin analogues **149**
insulin resistance 25, 46, 143
  secondary hypertension **37**
  see also diabetes mellitus
insulin tolerance test 83, 167–8
insulin-like growth factor-1 23, 24, 71
insulinitis 143
insulinoma 9, 10–11, **10**, *11*
  management 11
interferon-alpha 34
intermediate-density lipoproteins 125
intracytoplasmic sperm injection 124
intrauterine insemination 124
intravascular volume depletion 61
iron overload 131
ischaemic heart disease, Turner's
    syndrome 115

K

kaliuresis 85
Kallmann's syndrome 20, **20**, 44, 110,
    111
  hyposmia in 20, 44, 112
karyotype analysis 19, 21
  delayed puberty 110
  Klinefelter's syndrome 21, 45
  Turner's syndrome 19, 53–4, 115–16
ketoconazole
  side effects
    blockade of steroid synthesis 70
    gynaecomastia **12**
Kimmelstiel-Wilson nodules 155
Klinefelter's syndrome **12**, **20**, 44, 110,
    111
  karyotype analysis 21, 45
kyphoscoliosis, Cushing's syndrome 68

L

Lawrence-Moon-Biedl syndrome **25**, **81**
laxatives, and hypokalaemia 38
left ventricular hypertrophy, ECG *36*
legs, proximal myopathy **65**, 66
lethargy *see* tiredness
letrozole 13
levothyroxine 99
light-headedness 8–12
    arrhythmias 9
    drug history 9
    investigation 10–11
    management 11
    referral letter 8
    social impact 9–10
liothyronine 99
lipaemia retinalis *127*, **128**
lipid lowering 36
lipid storage diseases **65**
lipoatrophy 149, *150*
lipohypertrophy 149, *150*
lipoproteins 125
lipoprotein lipase deficiency **126**
lipoprotein(a) 125
    metabolism 125
liquorice excess **39**
lithium, and nephrogenic diabetes insipidus 7, **81**
Looser's zones 135, *136*
loperamide 34
low blood pressure 42–3
    endocrine examination 42
    pituitary mass lesion 42–3
low-density lipoproteins 125
    metabolism 125
Lugol's iodine 63
lung cancer, and syndrome of inappropriate antidiuresis 58
luteinising hormone 19, 21, 83
    delayed puberty 110
lymphadenopathy 40, *41*, 49
lymphoma 49
    thyroid **108**
    weight loss 27

M

macroprolactinoma **73**, *74*, 75
maculopathy, diabetic 154, **154**, *155*
main d'accoucher 142
malabsorption, weight loss **27**
male hypogonadism 20–1, 43–5, *44*, 111–13
    aetiology/pathophysiology 111
    androgen status 112
    cause **20**, 44–5
    clinical presentation 112
    cryptorchidism 44, 111, 112
    endocrine examination 44
    eunuchoid appearance 44

history 20
investigation 20–1, 112–13
Kallmann's syndrome 20, **20**, 44, 110, 111
Klinefelter's syndrome **12**, **20**, 44, 110, 111
management 21, 113
physical signs 112
pituitary status 44
pubertal development 44–5, *44*
referral letter 20
mastocytosis
    and osteoporosis **132**
    systemic **32**
Medic-Alert bracelet 56, 84
menopause
    premature 16–17, 113–14
    symptoms **9**
menstrual disorders 14
    amenorrhoea *see* amenorrhoea
    oligomenorrhoea 15, 27, 40, 113–14
metabolic syndrome 36–7
    diagnostic criteria 37
metanephrines 90
metastatic cancer
    bone 4
    pituitary *8*
metformin 15, **151**
    polycystic ovarian syndrome 117
methyldopa 161
α-methylparatyrosine 92
metoclopramide, and hyperprolactinaemia **73**
metronidazole, side effects, gynaecomastia **12**
metyrapone 70
microalbuminuria 155, 156
microprolactinoma **73**, 75
micturition, frequent 6
migraine 6–7
milk-alkali syndrome **3**
mineralocorticoids, deficiency **94**
mirror movements 112
moon-like facies 68, *69*
multiple endocrine neoplasia 162–3, **162**
    management 163
    screening 163
    type 1 4, 5, **162**
        insulinoma 11–12
    type 2 48, 49, 89, **162**
multiple myeloma 4
muscle weakness 65–7
muscular dystrophies, inherited **65**
myeloma, and osteoporosis **132**
myocardial infarction
    drug history 35
    family history 35
    history 35
    investigation 35–6
    prevention 34–7
        antiplatelet therapy 36

    blood pressure control 35, 36
    diet 35, 36
    exercise 35, 36
    lipid lowering 36
    stopping smoking 35
    weight control 35, 36
myopathy, proximal **65**, 66
myositis, infective **65**
myxoedema, pretibial 48, *102*
myxoedema coma 97
    treatment 99

N

nateglinide **151**
nausea and vomiting
    and hypokalaemia 39
    weight loss 40
neck lump 48–50
    causes 49
    endocrine examination 48–9
    fine needle aspiration 49
    investigation 49, *50*
necrobiosis lipoidica diabeticorum 159, *160*
nephroalcinosis, hyperparathyroidism 138, *139*
nephrolithiasis, hyperparathyroidism *139*
nephropathy, diabetic 155–7
nerve root irritation 66
neurofibromatosis type 1 **89**
neuroglycopenia 9
neuroischaemic foot **158**, *159*
neuropathic foot **158**
neuropathic joint 159
neutropenia 95
nicotinic acid supplements 34
night sweats 40
nocturia 5
non-compliance 55–6
normochromic normocytic anaemia 95

O

obesity 54–5
    central 68, *69*
    centripetal 45
    and Cushing's syndrome 65
    drug treatment **26**
    and myocardial infarction risk 35
    see also weight gain
obstructive sleep apnoea, acromegaly 23, 71
octreoscan *33*
    Cushing's syndrome 70
octreotide 34
    acromegaly 72
oedema
    periorbital 29, 48
    pulmonary 39
oestradiol, delayed puberty 110

oestrogen therapy 114
'off legs' *see* immobility
oligomenorrhoea 15, 27, 40, 113–14
  differential diagnosis **114**
oocyte donation 124
ophthalmoplegia 29, 46, 48, *101*
opioids
  overdose 56
  porphyria 129
oral contraceptive pill 14
  and amenorrhoea 16–17
oral glucose tolerance test 169, **169**
  acromegaly 171
oral hypoglycaemic agents 149, **151**
orlistat **26**
osmotic diuresis **6**
osteitis deformans *see* Paget's disease
osteitis fibrosa cystica 138
osteoclast-activating factor, ectopic **164**
osteogenesis imperfecta, and
    osteoporosis **132**
osteomalacia 65, **65**, 66, 67, 134–6
  causes **135**
  clinical presentation 135
  epidemiology 135
  investigation 135
  management 67
  pathophysiology 134–5, *134*
  physical signs 135
  prognosis 136
  treatment 135–6
osteopenia, premature menopause 114
osteoporosis 131–4
  clinical presentation 132
  epidemiology 132
  investigation 132, *133*
  pathophysiology 132
  premature menopause 114
  prophylaxis 134
  secondary causes **132**
  treatment 132–4
  Turner's syndrome 115
ovarian hyperstimulation syndrome 124
ovarian tumours 17
  virilising *88*
ovaries, premature failure 16–17
ovulation induction 124

P

Paget's disease 136–7
  aetiology/pathophysiology 136
  clinical presentation 136
  complications 137
  epidemiology 136
  investigation 137, *137*
  physical signs 136–7
    bony deformities 136
    increased vascularity 136–7
    nerve entrapment 137
  treatment 137

pallor 42
palpitations 8–12
  drug history 9
  history 9
  investigation 10–11
  management 11
  referral letter 8
  social impact 9–10
  thyrotoxicosis 27
pamidronate 61
Pancoast tumour 58
pancreatitis
  acute
    hypercalcaemia 4
    and hypocalcaemia **141**
papaverine 122
paraganglioma 49, **89**
parathyroid glands
  adenoma 5, *140*
  hyperparathyroidism *see*
    hyperparathyroidism
  hypoparathyroidism 105, **105**, 131,
    141, 142
parathyroid hormone 4, 138
parathyroid hormone-related peptide,
    ectopic **164**
parathyroidectomy 5
Parkinson's disease 22
  bradykinesia 45
  coghweel rigidity 45
  resting tremor 45
patient education 55–6
pegvisomant, acromegaly 72
pellagra 33
penile curvature 121
pentagastrin stimulation test 168–9
pentamidine, side effects, hypoglycaemia
    10
peptic ulcer, and hypercalcaemia 4
periorbital oedema 29, 48
peripheral neuropathy 157
pernicious anaemia, weight loss 28
Peyronie's disease 121, 122
phaeochromocytoma **3**, **9**, 89–92
  aetiology/pathophysiology 89, **89**
  clinical presentation 89–90
  differential diagnosis 92
  epidemiology 89
  familial 89, **89**
  flushing and diarrhoea 33
  genetic testing 91–2
  imaging
    ^{123}I-MIBG scan 91, *92*
    MRI 49, 90–1, *91*
  investigations 90
  physical signs 90
  prognosis 92
  secondary hypertension **37**, 38
  treatment 92
phenothiazines, and hyperprolactinaemia
    73

phenoxybenzamine 92
phenytoin, side effects, osteomalacia
    66
phosphate 4
phosphodiesterase inhibitors 121–2
pinpoint pupils 56
pioglitazone **151**
pituitary apoplexy 77–8
  aetiology/pathophysiology 77
  clinical presentation 77
  complications 78
  epidemiology 77
  investigation 77, *78*
  physical signs 77
  treatment
    emergency 78
    hormone replacement 78
    surgery 78
pituitary disorders *see*
    hypothalamic/pituitary disorders
pituitary mass lesion 42–3
pituitary metastasis 8
pituitary tumours 24, 44
  adenoma **68**, 70
    see also acromegaly; Cushing's
    syndrome
  macroprolactinoma **73**, *74*, 75
  microadenoma *72*
  microprolactinoma **73**, 75
  non-functioning 75, 76–7, *76*
    aetiology/pathophysiology 76
    clinical presentation 76, *76*
    complications 77
    differential diagnosis 76–7
    epidemiology 76
    investigation 76
    prognosis 77
    treatment 77
  physical signs 76
plasma
  ACTH 93
  aldosterone 86
  catecholamines 90
  free metanephrines 90
  osmolality 7, 58–9, 80–1
    calculation of 59
  renin 86, 93
plethora 68, *69*
polycystic ovarian syndrome 14, 15, **73**,
    113, 116–18
  aetiology/pathophysiology 116
  cardiovascular risks 117
  clinical presentation 116
  epidemiology 116
  hirsutism **119**
  infertility 123
  investigations 116–17
  physical signs 116, *117*
  prevention 118
  prognosis 16, 117
  treatment 117–18

polydipsia **6**, 80
 diabetes mellitus 144
 management 7
 psychogenic 8, 57–8
polygenic hypercholesterolaemia **126**
polymyalgia rheumatica 65, 66
polymyositis/dermatomyositis 65, 66
polyuria 5–8, 41, 80
 causes **6**
 definition 5
 diabetes mellitus 5, 144
 drug history 7
 history 6
 investigation 7
 management 7–8
 psychiatric history 7
 referral letter 5
 thirst 6
porphyria 128–9, **129**
 acute intermittent **129**
 clinical presentation 129
 congenital **129**
 erythropoietic protoporphyria **129**
 hereditary coproporphyria **129**
 hyponatraemia 58
 investigation 129
 pathophysiology 128–9, *129*
 treatment 129
 variegate **129**
porphyria cutanea tarda **129**
postural hypotension **9**, 48
Prader orchidometer *44*
Prader-Willi syndrome **25**
prandial glucose regulators **151**
pregnancy
 complications
  diabetes mellitus 161
  Graves' disease 101
  hypertension **37**
  hypothyroidism 99–100
  thyrotoxicosis 105
  hyperprolactinaemia 75–6
pregnancy test 17
premature menopause 16–17, 113–14
 aetiology/pathophysiology 113, **113**
 clinical presentation 113
 complications 114
 disease associations 114
 fertility 114
 investigation 114
 osteopenia/osteoporosis 114
 physical signs 113
 treatment 114
premature ovarian failure 16–17, **113**
 weight loss 28
pretibial myxoedema 48, *102*
primary pigmented nodular adrenal
  disease **68**
prognathism 46, *46*, 71
prolactin 74, 84
 polycystic ovarian syndrome 117

prophythiouracil 103
propranolol 92
 thyroid crisis 103–4
proptosis 47
propylthiouracil 63
proximal myopathy **65**, 66
pseudo-acromegaly 23
pseudo-Cushing's syndrome 45, 69
pseudohypoparathyroidism 142, *142*
psychogenic polydipsia 8, 57–8
pubertal development 44–5, *44*, 107
 Tanner staging system 44, 107, **108**,
  109
puberty, delayed *see* delayed puberty
pulmonary oedema 39
pulse, thyroid disease 48

Q

quadrantanopia 42, *43*, 46, 48, 71, 79
quetiapine 74
quinine, side effects, hypoglycaemia **10**

R

radiculopathies 157
radioiodine 104
radiotherapy, acromegaly 72
raloxifene 133
Rathke's pouch 78
renal failure, chronic 5
renin 86, 93
repaglinide **151**
retinopathy
 diabetic *see* diabetic retinopathy
 hypertensive *38*
rheumatoid arthritis 66
ribs
 notching 39
 'rickety rosary' 135
rickets 135, **135**
 treatment 136
Riedel's disease **106**
rimonabant **26**, 36
rosiglitazone **151**

S

'sabre' tibia 137, *137*
salicylates, side effects, hypoglycaemia **10**
salt-craving 41, 95
salt-loading tests 86
sarcoidosis, and hypercalcaemia 3
Schmidt's syndrome **163**
seborrhoea, acromegaly 46
selective oestrogen receptor modulators
  133
semen analysis 123
sex hormone replacement therapy 84
sex hormone-binding globulin 14, 118
Sheehan's syndrome **81**

short stature
 amenorrhoea 17–20, 53–4
 family history 19
 history 18–19, *18*
  growth 18, *18*
  illness 18–19
 investigation 19
 management 19
 social history 19
 Turner's syndrome 116
short Synacthen test 83–4, 165–6
 contraindications 165
 indications 165
 interpretation 165–6
 investigation 165
sibutramine **26**, 36
sick euthyroidism **98**
sildenafil 121–2
Sipple's syndrome 48, 49, 89, **162**
skin tags 46, *46*
smoking cessation 35
sodium iodide 103
somatostatin analogues 34
 acromegaly 72
spironolactone
 hirsutism 120
 hyperaldosteronism 86
 side effects, gynaecomastia **12**
splenomegaly, haemochromatosis 130
statins 128, 152
steroid treatment card *96*
streptozotocin 34
stress, and amenorrhoea 16
striae, Cushing's syndrome *69*
strontium ranelate 133
struma ovarii **100**
succinate dehydrogenase 89
sulphonylureas **151**
 and hypoglycaemia 10
supraorbital ridging 46
sweating 8–12
 acromegaly 23
 drug history 9
 history 9
 investigation 10–11
 management 11
 night sweats 40
 referral letter 8
 social impact 9–10
Synacthen test 4, 24, 95
 short *see* short Synacthen test
syndrome of inappropriate antidiuresis
 causes **57**, 58
 diagnosis 59
 and lung cancer 58
syndrome X *see* metabolic syndrome

T

tamoxifen, gynaecomastia 13
Tanner staging system 44, 107, **108**, **109**

tendon xanthomata *127*, **128**
teriparatide 133
testes
    assessment 44
    cryptorchidism 44
    undescended 112
testicular atrophy, haemochromatosis 130
testicular volume 112
testosterone 21, 93
    delayed puberty 110
    polycystic ovarian syndrome 117
testosterone replacement 21
thiazide diuretics, side effects,
        hypercalcaemia 4
thiazolidinediones **151**
thirst 6
thyroglobulin 106
thyroglossal cyst 49
thyroid acropachy 29, 48
thyroid antibodies 106
thyroid autoantibodies 49
thyroid cancer 48, *49*, 106, 107
    anaplastic **108**
    clinical aspects **108**
    follicular **108**
    lymphoma **108**
    medullary thyroid carcinoma **108**
    papillary **108**
thyroid crisis 101
    treatment 103–4
thyroid disease
    atrophic thyroiditis **97**
    goitre *see* goitre
    Hashimoto's thyroiditis 97, **97**
    hypothyroidism *see* hypothyroidism
    tiredness 30, **30**, 48
    weight loss 28, 29
    see also thyrotoxicosis
thyroid function tests 19, 36, 62, 98, **98**,
        102, 106, 171–2
thyroid gland, examination 49
thyroid nodules 105–7
    aetiology/pathogenesis 105
    clinical presentation 106
    epidemiology 105–6
    fine needle aspiration biopsy 107
    imaging 106–7
    investigations 106
    physical signs 106
thyroid storm *see* thyrotoxic crisis
thyroid-stimulating hormone 29, 40, 62,
        83, 84, 96
thyroiditis 102
    atrophic **97**
    de Quervain's **106**
    Hashimoto's 97, **97**, **100**, **106**
    postpartum **100**
    treatment 105
thyrotoxic crisis 61–3
    examination 62
    history 62

investigation 62
management 63
thyrotoxicosis **3**, 9, **9**, 100–5
    aetiology/pathophysiology 100, **100**
    clinical presentation 100–2, *101*, *102*,
        102
    and depression 45
    epidemiology 100
    flushing and diarrhoea 32, **32**
    investigations 102–3
        radioisotope uptake scan 103, *103*
        thyroid autoantibodies 102–3
        thyroid function tests 102
    management 29, 103–5
        surgery 105, **105**
    neonatal 102
    pregnancy 105
    proximal myopathy **65**
    weight loss 27, **27**
    see also Graves' disease
thyrotrophin-releasing hormone test
        166–7
thyroxine 29, 62, 84, 96
tiredness 29–32, 48
    Addison's disease **30**, 41
    amenorrhoea 39–42
    disorders presenting with **30**
    endocrine examination 48
    history 30, 40
    investigation 30–1, 41–2
    management 31
    referral letter 29, 39–40
    thyroid disease 30, **30**, 48
toxic multinodular goitre **100**
    clinical features **102**
tracheal displacement 49
tracheal stenosis 49
transcatheter arterial chemoembolisation
        34
transferrin 131
triiodothyronine 29, 62, 84
Trousseau's sign 142
tuberculosis, and adrenal insufficiency 94
tumours
    adrenal 17, **68**
    carcinoid 32–4
    ovarian 17, *88*
    Pancoast 58
    parathyroid glands 5, *140*
    pituitary 24, 44, **68**, *72*, 75, *76*
    virilising 87–8
Turner's syndrome 19, 53–4, 110, 115–16
    appearance *115*
    cardiac abnormalities 115
    ethical issues 116
    fertility 116
    hearing loss 116
    hormone replacement therapy 115
    hypothyroidism 115
    intelligence 116
    ischaemic heart disease 115

karyotype analysis 19, 53–4, 115–16
osteoporosis 115
renal abnormalities 115
short stature 116

U

ulcerative colitis, and osteoporosis **132**
ulcers, peptic 4
uncertain outcome, explanation of 50–1
unconsciousness *see* coma
urea, hyperaldosteronism 85
urinalysis, diabetes mellitus 145
urinary tract calculi 3
urinary tract infection, and urinary
        frequency 6
urine
    free catecholamines 90
    free cortisol 68, 87
    osmolality 7, 58–9, 80–1
    potassium 85
    sodium 85
urolithiasis 138

V

vanillylmandelic acid 90
vardenafil 121
variegate porphyria **129**
very low density lipoproteins 125
Viagra 121
virilisation 14
virilising tumours 87–8
    clinical presentation 87
    epidemiology 87
    imaging 88, *88*
    investigation 87
    pathophysiology 87
    physical signs 87
    prognosis 88
    treatment 88
visual field defects
    hemianopia 42, *43*, 45, 46, 48, 71, 79
    pituitary disorders 43, *43*
    pituitary tumours 76
    quadrantanopia 42, *43*, 46, 48, 71, 79
vitamin D
    deficiency **135**, **141**
    metabolism *134*
    osteomalacia 135
    osteoporosis 133
    sensitivity **3**
    toxicity **3**
vitiligo, Addison's disease 42, 62, 64
von Hippel-Lindau syndrome 89

W

water deprivation test 81, 172–3
water intoxication 6
weight gain 24–6
    cardiovascular risk 26

weight gain (*continued*)
causes **25**
drug treatment **26**
eating habits 25
exercise 25
and hirsutism 14
history 24–5
investigation 25
management 25–6
psychological/psychiatric disorder 25
referral letter 24
surgery 26

time course of 24–5
underlying physical disorder 25
weight loss 26–9
abdominal symptoms 27
and amenorrhoea 16, 39–42
causes **27**
diabetes mellitus 27, **27**, 144
drug history 28
gritty eyes 47–8
history 27
investigation 28–9
management 29

nausea and vomiting 40
referral letter 26–7
social history 28
thyrotoxicosis 61–2
weight reduction 15, 35, 36, 54–5
polycystic ovarian syndrome 117
Wermer's syndrome 4, 5, **162**

X

xanthelasmata *127*, **128**
xanthomata 112, *127*, **128**